IN BED WITH A. MANN

Part One – Pre-Referendum
By Anthony Mann

TROUSER PRESS

© Anthony Mann 2018
Cover design by Tim Harvey
Typesetting and colouring in of cover Tim Harvey (again!)

Published by Trouser Press

First published 2018

Printed in the UK by CMP (uk) Ltd, Poole, Dorset BH12 4NU

British Library Cataloguing in Publication Data
A catalogue record for this book is available from the British Library

ISBN 97809516501-9-6

Acknowledgements and Readers' Notes

One man's – or woman's – justice is another's injustice. Whatever one's opinion it is vital that we retain and enjoy a press free to challenge and provoke opposing views. For that is the basis of democracy and I am grateful to the national daily papers.

My thanks to Maureen, who has once again typed this book on our Apple computer, an Apple I feel more Bramley and English than an American Macintosh.

The entire contents of this book was handwritten, similar in rustic charm to "hand-battered cod", "hand-cut chips" and hand-finished pastry".

At Trouser Press we pride ourselves on our green credentials. The paper used for the printing of this book all came from trees that were old anyway and probably from a foreign country – or Yorkshire as some people call it.

The completed work shows no sign of being genetically modified and appears to be lactose tolerant, gluten free, tallow free, non-nut allergic, ceoliac resistant and "ism" free. You know, all those special needs we never knew we didn't suffer from during the fifties and sixties … happy days … Enjoy!

Welcome (Preface as was)

You've found everything to hand in the kitchen, have you? What's that? Yes, you'll find the biscuits in the tin marked "Coffee" as it's airtight, the biscuit tin contains the jar of coffee – or if you prefer hot chocolate, you'll find a sachet in the cupboard along with a wide range of Ainsley Harriott packet soups, just in case you're feeling so inclined later. (Croutons are on the left).

Well, drink it while it's hot and let's have a chat. I'll go first, shall I, seeing as you're still scoffing a custard cream and I'm writing this introduction. Not much has changed since the last book. Locally, another three public houses have closed. Nationally they're still building on Green Belt land like there's no stopping migration, and more branches of Aldi and Lidl are opening than M&S or Waitrose. Oh the march of the socially housed! Internationally, for many, the threat of terrorism and Trump appear to be held in similar vein. However, for every ray of hope that is extinguished during our lifetime, you can always count on Carol Kirkwood to brighten up the start to any day. (Weekends excluded).

So, settle down and join me as we chew the cud, cogitate, and attempt to make sense of the hype, the hyper, the over-blown and the under-stated. Another custard cream?

Contents

Chapter 1

That Socrates, Now He Was A Thinker!

What a week of pleasant surprises it's been so far. Not only did our erstwhile GPO deliver letters possessing unfranked second-class stamps on two consecutive days which, by the way, were deftly detached before you could say "privatisation", but my highly anticipated "My Waitrose" card also arrived courtesy of that very pleasantly disarming lady in red and blue uniform.

My only disappointment, if I'm honest, was the card not being delivered by private courier or possibly Ocado, but it's here now. The downside to shopping at my local Waitrose (Frimley branch) is that it does not possess a café and I've never taken to tea being consumed from a cardboard cup. Maybe I'm expecting a higher level of innovation from John Lewis Partnership than I'm entitled to, but is it really too much to expect them to hand over a ceramic mug to take home with the beverage of ones choice. The natural assumption being that you would return said mug upon your next visit. Now I am fully aware that some customers would not return theirs, but surely that problem would only raise its thieving head away from the home counties south – which is presumably why you do not find many Waitrose stores situated in the northern territories! JLP certainly know good marketing when they think of it. The customer avails themselves of a "free" paper and cuppa when spending over £5* during Monday to Friday and £10 at the weekend – and it's difficult not to! I returned to my car recently having parted with £68 for groceries and I only went in for a pint of milk and a quick look round!

* I am aware that between writing this book and its publication, the minimum amount to be spent prior to obtaining your free paper and cuppa has doubled, but that's inflation for you!

Just a thought, but wouldn't it be a nice touch if the selection of mugs for take home purposes had individual initials so that you could tell yours apart from your other half, should they also possess a "My Waitrose" card, of course.

Before I forget, a major change has happened within the family – no, none of the children have come back home – which is always good news, but we now have another rescue dog. For those of you who have read my previous book, you will know that we had a lovely border collie called Ben. He was with us for three years but sadly decided to become aggressive with our granddaughter, without any provocation, so unfortunately had to be put down as we could not risk that happening again, either to her or indeed any family member or visitor. The good news is that we have now adopted a mongrel called Chrissie. We acquired her from Battersea Dogs' Home – no, not their headquarters in London, as they have a branch closer by in Windsor. Her name on her arrival, when handed in as an unwanted mutt was Crystal, which to be honest, sounds as if its origins were on a council estate in some ghastly overspill town teeming with social housing! As you know, I'm not a snob but it really isn't the sort of name given to a dog that will be tethered outside Waitrose in Farnham. She is a cross border collie (according to Battersea). In reality she is a cross collie, lurcher, springer spaniel and terrier (her mother was very popular in Aldershot!) She is white in colour with flecks of grey and brown, with springer coating on her hindquarters and the ruff of a collie on her neck and shoulders. Her ears are distinctly lurcher, as are her whiskers. (Why does she remind me so much of my grandmother!) We have now had her for six months and she has become the third member of our household and is like most females, extremely manipulative. Joke, joke, as Maureen is typing this! She loves chasing a ball in the park and going for long walks along the canal and over the Ranges. The "ball in the park" is conducted with Maureen at the helm (or at the end of a lead) and I take her for the early morning walks. It clears the mind, no one around, just the dog and me and it's a perfect start to the day. There will be more stories anon.

I drove to deepest Kent earlier today in order to give a talk and found myself shouting at Radio 4 for the majority of the outbound journey. As ever, some complete arse wished to "downplay" as opposed to "play down" a situation. Whilst another interviewer informed listeners of the "Skedule" instead of the "Schedule" – bloody Americanisms! Trains were being diverted due to a signal failure and apparently such and such a "train station" would be affected. It's a railway station! Trains arrive and depart from a railway station. Someone else was describing distances in metres.... I really had a good journey! The return was little better. I argued with my father for over an hour. As many of you know, he died nine years ago but I still argue with him, and d'you know, the really sad thing is that I still lose the argument!

At the talk I attended the name Susannah Reid cropped up, probably when commenting on "Strictly". I haven't seen hide nor hair of her since she left the settee on the Black and Asian Broadcasting Corporation – or the BABC as I refer to it these days. Once newscasters or presenters move to ITV they are rarely seen again. Why would anyone watch a channel containing adverts? Now whilst I did watch Downton Abbey, I only did so once it had been pre-recorded. That way I could enjoy a whole episode in what was probably little more than 15 minutes!

Getting back to Ms Reid, I never did warm to her, as she sat there next to Bill or Charlie. Always felt she had an air about her, an air that was confirmed when she appeared on "Strictly". Funnily enough, I met her dad at a gentlemen's lunchtime club I was invited to as a speaker. Nice enough chap I thought.

Earlier this week it was announced on Breakfast News that my vision of a femme fatale with a Scottish lilt, Carol Kirkwood, would be joining the Strictly Come Dancing line up. I haven't been on such a high since the announcement of Margaret Thatcher's passing.

Now, mention must be made of Louise Minchin or "The Minchin" as I refer to her. She is an entirely different cup of tea, a bit like one served in a subtly coloured ceramic mug, attractive though not pretentious. Ms M appears homely, the archetypal nice-girl-next-door. Hopefully she will be on the settee tomorrow as she gets a tick in her box from me, and no, that's not a euphemism nor a medical condition contracted through visiting Bangladesh or Harlow. Which reminds me, I recently visited an Essex village in my capacity as speaker and found myself on the outskirts of Harlow during my return journey. I encountered a bus sporting a destination roller blind proclaiming "Town Center". Who on earth sanctioned that American spelling on an English bus? Do they not know, or do they just not care? What you do know is that the person responsible for this heinous act will have an A star in English, along with twenty-five other subjects. In today's lack-of-educational world, it's merely a case of entering your password and downloading the doctorate in whatever subjects you wish to choose – and in many cases, pay for.

The Royal Mail is no better. They delivered a parcel to me earlier this month which had a postage paid label, including date, order number, references, two bar codes, depot number, tracking number, my address, which by the way stated Aldershot, Hants, and not Surrey – so you can imagine how I felt about that – but worse, if you can believe it, was still to come. There was a box in which the following was announced. "Safe place – please leave out of sight/under cover (eg with a neighbor)" Neighbor! Not neighbour.

Is spelling now considered to be part of the cutbacks? Right! I'm orf to bed now, as Tim Wonnacott would put it. However, before I go, a little jollification.

A man with a completely bald head and only one leg is invited to a fancy dress Christmas party. He doesn't know what to wear to hide his head and his wooden leg, so he writes to a fancy dress company to explain his problem. A few days later, he receives a parcel with a note. "Dear Sir, please find enclosed a pirate outfit. The spotted handkerchief will cover your bald head and with your wooden leg you will be just the ticket as a pirate". The man is offended that the outfit emphasises his disability so he writes a letter of complaint. A week passes and he receives another parcel and note. "Dear Sir, sorry about the previous parcel. Please find enclosed a monk's habit. The long robe will cover your wooden leg and with your bald head you will really look the part." The man is now incandescent with rage as the company has gone from emphasising his wooden leg to drawing attention to his bald head. He writes a really strong letter of complaint this time, to which a few days later he receives a very small parcel from the company, with the accompanying letter. "Dear Sir, Please find enclosed a tin of Golden Syrup. We suggest you pour the golden syrup over your bald head, let it harden, then stick your wooden leg up your arse and go as a toffee apple!" Good night.

It's six hours later, or thereabouts, so good morning, I trust you slept well. I didn't, but then I rarely do. I dream a lot. Funny, but in my dream last night I was having the whole of the house rebuilt, though it wasn't the house I actually live in, there was far more brick and low ceilings. The dream ended with me thanking the builder and looking at the amount of rubbish I had to dispose of once he'd gone. By the way, the builder was played by that jazz chappie, Jamie Cullen. Don't know him, never met him, never listened to him, so why I should employ him as an "in-dream" builder is beyond me. There we go!

Right! We'll start where we left off with a thought for the morning: "By all means marry, if you get a good wife, you'll be happy, if you get a bad one, then you'll become a philosopher".

That Socrates, now he was a thinker, wasn't he!

No talks today, although there's a brewery tour at six-thirty. Readers of previous books in this series will probably remember that my dad came from Aberdare. As there was no longer a league team in the town come the late nineteen twenties, his allegiance switched to Cardiff City. As a teenager, I travelled from Clapham Junction Station, paid for by mum and dad, naturally, to Cardiff City's erstwhile ground, Ninian Park, with my best friend – whose parents paid for him. It was a great treat for the pair of us come the Saturday concerned, Clapham Junction to Waterloo, Waterloo by Underground to Paddington Station and then by steam train to Cardiff General (Central as is). Then we changed for the "Football Special" to Ninian Park football ground where we cheered on the local heroes. On the train up from Paddington our parents paid for us to be fed, not sandwiches but a full dinner served in the restaurant car. We were the bees knees at fifteen, I can tell you.

Following the match and return from Ninian Park to Cardiff General we finished our day in Wales with fish and chips at the café just outside the station, before making our way back to Paddington, Waterloo and ultimately Clapham Junction. Happy days and incident free.

My father's affinity with Cardiff City rubbed off on me to the point where, from my armchair, I would always note their results along with those of Swansea and Newport County. Wrexham was the last of the four Welsh clubs whose result I would glean as they were north Walians as opposed to the south. When thinking of Aberdare, it's worth mentioning at this point their football team. They were the first professional football team in Wales and paved the way for football, as opposed to rugby being the only major sport played in the principality. The team was called Aberdare Athletic and I have in my possession a souvenir, well, not a programme, but a four-page pamphlet in what we called quarto size and it is a souvenir of a schoolboys' international match between Wales and Scotland, played at the Athletic Ground, Aberdare, on Saturday, 14th May 1921. The attendance for this match was 22,584. This was part of their efforts to garner support to enable them to rise from the Welsh League and the Southern League in which their teams played, into the Football League Division 3. Aberdare Schoolboys' team was the Welsh Schools' champions in 1919-20 and 1920-21. The letter on the inside of this pamphlet is quite revealing. It is signed by John D. Herd who was the Hon. Secretary of the Scottish Elementary Schools Football Association. The letter reads,

"To the Aberdare Athletic Club":

"Allow me on behalf of the Scottish School-boys and Council to thank the people of Aberdare for the especially warm reception extended to them. Everybody seemed to vie with each other in doing what they could and the visit will be long remembered by us all.

The arrangements on the ground were perfect. You have a good pitch, a commodious, well-equipped pavilion, and once the grand stand is completed your ground will well compare with most of those I have seen.

It is the wish of my Council that Aberdare should be included in the Third Division of the League, and should that be an accomplished fact, the league will have a club distinguished for courtesy and kindliness, and nothing will please us better than to be invited to play our next game at Aberdare. I am, yours sincerely, John D. Herd."

Interestingly the address Mr. Herd gives is his home address, as it is 36 Seymour Street, Crossmyloof. It doesn't give a county or, indeed, mention the fact that it is in Scotland. I must look this up on Google.

Following on from that, my only other piece of paperwork from Aberdare Athletic Club's history is the illustrated handbook issued "in support of application for Associate Membership of the Third Division Football League Southern Section." This is quite a comprehensive folder, telling you about the town, the fact that the ground is situated within a three minutes' walk of both stations – Great Western Railway and Taff Vale Railway – and that the ground extends to six acres and is freehold property. Pictures of the ground show its completed grandstand, with scaffolding alongside in order to extend. It lists the income taken from gates with a telling comment that "We have 1,500 shareholders of the Working Class alone." There

6

are views of the field, a match in progress with hordes of spectators along with publicity photographs of the changing rooms and referees' room. There is also a letter published at the end on behalf of Cardiff City Association FC Ltd in support of Aberdare's ambitions. The most interesting and quite surprising aspect is that their ground in 1921 held 35,000 spectators and according to the comments here, state that "When completed will comfortably accommodate 65,000 people and thus will be one of the best equipped grounds in Wales." The grandstand itself will have a seating capacity for 1,000 people.

What a pity their stay in the Third Division South was a mere six seasons. Sadly, they do not look like re-entering the league at any time soon.

When living in London I used to regularly travel across the river to Chelsea but I always felt they were too big a club and without going over ground covered in previous tomes I ended up supporting Charlton before moving to near Aldershot, which in the early seventies appeared a quiet, sleepy market town. I then supported them as my local team, whilst still looking at Charlton's results along with the Welsh clubs. Looking back now I cheered from the terraces at Aldershot's Recreation Ground more times than I care to remember, and in the eighties I visited The Valley when time and work allowed and there was even the odd foray to see how Newport County were getting on in the old Division Four towards the end of their life in the Football League. So it's nice to see they are now back after a near thirty year exile. I have never been in favour of poncy monikers such as "Premier" and "Championship". It divides and rules and stretches the money. Divisions 1, 2, 3 and 4 kept it simple and the money flowed far more seamlessly between those at the top and those struggling at the bottom, but as ever, once big business got its grubby little mitts on sport you knew darned well that those who have more will end up with more and those that have less – well, you know the rest. The saddest observation is that those who have never kicked a football are the ones who will have made the greatest fortune out of the game – bastards!

So, as Cardiff City progressed from the depths of despair back through the ranks, it was down to Dave Jones, a manager I've admired over the years at Stockport County and Southampton, to make that final push to the top division. So close, but sadly, not close enough. Mr. Jones was replaced by Mr. McKay, a genial Scotsman who ultimately took Cardiff to glory and a place in the Premiership. A new ground and a new foreign owner! Ahh … foreign owner generally equates to a total disregard for a club's history or heritage. Cardiff City have always been nicknamed the Bluebirds, this not unsurprisingly is because they play in blue. Enter a man wearing dark glasses from foreign climes and bugger tradition! He wanted them all in red, due apparently to it being a "luckier" colour than blue. Arse! Never underestimate a club's supporters. They turned up in blue and at last with Mr. McKay sacked and yet another man at the helm, blue has won the day and red has been consigned to the bin as Cardiff were relegated after just one season. One questions what price lucky colours are now. The man alienates the fans with his roughshod treatment of the Club's history and then sacks the man who had taken them into the top flight and looked like doing a good job. Never trust a foreign owner. We have enough untrustworthy ones of our own, but an owner who continually wears dark glasses and sports a moustache, well, this is in my book only one step away from being sectioned – or possibly offered a peerage, a choice often too close to call.

Here's an appropriate footballing anagram. Did you know that "West Ham United" equals "The New Stadium"?

Right! Let's have a look on the computer to see if there are any new book orders…. No, bugger all, but what we do have is an email in Spam from Walgreens advising me that my points are expiring. Wasn't aware I had any. There's another from Amazon Gifts informing me that a friend has sent me a $50 gift card. That's suspicious – I don't have friends! Frank, who is he?, has asked, "What would happen to your family if you died?" Not sure, really, but they would certainly be able to sell off my model railways, but other than that life would just go on as normal, I suppose, with the added savings of less birthday and anniversary cards. But thank you Frank, for asking. Wait … Another two have just come in. VA Loan hashtag 13387593541 informs me that their "processing center" is waiting for my response. Spell "centre" like that matey and you will be awaiting my response for ever! And finally, Teddie Dietrik is asking, "Do hot cuties ignore you?" Well, yes, they do, actually – especially with my diabetes! Next!

I'm off to the Post Office and the bank. Since I last wrote to you (no, not the last paragraph, the last book) our post office in Ash

Vale, or as we prefer to call and pronounce it, Upper Arsh Vale, has moved from the newsagents to Budgens. We originally had two post offices within our urban sprawl, one in the urban sprawl centre and one right outside the railway station, but due to the cutbacks and the need to transfer money to third world developing areas such as Tower Hamlets and the north, they both closed. The one in the urban sprawl transferred to what was the old NSS Newsagents in Shawfield Road. That came to a sticky end a couple of years ago now, so the new post office is located in Budgens where you queue along with shoppers who want nothing to do with post office requirements, but everything to do with lottery tickets, cigarettes and alcohol. I thought our country was in the midst of a giant cutback? Not, however, if you're on benefits. The queue always includes shifty looking coves whom you know have never done a day's work since they first filled in the welfare claimant forms. Just an observation … I generally end up replying when the assistant apologises for the wait, "I was clean shaven when I joined the queue!" I really must go. See you later – don't want to miss my place in the queue, do I?

Okay, back now. D'you know, I have been with the HSBC, Midland Bank as was, for over forty years. My holding branch is Aldershot, but for the last two years I have not ventured into that ghastly town. The staff in the bank has always been very, very pleasant. I also noticed that on more than one occasion I was literally the only white face in the bank, save for two stalwart members of their staff the other side of the glass. There are so many Nepalese, Somalis and other swarthy worthies. I never thought I'd feel like a minority. It did cross my mind that I could be next in the international kidnapping racket and sold on to the white slave trade (mature male division). I wonder if they have a sub-section dealing with diabetics?

Talking of diabetes, I remember when Paddy, the Irishman, decided to take up boxing and went for the required medical. A few days later the doctor phoned him and said, "Paddy, do you realise you have sugar diabetes?" Paddy replies, "Nice one, when do we get to fight?"

My adopted branch is now Frimley, which for those of you who may not know, is in Surrey, as opposed to Aldershot, which is Hampshire, so it's nice to know that one is conducting all transactions "in county". Aldershot is such a hole nowadays that on one of my last visits I ventured into Rymans for some stationery. The very pleasant, smiling lady behind the counter welcomed me with a warm "May I help you?" My response was as bright and equally warm. "Yes, you may, and isn't it nice to hear English still being spoken here!" Joanna Lumley – no longer Lovely – has a lot to answer for, having taken over the post of Immigration Minister during the last Labour Party's term in government. The joy of the HSBC branch in Frimley is that it is never busy, has a nucleus of, I think, four ladies, two of which are at their posts at any one time. Always pleasant, it's a joy to visit and pay in money and, of course, the added bonus is that you can park for free across the road in Waitrose!

I read that there is a new European directive No. P456123, if you care to look it up. It appears that in order to meet the newly passed harmonisation law, all UK and Northern Ireland citizens should be aware that the phrase "Spending a penny" is to be phased out and in future we will all be "Euronating!" Yes, I know....

I've also just read how you can tell the sex of a fly. Apparently a woman walked into the kitchen to find her husband stalking around with a fly swat. "What are you doing?" she asked. "Hunting flies," he responded. "Killed any yet?" "Yes, three males and two females." Intrigued, she asked "How do you tell them apart?" To which he replied, "Easy, three were on the beer can and two were on the phone!"

Note, you can tell that little joke was set outside of Surrey as if inside she would have enquired, "How does one tell them apart?" Class and breeding will out, you know!

Well, we've taken the brewery tour and as ever, a nice group of eager beavers, so it's now 9.15 pm and I'm about to consume a Waitrose Prawn and Mango Curry, complemented by a Waitrose Allo Slag (as I call it) and a Waitrose Lemon Pilau Rice. This will be accompanied by a Waitrose purchased Sharwood's Green Label Chutney, Sharwood's poppadoms (coriander) and a Waitrose Merlot. Now, I'm fully aware that you can buy Sharwood's poppadoms in Sainsbury's but I always get the feeling that more effort and taste goes into those they pack for Waitrose. Out of interest, I also purchased a punnet of nectarines to ripen in the bowl, so they should be ready for Christmas.

It is now an hour later. Mmmmm ... that was nice. In fact, that was very, very nice. And now for an episode or three of Not Going Out, recorded from one of those funny channels, and then I'm off to bed.

You remember my comments about Socrates earlier – yes, you do, it was only this morning for Christ's sake – what's wrong with you. Anyway, I found an email concerning the great philosopher. This was sent to me by my very good friend, Peter, now resident in New Zealand as he and his wife, Marion, have emigrated at the ripe old ages of seventy, or thereabouts, to live alongside their son and daughter-in-law. They used to live in Cornwall so whilst we didn't see them that often, we now don't see them at all. Oh, for emails. So, here's the story:

To set the scene, it's Ancient Greece. Socrates, by the way, lived from 469 to 399BC, that's according to the email. He was widely lorded for his wisdom, as you know. One day, an acquaintance ran up to him excitedly and said, "Socrates, do you know what I've just heard about Diogenes?" "Ah", said Socrates, "just one moment. Before you tell me I'd like you to pass a little test. It's called the triple filter test." "Triple filter?" quizzed the acquaintance. "Yes, that's right," Socrates continued (for he was very well mannered). "Now, before you talk to me about Diogenes, let's take a moment to filter what you are going to say. The first filter is truth. Have you made absolutely sure that what you are about to tell me is true?" "No" the man said, "actually I've only just heard about it." "All right," said Socrates, "so you don't really know whether it's true or not. Now let's try the second filter, the filter of goodness. Is what you are about to tell me regarding Diogenes something good?" "No, on the contrary…". "Ah," Socrates continued, "so you want to tell me something about Diogenes that may be bad, even though you are not certain it is true?" The man, a little embarrassed, shrugged his shoulders as Socrates persisted. "You may still pass the test, however, as the third filter is the filter of usefulness. So, is what you want to tell me about Diogenes going to be truly useful to me?" "No, not really." Socrates clasped his hands together under his chin, relaxed back into his chair and concluded, "Well, if what you want to tell me is neither true nor good, nor even useful, why tell it to me or anyone at all?" The man was bewildered and felt not a little ashamed. This is an example as to why Socrates was such a great philosopher and held in such high esteem. It also goes some way to explaining why Socrates never found out that Diogenes was shagging his wife!

Good night.

Good morning. Up with the lark, well robin and blackbird anyway. It's now 6.20 am. I've fed the birds a mixture of mealworm, mixed seeds, suet pellets, peanuts and sunflower seeds. As well as the hanging containers there is a plate on a bird station staked close to the patio and I try to ensure that they always have a good mix, quartered to provide nourishment, vitamins and a balanced, healthy diet – well, that's what it states on one of the packets anyway. In the centre of this veritable feast are specially selected surprises. All this daily dosage is apart from the suet balls, a suet block in its own cage and separate cages hanging from the pole with mixed seeds, niger seeds and a half coconut full to the gunwhales with its fat filled treat, not forgetting of course the water dish, which seems to continually supply liquid for thirsty magpies. We have friends who have a similar bird station in their garden in Camberley but they have built wire cages around theirs to prevent magpies, pigeons, collared doves and squirrels from enjoying their offerings. We're not like that. I think it's important to look at our birds and squirrels in a more rounded holistic manner, embracing all forms of wildlife with equal enthusiasm. I think I read that somewhere in a magazine whilst waiting in the doctor's surgery! We are all things to all birds, not humans obviously, but birds, yes.

We actually seem to spend more on their welfare than is good for the household budget. Last week we crossed the border into north Hampshire and ventured into The Range. It's only saving grace is that it is on the outskirts of Aldershot, that is, you can get across the county border, purchase your goods and get back without exhaling. North Lane, home of The Range, is also the location for Turner's butchers. Now they sell a wide range of award-winning sausages, two of which contain beer from the brewery where some of you know I have been a tour guide for many years – thirteen and rising. One of the sausages is called "Hair of the Hog" and the other, "Pickled Pig". Very good they are too. If you wish to seek out Turner's butchers, the shop lays back on the right, if approaching from the barracks end of town. The landmark is the building almost opposite. It used to be a public house called the Prince Albert. It closed many years ago to become Barry Phillipe (I wonder if in a previous life he was plain Barry Phillips – I do hope so). Anyway, you can't miss the premises as it's painted in a garish yellow. Primarily a hairdressing and tanning centre it also includes colonic irrigation amongst its treatments – which never ceases to amuse me, what with it being opposite the sausage shop an' all....

What's that? How did I get the job of a tour guide? Oh, well, I saw the role advertised in the Surrey Advertiser. If it had been in the Aldershot News I would never have seen it…. One does have standards….

Getting back to The Range, I was going to say before I became sidetracked by the metaphorical smell of sausages a'frying, that we were out of suet blocks, so off to The Range we went. But they were out of stock. We did, however, pick up some other birdie treats we thought they would enjoy, but sadly, no suet blocks. So, back across the border into Surrey, exhale and travel to Squires Garden Centre (Caffyn Parsons as was) in Badshot Lea, where there was a wide choice for our feathered friends. "Oooh," we cooed, "they'd like that. Oh, and that," Maureen enthused. Well, bugger me with a fish fork and call me Delilah. The Range cost us £34 and Squires £101.50! Don't even think about it! At least we won't need to buy any more bird food for a few weeks.

Better put the pen down now as I have a blood test at 9.20 am at our local surgery, then it's the day to myself, followed by a talk this evening in Ruislip, Middlesex. Oh, how I shouted at BBC One earlier this morning on Breakfast Television when someone announced an incident as taking place in Uxbridge, West London. "Middlesex", I shouted, loud enough to frighten the dog. "Fulham, Hammersmith, they're in West London." No-one responded. As many of you know, I was born in Limehouse, East London, but only because I was late. I should have been born in Kensington – my mother's preferred birthing location. She never really forgave me for that but I did spend my first 21 years in Battersea – or north Surrey as we now think of it.

Well, that was quick. Sat down in the waiting room, and before I could say "Carol Kirkwood", let alone think about her, my name was called, arm jabbed, with me looking away, and then home. Eighteen minutes in total, including travel. Who said the NHS was failing.

I've just arrived in Ruislip ahead of time and am parked outside the hall awaiting the throng of ladies as they make their way towards the church hall entrance. And so the evening will commence, parish notices, the talk and then what for all of us will be the highlight of the evening – tea and biccies. On the way over a Radio 4 continuity announcer mentioned a forthcoming programme involving Bear Grylls. I really do think you have to be a very long way up your own backside to be happy at being referred to as "Bear." His name was first conferred upon him apparently by his sister when he was a baby.

Why? Did he remind her of a panda, a koala or was he just plain grizzly? Who knows, who cares?

I do remember his father, the knighted Sir Michael Grylls, whose career became enmeshed in a "cash for questions" investigation during the 90's. He was the archetypal politician, upright, well spoken, charming and you wouldn't trust him any further than you could throw him. I gleaned further information on his offspring whilst wading through Wikipedia some little while ago. Not surprisingly, our Bear, who was born in Bembridge, Isle of Wight, was educated at Eton and Birkbeck College and has a degree in Hispanic studies. He speaks English, apparently – well, even in Bembridge it's still the first language – as well as French. His father was a member of the "prestigious" Royal Yacht Squadron. No, I'd never heard of it either. Naturally, young Bear became a sailor and a climber. As a teenager he sky-dived and achieved a black belt in Shotokan, which apparently is a type of karate. There was me assuming it was a 1970's black disco group! He was also a cub scout at 8 (presumably that's good?). Oh, yes, it definitely is good as he became the youngest chief scout in the history of chief scouts – well, scouting, anyway. In 2004 he was awarded the honorary rank of Lieutenant Commander in the Royal Navy Reserve (didn't know we still had one) followed nine years later by his promotion to Lieutenant Colonel of the same outfit. So far, so jealous! How can people get things so right and be as near bloody perfect as you can get when there are people like us – all right, me. I struggled to get the sack from my first job. I tried that for three and a half years and still failed. Anyway, back to Bearsix. He is married to Shara Cummings-Knight. My dad would have loved that. "Class," he would have said. But he would have been right. It sounds nicely upmarket. Not so sure about the naming of their offspring, however. Jessie, Marmaduke and Huckleberry. Now these are names that are bordering on child abuse. I'd have them taken into care, renamed and re-housed until their parents admit that they are not perfect. India, Piers and Toby would have been much more acceptable. Still, if you are looking twenty years ahead and thinking of a society in which these children will be mixing, it will be a world full of Shabnams, Ahmeds and Mohammeds.

You remember I mentioned that Carol Kirkwood, she of my wildest fantasies and BABC weather-forecasting fame, had been selected to indulge myself if not herself, in "Strictly Come Dancing?" Well, earlier this year there was a breakfast television article concerning new research into our pasts. Tests using DNA can apparently track down our heritage and tell us where our ancestors were a thousand years ago. Now, I don't mean it's as exact as confirming that your forbears lived at 35 Stone Lane, Avebury, Wiltshire (pre post code obviously) but towns – yes! It was most gratifying to learn that our Carol had been selected for the trial. Carol (fifty something but looking remarkably younger) was thrilled to discover that her origins lie in the highland town of Crieff, near Perth. Crieff, by the way, is only one hundred and twenty six miles from Carol's birthplace of Morar, near Fort William. Isn't that nice for her?

Of course, you do tend to think to yourself, a thousand years on, as a family, they didn't get out much, did they. Then again, when I told 'er indoors of the interview with Carol and my pleasure at her being one of the recipients of the test, I asked, "Guess where Carol's ancestors came from?" And Maureen who, as you know is not a fan of my comely Scottish femme fatale, replied wearily, "A mammoth probably?" Ouch!!

In between these notes I am partaking of a packet of Walkers deep ridged flame grilled steak flavoured potato crisps, the ridges of which are apparently now twice as deep, according the blurb on the packet. What as? Loch Ness, the Atlantic, or deeper, a lady's handbag? Or could it just be the normal depth of their crisps prior to re-marketing. Anyway, with curiosity and boredom probably getting the better of me, I have perused the rear of the sleeve that holds the five packets of comfort food. At the top is information relating to "typical nutritional information." Under which it is listed in percentages, grams, Kcal's and KJ's (whatever are the latter two?) It also lists energy, fat, carbohydrates, fibre, protein and salt. Other than me, during this bout of total brain fade, does anyone ever read this? The ingredients list contains all the usual suspects, as did the "Allergy advice", directing the reader to "see highlighted ingredients", which incidentally were dried milk and butter extracts. The words "milk" and "butter" I assume being highlighted to indicate just how heinous a crime it is for them to be part of the mix and presumably for the consumer to feel guilty for purchasing a snack so politically incorrect. The information then goes on to tell us, the potential purchaser/eater, that the crisps are made in a factory that also handles: wheat, gluten, barley, soya and mustard. That, I assume is for all those out there with intolerances. Seriously, we never had intolerances of a food nature when I was young. You just died, it was put down to natural causes and it freed up the housing market. Life back then was much more simple. I'm sure food allergies are a way of attracting attention if you don't get out much and wish to get out even less. I have to admit that over recent years I have grown extremely intolerant of those with intolerances. Get over it or queue for a colon transplant or whatever cure is on offer that week!

Getting back to the Daily Express's front page, I have just looked again at the photo of our Carol in a blue dress and looking dancing fit. Ahhhh....

The main story to the left of this picture proclaims that the UK population is set to soar by 21 million to "an incredible 85 million by 2080." Eighty five million, eh! It's unlike the Daily Express to underestimate so heavily.

And on that note, isn't it a pleasure to read that £3.6 million of EU taxpayers' money, you know, that garnered from "hardworking families," has gone to building "better" camps in Calais to enable migrants to enjoy a more comfortable stay before embarking on their final lap of their journey – England, and a financial exploitation of some very real "hardworking families."

Well, it's time to put down pen and sally forth. Having raised my backside from the driver's seat I note that the ladies are arriving for an evening of hoped for fun and frolics. Or, as I said earlier, a talk, followed by a cup of tea. See you later.

As expected, it is now later. Back from Ruislip – where I never saw a tropic by the way – and time for a home brewed cuppa before I take the stairs to Bedfordshire. Here's a little thought to ponder upon whilst I await the kettle's whistle. What have holidays, new clothes, computer games consoles, horse-riding lessons, art classes, massages, aromatherapy sessions and the building of summer houses got in question? Answer: No, not MPs' perks, but they are all services now paid for on the NHS as part of the "healing process for the country's depressed." Apparently, the aim is to give patients (you'll love this!) "Greater choice and control over the health care and support they receive."

What a pity that those who hold the relevant purse strings couldn't put the money to better effect, like real medicine for real patients. This pandering, by way of comfort frippery, only encourages those with the yearning for getting something for nothing, to become so clinically depressed that they can then be cured of something they never had in the beginning. I've always been of the opinion that mental illness is "all in the mind." Get a life – preferably somebody else's!

Just had a quick look at the full line up of "Strictly" this year. Other than CK, I know Ainsley Harriott, Jeremy Vine, Katy Derham and Anita Rani from Countryfile. Of the others? The name Peter Andre vaguely rings a bell. Daniel O'Donnell must have been a favourite of my mother, as during a clearout of her house after her passing, I discovered a mountain of CDs in a drawer. Several of them DO'Ds. She never said she liked him. Too embarrassed or couldn't remember, I imagine.

Right! I'm off! But before I say goodnight – a quick thought. "When a man steals your wife there is no better revenge than to let him keep her!" Good night....

Well, it's a grey'un this morning. I'm perusing the papers and smiling with the usual mix of amusement and amazement. The first, because this story sounds like a joke and the second, because I know it is not.

The West Midlands Police Farce, sorry, police force, apparently use 1.3L Vauxhall Corsas, not just as panda cars – as we affectionately remember them – but for emergency usage as well. Yes, that's right, the very car that Bert and Doris would poodle off down to Lidl or Aldi in for their weekly shopping, or a day out visiting family in Solihull, is now fitted with blue lights. The problem is that the Corsas are not fitted with sirens, so if there is a need to attend an incident of a serious nature they are legally bound to adhere to the appropriate speed limit. One officer commented that he'd arrived at a scene too late to stop a drunk driver from assaulting his victim due to "road safety constraints!" Peter Harkness of the West Midlands Police Federation said, "The Corsa is fine as a family car {which is just what I said about Bert and Doris} but I don't necessarily think it makes the ideal police vehicle. The lack of a siren creates huge frustration among the officers driving them. It makes officers feel that we are letting the public down." Trust me, Sunshine, it's not the police in this case who are letting us down. It's the government of the day – of all party colours, who throughout the years have brought this country to its newly acquired third world knees.

It is never many pages into any book of mine before the Catholic Church is given reading space. The Pope has apparently offered "forgiveness" to women who have had an abortion and the medical staff who performed the service. I am sure everyone concerned will feel so much better due to his pronouncement. Arrogant sod! There is the Vatican and then there is the real world....

Just a thought, but were you aware that the word "evangelist" is an anagram of "evils agent" and that "Presbyterian" is "best in prayer."

And doesn't it make you laugh. Nothing stands in the way of the Son, the Father and the Holy Gross! I read that 3,400 priests have been disciplined by the Catholic Church in the past ten years for rape and molestation of children. Of these, 848 were defrocked and 2,572 given lesser sanctions. These of course, are the ones who are known about, or have been uncovered. What is it about these people and their faith that breeds such hypocrisy. Just another thought, but isn't it playing into their hands by disciplining them? What does that entail? A week of daily caning – they'd love that – or a real punishment, like a week without access to a child and a turned blind eye. The phrase "defrocking" always makes you think. Does it entail being thrown out of the cult or merely being made to undress in front of the committee? Will their pleasure never end? No punishment seems to be too pleasurable for the priesthood. I remember a couple of years ago when over the "nailing" weekend huge crowds gathered in Vatican City to witness a historic ceremony where two popes, not one you understand but two, John Paul II and John XIII were declared saints, which must have been nice for both of them. The mass, co-celebrated by Pope Francis and his predecessor, Pope Benedict, was watched and listened to live by one million pilgrims and a large TV and radio audience. Royal dignitaries, heads of states and foreign delegates attended. Apparently it is the first time that two popes have been canonised (as opposed to sodomised) at the same time. Still think being fired out of a canon would have been more beneficial to the masses....

I can only assume that the Anglican Church is lagging behind in the popularity stakes, as Rowan Williams commented some little time ago, "Britain is now a post-Christian country, adding that we are no longer a nation of believers and that the era of widespread worship was over." Thank Christ for that, I say....

Interesting that his comment was made shortly after David

Cameron stated that Britain should be "confident" of its status as a Christian country, which was nice of him. So who should we believe? A believer or a politician? I'll say no more.

Now, if ever there is somebody who should be given a "thank you" accompanied by a large bunch of flowers from the government – or at least by her employers – it's Kathleen Buckley, aged 64, who is a lollipop lady. She was throttled in a street by a 45-year-old jobless thug when he turned violent through the effects of drink. Having consumed 12 bottles of beer he grabbed Mrs. Buckley, knocked her to the ground and held her in a stranglehold until she was rescued by a passing motorist – who fortunately didn't pass by. Mrs. Buckley has waived her right to compensation, saying she didn't want to be associated with claimants who exaggerate injuries to receive payments from the public purse. What a pity Daniel Vale, the thug in question, who at 45 years of age should know better than that, didn't think of the public purse when he acquired his latest bottles of beer. You and I have paid for all of these, plus all of his previous bottles, but then, that is why the shirking class can live in a manner that the working class can only dream of. What's the betting that this Vale character doesn't smoke or do the lottery....

On the subject of benefit cheats, here is another example of selfish Britain today. Kevin McEntee, aged 64, has managed to extract £68,924, of which £45,000 has been over the last twelve years. He's been claiming for his continuous disabilities. When the authorities looked a little closer, it became clear that his disabilities weren't quite so disabling as it once appeared. He cited being barely able to walk, requiring a stick or walking frame. In fact, so ill was he that he couldn't write. Strange, as it never appeared too much of a problem when filling in the claims forms, but then, what an incentive. Forty eight thousand pounds of that grand sum mentioned earlier came from his own claims, the other twenty thousand was for his wife, for whom he also filled in a form – his writing ability was good that morning too! He claimed that she was also disabled and mainly housebound. Interesting therefore that over the twelve years of deception, the couple went on nineteen cruises, were witnessed cycling, dancing and generally feeling all the effects that a magical trip to Lourdes would have given them.

I assume coach loads still visit Lourdes, do they? Naïve punters, desperate for a supernatural cure. I wonder if anyone really has been the subject of a genuine life-changing moment through the magical properties of its waters? Just a thought, but you do realise that "Evian" is "naïve" spelt backwards!

Anyway, back to the McEntee's. It's depressing to think that this couple, like thousands of others, can fool the authorities for so long a period. Are checks not made? Do they rely on whistle blowers? And all the time, the do-gooders moan when the government introduce checks and interviews for all registered disabled to examine if they cannot work in some capacity or other. No wonder there are 1.8 million out of work!

Bugger! So far yet not far enough. That's how I feel about today's snippet concerning a woman called Zahera Tariq, aged 33, who has been located along with her four children in Turkey and is about to "return" to the UK. She is suspected of leaving our septic isles with her brood in order to join Islamic State. Frankly, I have to ask, why on earth would we wish to stop her and even worse, make sure she comes back to somewhere she obviously doesn't like? Allah Almighty! If we could only get another 3 million of them in this country to feel the same we might not need to build another 200,000 houses a year, until the country has been completely concreted and bricked over – bastards!

Aahh.... Now I have mixed feelings with this one. Apparently, Britain's national sperm bank is having trouble attracting donors. In 2005 the UK changed the law, removing anonymity for sperm donors. As we know, everyone has rights but the donor, since this change, does not. Now that is the down side to the article. The up side is that the bank now has only 9 donors on its books. Isn't that good. The last thing this country needs is even more sperm flying around the banking system. There are enough tossers in the country as it is. It all boils down to a huge rise in demand from older women – which I consider selfish in most cases – and same-sex couples. Despite my abhorrence at the thought of same-sex couples getting married, let alone being allowed children, I fairly fume at the arrogance of the demands of these people. Laura Witjens, the bank's Chief Executive – and every bank needs a chief executive – stated that some sperm-banked would-be parents demand six feet tall donors because they want tall offspring. Among other demands made are that donors be doctors, barristers, etc. so that they will "inherit" a ready made professional. Surely these people should never be considered as potential false parents. Frankly, I wouldn't allow them to own a dog or a cat. Can you imagine the pressure any child of theirs would be under to succeed like "mummy and daddy" – or, "daddy and daddy" – or just for lesbian equality sake – "mummy and mummy." I suspect that for these people, good old-fashioned adoption is too risky a business. You could end up with a child who might become a shelf-stacker, a dustman or, worse than that, a Millwall supporter. The problem with this gene pool is that there is no lifeguard.

Right! I feel a story coming on and then I'm out for the rest of the day. This one concerns a gentleman who resides in one of our former territories and a heathen. (I'll let you work out which one is which!) So, to set the scene, we have a Scotsman and an Arab sheik. Strange bedfellows you may think, but less so in this story.

An Arab sheik was admitted to hospital for heart surgery, but prior to the operation, the doctors required to have some of his blood type stored in case the need arose. As the gentleman had a rare type of blood, it couldn't be found locally so the call went out for a donor. Finally, after much searching a Scotsman was located who had the same rare blood group. And to be fair, the Scotsman concerned was willing to donate his blood to the Arab. After the surgery, the Arab sent the Scotsman, as appreciation for giving blood, a new BMW, diamonds and £100,000 in cash. A couple of days later, once again, the Arab had to go through a corrective surgery procedure. The doctor telephoned the Scotsman again who was more than happy to once more donate his blood. After the second surgery, the Arab sent the Scotsman a thank-you card and a box of Quality Street chocolates. The Scotsman was shocked that the Arab did not reciprocate his kind gesture in the manner previously shewn. He telephoned the Arab and asked, "I thought you would be generous again. I mean, you gave me a BMW, diamonds and money, but on the second occasion I received a thank-you card and a box of Quality Street." To which the Arab replied, "Aye, laddie, but I noo have Scottish blood in my veins."

It's late afternoon and I am off to Barking in East London, though I do have a few local journeys to make en route.

Don't know what happened there, as time has slipped by quite unnoticed. I did get to Barking and I returned. The M25 wasn't kind and yesterday I gave a talk in Folkestone before taking an evening tour of the Brewery. It is now Friday and I am without either, so a lot of reading, and I hope not a little writing.

Chapter 2

'He's Behind You!'

So, "Good morning", or if you are reading this in Australia, "Good night". Before I wander down to the kitchen and brew a cuppa – Yorkshire tea bags, naturally – I'll peruse the in-box and see what's come in overnight. Mmmmm, mmmm, oh, that's good. A lady would like me to give her club a talk in Hornchurch, Essex, a part of the world I'm very familiar with. There is also a book order from one of the wholesalers I deal with. Sadly, that's where the positives end, I'm afraid. Sam's Club has informed me that I've won a $50 Sam's Club gift card. The "new blue pill" is inviting me to send details of my shipping address for my "blue pill trial period." "Vehicle Services Contracts" are advising me that I'll never pay for auto repairs again and Sonia is a beautiful Brazilian lady, apparently, who is looking for love, which is nice for her … Crap, utter crap!

Well, the day's reading hasn't started well. TV of all channels and papers of all political hues are concentrating their headlines on the latest wave, literally of migrants reaching Europe. The Daily Mail doesn't help the emotional sway, with its front page photo of two boys with a teddy bear between them, so evocative, so disarming, so beneficial to those still naïve enough to think that importing the world's waifs and strays into our tiny island will help their plight and my blood pressure. What a pity the Daily Mail didn't show a photo of a green field with a superimposed sign reading "Reserved for Syrian refugees – coming to a field near you!"

This sort of emotionally draining exposure is just what we don't want to see. It's not our problem! These two children, along with their mother, have drowned, whilst their father is alive and telling his story to the world's press. An international outcry is unfolding with demands for help – and even worse – housing. I ask again, do those in power really believe that by allowing hundreds of thousands of so-called refugees from Syria, Afghanistan, along with those from

Africa, who also apparently have a problem, into Britain, their own country's stability or future will become more secure? And that's not taking eastern Europeans into the equation who are, through an act of gross stupidity legally allowed into our country. No-one during interviews on TV, or from what I read, ever discusses the pressures on our own land, water, NHS, transport, etc. Every aspect of our waking and sleeping lives is affected by successive governments ineptitude towards the country's burgeoning population. If only wildlife could muster support as yet another field is turned over to concrete in order to house those who have no right to be here in the first place, second place, third place....

I really am of the opinion that every prime minister back to, and including Edward Heath, should be tried for treason against the state and yes, I realise, in most cases posthumously. Not one of them has ever safeguarded this country, having signed away more of our sovereignty to Europe and not one of them has ever had the common sense, let alone vision, to see a yard in front of them when assessing the effects of their short-sighted policies, which seem to benefit everybody the world over, but not the poor sods who were born here and pays his or her way.

Right! Kettle's boiled and, I think, so has my blood pressure.

Well, Barking was both an eye opener and an eye closer in equal measure. The ladies group, at which I was the speaker, meet in the beautiful Eastbury Manor House. Built in the 1570's and currently owned by the National Trust, the building is an absolute gem. The chappie I met on warden/caretaker duty had led a varied and interesting life and was extremely hospitable. The offer of a cup of tea on my arrival by someone who was not part of the group, but merely looking after the building, was above the call of duty – thank you again, sir, it was much appreciated. If you look on the computer, all photographic references to this building show it to be in splendid isolation, surrounded by hedges and trees. I am sure it hasn't been photo-shopped, but sadly the isolation is limited, as gaze around and you are enveloped by an estate without splendour, though it has a very calming influence which makes you feel very warm and relaxed. Once back in the car and the engine on, that feeling of calm dissipates very quickly as you join the throng of vehicles travelling into, or in my case, out of east London. The people are lovely but the area is not a pretty sight , more a site!

I see that gutless Cameron is showing his trademark lack of leadership by continuing to be all things to all people and nothing to anyone. Having previously stated that allowing more migrants into this country is not the answer, he has now bowed to pressure from that idealistic but unrealistic opposition, the Liberals and the most galling of all, the church, and stated that we will "play our part, do our duty and take in more refugees." Yvette Cooper has written to all MPs, asking them to take a photograph of themselves proclaiming that they would welcome more refugees to Britain. Unbelievable! British wedges and European thick ends spring to mind!

Remember, of course, that Yvette Cooper and that hapless husband of hers, Ed Balls, were both ordered to repay £1,363 in relation to the mortgages for which they both overclaimed. Just to make sense of those heady days before they were all caught with their grubby little mitts in the expenses trough, these two reprobates – or should that be retrobates – changed the destination of their second home three times in 24 months. Whilst exonerated by the government sleaze committee, it was interesting to note that John Lyon, the Standard's commissioner, said that although they had paid capital gains tax on their property and were not motivated by money (really?) they had purchased a four-bedroom house in Stoke Newington and registered this as their second home. This registration, rather than their home in Castleford, Yorkshire, qualified them for up to £44,000 a year to subsidise a reported £438,000 mortgage. They claimed under the House of Commons "additional cost allowance" scheme for the not insignificant amount of £24,000 – it is all perfectly legal, apparently, for children of a greedier god.

You wouldn't trust either of them, even if I was a Syrian refugee, any further than you could throw them – a comment to be fair that could be laid at the second home of virtually all MPs. Work on the basis that they are all lying bastards and you won't be far wrong – or disappointed!

Oh, this is a hoot. That great self-publicist, Bob Geldorf, who described the current migrant situation as "an absolute sickening disgrace" has offered Syrian families the chance to live in both of his London and Kent properties. That's nice, isn't that nice! He said the following, after perusing the photo of a 3-year-old's body washed ashore in Turkey, "I look at it with profound shame and a monstrous betrayal of who we are and what we wish to be. Me and Jeanne would be prepared to take three families in our place in Kent and a family in our flat in London, immediately, and put them up until such time as they can get going and get a purchase on their future." Perhaps Mr. Geldorf should make a priority of attending lessons for diction and grammar. Shouldn't he have said, "Jeanne and I would be prepared...". Also, if he wishes to hand out rent free accommodation, are there not any deserving British families worthy of re-housing? And during that quote I failed to find one foul-mouthed expletive. Sure he hasn't grown up yet, not with that hair?

I'm sitting here just awaiting news of Bono, the Bishops of York, Durham and anyone who has ever had anything to do with the Liberal Democrats holding up their Mecca-waving mitts and make similarly misguided overtures.

As I write, it's now a case of Germany calling ... Germany calling. "Angular" Merkel has announced her government's decision to accept 800,000 refugees into the Fatherland. Mmmmm. I wonder what the general response will be behind closed doors by the good burgers and citizens of that beacon of European dreams? Has she asked those who will be affected, or is this part of the new order – or in Germany's case, a very old order – where decisions are made irrespective of the wishes of the taxpaying public. We shall see.

Getting back to the Lib Dems, or the pointless ones as I've always considered them, you cannot begin to understand the sheer joy, relief and gay abandon (though not in a homosexual context obviously) that I displayed during that heady Thursday night in May as the election unfolded. I had just left a venue in Eltham, ex Kent and now south-east London, when I tuned into Radio 4 only to learn that the exit polls weren't exactly as previously forecast, and that it didn't look overly good for those sporting a yellow rosette, a colour so appropriate to their ideals. As the night unfolded, along with copious amounts of tea, pork pies, flame-grilled steak flavoured crisps (them again) and pickles, I immersed myself in the pleasure of witnessing the gradual whittling down of Lib Dem MPs, as one by one, and then two by two, they lost their seats and Paddy Ashdown offered to eat his hat if they ended up with less than ten seats. They did, and to my knowledge, he didn't. Ideally, a UKIP government would have been desirable, though unattainable – one MP being a tad of a disappointment. I am, however, realistic enough to believe that from small acorns, etc. – and despite a lot of negative comment from the BABC, it will take time to consolidate and raise their collective profile. It is not good when the name Nigel Farage is basically the only UKIP name that the general public have heard of, their sole MP being elected originally as a Tory and then defecting. A lot of votes were garnered but alas with no impact or leverage – this is to be read as leeverage (English) not levverage (American).

The big question, getting back to the pointless ones, is how did they manage to retain eight MPs? Who on earth voted? Were/are there really those with a thought process who believe in Lib Dem policies: policies so destructive to our society and costly to the tax payer. So, it is with great pleasure that I read of this government's determination to scrap the free school meal programme, introduced by the ex (how I love saying that) deputy prime minister. What was the point? We, as a country, are broke – or that's what the powers that be continue to inform us. We have cut back on everything that made this country the society it was, so how can we even consider offering free school meals for all and extremely sundry? Life should be so much more simple. If you can't afford children, don't have them. If you do, deal with the consequences, you should never expect hand-outs from the state. Because … (I'm looking around to see if anyone's listening) those free hand-outs only encourage common people to breed! Just remember, this little sop to those without conscience costs us £600 million every year – and we need that just to house the migrants that continually knock on the Euro tunnel door, plus those making their way across Europe seeking a better life on a bigger benefit. Maybe Buckingham Palace could help out – there must be a spare room or two.

Right! It's time for a little story and it concerns a Greek and a Scotsman this time. Those Scots, they'll talk to anyone, won't they. I hope you're sitting comfortably. Okay. A Greek and a Scotsman were sitting in a Starbucks café discussing who had the superior culture. Over triple lattes the Greek says, "Well, we Greeks built the Parthenon" and slowly arched his eyebrow. The Scotsman replied, "Well, it was the Scots who discovered the summer and winter solstices." The Greek retorted, "We Greeks gave birth to advanced mathematics." The Scotsman nodded in agreement and said, "Ah, yes, but the Scots were the ones who built the first timepieces and calendars." And so this went on until the Greek came up with what he thought would be the end of the discussion and with a flourish of finality he said, "But it was the Greeks who were the ones who invented sex!" To which the Scotsman replied, "Aye, that is true, but it was the Scots who introduced it to women!"

Yes, I liked that one too!

Interesting follow-up to the West Midlands police using Vauxhall Corsas without sirens, I read today that forces are issuing allocated vehicles with blue lights and sirens to civilian staff in order to reduce the recipient's tax bill. Apparently, HM Revenue and Customs, does not impose tax on emergency vehicles. The driver concerned can save up to £2000 per annum in tax, but is not required to be qualified to use the equipment in response to a 999 call. Yet another erosion of trust in our rulers, methinks.

Well, some good news this morning, three Jihadi supporters have been killed in a drone strike ordered by David Cameron. This good news, however, is marred by the description of these three terrorists as British subjects. Anyone less British, it's hard to quantify. That they hold British passports, that they may have been born here, that is not in dispute, but in the eyes of many, that will never make them British. It makes them foreigners who have been allowed to stay here after birth. They do not like our customs, our respect, our sense of fair play or our democracy. Common sense isn't helped either when you read that Kate Hudson of the Campaign for Nuclear Disarmament, and in my opinion a very silly lady, describes these deaths as being "An extra-judicial killing." I consider the act to be more of an extra-Jihadi killing!

It's difficult to defend the Beeb when you read that Alan Yentob is being paid £330,000 a year for advising on the creativity of its services. Not a bad salary that. I don't know, but I doubt if the job is full time, but one man defending the continued appointment is James Purnell who has the title of "Strategy Chief." Mmmmmm .... With its continual reviews, cuts – though to my mind rarely in the right places – this government, more than most, will reduce the corporation to a shell of the world communicator we knew and loved for decades. Not being a privatised organisation is irksome for the Tories. The ongoing question of whether to make non-payment of the TV licence a civil, rather than criminal, offence devalues our services even more. Shutting down

BBC 3 and transferring it to an online service is definitely something I'll not complain about, but surely BBC 4 should be expanded or merged with BBC 2, in order to raise the standard of programmes. They could cut the Asian network out altogether. What a waste of taxpayers' money. Why should this group of current minorities and soon to be majority, have their own station? I wonder how many white people are employed on their programmes and programming? Ye Gods, if it was the other way round, could you imagine a white English network service. There'd be all hell to pay.

Oh, I've just seen this. Doug Richard, who used to be one of the Dragons in the Den, has been charged with sexual offences against a 13-year-old girl. I remember the gloating and satisfaction I felt when Max Clifford was convicted. Having spent his life digging in the dirt in order to ruin other people's lives and livelihoods, the good citizens of Hersham (along with the bad) are now able to wake up to a cleaner, fresher, Clifford-free village than has been the situation of late. He really does engender a dislike by the public, rarely witnessed since Alan Bradley was so beastly to Rita all those years ago in Coronation Street. In fact, a nastier, common, more odious cove it is hard to find, though of course, there's always the Peters, Hain and Tatchell, Elton John and his … well, … you know … friend … Funny how your mind wanders….

But, back to those who have used their fame as a lever in order to carry out their crimes, they all seem to be coming out of the woodwork closet now. Jimmy Savile, Stuart Hall and, of course, Rolf Harris. Now, I never considered that his trial truly answered the questions we all asked. For instance, those two little boys were never mentioned in court! There was no explanation regarding Jake with his "extra leg." Was that a euphemism? Was that a nudge, nudge, wink, wink? And what about that kangaroo that was tied down? Was it consensual? Was it a joey? Was it still in the pouch? These are questions to which we will probably never receive an answer.

In today's papers there are more new stories of child sex gangs being jailed, this time in Aylesbury. We've already seen Oxford, Telford and Rochdale brought into the headlines over similar stories. One aspect common to all cases is that the victims are white and the abusers, Asian – or, as the BABC describe them – "men of South Asian heritage." What total bollocks, they are Asian, impure and not so simple. What they definitely are not is English. Interestingly, of course, and not surprisingly, is that none of the offences is considered racial, remember, it's black/brown/coloured on white, not the other way round, which, as sure as black is black, would have been racial.

What galls the reader of these stories is where you read that sex attackers who assault Asian girls can be given longer sentences than those whose victims are white. I find this hard to believe but an appeal court judge ruled yesterday that the abuse of an Asian victim may be considered worse, as it could damage her prospects of an arranged marriage. The judge concerned is Mr. Justice Walker. He upheld a 7-year jail sentence on some cove called Jamal Mohammed Raheem Ul-Nasir, aged 32, for sexual assaults against two girls aged 9 and 14. The judge who had originally convicted him, Sally Cahill QC, had commented that the fact that the victims were Asian was "an aggravating feature" as they had suffered shame in their communities and damage to their marriage prospects. Apparently, these comments provoked an outcry from the NSPCC. They said that "British justice should operate on a level playing field and children need to be protected irrespective of cultural differences, regardless of race, religion or gender, every child deserves the right to be safe from sexual abuse, and the courts must reflect this. It is vital that those who commit these heinous crimes are punished to the full limit of the law."

This Ul-Nasir character, whose abuse of the girls took place in his house in Bradford between 2010 and 2011, had sought leave to appeal against the sentence for four counts of sexual activity with a child and two of sexual assault of a child. I mention it again, you can imagine an even greater outcry if an appeal judge was to say that attackers of white victims should be given longer sentences than those of an alternative Allah.

On a lighter note, the above reminds me of a mate of mine who bought a Jack Russell. The dog is brown and black, with just a small patch of white – he's called him "Bradford!" I know, I know....

Just a quick one before we change subjects, I remember reading a story that concerned a Wisconsin priest who had abused over 200 deaf boys at a school. Now I realise they may have suffered a bit of discomfort, but at least they never heard him coming....

It's only September and the Christmas PC lobby are out and about once more. This time it's the De Montfort Hall, Leicester, that is under scrutiny. The seasonal panto is to be Snow White and her Seven ... wait for it ... Friends. Producers of the show are reported to have "rebranded" the title as they believe the term "dwarf" is not something people feel comfortable with. Who did they ask? The panto-going citizens of Leicester, the panto-performing dwarf artistes within Equity? I doubt it. It's never bothered me whether anyone is termed a dwarf, a midget, an elf, a goblin, a pixie, a troll, a ... oh, all right, I know there aren't too many goblins living where we are in Surrey, but visit Norfolk and I think you'll find them to be the inbred norm – or should that be gnome?

All this reminds me of the time when a dwarf visited a very popular doctor and asked, "I know you're busy but do you treat dwarfs?" The doctor replied, "Yes, but you'll have to be a little patient..."

Of course, I am now further reminded of the time a leading actor in another pantomime, this time Aladdin, was anally raped by the gay genie on stage. I mean, it's not as if the audience didn't try to warn him...!

Anyway, continuing the theme from genies to arses, it is the time to mention an American arse. Does the name Walter Palmer resonate at all? No, probably lost in the passage of time, but this is the man, a dentist by profession, so even for an American not totally stupid, who shot a lion called Cecil whilst hunting in Zimbabwe as is, Southern Rhodesia, as was. After committing the barbaric crime in July, he has returned to work and had to face a barrage of protestors. Walter the Arse said, and I quote, "If I had known this lion had a name and was important to the country or a study, obviously I wouldn't have taken it. Nobody in our hunting party knew before or after the name of this lion." Should that really make any difference? Knowing that the lion you are about to shoot might have a name? Perhaps lions the world over – indeed all wild life – should be named in order to gain a modicum of protection from crass arses with more money than animal welfare organisations could only dream of. How anyone can derive pleasure from an animal's death by hunting is beyond me. No wonder the world hasn't yet grown up.

Ironically, I met with an American a short time ago and after listening to his list of pleasures, desires and objectives, all of which involved a rifle, I suggested that America was a far more civilised country before the introduction of white man. I was never sure he understood, but then it's always difficult attempting to keep a conversation to words of one syllable during a discussion with an American!

I had to read this next piece twice. Lord Lexton (who he, I hear you ask – dunno, either!) has suggested that siblings be allowed civil partnerships. My first thought was that this isn't something new as I am pretty certain they have been legal, indeed mandatory, in Norfolk for many years. However, it's nothing of the incest kind, but purely a tool for financial purposes, specifically inheritance tax. A noble thought, perhaps, but not 'arf as juicy."

Now here is an aspect of deprivation that I've never come to terms with. Well, certainly not the real, genuine need for, and that's the recent phenomenon regarding food banks. I read with amusement that in Royal Tunbridge Wells, those availing themselves of the free hand-outs are simply "too embarrassed" to go and collect, so a charity called "Nourish" are delivering to the doors of these very recipients. Talk about feeding the hand that bites and devours! No doubt it tastes sweeter if it's free.

I would love to visit the homes of those afflicted by this "free-for-all" bug that appears to be the latest rage for the feckless and lazy. (If you are one of those I am referring to and bought this book, shouldn't you have given priority to feeding your offspring – Roxanne, Chardonnay, Tyler and Taylor?) If I did manage to enter the homes of these affected families, I have absolutely no doubt that along with the free food I would find formidable stocks of lager, fags, lottery tickets and an up-to-the-minute smart phone owned by each and every member of the family, including Summer, aged 4 and drenched in bling. There would be a plethora of celebrity magazines and delivery details of the latest food drop offers and requests for those of a vegetarian, vegan or nut cutlet variety. You'd then have the alternative list for those with allergies – nut, wheat, gluten – and another for those suffering from celiac disease. If the recipients in Royal Tunbridge Wells aren't prissy, lazy or embarrassed enough as it is, a spokesman for The Trussell Trust – another do-badding food bank organisation – said that residents in Ascot fear the shame if it be known they receive food parcels, so they travel to another town to collect theirs. I bet it's Bracknell and I also bet they arrive in their four-wheel drive BMWs or Audis. Serious point – as if the aforementioned were not – surely, if you cannot afford food, how then can you afford the petrol or diesel to enable you to travel miles to collect your goodie bag. Just a thought!

I see that "SD" or Spineless David, has capitulated again to those who care nothing for our continuingly less green and increasingly less pleasant land. He has announced that 20,000 Syrians can be added to our over-populated burden. Oh, yes, and he has also agreed to give £1 billion in aid – where the hell did that money come from? I wonder which government department is finding itself £1 billion short – Police, NHS, transport, libraries, cemeteries and lighting? Who knows? What you do know is that the overseas aid budget will be ring-fenced.

Right! Time for a little story, I feel. This little tale concerns the ecstasy being felt by the husband as his wife became intense and flushed ... Read on....

The husband was in pure ecstasy ... A far away, contented glaze in his eyes and a huge, gentle, knowing smile on his face, as he softly murmured. He was obviously "totally in the moment" as his wife moved rapidly forward towards him ... then equally rapidly backwards away from him. She was moving in that steady, undulating rhythm that he had come to know so well ... first, teasingly rapidly forward, then slowly backwards, only to be repeated with increasing pace and anxious determination. Again ... back and forth ... back and forth ... in and out ... in and out. Sometimes in one long steady drawn out motion and sometimes in a series of short, urgent spurts of movement ... but always keeping her focus on the same objective. Her heart was pounding ... her face was flushed ... she was starting to sweat but she was so totally engrossed in the act that she never recognised it, nor would she have cared even if she had recognised it ... Her focus was solely and totally upon her husband. Giving way to her inner feelings, she started to moan ... at first, a soft, barely audible whimper escaped her tightly pursed lips, then, with intensity and passion rising almost as rapidly as her inhibitions were escaping her, she abandoned all pretence. Her moans rising in volume and frequency, she began to groan louder and louder. She began mumbling obscene phrases that would make a veteran sailor blush ... she was now totally oblivious to the world around her. Finally, totally exhausted, she could control herself no longer. She let out an almighty ear-piercing scream and shouted, "OKAY, OKAY! ... YOU'RE RIGHT!! YOU DO IT YOU SMUG BASTARD, YOU PARK THE SODDING CAR!!"

That little story was sent to me by my friend, Peter. You know, my very good friend who migrated to New Zealand. I expect you feel you know him well by now.

Politics in this country has rarely been as interesting for many a year, but the emergence of Jeremy Corbyn as Labour Party leader has produced a very intriguing situation. What odds were there on him winning the Labour leadership race only four months ago, when the brother who would be king failed in his bid to topple the Tories. An immediate resignation by Ed Miliband provoked a fascinating selection of ever-hopefuls. What anyone has to ask, of any political persuasion or colour, of their prospective leader is: Are they statesmen – or statesmen-like? Sadly, none of the recent contestants were anything like. Andy Burnham dressed smartly, but I always felt lacked conviction and courage when confronted by an audience, so I would have no faith in his ability to hold his own with Messrs. Obama, Putin or Merkel. Then you had the ladies, Ms Cooper and Ms Kendall. When the total votes of registered supporters and affiliated supporters were tallied, Jeremy Corbyn accrued 59.5% of the vote. Andy (all things to all people) Burnham received 19%, Yvette Cooper 17%, whilst Liz Kendall licked her campaign wounds with a very disappointing 4.8%.

So, he who would be king looks exactly what he is and purports to be, an extremely left-wing, card waving, scruffy individual with a background in nuclear disarmament, anti-trident, pro-workers' rights – and very little sign of a tie. In fact, his sartorial elegance is matched and witnessed on a daily basis by anyone observing the arrival at school of your average comprehensive teacher. And teachers, in the main, are very average. As someone once said, "to succeed in politics, it is often necessary to rise above your principles!"

Right! Time for a joke before I turn in for the night. So, clearing your mind of left-wing activists and other unworldly nonentities (Nick Clegg, are you reading this?) try if you will to imagine the following scenario.

Alan had two of the best tickets for the Cup Final. As he sits down another man comes along and asks if anyone is sitting in the seat next to him. "No," he says, "this seat is empty." "That's incredible," said the man, "who in their right mind would have a seat like this in our biggest footballing event of the year and not use it?" "Actually," says the man, "the seat belongs to me. My wife, Wendy, was supposed to come with me, but she passed away and this is the first Cup Final we haven't been to together since we got married." There was an embarrassed silence before the man said, "Oh, I'm so sorry to hear that. It's terrible. Was there no-one else to take the ticket? A friend, a relative or even a neighbour who could take the seat." The ticket holder shook his head. "No, no-one was free, they're all at the wife's funeral." Night, night!

What's that? Oh yes, thank you. I did get a good night's sleep. Probably helped by the thought that with Jeremy Corbyn at the helm, Labour will be out of office for at least the next five years – or certainly unelectable until they ditch their master – who will "not" be at arms!

Anyway, good morning, dear reader. This is a corker and no mistake! The front page of The Times has a colour photograph of Mr. Corbyn with an Asian beauty to his right and two more to his left, no doubt selected to underpin his "inclusive" aspirations come the next general election – should he still be there, of course. Sporting traditional, colourful dresses, matching umbrellas or parasols and equally traditional embellishments to their foreheads, the photograph conveys the feeling that Jeremy Corbyn has just been appointed as the first white maharajah of an Indian province. The venue was, however, within his constituency in north London. Who would know?

Ah, ha! What goes round comes round. Germany is changing its stance on migrants, as of now, apparently. The German Interior Minister, one Thomas de Maiziere, said, and I nearly quote, "Ze great villingness to 'elp zat Germany haz shewn in recent veeks must not be overstated!" He vent on .... Sorry, he went on, "at zis moment ze Fatherland is temporarily introducing border controls again along national borders. Ze focus vill be on ze border to Austria at first." What he meant was, "Ze border to our Austrian territories first, followed by zose to Poland, the Czech Republic, Belgium, France ..." Even the Kraut government is witnessing a backlash from their own citizens concerning the mass invasion of foreign bodies. Mind you, they have had some experience of what to do in those circumstances before, I believe. See, what goes round comes round.

Appropriately, I have a little story about the Germans within the EU. I will continue.

The European Commission has just announced an agreement whereby English will be the official language of the European Union, rather than German, which was the other possibility. As part of the negotiations, the British government conceded that English spelling had some room for improvement and has accepted a five-year phase-in plan that will be known as "Euro-English."

In the first year "s" will replace the soft "c". Sertainly, this will make the sivil servants jump with joy. The hard "c" will be dropped in favour of the "k". This should klear up konfusion and keyboards kan have one less letter. There will be growing publik enthusiasm in the sekond year when the troublesome "ph" will be replaced with the "f". This will make words like fotograf 20% shorter. In the third year, publik akkeptanse of the new spelling kan be expekted to reach the stage where more komplikated changes are possible.

Governments will encourage the removal of double letters that have always ben a deterent to akurate speling. Also, al wil agre that the horible mes of the silent "e" in the languag is disgrasful and it should go away. By the fourth year, peopl wil be reseptiv to steps such as replasing "the" with "z" and "w" with "v".

During ze fifz yer ze unesesary "o" kan be droped from vords kontaining "ou" and after ziz fifz yer, v vil hav a reil senisvl riten styl.

Zer vil be no mor trubl or difikultis and evrivun vil find it ezi tu understand ech oza. Ze drem of a united Urop vil finali kum tru. Und efter ze fifz yer, v vil al be speking German like zey vunted in ze forst plas.

Ve do hop zis mad u smil.

Maureen is not a happy bunny, having just had to correct the computer that wanted to correct Maureen with the spelling!

Right! I'm off to Iver, in Bucks, this evening for a talk to a local WI. I've been there before, so I know the route to the hall. Why is that, you ask? Have you given a talk to these ladies before? Oh, no, it's not that simple, more a case of me being simple. Some time ago, the WI's Speaker Secretary rang me to ask if I could change the agreed date, which was earlier in the year, to tonight. Everything was fine except that when I put the phone down after our conversation, I forgot to alter the date in my diary, or the appropriate paperwork. Thus, I turned up two months early and started putting out my books on what I thought was an over-generous set of tables, totally unaware that they were awaiting the arrival of an auctioneer who was going to value their wares, so to speak. You do feel a fool, still I'm confident I have the right night tonight.

Back now, and yes, I did. Lovely group of ladies, very enjoyable evening.

Okay, continuing where I left off in today's Times, it saddens me to see "ordinariness" swept under the politically correct carpet – one that's so clean as to be almost transparent, without character or sense. I read that the Care Quality Commission – otherwise known as those who care about minutiae, but fail to recognise the use of bullying – have criticised staff at the Brackenley Residential Care Home, and consider that the staff require improvement. What, I hear you say, is wrong with that? Well, their report highlighted the "overly friendly and affectionate way" some staff reacted to patients. So they weren't surly, dismissive, cold, uncaring, intimidating. They weren't late in responding to a cry for help, they weren't physically or mentally abusing their charges. Oh, no. Their crime was far more heinous. They called their residents "love", "darling", "sweetie" or "handsome". The CQC contest that these phrases can be misinterpreted as demeaning or patronising. I suppose the role of a care home inspector instils such a depth of cold, clinical, box-filling and form-filling, that the very reason why care homes are there – ie to care – is lost on these grey, faceless individuals. Still, they work for a commission, and I suppose that says it all.

Incidentally, a little while ago and nothing to do with above, when I was paying for fuel at a Sainsbury's store, I noticed a chap in front of me, similarly dressed, you know, suit and tie, and as he departed the lady behind the counter said, "Goodbye, sir." She smiled at me, as I moved into pole position, the transaction was completed and credit card removed. I said, "Thank you" and she said, "Cheerio, love." You see, some of us are destined in life to be addressed as "sir" and others, like me, "love", "ducks" or as happened once, "chuck", pronounced chook. It wasn't as though I was even up north when this happened. This was in Sidcup, Kent. However, I suspect the lady in question was a native refugee from Rochdale. I have a theory that Sainsbury's train staff in order for them to tell which customers hail from Chelsea and which are from Battersea – a sort of "wheat and chaff" test!

Not belonging to a union is like not believing in a god. You feel cleansed, open, unfettered, in short, free. Getting back to Mr. Corbyn, those of a left wing persuasion are rubbing their work-shy hands, basking in the thoughts of a Trotskyist revolution in industry, commerce and every other aspect of society they would see brought down. One of those union arses, a chap called Mark Serwotka, nice English name, says it's time to "stop austerity in its tracks", adding "let's seek co-ordinated strikes and demonstrations in a matter of months to try to topple the government."

So, when a democratic vote doesn't go your way and give you the desired result, let's resort to that good old-fashioned standby, anarchy. I really do hope the Tories manage to press ahead with union voting reform and get it through the Commons and the Lords. For too many decades union power has brought this country to its bloodied knees. The worry is that previous strikes have seen whole industries paralysed before contraction and eventual closure loses everybody their jobs. British Leyland RIP.

I've just turned to page 11 where there is a colour photograph of Jeremy Corbyn supporters displaying banners and in one couple's case, a small child accompanies them. The assembled crew appear extremely suspect. There are both female and male examples with serious hair problems, men wearing it too long and women with it lesbian-like short. Many are sporting Jeremy Corbyn red sweaters, all are in casual clothing and not one tie to be seen. I rest my case!

Right! Let's see what latter-day emails we have unopened today. Aaah, bugger all in the Inbox, but wait: no, I am still worthy ... there are three spams. One is from a digital media company offering me something I never knew I didn't need, the second is a fantastic offer from a web posting outfit and the third is from somebody called A. Fanthorpe – all in capitals actually – which says, "From A, good evening," followed by a series of letters, numbers, symbols and slashes, both forwards and backwards. Who are these people, for spam read scam – bastards!

One click – all deleted. Oh, the power at one's fingertips. Now, I'm going to tell you a quick joke before dinner is served, or in my case, the microwave pings. This little story is called "Obsessions."

A psychiatrist was conducting a group therapy session with five young mothers and their small children. "You all had obsessions." He observed. To the first mother, Mary, he said, "You are obsessed with eating. You've even named your daughter, Candy." He turned to the second mum, Anne, "You're obsession is with money and that manifests itself in your children's names. Penny, Goldie and Frank." He then turned to the third mum, Joyce. "You're obsession is alcohol and this too shows in your choice of children's names. Brandy and Sherry. You even called your cat, Whisky." He then turned to the fourth mum, Jude. "Your obsession is with flowers. Your girls are Rose, Violet and Poppy." At this point the fifth mother, Cathy, quietly got up, took her little boy by the hand and whispered, "Come on, Dick, this man has no idea what he is talking about. Let's just go to the nursery, pick up Fanny and Willy and go home."

Ping! Munch, munch, good night....

Good morning, or for the lysdexic reader, mood gorning!

Not much time to spare, I'm afraid. Two talks to be given, one in Wallington, Surrey, and the second in Shenfield, Essex. Looking forward to both, so I'll see you later. Byeee!

As you can guess, unless you are under eighteen, or recently left your lack of education, it's now later. The Wallington talk was very enjoyable and I'm currently sitting outside the hall in Shenfield. It's just turned 7 pm on this warm, sunny, very pleasant evening. "The Archers" is about to start and the story of Rob the rascal continues to smoulder, with no one in the cast apparently aware of his true history or personality, but not surprisingly, several million listeners (me included) have had their suspicions for some time. Funny that. Shhh, it's just starting.

It's 7.15 pm and all over for another day. I've probably said this before but it is the only serial I know where you can miss 20 plus years of episodes and still pick up the storyline within 30 seconds, and you know that the sun will still be shining over Lakey Hill.

The doors open at 7.30 pm so let's have a quick butchers through the paper. Ah, yes, Germany has been calling again. They are to reintroduce passport checks as the EU's No1 of 28 can no longer cope with the influx of migrants. Cue wry smile.

Now this is a surprise, the so-called VIP abuse probe into activities of a sexual nature by prominent politicians, most of whom are dead, is still ongoing. Though looking somewhat short of any real evidence it will be such a pity if Messrs. Leon Britton and Edward Heath are not found to be up to their collective nether regions in some sort of sordid act. I've never taken to either of them, finding both to be most unedifying and distasteful. Now, you, dear reader, may consider that any dislike for political reasons should not necessarily lead to a guilty verdict "just because", especially as neither are able to refute any claims due to their passing, but in my books (literally) it's a very short jump from Europhile to paedophile! Also interviewed was Harvey Proctor, who claimed the police were pursuing a witch-hunt against homosexuals. Oh, right, that hoary old chestnut. No different from a black person making the same comment due to colour. It's always a witch-hunt if you're a minority. Blame everyone else and never listen to what history teaches you....

Right! Doors are open. On with the motley .

Back home and time to relax with a cuppa and a comment. On page 23 of today's Daily Mail there appears "before" and "after" shots of a field. The "before" was taken prior to the arrival of some 15 or so (and that is fifteen, not IS) gipsy caravans. The "after" shot is taken when some four families still remain. The field is a complete eyesore. The owner has lost a season's worth of crops and he has had to go to court in order for eviction notices to be served. He has ended up with a bill of over £10,000 for his troubles, and he's had a lot of them. Why are these feckless, unanswerable spongers allowed to even turn off their engines and then set up camp? It isn't theirs, they don't own the land, they don't rent it, so why should it be so difficult and costly to remove them. The law, and even worse, the attitude displayed to these people by those who have the power to do something about it is inept at best. Once knowledge of occupation has been gathered, a verbal warning by the police should be given with a time limit of one hour to remove themselves. If this friendly advice isn't adhered to, then water cannons should be brought in and tow trucks in order to forcibly evict the unwanted and unsavoury occupants. Talk about a soft touch!

I'm going to tell you a goodnight story before I go to bed, but, before I do, I have to say, stories of religious affairs just never stop making the headlines, do they. Within the church the sexual sleaze continues. I read that a former prosecutor made a rather bad judgement some twenty-two years ago when deciding against putting a senior Anglican bishop on trial. This bishop, one Peter Ball, or Bishop Ball, or should he just be BB, was given only a caution by Dame Barbara Mills, then director of Public Prosecutions. Last week, at the age of 85, BB admitted two charges of indecent assault and an offence of misconduct in public office – as opposed to a public toilet – by sexually exploiting young men when he was "suffragan Bishop of Lewes." (What is a suffragan?) I'll look it up.... I have, apparently a suffragan is a bishop subordinate to a metropolitan or diocesan bishop – still none the wiser and doubtless, bloody pointless. What is worthy of note is that BB has friends in very high places, including the Prince of Wales. You do wonder if leverage is brought to bear in such cases, as I have learned over many years, never trust anyone. Okay, time for bed, but first that story I promised you. We continue our international theme with a little yarn concerning two wrestlers, one Irish and the other Russian.

So, a Russian and an Irish wrestler were set to square off for the Olympic Gold Medal. Before the final match the trainer of the Irish wrestler said to his charge, "Now, don't forget all the research we've done on this Russian. Remember he's never lost a match because of that 'pretzel' hold he has. Whatever you do, do not let him get you in that hold. If he does, you're finished!" The Irishman nodded in agreement. As the bout commenced the Irishman and the Russian circled each other several times, looking for an opening. All of a sudden, the Russian lunged forward, grabbing the Irishman and wrapping him up in the dreaded pretzel hold. A sigh of disappointment universally rose from the crowd and the trainer buried his face in his hands, for he knew all was lost and he couldn't watch the inevitable happen. Suddenly, there was a long, high-pitched scream, then a cheer from the crowd. The trainer raised his eyes just in time to watch the Russian go flying up into the air. His back hit the mat with a thud and the Irishman collapsed on top of him, pinning him down and winning the match. The trainer was elated and astounded. When he finally got the wrestler alone, he asked, "How on earth did you ever get out of that hold? No-one has ever done that before." The wrestler answered, "Well, I was ready to give up when he got me in that hold but at the last moment, I opened my eyes and in front of me a pair of testicles dangled, right before my face. I felt I had nothing to lose, so with my very last ounce of strength I stretched out my neck and bit on them as hard as I could." The trainer exclaimed, "And that's what finished him off?" "No, not really," replied the Irishman, "you'll be amazed how strong you are when you end up biting your own bollocks!"

I hope you slept well, I didn't, but then I rarely do. Too much on my mind to really relax. No talks today, but a brewery tour this evening. Mind you, there will be a trip to the bank and the post office. It's been a good week for book orders, actually. What's that? Yes, it's the bacon, I've just put it on. To be honest, dieting fads or not, there is little better than a bacon sarnie to start the day, providing, of course, that it's "dead, dead crispy", as they say in the northern territories. Thick white bread, Lurpak unsalted butter, bacon and copious dollops of Branston Rich and Fruity sauce .... Ahhh .... Sadly, every breakfast, of whichever variety, is now accompanied by tablets for diabetes and more recently, blood pressure. I know, can you imagine me needing blood pressure tablets? Oh, you can!

It all came as a bit of a surprise when I was diagnosed with diabetes. Of course, you won't know this but I now receive injections in my eyes every month – not always the same eye, you understand, as they have a choice of two. Looking at television when the reception is perfect is, for me, like watching TV when the signal is faulty and the pixels are all over the place. Letters are either missing or appear on the line below. It's not good. The injection draws off the excess fluid that retains my sight and ability to drive – I'm just grateful that buses are still big and red! For the first couple of years I received these injections at Frimley Park Hospital. About a year ago they opened a unit that trundles from town to town, car park to car park. The administration lady at Frimley Park Hospital asked patients if they would be prepared to attend this mobile unit instead. The sweetener was that appointment times would be reduced from the average two and a half to three hours at Frimley, to around one hour at the unit. The decision to move did not take a lot of thinking about and being a fully paid up supporter of the NHS, I will always do my bit to help their logistics. Basically, you have the eye test, after which the nurse applies eye drops. You then wait in another corridor whilst the drops take effect, then have a scan. You then walk back around the corner from where you started and wait for the consultant on duty to call you in for a review of your scan, and the current state of play – or vision in our cases. He or she then declares which eye, if necessary, is in need of another injection. And if not, it's really good news and you are free to go home.

On my first visit I was amazed at how many patients were receiving treatment. I stopped a nurse who was passing by and asked how long the process normally took from entrance to exit and she said about three hours. She then informed me that they had had over 70 injections in the morning and were looking at some 68 or so in the afternoon. It really was like a conveyor belt. She could tell that I was a somewhat nervous novice – I expect the wet patch around the seat gave it away (I jest). I said I was surprised there was the thick end of

140 patients a day, to which she replied, "Oh yes, by 5 o'clock the needle's getting ever so blunt." My look said it all, before she smiled and added, "Only joking, dear."

When they mentioned a unit parked in a car park I imagined and quite naturally, that it would be a supermarket car park. I also imagined that it would be a Waitrose car park. But, no, the choice of locations for me to attend were either Aldershot or Camberley Tesco, or Farnborough, which is Sainsbury's. As I cannot drive back from the appointment as the effects of the drops take six hours to clear, I require a lift to and fro. Sadly, Maureen, being my driver, stated that it didn't really matter where I wanted to go, due to the fact that as she was driving she would head to the nearest. That happens to be Tesco's in Aldershot. Can you imagine the embarrassment of being seen by anyone you know in Tesco's, let alone Tesco's in Aldershot. I was thinking, before my first visit, of going in full burka which would obviously allow me to mingle more easily, but perhaps that was stretching the situation a tad. Having made a recce the said unit is parked in what was a through road, but is now blocked at each end, access only being available through Tesco's car park, so not quite so bad....

As you get to know the nurses and consultants there is always the opportunity for a touch of mirth. I am always being asked my date of birth, if I am diabetic and if I have any allergies. The first two are easy to answer, providing, of course, that I'm not suffering from dementia. The third, regarding allergies was a problem. Never having had any I've recently started feeling slightly bereft. After all, in these modern times everybody appears to be suffering from an "ism" or an "intolerance" and I really wanted to be "included". So, the question of whether I am allergic to anything is now met with replies ranging from "My mother, B & Q, Nick Clegg, cyclists, the cast of Emmerdale, fridge magnets." Endless fun....

Right! I'm off to the brewery.

Two and a half hours later and I have returned. They were a nice group, made up of both chaps and chapesses, from Woking, Andover, Crowthorne and Redhill – somewhere people rarely admit to being a resident of. You'll have to excuse me now as I don't want my fish and chips to get cold, so we'll talk later. What? No! You can't help yourself – get your mitts off my chips!

Well, they went down very well with Episode 1 of "A Bit of a Do". I never saw either series first time round, so I'm just catching up with it now. Written by David Nobbs and fielding an excellent cast, it looked good on paper. One hour later, several relationships unfolding and I'm finding it to be very enjoyable entertainment. Good writing, funny lines and acute observations – and no bad language. Both series were produced in 1989 so I'm catching up fast. I have read very few books in my life, but two stand out, well, three really. Two were written by David Nobbs and one by his friend, Peter Tinniswood. "Pratt of the Argos" and "Going Gently" are both Mr. Nobbs's work, rich in character and observations, they make excellent reading. Mr. Tinniswood's offering is "I Didn't Know You Cared", written in the seventies and turned into a TV comedy. I have the first six episodes on DVD and still find the views and antics of the protagonists as deep, meaningful and sharp as ever. Both men were great writers and observers of the ordinary and mundane. Aspects of life, in other words, that we live through and witness on a daily basis. Episode 2 tomorrow night!

Right! I'm off to bed but before I go, a little story involving a couple invited to a swanky costume party.

So, just to reiterate, we have this couple that had been invited to a swanky costume party. Unfortunately, the wife came down with a terrible headache and told her husband to go to the party alone. Naturally, he protested, but she said that she was going to take some aspirin, go to bed and there was no need for his enjoyment being spoilt by her not going. So he took his costume and away he went. The wife, after sleeping soundly for about an hour, awakened without pain and as it was still early enough, decided to go to the party. Since her husband did not know what her costume consisted of she thought she would have some fun by watching her husband to see how he reacted when she was not with him. She joined the party and soon spotted her husband cavorting around the dance floor, dancing with every good looking woman he could and copping a little touch and a little kiss here and there. His wife sidled up to him and being a rather attractive lady herself, he left his current partner high and dry and devoted his time to the new babe that had just arrived. She let him go as far as he wished. Finally he whispered a little proposition in her ear and she agreed. Off they went outside to one of the cars and had a quickie. Just before the unmasking at midnight, she slipped away into the darkness, went home, put away her costume and got into bed, wondering just what kind of explanation her husband would make for his behaviour. She was sitting up reading when he came in, and she asked if he'd had a good evening. He said, "Oh, same old thing, you know I never have a good time when you're not there." She teased, "Did you dance much?" Her husband replied, "You know, I never even danced one dance. When I got there I met Pete, Bill Browning and some other chaps, so we went into the den and played cards all evening. But you'll never believe what happened to the lucky sod I lent my costume to."

Good night, sleep well.

So, how are you today? I trust you are bright eyed and bushy of tail. It's now Friday and it's been a very busy couple of days. Talks in Harrow, North Kent and deepest Kent, plus a couple of brewery tours. Today I am free to write. I am just going to peruse the papers and then tell you a few tales of talks "wot I've done!" When I first started giving talks some fifteen years ago it was a situation I'd never found myself in before. It all started at a signing session for a newly released (or should that be escaped) book at WH Smith in Woking. A lady came up to me and asked if I gave talks. I replied, "No, I've never given a talk in my life." She was very beguiling, smiled sweetly and added, "I run a care home, the residents aren't gaga but they're bored witless with bingo." She told me to "just come along and chat like we are now." If you say no you look prissy, if you say yes and then fall flat on your face you end up making a complete fool of yourself. The only thing was that as nobody knew me, I hopefully could keep that foolishness a secret. I duly trundled along some weeks later and I honestly can't tell you what it was like. I think I was too nervous to remember a thing, but at the end a lady came over, a very strong character, and asked me, "Are you on the circuit, dear?" I replied that I didn't know what she was referring to. She then raised her voice slightly and said, "The circuit, dear, the circuit. Are you on the circuit?" Still looking nonplussed she explained that she was referring to Surrey Women's Institute. I then replied that this was the first talk I had ever given. "Would you like to do more?" she asked. "Ermm, yes, please." She smiled and said, "I shall put you forward for the next audition." My heart sank. I had not been auditioned in fifty odd years and wasn't looking forward to the morning when I had to go to Guildford and stand on a stage for some 15 minutes and deliver a small section of a prepared talk. Again, I cannot remember what I said but I received a letter some weeks later that stated I had been accepted for inclusion in the speakers' list for Surrey WI. And that, as they say, is how it started.

I think in the first year I received about fifteen offers of venues, second year some twenty six and then it climbed steadily through the eighties and nineties until I have got to the state where speaking engagements are in excess of two hundred a year. I've never considered it a chore, as every meeting is different. One or two, of course, stand out for various reasons

One talk of note took place in a Surrey village to an audience of thirty seven ladies. Now, just to set the scene, talks normally take place prior to the highlight of the evening – tea and biccies, so once the talk is finished I tend to sit behind a pre-arranged table with my books and CDs and hope I might just sell a few. Irrespective of any sales, members of an audience usually come across to just have a chat. There's normally an empathy with where you came from, jobs, children, but at this talk there was nothing whatsoever. Thirty-seven ladies stood close to where the serving hatch was and I sat on the other side of the room. I remember one lady brought me a cup of tea but didn't stay to talk and even five minutes is a long time when literally, sitting twiddling one's fingers. I then noticed a redheaded lady wafting across the room. I'm always wary of women what waft, especially when their red hair is dyed! She had an air about her and she picked up a book, seemingly at random, and quickly flicked the pages from beginning to end, looked at me and said, "It looks very interesting." "Thank you," I replied, although quite how interesting a book can be when the "reader" hasn't actually stopped at a page to read a word is beyond me. Anyway, she then asked who did my publishing. "I do, I self publish." I had actually said that at the end of the talk but I am aware that not everybody is going to listen to or take in everything I say. "So, you're not a proper writer?" she stated. I didn't bite, I just added that whilst I didn't have a wholesaler or a publisher or an agent, I did enjoy what I do and am free of any time restraints without pressure to get it done. She then asked me how many books I had sold. I told her and she took one step back, beamed a most insincere smile and exclaimed, "Oh, well done you." My mouth replied, "Thank you." My inner mouth said, "You patronising mare!" She then picked up either the same book – or another, I can't remember, flicked again from one end to the other, before leaving with the parting shot, "I must look out for one in the charity shop."

I remember replying, "Oh, thank you, that will help me no end." By that time she had turned on her heels and was walking back towards the serving hatch.

Now, that situation happened some four years ago. Two years later I was taking a tour of the brewery, a group of Rotarians, and during the tour the leader of their group asked if I gave talks to clubs. I replied that I did and he asked if I had a card or a flyer. I commented that I would give him a flyer at the end of the tour and thanked him very much. We were chatting about talks and he said, "I expect you get the odd one which is a bit of a problem or doesn't go down well." I related the story that I have just told you. "Where was that?" he enquired. "Well, I'd rather not say, as I don't think it's fair." "No," he countered, "I fully understand and respect that." He had a glint in his eye, adding "But if I guessed, would you tell me if I was right?" Well, Surrey is a small county but we still have a fair few villages and I never mentioned which part of the county the village was in. "Okay," I said, "if you guess right, I'll tell you." Without thinking, he named the village. "Well," I said, "I've got to tell you, you are right but I also have to ask, how did you know?" His answer was interesting. He said, "I've spent my life working for Surrey County Council and you've just named everyone who lives there." Classic, huh!

Another time, a lady from Hampshire rang and asked me where I lived, in case her club was too far away for me to travel to. It was, in fact, only fifteen miles away and bearing in mind the distances I cover, was almost next door. The lady commented that she knew Ash Vale due to the fact that she and her husband had visited Vale Furnishers. Now, for those of you reading outside of this area, you may not be aware that Vale Furnishers is a very imposing building taking up the whole of one corner of the village centre, erected on what was a lovely little garage which sold Burmah petrol in its hey day and the adjacent pub, which was called The Bridge House. These were both lovely old buildings, of course, which had to go in the redevelopment of the site. The store seems to be awarded "Retailer of the Year" virtually every year and is very popular with people whose tastes in furniture are modern. Come to our house and it's pine mainly, the principle being that no two pieces should ever match. In fact, our furniture is not so much second hand, more house clearance! And if there's a table, chair or sideboard lurking under dust in the corner with three legs attached and a fourth somewhere "to hand", then we'll definitely buy it. Anyway, the point was that whilst commenting that she'd been to our area, she made the observation that during her one and only visit, she did find the houses in the vicinity to be what she could only describe as "dubious." Still, one person's dubious house is another person's happy home!

Whenever I respond to a speaker's secretary's telephone call, at a time I feel appropriate, I will always ask them to call me by my first name, a practice I've never found to be a problem and normally is greeted with, "thanks, call me Jim," "call me June," or whoever. On this particular occasion a lady who was slightly distant, not rude, but cold and clinical and with a voice that had a distinct "air" replied, when I asked her to call me by my first name, "I certainly will do that Mr. Mann" and never did!

I had forgotten this incident until several months later when I visited her club. I parked and made my way to the hall door, which when opened led me into an ante-room. I thought I was in the company of a flock of seagulls. It was not the most human of sounds. I entered and the lady concerned made herself known and welcomed me in a very theatrical pose, with arms wide open and explained how pleased she was to meet me. I counted the number of ladies present and including the speaker's secretary, it totalled twenty-two. The chairs were formed into two arcs of eleven and when everyone sat down I realised that with the exception of the organiser, they appeared to be cloned. They sat, knees together and feet apart, handbags poised on laps and whenever I said something that, from experience, audiences tended to find amusing they looked at each other to see if it was! In other words, they didn't react individually. It's difficult when you receive little eye contact from an audience and you find that they are looking to each other for permission to laugh. I did find out, latterly, that the lady who rang me was, in fact, president, chairman, speaker's secretary, social secretary, outings secretary and treasurer. It was, in essence, her club and I would imagine, woe betide anyone who had the temerity to make a suggestion. At the end of the talk, the said speaker's secretary, again with arms flailing, exclaimed, "Oh, Mr. Mann, I have to tell you we did you find you awfully amusing." The "awfully" by the way was accentuated quite theatrically. She then came out with the phrase, "I'm sorry we didn't laugh out loud. It's just that we don't do that sort of thing harr." Only in Surrey would you get people who don't do that sort of thing "harr." And yes, the "hear", was actually pronounced "harr".

I will tell you more another time but I'll leave you with this amusing little snippet. I gave a talk to a ladies' club in Sussex which, I have to say, appeared to have been received very well. I left the hall with my box of books and was putting them into the boot of my car as ladies were waving cheerio and shouting out, "Thank you," "Lovely to see you," etc. A bespectacled lady wearing a cloth hat sprouting a stalk from the middle, made a beeline for me and said, "We've had a cracking afternoon," to which I replied, "Thank you very much." She then added, "We haven't laughed as much in a long time." To which I replied, "Thank you, that's a very nice thing to say." She then looked round, as if to check that no-one was within earshot, moved more closely towards me and said, "Mind you, we've had some lousy speakers." If ever there was a case of quitting while you're behind, that was it!

Hang on, the dog is getting restless, it's sitting with ears pricked and right paw raised, emotional blackmail, that's what this is. OK, I'll stop here and take her round the block otherwise there will be no peace for the wicked – or me!

Chapter 3

Strangers on the Shores

With cuppa in hand I have perused the papers as stated earlier. Cuppa has now been devoured and the following is proof, if ever needed, that corporate greed feeds only greater greed of the corporation and is against fair competition and choice.

Apparently, there is a rugby competition starting shortly, involving countries from all over the world – in short, it's known as the Rugby World Cup and is to be held at selected stadia in a city or town near you – which will be nice if you like rugby. Heineken has bought the rights to provide beers and lagers for all thirteen venues to be used throughout the length of the competition. This means that punters will have a staple choice of Murphy's stout, Heineken lager, John Smith's beer, Strongbow and Bulmers cider or MPC – mass produced crap, as I refer to it. That's it. That's your choice. Nothing locally brewed close to any of the stadia that could introduce visitors to a local flavour and therefore boost the local economy. No, just corporate brands, served cold, without taste, and I read will cost £5 a pint. What a rip off! No thought is given by the British rugby authorities as to choice or cost. For them, it is merely the income from some faceless, country-of-originless, international conglomerate that made the highest bid in order to swell the RFU coffers. I wonder just how much "greedy corporate bastard PLC" will make out of the hapless punters? Rugby, football, cricket … they are all the same. They sell their sporting soul to corporations who have very little interest in the game but a great deal of interest in profit.

You have to laugh – no, you really do! The immigration bill includes the requirement for migrants to be banned from public sector jobs unless they speak English fluently. Well, that should have half the staff of Frimley Park Hospital seeking alternative employment. Door, horse, bolt, spring to mind. Oh, yes, and in another article about our "very British problem," it seems that detainees, about to be repatriated to their country of origin, are not happy bunnies. Not just because they are part of that rare specie that is being repatriated, but because the food served to them in British detainee centres is – you have to laugh – too British! These wastes-of-taxpayers'-money originate from over eighty countries and nearly three-quarters of the 575 migrants housed at Verne Immigration Removal Centre in Dorset have told inspectors that they are unhappy with being served Shepherd's Pie. The centre has, not surprisingly, been advised to be "more culturally diverse" with its dishes! Bloody cheek. I am sure there are a lot of British pensioners – that's British, you know, those who look like you and me – who would be delighted to receive a free Shepherd's Pie. After all, they have paid in all their lives towards that Shepherd's Pie, unlike the buggers at Verne!

Several questions are raised in this article. Firstly, what has the county of Dorset ever done to deserve a "removal centre?" If the migrants were arriving by plane their collective feet wouldn't be allowed to touch the tarmac before a swift reversal of destinations. The same would apply to those found stowed away in a lorry if arriving via the Channel Tunnel. Secondly, why is HM Inspector of Prisons kow-towing to these "unwanteds". It doesn't impress the taxpayer, although I am sure the Howard League for Penal Reform will be rubbing their hands gleefully, alongside those from Liberty and every other organisation with a misplaced sense of loyalty. Thirdly, why are there only 575 occupants at The Verne? If ever there was a case for overcrowding and ensuing discomfort, it's here. For Christ's sake don't make the buggers comfortable. They'll all want to come! Oh, sorry, they have, haven't they.

And on a similar theme, here's another couple of miscreants worthy of a recycling visit to Verne. This little piece concerns a 75-year-old grandmother, Rachelle Harris, who withdrew money from a cashpoint in Cardiff and was waiting to board a local bus some short time later. Unbeknown to her, a 28-year-old female Romanian – yes, them again – was standing behind her in the queue at the cashpoint. This female then phoned her brother and his wife, who followed Mrs. Harris to the bus stop. As she was about to board the bus, the Romanian couple barged into her and the 43-year-old wife of the brother slipped Mrs. Harris's purse out of her handbag – experienced or what! They got away with £250 – bastards – or, in this case, Romanian bastards! While there is some good news insofar as the theft was captured on CCTV, the Romanian family (I use the term loosely) have been sentenced to 20 months in prison, which we all know will be less than a year before they are able to rejoin their kith and thieving kin and continue their life of opportunity in the land of plenty. What really adds insult to theft, is that this family of Eastern Europeans have only been in this country for two months – two months! Why the hell were they not made to pay back every penny, plus compensation, for everything lawyers can find – and it cannot be too difficult. They should never be allowed to touch English or Welsh soil again, being placed on the next flight back to Romania. Sadly, due to this country's collective gutlessness we will no doubt be paying for this family for years in one form or another. And do you think this situation will every change? No, neither do I!

I'm not sure if I mentioned it just now, but the offenders were Romanian, you know....

Talking of migrants, there is a very informative map of "that" part of the world currently affected by all this movement of bodies. Basically, the story is told in two colours, light green and orange. Light green covers countries not affected by the tide of financial and social terror – as opposed to terrorists – although one can never be sure they are not one and the same, whilst orange reflects those countries that are affected. Arrows mark the direction in which the unhappy, though expectant, hordes are marching.

The map actually reminds me of the title scenes from "Dad's Army" but with greater social cost and fields lost to development in order to house the unwanted wretches. Surprisingly, Syria, the assumed country of origin is in the light green area. Turkey, however, appears in orange and is the starting point for many a migrant's trek, the new silk road towards Greece, Serbia, Hungary, Czech Republic and Germany. Some continue north towards Sweden and Finland. What have the Scandinavians ever done to deserve this divisive and destructive onslaught of strangers on their shores? It seems that nothing will appease those in power who wish to change forever the social structure that was once the cornerstone of democracy and freedom of speech ...

The map also shows a "branch" of this wave involving Croatia and Slovenia before arriving in Germany. A third way is reported through Italy, France ... and ... oh, yes, us poor sods. There are currently reported to be 3,000 lost souls in Calais and 1,000 in Dunkirk, awaiting their chance to arrive in Blighty. Dunkirk? If our boys in the Second World War had known what was to befall our nation all those years ago, would they have so readily stood up and been counted and then, more than likely to fall.... It's a sobering thought.

Mmmmm, according to the map very few of these migrants from the Middle East appear to be heading towards Bulgaria, Romania or Poland. Now, this could have something to do with the first two countries having a less than enviable reputation for thieving, and migrants could end up with less than they arrived with. In Poland's case it's possibly more to do with Germany getting really fed up with Angular Merkel's policies, overthrowing the elected government and resorting to form by invading all and sundry, and let's face it, for the Germans all others are sundry!

I was talking to a lady recently at the end of a talk who, judging from her sympathies for the world's displaced, was suffering from a severe bout of left-wing leanings, luckily this state can be cured if the patient is subjected to a rigorous dose of common-sense and given a reality check. She asked me for my views on overseas aid. I replied that I was all in favour of funding major projects. Well, one actually. She looked enthusiastic as she awaited further details. Her face changed when I expanded that funding should be confined to the electrification of the fencing in Calais. She never did buy a book – funny that!

What else was there? Oh, yes, I read that BT is to bring back call centres to the UK. About time. I always ask to speak to someone in the UK when on the line to BT, whilst waiting to complain about Broadband, or the lack of it. I am learning. Whenever I decide to change my energy provider, insurance – house, car, pet, etc – I always enquire as to the location of their call centres. If they are not UK based, they do not receive my business. Another golden rule when choosing one's service provider for whatever service – or lack of it – always make sure the number is 0800, ie a free phone. I refuse to pay for a phone call in order to pay for a service I may, or more likely, may not receive in the future. Where is the incentive to answer a customer, valued or not, when your corporate profit is enhanced by the minute every time you delay answering the poor sod – or in my case, me! It's bad enough listening to music periodically interrupted by a (normally) female voice informing you that your "custom is valued" and that "we are busy dealing with other customers" and that "someone will be with you shortly," but when I'm assured that the "someone" will be one of their "customer associates" or "service advisors" I find myself shouting down the phone, "Just put me though to someone, anyone, even if they just happen to be passing, for Christ's sake…"

This response is particularly appropriate when holding on for an "assistant" at HM Revenue and Customs, an august body, well known for complaints via "You and Yours" the consumer programme on Radio 4…. Ahhhh, just taking a moment out to chill and immerse myself in the sexy, sultry voice of Winifred Robinson …. Okay, back now! Right, time for a little story.

This little tale concerns two elderly residents at a nursing home. I will begin. There are two elderly residents (told you!) a man and a woman, who are alone in the lounge of their nursing home one evening. The old man looks over and with a glint in his eyes says to the old lady, "I know just what you're looking for and for five pounds I'll have sex with you right now, over there, in that rocking chair." The old lady looks surprised but doesn't say a word. The old man continues, "Or, for ten pounds, I'll do it with you on that nice, soft sofa. Alternatively, for twenty quid I'll take you back to my room, light some candles and give you the most romantic evening you've ever had in your life." The old lady says nothing but after a couple of minutes starts digging around in her purse. She pulls out a wrinkled twenty pound note and holds it up to the old man. "So, you want a really nice romantic evening in my room, do you?" "Sod that," snapped the old lady, "it's four times in the rocking chair!"

Talking of jokes – well, political ones anyway – I see Jeremy Corbyn has taken a lot of flack from the press and to be fair, he appears to have brought most of it upon himself. His continuing support for those who pay nothing towards the system and yet take all, really grates with us taxpayers. However, on the basis that no one party has the exclusive rights to all the good ideas at the expense of other parties who have none, I really do sympathise totally with Mr. Corbyn's desire to re-nationalise the railways. It was privatised on the premise that the taxpayer could no longer afford to support a state-owned British Rail (Railways as was!). All these years on and the subsidies paid by those very same taxpayers are far in excess of what we apparently couldn't afford when we all owned it. The most galling aspect in this accountancy farce is that we have a posse of fat cats taking salaries, bonuses, shares, dividends and any and every other financial gain imaginable. Chief executives, directors and shareholders, all with their collective snouts in the increasingly electrified trough. The same is true of the gas, electricity and water industries. I can at least shop around for a so-called better deal with the first two mentioned, but water? Tell me where I can go for an alternative supply. Tell me who wins here, other than the aforementioned chief executives, etc. It is certainly not thee or me!

Just looking in the diary, I've got a busy weekend at the brewery. Three tours tomorrow and two on Sunday, so I'll bid you cheerio and leave you with a little story concerning an elderly gentleman and a fishing rod. Oh, help yourself to tea, won't you.

The rain was pouring and there was a big puddle in front of the public house. A ragged old man was standing alongside holding a rod with string attached, which he hung in the puddle. A tipsy looking gentleman came across out of curiosity and asked what he was doing. "Fishing," said the old man simply. The gentleman thought, "Poor old fool" and invited the ragged old man into the pub for a drink. As he felt he should start some conversation whilst they sipped their whiskies, the gentleman asked, "And how many have you caught so far?" The old man replied slowly, "Well, you're the eighth today!"

Well, the weekend has passed and was as busy as I expected. Monday has become yesterday and so therefore, unless the EU has intervened and I've got it wrong, today is Tuesday. It's all Germany today in the papers. A furore has erupted over the VW motor group making false "clean fuel" readings in order to pass USA emission tests. Icebergs and tips spring to mind. Time will tell as truth will out.

The following story is a continuation of a long line of stories that will only end when the last suspect dies.

A 91-year-old lady living in the Fatherland has been accused of being an SS radio operator at Auschwitz and could now possibly stand trial for playing her part in the deaths of 260,000 Jews. It's 70 years ago! What is the point, she is 91. What is to be gained by the authorities? Should there not be a time limit for alleged war crimes to come to court? Maybe the turn of the last century would have been as good a time as any.

Nearer home, isn't there a case for limiting the time allowed for bringing to court accusations of historical abuse? Whether those who support this principle like it or not, society has changed, it does in most walks of life – probably all walks of life. Every case is on its own merits. The likes of Jimmy Savile and that other disgusting haemorrhoid on the face of society, Cyril Smith, managed to muscle their way through life without ever being taken to task due to who they were and whom they knew. Other, well-known personalities probably did err on the side of assault by flattery, but it was the sixties, it was a different culture and it was over fifty years ago. I still consider six years to be the limit for bringing a case to court. Anything over that – move on.

On a lighter, though not brighter, front, I read that bridge players are still pushing to make the card game a sport. They argue that if darts or model aircraft flying are sports, then their card game should be also. I was aware that darts is considered a sport, although it feels rather spurious to be categorised thus. It is, after all, a game found in pubs, ie a pastime, a hobby. As for model aircraft flying, surely this is nothing more than a hobby. It may be competitive but a sport? Nah! If however these card-playing coves get their elegant way and bridge is deemed a sport, I understand it's then in line for Lottery funding – so that's their game!

Question: Why is sex like the game of bridge? Answer: Because if you have a great hand, you don't need a partner!

Talking of funding, I read that David Cameron and George Osborne appeared to be having very meaningful relationships with China this autumn. We apparently want them to be our new friends, our special friends, as America once was – when it suited both parties, of course. Friendships made between extremely different cultures come at a price, often a very heavy one – one our government considers worth paying, whilst China considers worth accepting. As cut backs continue to be announced for UK taxpayers, we, those same soppy saps, are to contribute £3 million to China in order to increase "awareness" in English football. Have you ever heard such tosh? Just another branch of the overseas aid tree I suppose....

Oh, I love the following: apparently, an Iranian has walked into a police station in Manchester and asked the police to deport him back to his own country as he's had enough of Manchester. He said he was desperate to leave because of the rudeness and violence in the city. That's a hoot, isn't it? Let's just hope his views are shared by others of his foreign ilk – in all about 3 million of the buggers!

Mmmm, the Bank of England, who I always assumed forecast

what will happen, now appears to be bringing up the rear, so to speak. They have just announced that the mass influx of foreign workers to these "septic" isles over the past few years has depressed average earnings. Well, there's a scoop and no mistake. With net migration up 300,000 in the twelve months to March this year, that trend looks set to run and run. Nice to know that the Bank of England is catching up with reality. Facing the consequences, however, is always harder.

I always love a good laugh and just occasionally ones comes one infused with a hefty dollop of gloating. As you know, I am not a gloater by nature, but when I read that Tim Farron, the pointless "leader" – a term I use loosely – of that pointless Lib-Dem party, encourages his fellow losers to believe that they can be "back in power" within five years, you really do feel a sense of incredulity creeping in. His assumption, I presume, is that as a Jeremy Corbyn led Labour Party shifts to the left, the Lib-Dems' remaining eight MPs will take the centre ground. Really? I suggest he means this merry band of brothers and sisters will be where they have always been – fence sitting. He added that he was proud of his party's record when in government. That must mean that Tiny Tim is proud of being instrumental in introducing free school meals, when as a nation, we are continually being informed that we are potless. As we are all too well aware, we close community centres, libraries, care systems break down, but we still give free school meals. If you want children, pay for them, put up or shut up! Note to parents: This country does not owe you or your children a subsided meal or three. I assume, also, that Tim Farron is proud of his previous leader's lack of support when the then Tory administration attempted to increase sentencing for knife crimes. I recall Nick Clegg's sickeningly inadequate response during a radio interview to a mother whose son had been knifed to death. What a lack of contribution to our society the Lib-Dems really make. There you are – another anagram! Liberal Democrats – Pointless Bastards!

Hypocrisy is nothing new, of course, and not confined to politicians either. Even I must admit to a small degree of double standards, though with a firm caveat and mitigating circumstances to boot, obviously. I remember writing in one of my previous tomes of a case where a boy was seduced by his female teacher. She was sacked and the boy's parents were not overly happy with her behaviour. My thoughts were, and really still are, that he was extremely lucky to be the chosen one. I would have loved to have an older, experienced lady teaching me the facts of life first hand – so to speak! Here comes the hypocrisy. It would, however, be an entirely a different proposition if it were my daughter being seduced by a male teacher. I'll not comment on cases where the seduced is of the same sex as the seducer, as you might be reading this book before the nine o'clock watershed and I'd hate to get into trouble with the authorities. I'll not be responsible for the resulting trauma and compensation! If it's a male teacher and a schoolgirl of fifteen, then to be fair, (a) he should have waited until she turned 16, or (b) thought twice about his school career, but not necessarily in that order. Society would think, "what an arse" and what a pity the young girl was taken advantage of.

Now, in the case relevant to this story and in today's papers, it concerns a schoolboy of fifteen and a female teaching assistant of thirty years of age, who has just admitted two counts of sexual activity with a child. She has been handed a two-year suspended sentence and has obviously lost her job. Along with this sentence she also has to face 250 hours of unpaid community work. As a chap, I am just looking back at those days at school, nearly 16 years of age, nearly legal and with several million hormones playing havoc, along with testosterone levels soaring higher than a rocket to Uranus – or anyone else's come to that! There is a photograph of the very slim-lined lady in question and if I was 15 and selected, I'd have thought my lucky number had just been picked. As many of you know, I went through school at Spencer Park Secondary Modern on Wandsworth Common and we all salivated over the cracking school secretary we had. How many dreams did I have of her – and not in a dry way! What happened? Bugger all – life can be so cruel.

You can't say anything, can you? The American President, that coloured chap called Obama, you may have heard of him, has had a meeting with the leader of that rather sad cult, the Catholic Church. Now, Channel 4's presenter, Matt Frei, has been forced to apologise as he has made a comment that is … well … not on, apparently. He described Mr. Obama as "smiling like a split watermelon." Do you see anything wrong in that? I thought it was quite an imaginative comment, but no, it's racist, you see. And weren't those offended quick to point it out. This insult dates back to a stereotype that watermelons were a staple favourite of black Americans. So? Mr. Frei will have to go back to that good old British classic, "grinning like a Cheshire cat," unless, of course, that is now considered a slur on Cheshire as a county, or demeaning to the cat as an animal or both at the same time. Ye Gods, these complainers should stay in more.

On a far more serious subject, I note that there has been an increase in the number of acid attacks on people, with females being targeted in the main from this horrific form of violence. A case today highlights a mother of six who is likely to lose an eye after acid was thrown in her face. How could anyone do this? Police are currently looking for two brothers who attacked the lady outside a nightclub in Southampton. To my mind, anyone convicted of such an evil crime should be given a life sentence – bastards!

Right! Let's have a quick check on the computer to see what's in the Inbox.

Aha, my friend, Peter, in New Zealand has sent Maureen and I a lengthy tome, which I will read in full shortly, always a joy to sit and immerse one's self in his news and not a little wit. What else is there? Hattons of Liverpool have sent me their latest newsletter containing details of impending model locomotive releases from Bachmann and Hornby. That'll make a dent in the pocket – or to precise, the joint bank account! The Cartridge People are confirming delivery of my black and colour inks, which is good news. Thinking about it, it's probably the only time you can use the words "black" and "colour" in the same sentence without being referred to the Race Relations Bureau of Minority Preference – or whatever they are currently branded – and if only some of them were! What else? It's all downhill from here I'm afraid. Something headed "Spy Cameras" is informing me that "Internet hidden cameras let you watch from anywhere" apparently. Federal Tax Settlement states that "tax relief is now available." Divorce.Attorney tells me that "the right divorce attorney is for me." Certainly better than the wrong attorney, I assume. There's also news of "discount dental implants near you." There's Nugenix, which apparently is GNC's number-one product. A shocking boost for men. That's nice! And finally, there's a McDonald's reward voucher awaiting me. I think that can wait a little longer. As you know, I wouldn't soil my shoes on their bloated corporate doorstep.

I saw a programme about that very company last year and in one episode they were coming up against opposition from local people to a store opening. I think it was in Derbyshire. Anyway, despite stiff opposition they still won and I remember the gloating they showed when someone mentioned that despite having a restriction on opening times, they really didn't see a problem in expanding very shortly afterwards. And sadly, that's what happens. They never know when to stop. Corporate greed only sees a barrier as something it intends to hurdle.

While I am just getting the metaphorical taste of McDonalds out of the system, another email has just come in. According to the Replacement Window Company my replacement windows have just arrived. Strange, really, as I've never ordered any and even in my advanced years I think I might have remembered. Here's another one. Pet Food Coupons are telling me I can save on pet food. I can do better than that if times get hard. I'll just have the dog put down – joking! There's also an invitation, with flashing pink hearts, to chat with "Lovely Russian and Ukranian beauties." Well, that's an offer I won't be taking up. I'm still struggling with Kaylee Does Kendal – a low budget video. And finally, Inogen, not Imogen, asks if I need a new oxygen concentrator. I assume that's what you purchase after chatting with either a Russian or Ukranian beauty?

Just getting back to last Saturday, "Strictly" started its new series and despite Bruce Forsyth's dreadful jokes scripted for him along with his continuing self-important references, I do feel that the show has lost some gravitas with Tess Daly and the zany Claudia Winkleman as co-hosts. I find little wrong with Ms Daly, but I do feel she is too lightweight of presence. In other words, never the captain but always the captain's mate. For me, Paul O'Grady would have made a good show host, or possibly from within, Anton Du Beke. I could certainly see him making a fist of it. A few years ago Ronnie Corbett, maybe. I have no problem with two females hosting the show, I just struggle with finding examples who would be empathetic and not too bullish. Having said that, Jo Brand springs to mind as a candidate worthy of consideration. So, this coming Saturday, the first contestant will be eliminated. Exciting or what!

As we are in fairly light mode, I feel it's time for a joke or two. The first of these concerns a burglar and a parrot.

A burglar broke into a house one night. He shone his flashlight around looking for valuables when a voice in the dark exclaimed, "Jesus knows you're here." He nearly jumped out of his skin, clicked off his flashlight and froze. When he heard nothing more he shook his head and continued. Just as he pulled the computer off of the desk so that he could disconnect the wires, as clear as a bell he heard, "Jesus is watching you." Now freaked out, he shone his torch around frantically looking for the source of the voice. Finally, in the corner of the room, his flashlight beam came to rest upon a parrot. "Did you say that?" he hissed at the parrot. "Yep," the parrot confessed and then squawked, "I'm just trying to warn you that he is watching you." The burglar relaxed. "Warn me. Who in the world are you?" "Moses," replied the bird. The burglar laughed. "Moses, what kind of people would name a bird Moses?" The bird rocked on his feet very slowly, looked up at the burglar and replied, "They're the same kind of people who would name their Rottweiler Jesus!" Yes, I liked that too.

Now the second story centres around a crocodile. Why a crocodile and not an alligator, I know not, so please just accept the story for what it is. I thank you!

A drover walks into a bar with a pet crocodile by his side. He puts the crocodile up onto the bar. He then turns to the astonished patrons. "I'll make you a deal. I'll open this crocodiles mouth and place my manhood inside. The croc will close its mouth for one minute, then he'll open his mouth and I will remove my manhood unscathed. In return for witnessing this spectacle each of you assembled here will buy me a drink." The crowd murmured their approval. The man knelt on the bar, lowered his trousers and placed his manhood and related parts into the crocodiles open mouth. The crocodiles mouth slowly closed and the crowd gasped. After a minute the man grabbed a beer bottle and smacked the crocodile hard on the top of its head. The croc opened its mouth and the man removed his genitals unscathed as promised. The crowd cheered and the first of his free drinks was delivered. The man stood and made another offer. "I'll pay anyone £100 if they are willing to give it a try." A hush descended over the crowd. After a minute of mumblings a hand went up at the back of the bar and a blonde woman timidly spoke up. "I'll do it," she said, "I'll try. Just one thing, though, please don't hit me so hard over the head with the beer bottle."

Yes, I like that one too.

I have a mid-week with only one talk in Buckinghamshire and an evening brewery tour, so have time to catch up with some domestic interests. Firstly, did I mention that I had bought a new car? No? Well, I have. It's another Kia Carens. The previous model was over 3 years old.

What? No, I realise that in itself isn't a good reason to change vehicles but the right hand windscreen wiper flew off on the slip road of the M25 and the A3 at Wisley. What happened was that I was returning from a talk in Kent a couple of weeks ago when, in pouring rain, I turned left onto the A3 when the wiper "clunked" and then flew over the roof of my car before landing on the bonnet of the vehicle behind and finally being run over by several vehicles after that. I feared that the arm was starting to scratch the screen, so I pulled over into what is a lorry parking area and raised the arm away from the screen before driving back to Ash Vale. I had to keep leaning to my left to see through the screen as it was still being wiped by the remaining functioning blade. The rain subsided as I approached the Kia dealership – the Dover Garage. This, by the way, is where I have purchased my previous Kia vehicles. Parking up in their car park opposite the showroom I quickly made my way to Reception, as by now it was approaching "going home" time. A quick word with the Service Manager saw him deftly search for a replacement blade. Luckily, he had one in stock. "Would you be able to fit it for me?" I enquired. As you know, technology and I are not good bedfellows. Always helpful, he summoned a mechanic who went across the road to affix the said blade. Now, it was at this point that boredom set in and I wandered to the Cars for Sale section of the park and there stood a demo model – an updated model to boot – in black, with tinted windows, half-length sun roof, and it all looked very nice. I enquired about cost and agreed to come back the following day for a test drive. The following day, having tested it, I then thought, "Yes, this is very nice. All these gadgets I've never had, never knew I wanted, definitely don't need and will never use, but they're there". Having said that, there were one or two which were distinctly advantageous. Electrically heated front seats and electrically heated steering wheel. I don't know why I'm emphasising "electrically" as they are hardly likely to be coal fired. Oh, yes, and sat-nav, that'll make a change from stopping in lay-bys every three minutes as I near a destination so as to check the exact location of the street/road required.

So, a £16 supply and fit wiper blade ended up costing just a few bob more. No, I hadn't planned on purchasing a new car or even a demo. However, the mileage on my existing Carens had reached 91,000 and the warranty extends to 100,000 or seven years, whichever is the soonest. Well, for me, it's always mileage limit first. The fact that my current Carens still possessed 9,000 miles of warrantable mileage proved beneficial when negotiating a trade-in price. So, for the last week or so I have been finding out what is and what is not available to me by way of gizmos and gadgets. Certain aspects of travelling by car are mandatory. One is that information regarding miles left before you need to fill up and distances to your destination should all be in, well, miles and not kilometres. Luckily that was all changed before I took delivery. I also have to find time to locate the English section within the owner's manual, as I need to ascertain if and how I can receive my temperature in Fahrenheit (a good old fashioned English name) as opposed to the foreign Celsius.

Having told my children that the car had heated seats they assumed it was a fairly recent innovation. I related the story of the first car I ever had with heated seats and that was a Ford Granada in either 1978 or 1979. They were quite surprised. I remember it well, because at that time I was working for Heath & Wiltshire, a Talbot dealership in Sandhurst, Berkshire. The best medium for selling new and used cars was the Auto Trader Magazine – in our garage's case, the Thames Valley edition. Each week a young lady – it was always the same young lady – would visit our garage to collect the copy for the following week's edition. Over the months, and Heath & Wiltshire's spending being not an inconsiderable amount on advertising, the young lady would arrive and she and I would motor off down to the Bird in Hand public house in Bagshot on the A30, where we would lunch (Auto Trader paid). We would then sort through the advertising content. One day, I took her to the Bird in Hand in the Granada and showed off the heated front seats. "How does it feel?" I enquired – or words to that effect. "Oh, it's lovely and warm," she replied, "especially as I never wear knickers." And that was word for word! You never forget moments like that. We always got on very well....

Do you read a lot? I don't, sadly. I know, you're about to say, "Yes, and it shows in your writing!" I've sometimes started a book, read to page 40 and then thought, "I've no idea what I've been reading" as I appear to have lost concentration shortly after the Forward. It's a bit like when I'm at the theatre or a cinema. I always know when I've enjoyed a production because I haven't been searching for the green exit signs to see how many there are. I believe the number of books I have read as an adult may still be in single figures.

What's that? You want to know which ones? Mmmm, well, let's see now. Counting from first to most recent, in the 80's I had a minor operation which necessitated my staying in Frimley Park Hospital for a couple of days. What was wrong with me, I hear you ask. Well, it was nothing drastic, but it was painful, a cyst at the base of the spine, where your tail would start if only you had one. Anyway, the book I took in with me was "Hello Sailor" by Eric Idle, and very funny it was. At some stage during the 1990's I read "Signalman's Morning" and "Signalman's Twilight" by Adrian Vaughn, a must for any follower of the Great Western Railway. Arthur Lowe's son, Stephen, wrote a biography on his father, which was extremely insightful and a very interesting read. I know I have told you about the next two books, but here is a little more detail. Having met the writer, David Nobbs, in 1995, I purchased a copy of his novel, "Pratt of the Argus" which I found warm and witty. I have also read "Going Gently" by the same author, a beautifully written novel with an imaginative story line and terrific twists and turns. A friend of mine is currently reading it – must remember to get it back! "I Didn't Get Where I Am Today", David Nobbs's autobiography was a sheer joy to read and has meant that he has now become my most read author – by dint of three books being read! Also thoroughly enjoyable was Barry Cryer's autobiography – "You'll Never Believe This But …". I also possess and have read what I consider as reference books, for example "Are You Being Served?", the "History of TV Comedy", "The Archers – A True Story", as well as two books on "Dad's Army", one by Bill Pertwee and the other by Graham McCann.

Oh, yes, and the other one I mentioned earlier was from the 70's. This book was picked up in a second-hand bookshop when my excursions into reading – as opposed to Reading, where I excursion very little! – was still very tentative. It remains one of my favourite books and is read and re-read for the pure entertainment I derive from its pages. Cue drumbeat ……… The book is – "I Didn't Know You Cared", by Peter Tinniswood, who was a long-term friend of David Nobbs, by the way and sadly, no longer with us. The novel was turned into a 70's sit-com, starring Liz Smith, John Comer, Robin Bailey and Anita Carey. And, let me tell you, I fell in love with Anita Carey who played Pat, the daughter-in-law. And funnily enough, never really fell out of love with her! She was in "Doctors" for some years, not that I watched it for myself, you understand, merely on behalf of a friend.…

Anyway! My latest reading material is " Left Foot in the Grave" by Garry Nelson. Mr. Nelson is not so well known in literary circles as that overrated Shakespeare chappie, but for those not familiar, Garry Nelson was a football player during the 80's and 90's, ending his playing days at Charlton Athletic under Alan Curbishley. The book in semi-diary format details his tentative first steps into football management at Torquay United. Officially second in command, he highlights the plight of clubs at the bottom of the league, trying to survive on a shoestring from day to day, against the backdrop of the riches enjoyed by the clubs at the top. He laments the rise in the number of foreign players coming to our country and he feels it affects the chances of home grown talent. He also criticises the effects that the moneymen (agents) have taken out of the game, draining it of essential funding. This book was written in 1997, so nearly 20 years on and the fears and warnings expressed then have multiplied one hundred fold. We have few English players in the Premiership and even fewer English managers. It's a case of all money, no ethics, no principles and no moral leadership. Still, as we know, what goes round….

Another footballing aspect Mr. Nelson comments on, is the "involvement" of the police during the Hillsborough disaster. He reminds us that the Court of Appeal found 2 to 1 in favour of the police who helped with the removal of corpses, being paid compensation for post traumatic stress disorder. A slightly different story now emerges after inquest after inquest, showing that the police weren't quite so whiter than white after all. Altered statements, lost paperwork, and downright lying, by those they trusted.

On a more general basis, I've never understood why the police – or anyone come to that – should be given extra payment for doing the job they are employed to do. As I've said in previous tomes, we never sued Mr. Hitler and I mean, it wasn't as if we didn't know where he lived, although of course it might have been difficult to serve papers! Oh, no, we arose from our collective Anderson shelters, saddened we didn't have a home any more, gladdened that the dog was still alive and all of a sudden the world wasn't such a bad place after all. But back then, when we were English, we were stoic, we had backbone and we were stiff of upper lip….

With regard to compensation claims and the police, I remember a case where a former police motor-cyclist was awarded £6,500 after he convinced the powers that be that he had suffered permanent hearing damage due to the noise of his British Transport Police issued motorbike. Having ridden for 12 years it was only near the end of his career that he was issued with earplugs. Sadly, it meant he couldn't hear the police radio. Life's a bummer, and then you sue! It must have been a Red Letter day for police trauma cases as about the same time, two policewomen "won" £35,000 due to their pistols being "too big for their hands!" What on earth do they expect? Are they anticipating Smith & Wesson producing tailor-made girlie guns, light of weight, possibly with fur lining, a picture of a cuddly bunny on the handle and the barrel sporting a rather relaxing pink hue?

Everybody seems to be in on the act. Prisoners are routinely handed wads of cash by the authorities because of this or that. Now, this case, I read about a couple of years ago and it took my eye, though not fancy, due to the prisoner involved being described as a "serial claimant." His name is Kevan Thakrar, so he doesn't sound as if he's one of us but I'll continue. He is a triple murderer and he received £800 compensation in his latest round of compensation claims which, to date, number almost 250. The district judge, one Neil Hickman, of whom I would have serious reservations as to his ability to judge anything from a beauty contest to a flower arrangement, ordered the payment for lost or damaged belongings. I will elucidate. Apparently, the said Thakrar chappie was being transferred between prisons when some of his possessions were lost. These items included nose hair clippers, cranberry juice, an alarm clock, photographs and other unspecified "priceless items." I was just waiting for a cuddly toy and a set of sliding doors!

Anyway, the good Mr. Hickman, who is obviously very free with taxpayers' money, awarded the murderer £224.97 for damage to his stereo, alarm clock and nasal clippers. Another £90 was added for the loss of the cranberry juice, protein powder and toiletries, as the loss of these items caused him to be "stressed." It gets worse! The district judge, you know, Neil Hickman, commented that there had been a "cavalier disregard for Mr. Thakrar's rights. {ahh, them} and for his property." He then promptly awarded a further £500 to compensate him for the loss of photographs and personal items. That totals £814.97 from our hard-earned taxpayers' money. Mr. Hickman went on to say, "Had the defendants said promptly and sincerely to Mr. Thakrar that they deeply regretted the loss of his personal items and understood his distress, the loss of them would not have been aggravated in the way it has been." Unbelievable! How do these people like Mr. Hickman, educated and with a modicum of common sense, get taken in by these prisoners? Incidentally, in 2011 Thakrar was paid £75 for distress after some milk went missing. What sort of support and confidence does this give to the Prison Service? Having attacked prison staff with a razor-sharp broken bottle, one of the injured prison officers is still awaiting compensation and hasn't worked since. To paraphrase my hero, John Le Mesurier, "He really doesn't sound an awfully nice chap at all!"

With solicitors doing their democratic best to get their clients off any charge brought against them, from judges like Mr. Hickman who, I would assume, votes Liberal Democrat, to the Howard League for Penal Reform, those in day-to-day charge of our miscreants are at a very great disadvantage. Talk about pampered. I recall a spoke for the Howard League for Penal Reform commenting on prisoners' clothing and sizes. Her name was, and probably still is, Frances Crook (wry smile time). She said, "Prisoners not within a narrow size range cannot get clothes to fit, so if a man is on the large size, they have to wear trousers that don't do up and T-shirts that don't cover up their tummies." Just a thought, but it was nice to read the word "tummies." Now, you wouldn't be at all surprised if she started off life in Surrey, would you.

Sadly, the rest was typical left-wing, namby-pamby-pinko waffle. Or, what you would expect to hear at the NUT Conference or the Lib-Dem AGM. Interesting to note, of course, that Britain's 4000 female prisoners are allowed to keep their own clothing (so much for equality) as are trans-sexuals – well, they would be, wouldn't they. "Ooooh, now who shall I be today? Martha or Arthur, Doris or Maurice, Dickie or Vicki. Should I be both at the same time?" I trust you read all this in camp tones, whilst fluttering your eyelashes and flailing a limp wrist.

Which reminds me – did you hear about the fat, alcoholic transvestite? All he wanted to do was eat, drink and be Mary! And while we're about it, I see that the local police force have been hunting the "knitting needle nutter" who has stabbed six people in the backside in the last 48 hours. The police say they believe the attack could be following some kind of pattern!

And news just in – A Muslim has been shot dead with a starting pistol and the police say it is definitely race-related!

And another? Okay. I read that a man charged with murdering

another man with sandpaper said in mitigation, "that he had only intended to rough him up a little"

Enough, I hear you say! Not long to Strictly. I have one more brewery tour at 3.30 pm which will finish around 5.15 pm. I will then clear up, clean up and then get back for the football results before tea and Tess. The last tour, by the way, was the 1 pm, which finished ten minutes ago, so it's a quick cuppa in the Hospitality Suite, or Hostility Room as I call it, and write the notes you are reading now.

Well, that's all over for a second week, results tomorrow. I certainly wasn't impressed with Ewan Thomas, although he appeared slightly more impressed with himself than the judges were, so here's hoping he won't last long. Time before Match of the Day to peruse the papers and find out what didn't happen in the world today. Well, I am reading The Daily Mail.

Firstly, there is a lovely photograph of a black fox filmed in North Yorkshire. There is only a handful and the dark colouring is due to some genetic defect. The animal looks absolutely stunning. Having said that, the photographer has to keep the location secret so as to deter hunters. How sad is that.

Now, here's a nice little statistic that ironically is probably understated. An article on immigration states that 38,000 migrant children will be requiring school places this year, some 160% up since the start of the decade.

There is an entertaining page containing 12 photographs of faces, six male, six female, well, they naturally don't want complaints about sexist bias. Anyway, you have to look at the faces and determine which six, presumably three male and three female, have been unfaithful. Yes, I realise it's shallow and vacuous but it probably suits me quite well. So, here we go, let's take a gander. Interesting, but there are no ethnic minorities in the line up. So what does that tell us? Only white people are unfaithful? Surely not. They have names like Malcolm, Ryan, Angela and Abbie…. Mmmmm, the first photo is of a lady named Mel. Now it couldn't be her. I'm very close to someone called Mel and he's not the type. Right, I've chosen my six based purely on their eyes. Are these eyes that can lie, I've asked myself and on that basis, be my judgement. So, it's No. 2 Malcolm, 3 Hannah, 5 Ian, 6 Laura, 9 Hannah (there are two Hannahs) and 12 Julian. Before I turn over the page and check my percentage of correctness, it would have been easy merely to have suggested the six females, but I suppose that could have been described as bias – or possibly experience. Ha, would you believe it, I got three right, 50%. But the ones I said cheated and got correct were Nos 2, 5 and 12, ie all the males! The two Hannahs were apparently completely innocent, as was Laura. My sincere apologies to all three ladies. As for No. 1 Mel, 8 Angela and 11 Abbie, well, you all fooled me. There is an observation to be made here insofar as the three lady "cheats" are all smiling brightly, whilst the "innocent" ladies are "bland to warm". Am I therefore to deduce that ladies wot cheat are happier? They certainly look it.

The pictures of intimidating refugees in Germany make "told you so" reading for those of us aware of the pitfalls of mass immigration. Also of interest is the gradual mood change in the Fatherland from the Heiling, sorry hailing of Angular Merkel on her brave pro-immigration speeches to the scenes unfolding only several weeks into the policy being seen for what it is.

I remember when Mr. Berlusconi caused another one of his many upsets when he said that for the Germans concentration camps never existed. He was apparently referring to a previous comment in which he told a German MEP that he could play a Nazi concentration camp guard in a film. The German Family's Minister, probably the equivalent of Eric Pickles, stated that Mr. Berlusconi's "attacks against Germans" were "unspeakable" – as opposed to Germany's attitude towards Poland, which was more of an everyday story of German dominance! This all reminds me of the tale of a chap who was sitting at a red traffic light minding his own business and patiently waiting for it to turn green, even though there was no oncoming traffic. A car load of bearded, young, loud Muslims, shouting anti-British slogans and sporting a half-burned Union Jack duck-taped to the boot lid of their car and a "remember 9-11" slogan spray-painted on the side, stopped next to him. Suddenly, in unison they yelled out "Allah Akhbar!" They stormed off before the lights had changed. Out of nowhere a bus came speeding through the junction and ran directly into their car, crushing it completely and killing everyone in it. For several minutes the man sat in his car thinking, "Bloody hell, that could have been me." So later that morning, he went down to the depot and got a job as a bus driver!

And while we're at it, there was a conversation between David Cameron and President Obama. The pair of them were sitting in a bar. A man walked in and asked the barman, "Isn't that Cameron and Obama sitting over there?" The bartender replied, "Yep, that's them." So the man hastily walked over and said, "This is a real honour. May I ask what you guys are doing in here?" Cameron said in his perfect English, "We're planning World War 3." The man said, "Really, what's going to happen?" Obama sat back in a relaxed manner and said, "Well, we're going to kill 140 million Muslims and a blonde with big tits." The man looked aghast. "A blonde with big tits? Why kill a blonde with big tits?" Cameron turned to Obama and said, "See, I told you, no-one gives a shit about 140 million Muslims, but a blonde with big tits…!" I do realise that some people may be offended by that little joke, but rest assured, no blondes – with or without big tits – were harmed in its making or telling.

Now, what else is in today's paper? Oh, yes, just a little story but one that sums up the declining standards of those who should know better. This piece surrounds the mayor (or mare?) of Weymouth and Portland who supports refugees and is of the opinion that residents within the area of her mayordom (?) should donate goods for newly arrived migrants! You know what I think, so I'll just sit here and quietly seethe. However, and not unsurprisingly, some residents were not wholly behind the idea and a debate ensued on that ghastly Facebook. When criticised for her plans she went online and told the critics to "shut the f… up!" There is a colour picture of the said mayor, one Christine James, who in full mayoral gown and regalia looks worryingly like an 18th century highway woman, though with a much more sour look to her. She doesn't appear to be an overly nice person, as she has previously been given an 18-month conditional discharge for assaulting her husband. Wry smile time, methinks! But it didn't go unnoticed that she is a Lib-Dem councillor. I rest my views.

Seriously though, it does go to show how standards of those in office have slackened over the years, no decorum, no manners, no respect for other opinions and no regard for position. It also shows the dubious face of Facebook, which hereafter will be called Fastbuck, or Twitter, which for me is Twatter and no, I don't have and never will have a page telling everyone what I've had for breakfast or when I last went to the toilet.

Right, MOTD beckons. Night, night.

Chapter 4

Class wars and a lack of eastern promise

It's now Monday and no work today. First, the good news. Whilst my heroine Carol did not perform overly well, at least she is still on the retained list. He who seemed pleased with himself was duly eliminated at the first opportunity, so onwards and sideways for our Scottish lass. I don't know, but I'm not really sure she will ever improve that much, although of course her smile can forgive all ...

It's interesting to note that we, that is the UK in general, and thee and me in particular, are contributing £10 billion to help third world countries to deal with climate change. Ironic, really, as this comes just at the time when our government has cut back on our own green policies causing industry to withdraw from expanding cleaner fuels for our own islands. Funny that.

I see that the worrying trend of total disregard for other people's rights is alive and well and currently being practiced in East London. There is opposition to the so-called "gentrification" of the area by some and they may well have a point. What is totally unacceptable is their form of protest. Aggressive banners and flaming torches are bad enough, but paint and smoke bombs being thrown at customers in a café is nothing less than intimidation and violence. Hundreds of these "people" (I use the word loosely) rampaged down Brick Lane, many wearing pig masks, organised it seems by a group calling themselves "Class War" which I think you will find is an anagram of both "unemployed scum" and "left wing oiks." The café at the centre of their ire is the Cereal Café, where you pay £5 for a bowl of cereals. Now, I would never use the services of a café charging that sort of money for that sort of fare, but there are those who obviously will, and whilst I consider the prices obscene, the answer is to vote with your feet, or in this case your bum. There's always a tell-tale sign with those banging on about democracy, they rarely wish it to be conferred to those of a differing opinion.

As you are aware, being born under the star sign of Libra, I do try to be fair. I see both sides of an argument and generally come down fairly heavily on one side or the other, there being few times when I umm or ahh about a situation or spend time fence-sitting. There's nothing remotely Liberal Democrat yellow about me!

So, the pictures of Jeremy Corbyn, his wife and a few others swirling along in his wake make you take stock of the prospects for us under any future Labour government. The contrast in the photographs between him and his wife couldn't be more noticeable. He, on her left (appropriate I feel) looks unkempt, shoddy, with un-creased trousers and an ill-fitting jacket over a tie-less shirt. In short, he looks like a cross between a CND protester who has just walked 50 miles, a candidate for care in the community and someone who is homeless and seeking a squat for the night. She, however, Laura Alvarez, looks classy, trim, sporting black trousers, black top and a yellowy, mustardy jacket. All in all, you wouldn't put them together. They probably have the same political views but they are certainly poles apart when it comes to sartorial elegance. There is an article accompanying the photographs, which becomes slightly worrying when you read that Mr. C would like to see the school curriculum re-written so as to teach children about the "evils of the empire." That's the one we had, I suppose. He feels we should inform them about our "incredible socialist tradition." I would happily see the "evils of empire" being taught if it showed what happened to the native peoples – American Indians, Maoris, Aborigines, etc, the destruction of native tribes, animals, forests, etc. It would also be useful to teach children that what goes round, comes round and that if we hadn't colonised so many places we wouldn't have the immigration problems we have with former colonial natives now being deemed "British" just because they live here and were issued with our passport. JC's attitude to the IRA in the 80's and 90's was not at one with public feeling at the time. Now, I'm fully aware that you don't have to be in the majority to be right and I have great sympathy for a united Ireland, but when innocent civilians in this country are being killed just because they are British, then you are going to win very few friends – as he and the IRA didn't at the time. His number 2, Mr. John McDonnell, has an equally worrying history of inflammatory views and if in government I will bet a pound to a penny that he would revert to form. Mark my words – you would not want to live in this country should the likes of Corbyn, McDonnell and their "hungry for blood" co-conspirators ever take to government. Freedom of speech would be the confine of very few and all of like mind.

Oh, I see there's been a shooting in East London – Hackney to be precise. The murder is being dubbed in the Press as a "gangland execution." Not very nice, of course, for members of the public forced to flee the streets in terror, but at least it's one gang member taken out of the equation. Frankly, I can't imagine anyone wanting to live there. Give me Farnham, Guildford or Dorking any time....

I'm going to break off now for a cuppa and a biccie, seeing as you made one ten minutes ago and didn't ask me. So obviously will have to make my own. What's that? You didn't think I wanted to be disturbed? When have I ever refused the offer of a cuppa? No, too late now, I'll do it myself.

Three minutes later – slurp, slurp, slurp. Right, back to business. We really are living in a new "puritan" age. The "Thought Police" are everywhere, and they come in many shapes, sizes and both sexes. Now, Anthony Horowitz, a renowned and accomplished writer, has been commissioned by the estate of Ian Fleming to write a new James Bond novel. Well, he has and he decided to show it, or share it, with his wife, a lady called Jill Green. Having read the first draft JG as we'll call her, was "infuriated by the spy's attitudes to women." AH says, "She was quite angry about some of the words I used and the descriptions," before sycophantically adding, "She was right, as she always is and I had to cut back." Firstly, can we be reminded just who was commissioned to pen the novel. Was it he or was it he and she? Secondly, the story is set in 1957, not post-feminist 1987 for Christ's sake. Why should he have to alter anything to satisfy his wife's feminist lack of humour or, more importantly change a beloved character to suit a political correctness, not conducive to the time in which the story is set. This Green Lady, by the way, is a TV producer by trade or possibly – tirade! I rest my remote....

I read that 7-year-olds will be facing stiffer tests under new rules first mooted by Michael Gove when he was Education Secretary. I glossed through the minutiae, but it's basically checking the child's ability to understand punctuation, grammar and be able to read "accurately and fluently without over-sounding and blending." In other words, speaking English as we were taught all those years ago when we had proper teachers. In maths they should be able to mentally subtract two digit numbers, such as $74 - 33$, this being the

Daily Mail's example. My main interest was concerning the response by those who spend most of their time lurking at home with colds or stress, awaiting yet another inset day, yes, the teachers!

Aahh, here we are and guess what? No surprises. The qualified brethren have warned that the tests are too difficult and could damage children's confidence. A lady representative, and I am sure she is, of the Association of Teachers and Lecturers, one Mary Boustead, (as opposed to Ofsted) said the tests were "not developmentally sound." So once again teachers are true to form with their total lack of support for anything designed to improve the basis for learning. Methinks that increasing the standards of teachers employed should be one of the first tasks of any Education Secretary.

It seems to me that teachers will divert any responsibility for children's education, welfare and all-round citizenship wherever an opportunity arises. Their lack of enthusiasm isn't helped by a political society hell bent on targets. I have no doubt that, say, bullying is often hidden or sidestepped, rather than confronted, because it could call the school's ratings into question. League tables for schools and hospitals should be stopped immediately. It doesn't help anyone except the ministers who introduce systems they will never have to work with themselves and statisticians who need "comparable figures" like alcoholics needs lager or cider – or more likely both mixed together with just a dash of blackcurrant. Just for the record, "schoolmaster " is an anagram of "the classroom" and "dormitory" becomes "dirty room".

One area where I would love to see teachers assert themselves far more concerns the spread of radicalisation and the Muslim terrorist threat that grows daily across Europe. I remember making the point in previous books and it gives me no pleasure to.read of infiltration through school governorships in Birmingham schools. I am aware that Ofsted has investigated and is continuing to investigate but you know it will never lead to the deportation of those responsible for what is a quest to change British society as we know it and impose Sharia law in the not too distant future. Over-reaction? Hype? Panic or just plain fanciful? Wedges with thin ends have a habit of getting thicker if not trimmed. Would you have thought 20 years ago that we would read of school inspectors witnessing a situation where girls were made to sit at the back of the classroom? That's what they found at Park View School and that the GCSE syllabus was "restricted to comply with a conservative Islamic teaching," and that an extremist preacher had been invited to speak to the children. Five non-Muslim teachers have left their posts as schools were put under pressure to segregate classrooms and change teaching practices in order to reflect radical Islamic beliefs. According to Ofsted, areas of "collective concern" include "pressure" on head teachers (master and mistress as was) to adopt "certain philosophies and approaches" and a selective form of appointing teaching staff. There is also comment from Ofsted on the risk of "eroding the basic entitlement of children to a rounded education." To be fair, even ... EVEN the general secretary of The National Association of Head Teachers, a certain Mr. Hobby, got on his horse at that particular annual union conference and stated that concerted efforts had been made by Islamists to infiltrate schools in Birmingham and that they were part of a bigger plot involving schools in Bradford, Manchester and East London. When a statement from the NAHT refers to attempts to "alter the character of schools in line with Islamic faiths which includes sidelining parts of the National Curriculum and attempting to influence the appointment of Muslim staff", then I think we can safely say we have a major cultural and potential terrorist problem on our hands. Still, no government can say that whilst they didn't see it, Middle England has seen it coming for years.

Of course, the older you get, the more radical (I use the word in a wider sense) young people become. Primary school pupils morph into secondary school pupils, who then morph into students. This is where the great change appears to lie. Students become left-wing, anti-establishment provocateurs and join the Labour or Communist party and those with little else to do but prevaricate join Class War and throw paint bombs at every given opportunity.

David Cameron reminded universities of their duties to clamp down on "hate preachers" when speaking at recent events. Last year over 70 of these so-called preachers attended venues in order to spout their views at student meetings. Imagine if a member of UKIP were to be invited. Christ, all hell would break loose but you have to ask, who are these people who invite the preachers in the first place?

Well, the worst offending colleges appear to be Queen Mary, King's College, the School of Oriental and African Studies and Kingston University. As ever, the worrying aspect is the view taken by the National Union of Students who oppose any anti-radicalisation strategy. They maintain it will create a culture of suspicion at academic institutions and restrict freedom of speech. That's rich! Do they not see that that is exactly what these preachers are proposing, a complete lack of equality for females and an undermining of our values of democracy and tolerance of others and the views they hold.

For many years I have been of the opinion that successive British governments of all political hues have treated the threat of Muslim extremism in this country in the same way as Chamberlain treated Germany, just prior to that little contretemps that escalated into six years of world war. We appear to have adopted a principle of burying one's head in the sand and hoping that a tinkering at the corners of the problem and a brief finger-wagging will solve all. It won't, we need a strong, relentless campaign against anything considered harmful to our democratic values and it should be addressed sooner rather than later. Who were these mealy-mouthed do-gooders who supported Abu Hamza in his attempt to halt his extradition order? As ever, our country is not helped by the grossly one-sided "human wrongs" legislation with us blindly signing up to it because it probably seemed the right thing to do at the time. Extremists have issues and agendas, normal people do not. That is why they breed and spread like the very worst cancers.

Mr. Cameron should make it clear that any teachings of religious fervour should be considered as "possible" acts of treason against the state. This is not, as I write, an Islamic state but I fear for my grandchildren. When I said a couple of sentences ago "that's why they breed" I meant exactly that. Look at the birth rate of Muslims in this country and as their numbers increase the choice of candidates in an election will most likely reflect that rise and tactical voting for those with a particular religious bent will ensue. We already have problems with postal votes and fraud. Intimidation and abuse of our democratic system will get worse – a lot worse. It will no longer be a case of voting for the person or party you feel best represents your views, but the candidate representing your religion, issues and/ or aims.

So, here's a little story called "Democracy and Racism Explained." I'll tell you this and then we are going to have a nice cup of tea. To be fair, after reading all that, you probably need it.

So, an illegal Muslim immigrant child, now relocated to Cardiff, asks his mother, "Mumma, what's the difference between democracy and racism?" Mother (hardly to be seen as she's in full burka) replies, "Well, son, democracy is when British taxpayers work hard every day so that we can get all our benefits. You know, like, free housing, free National Health, free education and grants to build mosques and community centres and far more welfare payments than British pensioners get. That's democracy." "But, Mumma," responded the child, "don't the British taxpayers get pissed off about all that?" "Sure they do, son, but that's what we call racism."

Well, the cuppa's going down well, thanks for that. What's that? Oh, yes, a couple of Hobnobs. Thanks! I didn't see them there.

I don't know why it is, maybe it's just the way my brain, or lack of it, doesn't work. I've just thought of another book I've recently read. The reason it didn't come to me earlier was due to the fact that I didn't own the book. I was loaned the book and yes, I did return it. Whilst a very funny and entertaining read at times, it was also frustratingly disingenuous at others. However, Jeremy Hardy's autobiography hit the spot for me and no mistake. For those of you not familiar with the chap, you will often hear him on Radio 4 panel shows, such as the "News Quiz" and "I'm Sorry I Haven't A Clue." He also had a radio series some ten years ago now, I believe, entitled "Jeremy Hardy Addresses the Nation." The book is called "My Family & Other Strangers." It is an interesting premise in a search through registers to see if there is anyone famous or of note in his family background. Very well written, I found myself laughing out loud on several occasions and then almost instantaneously fuming at his namby-pamby leftie views. He appeared on "Just a Minute" in 2000 and faced a very hostile Radio 4 audience. When given the word "parasite" by Nicholas Parsons on which he was to talk for sixty seconds he spoke about the Royal Family. I never heard the episode myself but I can imagine you are not going to make too many friends on a Radio 4 panel show with that analogy, although I do sympathise with his view on this subject.

Jeremy Hardy comments in his book of his disdain for Farnham – too white for his liking – bloody cheek. I think you'll find that that is why white people live there. If I want to live in Brixton, I'll move to Brixton. Sadly, he rants at everything and most people if it's white or pro-white or middle-class – taxpayers as we call them, whilst leading the charge towards a multi-cultural society (social engineering) and giving his full support to the lower classes (benefit claimants and the hard done by). He was actually born in Farnborough, so the lad is local but his family moved across the border to Surrey, which I suspect he hates just as much, and lived in Mytchett, just up the road from where I live in Ash Vale. Mytchett is located in the southern most part of Surrey Heath Borough Council and it borders Guildford Borough Council, to whom Ash Valians pay their rates. So when I receive a letter addressed "Ash Vale, Aldershot, Hants" it really grates and determines an immediate phone call – or almost immediate if I need to go to the loo, obviously – in order to correct the heinous mistake. So, it was a really good read – if you can imagine reading a book written by someone who enjoys ranting. Can you imagine!!

Aren't our police pointless? I see that an injured motor-cyclist was left by the roadside for 3 hours as three police forces decided the incident had not happened within their area of jurisdiction. Bedfordshire, Cambridgeshire and Northamptonshire police are the farces involved. They just passed the 999 call from county to county – unbelievable! At least being white, the motor-cyclist won't be suing the police for racial discrimination, so that's something they can be grateful for!

I remember many years ago, shortly after we had moved here, I was driving home in my ... wait for it ... Triumph Herald Convertible in lemon yellow, when a pig appeared in the road in front of me. I wasn't aware that in the early 70's there was still a working pig farm in Scotland Farm Road, near to where I now live. I rang Surrey Police, who appeared more concerned as to which part of the road in question the pig was ambling along, as it could be a Hampshire pig (no Hampshire Hog jokes, please) as opposed to a Surrey pig. They were reluctant and I had to ring Aldershot Police Station, who then referred me to Surrey. All those years ago now I cannot remember what happened at the end of the saga but I suspect, hopefully, that the little piggy went wee wee wee all the way back to Scotland Farm and lived happily ever after. Well, until next week when he was obviously bacon – but being the 1970's, non Halal.

Right! Time for a little light-hearted story or three. This is a nice follow-on from the last story. It concerns two farmers. Indeed, two Aberdeen farmers, Tam and Shughie, who were sitting in the farmers' bar in a little pub just outside Aberdeen. Tam turns to Shughie and says, "Do you know what, I'm tired of going through life wi'oot an education. The morn I am going awa doon tae the community college te sign up fer some classes." Shughie thinks it's a good idea and the two leave.

The next day Tam goes away doon te the college and meets the lecturer, who signs him up for four basic courses. – Maths, English, History and Logic. "Logic," Tam says, "What's that?" The lecturer says, "I'll show you. Do you own a strimmer?" "Aye." Says Tam. "Then logically because you own a strimmer I think you have a garden." "Well, aye, that's true, I dae ha' a garden." "I'm not done," the lecturer says. "Because you have a garden I think logically that you have a house." "Aye, I've a hoose." "And because you have a house, I logically think that you have a family." "I do." "And because you have a family, then logically you must have a wife." "Yer nae wrang, I dae hae a wife." "And because you have a wife then logically you must be heterosexual." "I am an' all," says Tam, "that's amazing. You were able te find a' that oot jist because I hae a strimmer."

Fair excited about the classes, Tam shakes the lecturer's hand and goes awa te meet Shughie doon the toon. He tells Shughie aboot his classes and how he was doing Maths, English, History and Logic. "Logic?" says Shughie. "What's that?" "Well," says Tam, "Dae ye hae a strimmer?" "No," replies Shughie. "Aha! That proves wha I always thought. You're a poof!"

And the second of the trio, whilst stitching a cut in the hand of a 75-year-old farmer after it was caught in a gate when he was working cattle, the doctor struck up a conversation with the old man. Eventually the topic got around to politicians and their role as leaders. The old farmer said, "Well, as I see it all politicians are 'post tortoises.' Not being familiar with the term the doctor asked him what a 'post tortoise' was. The old farmer said, "If you ever drive along a country road and you come across a fence post with a tortoise balanced on the top, then that's a 'post tortoise'." He saw the puzzled look upon the doctor's face, so he continued to explain. "You know he didn't get up there by himself, he doesn't belong up there, he doesn't know what to do while he's up there, he's been elevated beyond his ability and you just wonder what kind of arse put him up there in the first place!"

So, not so far from the truth after all.

And the third little story is one of innocence. A farmer drove to a neighbour's farmhouse and knocked at the door. The young son of 9 years opened the door to the farmer. "Is your dad or mum home?" he enquired. "No, they went to town." "How about your older brother, Howard? Is he here?" "No, he went with mum and dad." The farmer stood for a few minutes shifting from one foot to the other, mumbling to himself. The young boy, attempting to be helpful, said, "I know where all dad's tools are if you want to borrow one, or I can give dad a message." The farmer looked uncomfortable. "Well … no, I really need to talk to your dad about your brother, Howard, getting my daughter, Susie, pregnant." The boy thought for a moment and then replied, "Then you will have to talk to my dad about that. I know he charges £500 for the bulls and £150 for the pigs, but I have no idea how much he charges for Howard."

Please note that the above jokes involved only English and Scottish farmers, there being no place for the Welsh, who were notoriously preoccupied with their sheep at the time of telling!

Right! Time to head for the kitchen before we sit and watch "Not Going Out." Every episode is a veritable gem. Lee Mack is without doubt one of my favourite comedy actors. He is also extremely enjoyable to watch on "Would I Life To You?" opposite that inspired choice of sparring partner, David Mitchell. With "Uncle Bryn," Rob Brydon as anchor-man, it really works well. It's interesting the extra breadth of comedy he brought to the role after the TV passing of Angus Deayton – what is he doing now? So, it's four Weetabix with half a tin of apricots, drowned in semi-skimmed milk (good boy!) and doused with liberal sprinklings of sugar over the Weetabix (bad boy!) What's that? Oh, go on then, help yourself to a Hobnob and make a cuppa before we both sit down. TV is on and sitting back to eat. See you tomorrow.

We start tomorrow, Friday, with a couple of related observations. If at first you don't succeed, destroy all evidence that you tried. Or, alternatively, if at first you don't succeed, then sky-diving is not for you.

First things first, I am firing up the Apple Mac as we speak – or write – and what do we find? Having wended their way through the ether, we have the following emails:

Firstly, there is an invitation to give a talk to a ladies' club in Basildon. Another invitation to a Probus Club in Surrey and a confirmation of a talk already booked for next year.

There, a satisfying start to the day. The ladies' club has just one date available and yes, I can do it, whilst the Probus Club have offered me three alternatives. One of these dates is already taken but the other two are free, better get back and state a preference. Naturally, the obligatory spams are present. So what gems are presenting themselves today … mmm….

There is a reminder from a lady called Linda Ramirez telling me that my life insurance policy payment is due – didn't know I had one. Some unnamed cove is offering me coupons to buy "new tires." These coupons must be redeemed soon as they are about to expire – before my tyres, I trust. Next! Oh, that's interesting, there's another life insurance policy payment reminder. This time it's from Barbara Ramirez – must be a family business. Erica is inviting me to obtain a Russian girlfriend, adding that these ladies are "gorgeous" and suggesting that I review their profiles. I think not. There, already deleted! And then we have Starbucks (Greedy Bastards PLC), no it doesn't say that, obviously, that's merely an anagram but they are offering me "free ventisize cups of coffee on us – coupon enclosed." A, what is a "ventisized cup?" and B has no-one at Starbucks ever read my books, because if they had they would be aware that I would never soil my shoes on their doorsteps.

The paper I'm reading this morning is The Independent, so let's have a quick perusal. Mmmm, aha, ahum, aah, here's an interesting little statistic, offered up, not surprisingly, by the Office of National Statistics. It reveals that nationally 1.6% of all people identify themselves as either lesbian, homosexual or bi-sexual. In London the percentage is 2.6. Now, if I were to guess I would have thought that head for head (and no, that's not a euphemism) Brighton would have come out (and no, that's not a cheap aside) on top (and no, only 50% can be). Frankly, who cares? Who on earth orders their minnows to collate these sort of statistics, and why? Who benefits other than members of the National Union of Collators, and I'm sure there is one.

Now, the following does nothing to further REAL grievance by so-called minorities. There runs in California a train through wine-making country. On one particular trip eleven black women were ejected for laughing too loudly during an afternoon excursion last month. This is not the sort of behaviour that would take place during a wine-tasting trip in Surrey, obviously, although one can imagine it being par for the tracks through traditional wine-making areas such as Halifax, Todmorden or Wigan. I am sure, however, that they would have apologised for their behaviour but not in Nappa Valley. For the "black eleven" as I refer to them, have filed a racial discrimination lawsuit, each seeking $1 million in compensation. Now, if I were ever so slightly cynical I might just have a passing thought that they were playing the race card, but I could be right!

Now, I've always been fascinated by coincidences, none more so than the SS Titanic. Today it is noted that a menu for the last lunch served has just sold for £58,000. The first-class menu offered grilled mutton chops and custard pudding, corned beef with mashed, fried and baked potatoes and a buffet of fish, ham and beef. Afters included apple meringue pastry and a selection of eight cheeses. And that was lunch! As a youngster I spent a lot of time in Battersea Library. Being an only child it seemed easy to immerse myself in books. Looking back it seemed relaxing and one was without the pressure that parents always seemed to put upon me in one form or another. I may have written more on that subject, but on the basis it would have been in the first book and I never read anything I have written before, please forgive me if I've written about this famous steamship before.

Back in Battersea Library, all those years ago, I pulled out a book on The Titanic and the Forward mentioned a novel written some years before the great liner was launched, but the storyline and the dimensions of the ship were uncannily similar. That has stayed with me for all these years, although the details had faded. What did remain was the fact that the author's name was something Morgan, or maybe Morgan something, but that was it. Oh, the power of the Internet. I looked it up one day last year, having attempted to download Debbie Does Doncaster, followed by Edna Does Epsom – I am gradually working my way through the alphabet, I expect it will be Freda Does Frinton next – anyway, there is quite a bit on the web about both the book and the man. Firstly, his name was Morgan Robertson and the book surrounds the fortunes, or lack of them, of a man who held a high position but fell on hard times and was then employed as a deckhand on board a ship sailing for England from New York. The ship in the novel is described as the "largest craft afloat," crewed with officers of Royal Navy background, a professional standard applied to the personnel of the engine room and the stewards' department being equal to a first-class hotel. Two brass bands, two orchestras and a theatre company are also featured.

During the description it comments that "from the bridge, engine room, and a dozen places on her deck the 92 doors of 19 water-tight compartments could be closed in half a minute by turning a lever. These doors would also close automatically in the presence of water. With 9 compartments flooded the ship would still float and no accident of the sea could possibly fill this many compartments. The steamship 'Titan' was considered practically unsinkable." Yes, the Titan!

The description continues its uncanny resemblance to Titanic with references to the following statistics when read in conjunction with those of the Titanic. Firstly, the Titan was given as being 800 feet long, the Titanic was 882 feet and 9 inches. The Titan's fictitious speed was 25 knots, the Titanic's was 22.5. Both ships were built of steel.

The weight of the Titan was 45,000 tons whilst the Titanic was 66,000. The Titan's horsepower was recorded as 40,000 and the Titanic's was 46,000. As previously noted, the Titan had 19 watertight compartments, the Titanic had 16. The passenger and crew capacity was 3,000 for each ship. The Titanic's owners, White Star, showed much the same disregard for safety as that described in the novel, as both claimed their ships were unsinkable, thus 24 lifeboats were fitted to the fictitious Titan, whereas in reality, 16 lifeboats and 4 Engelhardt folding lifeboats were placed upon the Titanic. Both ships succumbed by hitting icebergs, both on their starboard bow and ironically both 400 miles off the Newfoundland coast. In the novel the iceberg was hit "near midnight", in reality the Titanic was hit at 11.40 pm. In the novel the full complement of 3,000 were on board the ship, of which 13 survived. On the Titanic the figure was just over 2,220 and over 700 survived. It was the uncanny nature of these coincidences, rather than the detail, that lingered in the back of my mind. By the way, both ships sailed from their respective ports during April, so you can imagine the interest I took when modern technology allowed access to the ship's remains and yes, I did buy the video and the book and two subsequent books. A year ago I received a gift of "The Wreck of the Titan" reprinted by Hesperus Press. The novella by Morgan Robertson is only 84 pages long, but it's the content that counts.

Interestingly, do you know what you get if you cross the Atlantic Ocean with the Titanic? Answer: About half way!

News just in! It's just been announced that Irish divers were amazed to find that after one hundred years of lying on the sea bed, Titanic's swimming pool was still full!

One final point, are you aware that "The Titanic Disaster" is an anagram of "Death, it starts in ice."

Writing these notes and memories of Battersea Library have reminded me that I obviously read more books than I previously imagined. Sadly, just what I read as a youth is now firmly forgotten. There seems to have been a large gap of reading between those teenage years and my mid-forties. Funny that.

And now for something completely different, though connected to the above in a manner not overly obvious at this stage! One of the finest comedy series I have ever watched was "Mrs. Merton and Malcolm" played by Caroline Aherne and Craig Cash. Panned by the so-called authorities, ie the critics, the comments arising from the six episodes caused obvious pain to the writers, the team consisting of Aherne, Cash and Henry Normal. "Time Out" magazine's reviewer described it as "Possibly the most disturbing show on television". Other critics considered Malcolm to be suffering from mental illness or a sufferer of infantilism at best and incest at worst, due to the close relationship between mother and son. With these comments and I suspect many more ringing in their collective ears, they turned their talents to a second series of the "Royal Family."

I mentioned "Mrs. Merton and Malcolm" because not only did it hit the spot for me, but it made me laugh out loud without the need of a studio or canned audience, suggesting what was funny and when. The timing and acting was superb. If only they'd asked me! Anyway, the point of bringing up this series in the first place was that throughout the many memorable lines, one was extremely pertinent. In this particular scene Malcolm is very keen on a young lady who works in the chemist, Judith Potts. He asks if he can take her to the pictures to see a film called "Titanic." She says yes, although she later lets him down. Malcolm turns to Mr. Malik, the Indian pharmacist, and asks him if he has seen "Titanic." "No," Mr. Malik replies, "I have very little interest in shipping." Classic! Oh, and yes, I did buy the DVD of "Mrs. Merton and Malcolm" and I regularly savour the six priceless episodes. Interesting, of course, is the fact that whilst the critics criticised Malcolm, no-one appears to have criticised Ian Lavender's portrayal of Private Pike in "Dad's Army." Yet, he was a mummy's boy. Oh, how politically correct times have changed.

Crikey! Is that the time? Thanks for telling me. What? Oh, no, don't worry about me, you just go and make another cuppa. I had better get ready. I'm off to Maidstone to give a talk to a mixed group. By that, I mean male and female, not mixed race! I'll catch up with you later – Byeee.

Back again. A lovely, receptive group who made me most welcome, and with a cuppa on arrival you can't go wrong. Incidentally, I usually have a freshen- up when arriving at a venue, sometimes preceded with a wee first. As a rule, there is a sign that reads, "Please wash your hands" or "Now wash your hands." A village hall toilet I once used in East Sussex proclaimed, "Now wash your hands in the sink." I did wonder what the other possibilities were, but ended up taking their advice. Of course, if you visit a public toilet in Surrey you'll find it reads, "Would you mind awfully washing your hands – that really is most kind of you."

I arrived at the hall in good time – time enough to consider the wedding plans of swimmer Tom Daley and his – I struggle with this – boyfriend, one Justin Black. This is quite amusing on its own as he could have been Justin Green or Justin White, the latter of which he will no doubt be in at their wedding. The colour photograph shows the two men, Daley to the left with his left arm behind his "other half." They've just announced their engagement. Daley is 21 and his intended 41. If Daley was a girl no doubt Mr. Black would be considered a cradle snatcher, but as they are both of the same persuasion I suspect that I'm now the last man standing who finds the idea of same-sex marriage totally repulsive. There actually are others like me but similarly with immigration and race, "nobody likes to say anything now, do they?" The "Archers" has been politicised to the point that everybody was cock-a-hoop (probably the wrong phrase) when Adam met the man of his dreams. No dissenters, no adverse comment, just total adulation for a marriage made in abnormality. As you know, I have nothing against two members of the same sex living together but marriage and children, it frankly wants to make me throw up.

Now the following really pigs me off. Under the "courts" section of the Independent the headline reads, "British boy in terror plot was radicalised online by ISIS." It tells the story of a 14-year-old who plotted a massacre on Anzac Day in Australia. It's the use of the word "British". They all use it, the BABC, the press, they all like to include these people as "British." They are not British. As I've said previously, the fact that they live in this country (our country) possess a British passport and enjoy our democratic process, does not make them British. They are foreigners who happen through our own stupidity to be here. As I have noted before, even if I was born to white parents from Britain in Pakistan, it wouldn't make me a Pakistani, I'd still be British, although in my case of course, English. And, as we always say, any fool can be British it takes far more breeding to be English.

Whilst Oxfam, Amnesty International and the Archbishops of everywhere condemn this government for NOT taking in hundreds of thousands of refugees, it gives me no pleasure to record the news that over the past year 6,000 acres of Green Belt land has been lost to housing and still the authorities are hell-bent on building more. Unbelievable.

I am reluctantly early to bed tonight as I am leaving early tomorrow for Brecon. I have decided to take a couple of days off and stretch my legs in the Beacons, or possibly a pub bar but no matter, it will be a change of scenery from the south-east. So, a story aforebed, methinks. This little tale takes place on the Sussex coast so in your mind trot off to Victoria Station, take your seat upon the latter-day version of the Brighton Belle and you will be in good time to peruse the antique shops in The Lanes. You are now ready to read the story.

Four retired men are walking down a street in Brighton. They turn a corner and see a sign that reads, "Retirees Bar – all drinks 20p." They look at each other and then go in, thinking this is too good to be true. The barman says in a voice that carries across the room, "Come on in and let me pour one for you. What'll it be, gentlemen?" Behind him is a fully stocked bar so each of the men orders a malt whisky. In no time the barman serves up four malt whiskies and says, "That'll be 20p each, please." The four men stare at the barman for a moment and then at each other. They cannot believe their good fortune. They each joke about it being their round and eventually one of them hands over 80p. They finish their whiskies and order another round. Again, four excellent malt whiskies are produced with the barman requesting 80p. They pay but the curiosity now gets the better of them. Finally one of them says, "I've got to ask you, how can you afford to serve malt whisky as good as this for 20p a shot?" The barman places his arms upon the bar and replies, "When I retired I always wanted to own a bar and last year I hit the Euro millions jackpot, £125 million!" They were aghast, they repeated the figure and he nods. "Yep, that much, so I decided to open this place. Every drink costs 20p, wine, spirits, beer, it's all the same." All the men look at each other before one of the men exclaims, "Crikey, that really is a great story." As the four of them sip their whiskies they cannot help noticing seven other people at the end of the bar who don't have any drinks in front of them and haven't ordered anything the whole time they have been there. Nodding in their direction one of the four asks the barman, "What's with them?" The barman says, "Oh, they're pensioners from Scotland and they're waiting for Happy Hour when all drinks are half price!"

It's Saturday evening and I am writing these notes from a B & B deep in the Beacons. It's been a lovely day, weather-wise, journey was good. Stopped in Calne for breakfast with tea and a cake in Brecon. Dinner was partaken in Abercraf. Of course, it's rugby World Cup time at the moment and tonight it was England's turn in the limelight. The match was unfolding as I tucked into my steak with peppercorn sauce and I'm glad to say two large onion rings. It was interesting witnessing the scene in a Welsh pub. During the match the Welsh bayed, and every time the opposition got the ball, oh, how they cheered. As I've said before, I've always backed England first but if they were to be knocked out of a competition, then I'll root for Scotland, Wales, Northern Ireland and Eire. You never find a Scot or a Welshman rooting for England. It's always a case of "anyone but". I can't speak for an Ulsterman as I'm not sure I know any, but I would surmise support, or lack of it, being given dependent upon your religious persuasion – that harbinger of hate.

My new car, as you know, is all but a few weeks old. When I arrived in Brecon I parked in the main town car park before making my way to the meter. My heart sank. It's one of those that requires you to enter your vehicle registration number. As you also know I owned my previous Kia for nigh on three years and I never got to grips with that one's registration number. So, back I trudged from the meter, making a mental note of the number before retracing my steps to the same ticket machine. Tapping in the number of the vehicle and placing my coins in the appropriate slot I then pushed the green button. All of this technological philandering was, I have to say, under the much-appreciated supervision of a local lady who helped me through this very tiresome and unwieldy procedure, but through it we got. Back I went to the car clutching my precious ticket, pressed the key fob and lo and behold the indicator lights flashed on a car two up from the one I had taken the number from. Well, the Audi was black and had five doors! Bugger! Back I went towards the ticket machine where I espied two car-parking attendants. I explained the situation, you know, that I was new to the area, just bought my car and no, I don't appear to know the difference between an Audi and a Kia, before mentioning that we don't have machines like this in Surrey. I think it was the fact he realised I was English that he then gave me a sympathetic look and he was, to be fair, sympathetic enough not to take the mickey and said, "Don't worry, I've made a note and I'll tell my colleague." Being of a slightly cynical nature, as you know and never trusting the Welsh anyway, I did wonder if I would come back to find my car with a parking ticket on it but no, all was fine and dandy and my windscreen unfettered.

A walk into the High Street, a street I hadn't visited for many a year, found me outside what I believed to be the old town hall. Anyway, standing on the doorstep was a white man handing out flyers to passers-by. There was a smell of spicy food wafting and music, not penetrative but inviting. "Would you like to take a little time," he invited, "it's a fair trade fair, crafts and food – it's free entry." "Fair trade?" I retorted. "Yes," his eyes lit up with enthusiasm. "It's fair trade, all the profits go directly to those who produce the goods and food. There are no middlemen." (I should have enquired about middlewomen, but it seemed churlish). Now this is where it's difficult not to enjoy oneself. "Oh," I said, "fair trade? I've always been a great supporter of slavery myself. You know where you are with slavery. Everyone's in bed at the same time, chained, no skiving off, ready for the fields come daylight." His face was a picture. "And, of course, the advantage with slavery is that inflation always remains low. You're competitive and the worker takes what he's given and is grateful!" I left it at that. Funny, but he didn't say anything else. I did actually wander around the floor upstairs and yes, if you like wooden, tribal knick-knacks, bling object d'art and garish clothing that would no doubt frighten the horses, then it was all very interesting but on the whole, there was nothing I found comparable to clothing found in Orvis, Joules or Fat Face in Farnham.

Tomorrow I shall go for a ride on the Brecon Mountain Railway, along with hundreds of others and it looks like being another fine day, though not, I suspect, for England's rugby team or their supporters. Being beaten 33 points to 13 was not good, although it was naturally good for the Welsh. Funny, but I didn't know the rugby World Cup was on until the Hog's Back Brewery produced another brew of "England's Glory". It's really the only way I become aware of yet another impending sporting disaster but hearing the cheers in that pub every time Australia scored was hard to take and as nations we do live next door to each other. Still, the Welsh are, in the main a small-minded nation....

I'm just reading a few stories before I turn in and say goodnight. Some people have some neck don't they. There's a couple that moved home in the West Midlands and hired the services of a "man with a van" who they found on Fastbuck. He and his mate loaded the van in record quick time and left the flat never to reappear at the pub the couple were taking over. It is sad, it is mean, but I have to ask – who in their right mind hires a removal "firm" from Facebook with a nonsignwritten van and a driver who charges £40. Still, thinking about it, it is the West Midlands and probably quite expensive by their standards.

The second story of note concerns a woman called Janine Adeleke, another well established English name. She ran an escort agency that brought her in some £1.5 million over an eight-year period. I have no problem with her income, what I do have a problem with is the fact that this very greedy lady received over the same period £117,000 in benefits, tax credits and carer's allowance. She claimed to be a single mother of five children with an elderly mother to look after. Greed, sheer unadulterated greed. I would deport her, her children, any children's children, her mother and all who sailed in her. I wouldn't care that she was born here – remember, they may hold one of our passports but they'll never be British, let alone English. What's that? Yes, I am feeling slightly pious.

The next page contains a story of historical guilt, or "chancing your arm" as I see it. David Cameron has visited Jamaica. Of course, any visitation to black inhabited former colonies reveals calls for money. Who are these lobbyists who continue to seek apologies from those who never owned slaves and billions in compensation from a country whose current natives had bugger all to do with it in the first place. My message? Get over it! Go out and work for your living and stop campaigning and complaining. If you really want to garner a few "readies" there's a lady who runs a model agency who could give you a few tips!

Well, it's time to say goodnight. Just to tell you that it's so peaceful here. The lady who runs the B & B keeps chickens that are let out at 7 am and penned (or should that be henned) at dusk. The view from my bedroom window is stunning. So glad I found this place. No noise and a clear sky. Heaven.... Good zzzzzzzzzzz.

Since I last wrote I have awoken, scratched, showered, breakfasted and collected my belongings and refilled my car. I'm off to Merthyr. I feel the need to self-inject a huge dollop of plight. Last time I was here I felt it was the kind of town that gave Aldershot a good name. It is dour. However, the sun is shining, it's warm and the Brecon Mountain Railway beckons. I suppose it beckons in Brecon!

It's late afternoon, a brisk wind, kites soaring above the moors and a very pleasant ride behind a steam locomotive, or choo-choo as a friend of mine refers to it. Time to wend my way back towards Abergavenny, over the bridge and then home. I'll talk to you later.

It's now later, much later and the kettle's just boiled. Aah, nothing like a cuppa after a long journey. I have a biccie to dunk and then it's upstairs to Bedfordshire. I'll leave you with a thought. A clear conscience is usually the sign of a bad memory. Night, night.

Hot on the heels of reading that 6,000 acres of Green Belt land has been lost in the last year, George Osborne has pledged to "shake Britain out of its inertia" by making it harder for rural and provincial councils and "nimby activists" to frustrate building developments. Bloody cheek. We ruin this country at our peril. I'm not going to harp on – honest – but it's a crying shame that we have no-one in authority or government, as it likes to be called, who cannot see the same view as that which is obvious to millions of true Brits.

It's Monday morning and no work today. Now, this is what gets racism a good name. There's a chap called Adam Dinham, nice enough sounding name. He is Professor of Faith and Public Policy at Goldsmith's College, University of London. He has drawn up a religious literacy programme due to be unveiled to employees shortly. He contends that when preparing food at corporate do's, one should be careful not to offend any religious group by making sure that Kosher food is not placed next to Halal. Both foods should be certified and thought given as to whether or not to provide alcohol. This programme has been commissioned by the interfaith group

CoExist House. They also deal with clothing and which religious artefacts are right or not quite right to wear. It's people like these at CoExist and professors like him who fuel resentment from the native population. Apparently it's not a good idea to microwave sausages in the office microwave in case it causes offence to fellow workers of other religious persuasions. If they don't like it, bugger off! Another area for discrimination appears to be concerned with religious days off – or shirking as I call it. Naturally, the equality and human wrongs commission states that "If you refuse everyone's request to take time off on a particular day which happened to be a special observance day for workers of a particular religion, this may be indirect discrimination unless you can objectively justify your refusal." Christ Almighty! It's all quite justifiable. These coves are employed to work, not shirk. Get on with your job and visit your temple, or whatever it is you visit in your own time after work. Needy or what!

Now here is an area where you could make some money from those dropping litter. Under new legislation those caught can be fined £100, an increase of £20 from the current £80. It really is a scant deterrent. Make it £500 and those thoughtless bastards might think again.

Now, this made me smile – and sigh. There is a chart outlining fees charged by well-known personalities for after-dinner speeches. John Humphrys, for instance, charges between £5,000 and £10,000, Melvyn Bragg £11,000 to £16,000, Gary Lineker £25,000, whilst Stephen Fry is £50,000. Good luck to them all but it certainly puts my meagre amount, inclusive of travel, into perspective. Bugger!

Oh, doesn't it warm the cockles. I read that Hungary is to build an iron curtain to deter immigrants. The country's prime minister has said they are doing it so as to avoid multi-cultural Britain's mistake. As they say, if you are being overrun you cannot continue to accept migrants. Those Hungarians, they know a thing or three.

You remember the man with the van who moved a couple's personal possessions from a flat to a pub – but didn't – well, there's a chap in London who contacted a "man with a van." Sounds like the same man as they both had a West Midlands accent and both charged £40. This chap in question has just lost £8000 worth of champagne and yes, I know I shouldn't be smiling, but would you trust anyone with a West Midlands accent to move your furniture? I ask you!

Well, it's a bright start to the day and I have a talk this afternoon in north Kent. It's back to Bexleyheath. One of my favourite comedians was Linda Smith and it's now nine years since she died. I remember travelling to a talk in Burgess Hill when Radio 4 presented a half-hour tribute to her. Several snippets from her "one lady show" were broadcast. They featured good, clean, observational humour without the almost mandatory four-letter words. She never needed to lower her standards unlike many of today's comedians in order to obtain a very cheap and often unworthy laugh (Apollo comedians take note). One of her most poignant comments concerned her home town of Erith. She said, "I come from Erith, Erith is either in north-west Kent or south-east London, dependent upon whether you rent or you are private. Erith is boring, Erith is so boring it isn't twinned with anywhere, though it does have a suicide pact with Dartford." Classic.

Today's front page shows a lovely photograph behind which lies a tragic story. The picture shows mum, dad and two smiling children. Sadly, the father, a policeman, was murdered by burglars who ran him down in their attempt to escape the scene. They would hang if I had my way.

Nice to see Theresa May stating the obvious. She has commented, "When immigration is too high, it's impossible to build a cohesive society, or for schools, hospitals, housing and transport to cope...." Well, other than the left and the Lib-Dems, no-one would disagree but will anything be done, other than encouraging George Osborne to make it easy for developers to build over the Green Belt? I rest my bulldozer.

Ah, now, this is good news. Robert Peston is to change sides and go to work for ITV. Perhaps we will have a political reporter on the BABC who speaks with continuity, clarity, flow and without intermittent crescendo. I've never understood those who consider him a joy to listen to and by moving to ITV he will join the ranks of Susannah Reid et al. Once unseen, never remembered.

Well, reasonably early to bed as two talks tomorrow, a ladies' luncheon club in Bexhill, followed by a WI in Surrey so I'll bid you goodnight, but before I go, a little story concerning a postman and a party. What's that? You're going to make a hot chocolate. Oh, well, you carry on while I tell the joke.

One Monday morning the postman was walking through the neighbourhood on his usual route delivering the mail and as he approached one of the homes, he noticed that both cars were still in the driveway. His bemusement was cut short by the home-owner, David, walking out with a load of empty beer, wine and spirit bottles towards the recycling bin. "Crikey, it looks as though you chaps had one hell of a party last night," the postman commented. David, in obvious pain, replied, "Actually, we had it Saturday night. This is the first time I've felt like moving since 4 am Sunday morning. We invited about fifteen couples from all around the area to have some weekend fun and it all got a bit wild. By midnight we'd all got so drunk we started playing the game 'Who Am I'." The postman thought for a moment before asking, "How do you play 'Who Am I'?" "Well, all the men go into the bedroom and come out one at a time covered by a sheet with only the 'family jewels', you know, meat and two veg, showing through a hole in the sheet. The game is that the women then try to guess who it is." The postman laughed and said, "That sounds like fun, I'm sorry I missed it." "It's probably a good thing you did," responded David. "Your name cropped up seven times!"

The morning has started as yesterday finished. David pointless Cameron has announced a crusade. Not one, of course, where we repel all borders or return from a foreign land with treasures and slaves, but one to house the buggers. He has pledged to build hundreds of thousands of homes in the hope that it will boost "social mobility". Can anyone explain to me what that really means, as I have absolutely no idea. I suspect it's a phrase concocted by an expensive marketing team employed to make any government appear to be actually doing something. It's similar to that cringe-making phrase "northern powerhouse". All a high-speed link does at £36 billion and rising, is to encourage those in the north to get to the south quicker and those with a somewhat twisted bent to arrive in Birmingham half an hour earlier than previously. As you must be aware, I've never understood the need to be taken like lemmings to the West Midlands and be subjected to the most horrendous accent in Christendom. What on earth did the inhabitants of that most unfortunate geographical area do in a previous life to be condemned to an existence speaking with those grating flattened vowels. Hideous, simply hideous.

I read that in America – where else – a boy of 11 has been charged with the murder of his 8-year-old neighbour, and all because she wouldn't let him see her puppy – and no, that's not a euphemism. Can you imagine? Police confirmed that the gun used by the 11-year-old was legally owned. Pound for pound, America has progressed very slowly in social terms and is basically still a country consisting mainly of white rednecks, with a few rednecks dressed in suits. Many of those in suits are now at the forefront of American policies and the problem with leadership is that it doesn't always come with common sense or common good as part of the equation. Mr. Obama has never had an easy ride regarding gun control, what with their nation's obsession with gun ownership.

I don't know about you, but I really do feel there is too much government interference in the content, make up and all round character of the BBC (yes, I'll call it what it should be this time). I cannot imagine why any government should wish to dictate to that which has produced such a traditionally strong news history. The World Service has been a beacon of free speech and fair play throughout the world and I understand is regarded as such. It is a by-word for even-handedness. However, successive governments have sought to interfere over long periods of time. This Tory government looks set to cut limbs from its body and produce something it can manage and control. It isn't theirs! They seem to look at it as they did gas, electricity, water, railways and the Post Office/Royal Mail. They never learn.

My cup of tea is going down very well this morning. Actually, it's the second of the day and it's only 7.50 am. Carol Kirkwood looks as lovely as she did yesterday and last week … so I shall wait with breath of a bated nature to witness her performance on Strictly this Saturday … aaah….

Rights and freedoms haven't done much for a certain group of females, as "young ladies" they certainly are not. A fight between two girls over a boy turned into a mass brawl when up to 200 teenagers, mainly female, battled in a high street for over four hours. It took over 100 police officers to eventually contain the situation. Hair extensions were pulled and one girl was literally pole-axed. These were some of the scenes witnessed by passers-by. Interesting to note that local residents surmised that the girls attended Sir George Monoux Sixth Form College and Leyton Sixth Form College. The surprise to me is the use of the word "college". I was expecting to read of a reform school or assessment centre, correction centre or youth offenders' detention centre and all this outside Walthamstow Central tube station. There are no standards, no decorum. Such behaviour would not have been countenanced during the prime of Miss Jean Brodie.

I'm off to Edgware this afternoon and later on, Crowthorne. It's all go.

Oh, help yourself to a Jammy Dodger while I'm gone.

Now, you remember a few pages ago we were talking about women having sex with minors? That's minors, not miners, there aren't very many left. Well, here is a case in point where a female, aged 21, but described as "young for her age" had sex with an 11-year-old boy when she was babysitting. Now, this female, Jade Hall, has been sentenced to a six-month jail term suspended for two years. She will be on the register as a sex-offender for seven years. As the NSPCC spokesman said, "You have to wonder whether in the same circumstances a man would have been treated the same." Exactly! The father of the 11-year-old boy appeared to have few concerns as he commented that his "sex mad son" saw it as a "notch on his belt". I can understand the sentiment to a degree but I think 11 is a tad young, and as a father, wouldn't you want your son to obtain his first "notch on his belt" so to speak with a lass sporting a more upmarket name! Caroline, Camilla or Cassandra springs to mind. Thinking of names with C, which I obviously am, Carpathia is nice, isn't it? It means fruit, you know.

Those of you who know my views on animal welfare, or more specifically the lack of it, will no doubt join me in the sorrow one experiences when espying a photograph of rabbits in cages at a battery farm. When I was young I naively assumed that cages were the sole preserve of chickens but this sickening spectacle where rabbits are crushed up against one another is far beyond what one expects in this day and age. If the EU had any backbone or real moral fibre it would be addressing this situation with urgency. Interesting to note that since 2012 it has been illegal to keep chickens in battery conditions but sadly and remarkably, no such law exists to protect rabbits. This country's authorities should be holding their collective heads in shame as we apparently import meat and organs from around 300,000 rabbits annually. Most of these are "cage-farmed". The farms are in Italy, Greece, Czech Republic, Poland and Cyprus. No real surprise. These rabbits live their whole lives in cages, very often displaying behavioural problems due to the disgusting and inhumane conditions and have been known to chew off each other's ears, suffering fungal infection and ulcerated skin. The density is mind-blowing. It apparently works out at one rabbit per A4 sheet of paper, or 16 rabbits per square yard and three inches – just can't bring myself to say the M word! When contacted, all of the well-known pet food suppliers stated their collective concern but I wonder if welfare will take precedence over profits. No, I'm not holding my breath either.

And on the subject of welfare, I see that despite all the fish firms declaring "caught by sustainable methods" or some such non-reassuring drivel, John West, that's John West, still catches tuna in ways that kill dolphins, sharks and turtles. Interesting to note that whilst all the big supermarkets claimed 100% sustainability – that's M & S, Waitrose, Sainsbury's, Tesco, Aldi, Asda, Morrisons and the Co-op (figures provided by Greenpeace – so they could just be true) Prince's was only 25% sustainable, Lidl 20% and John West, that's John West, 2%!

It was no surprise to learn that of all those achieving 100% in the sustainability stakes – or should that be steaks – Greenpeace praised Waitrose and placed them at number one for ethical "sourcing". (Ghastly word). Apparently, all the tuna fished from the sea that goes to Waitrose is caught by pole and line, which means other fish and mammals remain unharmed. Greenpeace then gush, with justification, that Waitrose is "truly dedicated to providing customers with equitable tuna – its policies protect local workers and communities as well as the environment." Second place went to Marks & Spencer, third was Sainsbury's, with Tesco and Aldi fourth and fifth. In fairness to John West, that's John West, I reproduce their response to the question of sustainable tuna fishing. They responded thus: "We have found it extremely difficult to increase the proportion of John West pole and line tuna that we can provide at a price that consumers would be willing to pay." They went on to say, "John West is fully committed to the protection of the marine environment and to sustainable sourcing. Our over-arching sustainability promise has not changed – we believe our commitments are best achieved by employing a number of practices and innovations to minimise by-catch (fish caught unintentionally while targeting other species), protect stock levels, preserve oceans, improve working conditions and ensure safe and legal practices." Have you ever heard such waffle? It's funny, but if Waitrose et al can do it, why can't John West? That's John West.

Talking of the environment, I read with quite a degree of interest of a tree, a Cypress tree to be precise, that is having a somewhat hard time of it in Durham. As with many things past those who want to see the tree chopped down moved in many years after it was planted. This particular specimen is a Lawson Cypress, planted over one hundred years ago. The tree is named Elsee and lives smack bang in front of Durham Cathedral and some of the nearby residents are rather aggrieved at Elsee blocking their view. Without knowing any of the whinging wailers I have to say that I doubt if they have resided in the same location for over one hundred years, as Elsee has. Incidentally, I once had a Kia Carens called Elsie, but that was because the first part of the registration number was L C. U C? Sorry, you see?

Meanwhile, back in Durham, a lady called Beth Bell has organised an on-line petition to save the tree. Elsee, incidentally, rests within Durham Cathedral's grounds in what are allotments rented by Beth and her husband. She commented that a few years ago neighbours approached them, asking them to remove the tree as it was obstructing their view of the cathedral. They say they trimmed back the conifer and took down several others. Were these neighbours satisfied? No. But then these people never are. One of the complainers is a chap called Ronan Freeley, aged 60, whose view of the cathedral is "totally obscured". Move, dear, move! Another complainant, gutless this time as he remains nameless, described Elsee as "an eyesore". This Freeley cove approached the cathedral's management who were very sympathetic and agreed to enquire about its felling. A planning application has gone in and shortly a decision will be made concerning Elsee's future. I know who's future I'd be discussing.

We have a very similar situation here in Ash Vale, although in our case its outcome is known and it's not good for the public at large. There sits in Ash Hill Road the Victoria Hall, which possesses a fine clock located in a similarly fine turret made of old English oak. The three-sided clock possesses tubular bells that strike on the hour and chime on the quarter. In recent years Ash Parish Council has taken over responsibility for the upkeep of the clock and it is now fitted with an electric winding system. So far, so chiming. In 2014 a new resident comes to town, or in Ash Vale's case, urban sprawl. This new kid on the block apparently visited the house he intended to purchase five times before a deal was done. So, he should know that his newly intended homestead is right next to a hall, which has a clock. I know what you're thinking and you're right. Not one to settle in and be part of the local scene, oh no, this cove creates one by complaining about the clock chiming during the night.

The long and short of it is that the hall's management committee is to authorise the spending of thousands of pounds in order to silence the clock between 11 pm and 7 am. So, in a thrice, tradition is thrown out of the clock tower due to the whining of one inhabitant – sorry, one newly arrived inhabitant.

Dave Brown, Chairman of the Management Committee, said, "I'm told that legally I don't have a leg to stand on, as the Charities' Commission would be on my back if I fought an unwinnable case." The law has no respect for history. Not surprisingly, Health and Safety, that good old standby of the complaints brigade was cited as grounds for complaint. I do hope the said gentleman's stay is short and sour.

Aha! I've just scrolled onto the next page on the computer and lo and behold, I've come across the culprit. Surprise, surprise, he's not even local or English. What a bloody cheek! The complaining cove is called Steve Tai, who moved in with his wife, Yong Wong – no, really. Little wonder the Management Committee was wary of taking him to court. He is a case manager at the Royal Court of Justice. He contacted both Ash Parish Council and Guildford Borough Council threatening to sue because of the chimes. He said the couple was unable to sleep and felt depressed. Let me tell you, chummy, your joint depression is nothing like that felt by the residents of Ash Vale who work on the principle that when in Rome....

Eric Pickles, at the time Communities Secretary, said new guidance was being introduced enabling councils to prevent this sort of thing happening again. He said, "If you don't like the chimes of a bell that has sounded for generations, they should reflect on whether they want to live next door to it in the first place or consider the merits of double glazing." He's not wong, sorry wrong! There is a picture of this Tai man ensconced in gown and wig. What a pity that knowledge of the law and an ability to know how to win a case outscores common sense.

Right! I'd best be going – Edgware beckons.

Back not only from Edgware but Crowthorne as well. For someone who will never cross the threshold of a Costa, Starbucks, Café Rouge, Nero or any other brand of its internationally bloated ilk.

97

It was with warmth rarely felt unless reading that Charlton Athletic has not lost a match or that another 400 Muslims have left these shores to join IS, that I read the following. Costa has been rated as less than satisfactory by health inspectors in certain stores this year. They inspected the Costa branch at the Royal Hampshire County Hospital and found their paninis to be at risk of contamination with clostridium botulinum. Now this is a bacteria that has been known to cause paralysis and even death and all due to lax temperature controls. At their outlet in St. Paul's Cathedral mice droppings were found on shelves, surfaces and floors. Perhaps they were just leaving a sinking Anglican ship. Oh, and a dead mouse was found rotting in a back room. Not mice, sorry, nice! It beggars belief that two branches in Margate and Cheam were found to have no hot water for staff to wash their hands after using the toilet. Oh, how it gets better for dislikers of all things corporate. Their branches in Devizes and Warwick apparently had back rooms hoarding food debris, overflowing bins and walls and floors spattered with dirty stains. It does actually get worse but I'll not go on, I'm just sitting here with a very warm, smug smile.

The standard of politicians continues its downward spiral. I note that the Shadow Chancellor, John McDonnell, heaped praise upon a union member for spitting in her boss's tea. He deemed it "an acceptable form of giving it back to those in power." He added that the employee's behaviour was the kind of direct action that could help to force the government out of office. Really! Now, I understand these comments were made four years ago, long before either he or his lack-of-esteemed leader would have dreamt they were where they are today, ie keeping the Tories in power for the foreseeable future. My point is that a leopard, or in this case a virtual anarchist, never changes his or her coat for a non-red one. Personally, I could never see a situation whereby spitting would be considered acceptable, although I am sure many residents in Glasgow would consider it to be the norm.

Now, whilst spitting is unacceptable, sending rancid meat and rotting plums appears to be perfectly acceptable if two criteria are met. One is that the cause of the outcry concerns house building, and secondly, those owning the land to be built upon is the Church of England. Without as much as an open meeting with locals to discuss the possibility of land sale, the Bishop of Gloucester, the Right

Reverend Rachel Treweek has been accused of getting into bed, so to speak, with a building company called Gladman Developments. I don't suppose you'll find glad men or glad women in the village of Willersey in the Cotswolds. The population is currently 816, although development could increase this by 350 homes. Multiply that by the number of inhabitants and the village will be swamped with incomers. This is exactly the type of action that destroys towns and villages. There is no resident doctor, the school accommodates only 50 children, so once developed, the whole fabric of that society is changed forever and where will any sale money go? The plot is worth upward of £3 million. Will it buy a doctor's surgery, a school extension, a well or two in India – possibly an investment opportunity in an offshore account....

Ah, since I last wrote, I have been to Langley in Essex and taken two tours of the brewery. It's now Saturday evening and I'm waiting for MOTD. Didn't Carol do … Well, not that well, actually but she looked happy enough. I'll be going straight to bed after football. Oh, you're nodding your head. You will as well. So, I will leave you with the following story.

This little number is called the Blonde and the Lord. A blonde wanted to go ice fishing. She'd read many books on the subject. Finally, getting all the necessary tools together, she made her way to the ice. After positioning her comfy footstool she started to make a circular cut in the ice. Suddenly from the sky a voice boomed, "There are no fish under the ice." Startled, the blonde moved further down the ice, poured a thermos of cappuccino and began to cut yet another hole. Again from the heavens a voice bellowed, "There are no fish under the ice." The blonde, now worried, moved away, right down to the opposite end from where she had been sitting. Setting up her stool once more she tried again to cut the hole and once more the voice came over, "There are no fish under the ice." She stopped, looked skyward and enquired loudly, "Is that you, Lord?" The voice wearily replied, "No, love, this is the manager of the hockey rink."

Another? Oh, okay, but it will have to be quick as the Match of the Day theme tune is just starting. A man and a woman were enjoying a quiet, romantic dinner. They were gazing lovingly at each other whilst holding hands. The waitress, taking another order at a table a few steps away, suddenly noticed the woman slowly sliding down her chair and under the table, although the man stared straight ahead.

The waitress continued to watch as the woman slid completely out of sight. Yet still the man stared ahead. The waitress, feeling this behaviour be a little risqué and worried that it might offend other diners, went over to the table and tactfully said to the man, "Excuse me, sir, but I think your wife just slid under the table." The man calmly looked up at her and replied, "No, you don't understand, that's my wife who's just walked through the door!"

Phew....

Chapter 5

And Carol is Still With Us!

Sunday came and Sunday went. As did Anthony Agogo on Strictly. Our Carol lived to prance another week. Thinking about it, Monday came and went as well. It wasn't that I needed another day to get over Carol's survival, it just happened that way. So, it's now Tuesday and this afternoon I'm off to Chipstead. Yesterday, just for the record, I visited Swanley in Kent in the afternoon, followed by a very nice meal at a golf club with a talk afterwards in Hersham. Tomorrow, by the way, sees me in Basingstoke for 10 am and then winging my way up the M3 and around the M25 to Chatham for a talk at 2 pm. Let's hope the M25 is kind, eh.

Whilst we have a few minutes, I'll tell you of a conversation I had the other day with a friend of mine – yes, I still have the one. Anyway, strange to tell we were discussing songs that had been played at funerals. non-religious, of course. Once back in the car by myself, it got me thinking of mine, because it will happen and usually when you least expect it. My mind travelled, along with my car, conjuring up a whole train of thoughts on what I considered I would like to have on my gravestone, if I ever have one. I'm not sure, though, but if I did it might read something like, "He never made much of his life but he made a nice cup of tea." I like the sentiment as it's quite descriptive. Maureen suggested one some time ago which was, "Life passed me by, I think I was working at the time." Ouch!!

But, back to the songs. This thought requires one to consider the length of the service minus the obligatory chat, the eulogies. I certainly wouldn't want anyone religious taking it so on that basis I have worked out that you could probably get four to five songs in a 45-minute slot, that also allows for those who hope to get something in your will to wax lyrical about your charm, disarming personality and humility, whilst those who are only there to witness that you have finally gone can feel relief that it wasn't just a wind-up and that you really are dead.

Now, I do like words, as you know and I like words in songs that are said with feeling. I've never enjoyed listening to songs where "new" rhymes with "you" and "true" with "blue", "love" and "above" are in similar vein. My favourite group of all time is the Alan Parsons Project, their range of music and style differing from track to track, album to album. By not retaining a fixed lead vocal they have been able to marry singer with song. It's worked extremely well. So the four tracks I have chosen for my passing are three APP and one from Andy Fairweather-Lowe. "Wide eyed and legless" has always been a favourite of mine. It's timeless. I have, I hasten to add, never been addicted to alcohol that is what I understand the lyrics to be about. In fact, I've never been addicted to drugs, gambling or cigarettes, either. My only addiction is the Hokey Cokey but I've turned it around and that's what it's all about ... I know, I know! Back to Alan Parsons, the top three most appropriate songs are "Old and Wise", "Time", and "Limelight". If you don't know of any of these songs, or indeed the Alan Parsons Project, I implore you in a manner that you've never hitherto been implored to tune in on your computer radio and listen to their music on Youtube. Alan Parsons background is one of record producer, as well as instrument playing, writing and singing. His partner in song has sadly died but his lyrics and voice are there to be enjoyed by all. His name is Eric Woolfson, a most unlikely looking pop artiste, more accountant really, but oh, those words!

I have to admit, that whilst I have never played a game on the computer or even a computer game on a box, device or whatever is in vogue that day, the ability to research people and music is exceptional. For me, one of the greatest and sadly unsung names of the British music industry was Anthony Newley. Fire up your computer, gas mark 5, and watch his thankfully recorded performance on the Michael Parkinson show way back in the 70's. His singing and acting skills are sublime. The song in question is "The Man Who Makes You Laugh." This is the story of a sad, lonely clown, which unfolds very cleverly and with great observation of life's frailties. His voice was not to everyone's taste and I can understand that point of view but it was distinctive. Above all, it was honest. He had a very successful writing partnership with Leslie Bricusse that gave us great standards still enjoyed to this day. To sum up, no-one ever "acted" a song whilst never looking as though they were acting and Tony Newley never looked as if he was acting. I suspect most of his material truly reflected an inner torment and a life of uncertainty.

So, we've got the gravestone wording sorted, we've got the songs, we just need to name that day! Wait for it!

Chipstead and its club were very pleasant, with an extremely welcome cuppa to finish off the afternoon. I was back in time to take a brewery tour at 6.30 pm, which ended some half hour ago at 8.15 pm so it's now down to "catching up with the papers" time.

First irritation is reading that David Cameron has told police forces that they must keep separate records of hate crimes against Muslims. So, once again, they get preferential treatment in the statistics league. Our esteemed lack of leader reasons that this will help gauge the scale of the problem and enable the police to allocate extra resources in high-risk areas. This includes selective schools and mosques, apparently. Religious crime rose by 45% in England and Wales last year. Mmmm, only that much, eh, I'm surprised. Not surprisingly, there is a charity called "Tell Mumma." They check on anti-Muslim crimes. They state these have risen by 70% and comment that women who wear full-faced veils are the targets of "aggressive incidents." I would have thought that the bombings in London, the hacking to death of a soldier in Woolwich and the hatred portrayed by many Muslims given sanctuary within our shores, might well be considered "aggressive incidents" in their own wrong. But as we all know too well, it is black, blackish or coloured against white, which appears to be passively acceptable. It's not as if these Muslims have morals. I note that a terror suspect, one Jamal Al-Harith, was among a number of those interned in Guantanamo Bay. Having been released in 2004 he returned to the land of his lack of fathers, though he possesses our passport, and we give him £1 million in compensation. Is he grateful? Is he buggery? The cove has now joined IS. He has never played cricket, I'm sure. The man's a bounder!

Now, here we have a foreign story where I am at one with the country concerned. It comes under the heading of "When in Rome". Muslims in Britain please take note! I read that a certain Karl Andree, aged 74, is currently residing in a Saudi Arabian prison. His crime is that having been stopped when driving, police found bottles of wine in his car. Now, whilst we all know that corruption is rife, it does not pay for an Englishman abroad to cross the Saudis. We know the rules, no alcohol – unless you are in with the "in crowd" or you are plain arrogant. So, why whinge when caught? It appears that Mr. Andree was sentenced to 12 months' imprisonment some 14 months ago and is now likely to receive 350 lashes, which take the form of a public flogging. The report in the Daily Mail makes great play of the fact that he has had cancer, suffers from asthma and has a wife dying back home here in Blighty who needs constant medical care. Personally, I wouldn't have thought alcohol would have been what the doctor ordered. His son, Simon, aged 33, who should know better, bleated, "Our father has given 25 years of his working life to Saudi Arabia, and this is how he is treated. Until his arrest he has always been happy working there and felt safe. He is 74, has had cancer three times, he needs medical care for his cancer and asthma and there is no doubt in my mind that 350 lashes will kill him." He's worked there for 25 years? He doesn't know the system? Grow up, Simple Simon, your father erred.

All three offspring are banding together as one distraught family and pleading with David Cameron to "personally intervene and help get our father back home." Why? I really hope he doesn't. It's bugger all to do with this country or government time. Our society is not theirs and their society takes precedence in their country. Muslims in this country please note the fairness displayed by natives in Britain. Standing back and looking at the situation I have few doubts that Dave will intervene and a deal will be done. Well, more trade talks really, I suppose.

I really don't understand the powers that be in this country. What a pity they are not called to account at a public meeting. Let me explain. When there are so many in favour of making Britain an arm of Islamic state we really do not require the likes of Lord Neuberger or Lord Hoffmann, unless of course you are a supporter of miscreants, terrorists' rights and decisions which cost you and I millions in tax, though hopefully not lives. Lord Neuberger last week praised the Human Rights Act. This educated, decorated fool, who is the leading judge at the Supreme Court, stated that the Act had given judges the power to defy Parliament. He pointed to a 2004 case in which Law Lords ordered that terror suspects should not be held in detention, adding it "vindicated the importance of judges to the rule of law." That decision in 2004 led to the immediate release of twelve terrorist suspects, including that rather nasty cove Abu Qatada. It then took eleven years to deport the bugger. Seven months after their ill-conceived decision fifty-two people were killed on tube trains and a bus in London. The Neuberger fellow then congratulated the Hoffmann, or Oafman as I prefer to think of him, by declaring that the real threat to this country was not from terrorism but from anti-terrorism laws. He was chuffed as he stated how judges were using their "fundamental right to freedom of expression." We really do not need people like these within the judiciary, as ever they support the rights of those who err but care little for the bigger picture of the population as a whole.

Do we spawn "judicial arses" as part of the birthing quota in this country? On a similar theme I note that a dozen retired judges accompanied by more than 300 lawyers and academics (I suspect they graduated at Cambridge) have condemned the government for taking in too few migrants. Bloody cheek! These advocates of social engineering and change will never have them living near them. They will never attempt to sit in Aldershot or Camberley town centres and realise that all the seats have been taken by the Nepalese aimlessly eking out their lives in an expanding suburban sprawl, expanding in no small part due to the number here. They will never have to live next to a field developed to take in their Syrian, Afghan or Iraqi bedfellows. For them it is all about social conscience without reference to the native population. They will never listen to the man in the street who is born here, with heritage here and pays tax here. Yes, I'm bloody annoyed about it.

Now, to lighten the mood, here is a joke or five that will certainly not be told by judges after their gourmet banquets. You know, the banquets we pay for, plus their first-class travel, plus their expenses, plus....

Joke 1

Whilst strolling along the River Thames this morning I noticed a Muslim extremist slip from the river-bank and fall into the river. I knew he was a Muslim extremist because of all the explosives he was carrying and due to their weight, he was struggling to stay afloat. If he didn't get help I knew he would surely drown. Being a responsible British citizen and abiding by the law of the land that requires you to help those in distress, I informed the police, the Immigration Service and even the Fire Service. It is now 4 pm and he has drowned, yet none of these authorities has yet responded. I'm starting to think I've wasted three second-class stamps!

Next!

I was walking through the shopping mall and came across the "Muslim Book Store". I wondered exactly what was in a Muslim book store, so went inside. As I wandered around taking a look the shop assistant stopped me and asked if he could help. I imagine I didn't look like his normal clientele, so I asked, "Do you have a copy of a book referring to the British police attitude to Muslims?" The shop assistant said, "Sod off, get out and stay out". I said, "Yes, that's the title. Do you have it in paperback?".

And again....

I woke up to go to the toilet in the middle of the night and I noticed a Muslim sneaking through my next-door neighbour's garden. Suddenly, from out of nowhere, my neighbour appeared and smacked him over the head with a shovel, killing him instantly. He then dug a grave, put the body in it and covered it. Astonished, I got back into bed. Carol, my wife, said, "David, you're shaking, what is it?" I said, "You'll never believe what I've just seen., that bastard next door's still got my shovel."

It's not over yet.

Email from a man in Sheffield to his friend in Birmingham:-

I was fed up being burgled every other day so I tore out my alarm system and deregistered from the local Neighbourhood Watch scheme. I've planted a Pakistani flag in each corner of my garden and the large black flag of ISIS in the centre. Now, the Yorkshire police, the National Security Bureau, Scotland Yard, MI5, MI6, the CIA and every other intelligence service in Europe and the US are all watching my house 24 hours a day, 7 days a week. My children are followed to school every day, as is my wife when she goes shopping. I am followed to and from work myself, so no-one bothers me, I've never felt safer, and all thanks to Allah!

One to go....

The Liverpool manager flies to Kabul to watch a young Afghani play football. He is suitably impressed and arranges for the player to come over here. Two weeks later Liverpool are 2-0 down to Newcastle with only 20 minutes to go. The manager gives the young Afghani striker the nod. The lad is a sensation. He scores 3 goals in 20 minutes and Liverpool win the match. The fans are delighted, the players and the coach are delighted and the media love their new star. When the player comes off the pitch he phones his mum to tell her about his first day in English football. "Hello mum, guess what? I've played for 20 minutes today, we were 2-0 down but I scored three times. They call it a hat trick and we won the match. Everybody loves me, the manager, the players, the fans, the press, they all love me." "That's just wonderful," says his mother, "Let me tell you about my day. Your father got shot in the street, your sister and I were ambushed and assaulted and she would have been raped if it hadn't been for the passing police vehicle. Your brother has joined a local gang of looters and set fire to some buildings. And all this while you were telling me what a great time you've had." The young lad is very upset. "What can I say, mum, I'm really, really sorry." "Sorry? Sorry?", says his mum, "It's your bloody fault we came to Liverpool in the first place!".

Okay, it's late, time to take my tablets and off to bed. I trust you will sleep well and I'll see you tomorrow.

Morning, have you had breakfast yet? Oh, you have. What? Toast and marmalade? I hope it was Wilkins of Tiptree or Waitrose own. There's been some Robertson's at the back of the shelf for years. I'm about to have tinned plum tomatoes on toast. As you know, it's Basingstoke this morning and Chatham at 2 pm. I'll catch you when I'm back. Byeee.

The M25 was reasonably kind, with only a short delay between Junction 6 and 5 close to the Clacket Lane Service Station. It was only a small prang, we all slowed down, gawped and then speeded up again. It's traditional. So, I am sitting with a sandwich and reading with a mixture of sheer anger and incredulity that we poor sods have just funded the hire of a stretched limousine to ferry seven asylum seekers from a hotel we funded in Longford near Heathrow to their new homes in Manchester, which we will fund in the future. Whilst I have nothing but relief that they have been moved up north, I would love to know who at Serco, the company contracted to move these people, decided that we should be paying for this form of luxury transportation. The Home Office has stated that it is up to the contractor to bear the cost of the limo but "that it was totally inappropriate." The good news is that there was "no additional cost to the taxpayer!" No additional cost? What the bloody hell are we doing paying a penny for their transport in the first place. The only money I'd sanction is that leading to their deportation. Bastards!

Mmmm, I see that at the same time as David Pointless Cameron is publicly supporting the Brit sentenced to 350 lashes in Saudi Arabia, our government has cancelled an order worth £6 million to provide training advice for Saudi prison service staff. Where does that leave us? Feeling better as a nation due to a moral stance, or £6 million short of funds? The two must be linked. So, someone who errs in a foreign land can cost us a fortune in income – is that it? And if so, can that be right? While we reflect upon that very moral issue, the French have just completed trade deals with the Saudis worth £7.5 million. Would they have been so weak? I think not. A Gallic shrug at best, maybe. And while "Margaret Thatcher" is an anagram of "That Great Charmer" the best I can find for David Cameron is "Gutless Arse!", well, it nearly fits.

It really is a bad day for beer and lager drinkers as AB In Bev are set to take over SAB Miller. The "merger" will create the world's biggest brewer producing one in every three beers and lagers drunk throughout the world. The good news personally is that I never have nor ever will buy or drink their corporate "brands." Meantime Brewery was purchased by SAB Miller some little while ago, which means I would never buy any of their products either. Sadly, the same goes for "Doom Bar" brewed by Sharps of Cornwall. Again, Sharps has now been purchased by Corrs. I will never pay one penny to these faceless international conglomerates, any more than I would pay one penny to that Antipodean megawhatsit Rupert Murdoch. None of his papers has ever crossed my threshold, nor have I ever received Sky Television. You know me, as pure of principle as the driven snow – or should that be slush?

Footnote: Yes, I did read The Times, but it was for research purposes, certainly not pleasure or leisure. What we scribes do for our art!

Aha. The post has just arrived. We seem to have our regular post lady back at the moment. Sadly, it's not very interesting. A catalogue from Chums, a flyer from a double glazing company, who happen to be in our area this week, another flyer from Domino's, one from a Chinese takeaway who deliver within a three-mile radius – hopefully I'm further away than that – and an envelope devoid of name or address but when opened contains a letter inviting me to receive a free estimate for exterior wall waterproofing. I think not. I just feel sorry for the trees that were decimated for this rubbish.

Today's Daily Mail makes mention of a discovery by archaeologists. It seems that a site fitting the description of Soddom has been discovered in Jordan, which is all a bit of a surprise, as there was me thinking it had already been discovered and renamed Aldershot.

It's all change for presenters on quality programmes, both on TV and radio alike. Stephen Fry is to retire from QI and his replacement will be Sandi Toksvig and she, in turn, will be replaced on the News Quiz by Miles Jupp. Very good moves for the latter two who never fail to amuse and entertain. As it happens one of the staff down at the brewery has had a clear out of videos and passed me the complete set of 23 episodes of Jeeves and Wooster so I'll be Frying for a while yet. What a wordsmith and all-round worthy Mr. Fry is. I like words and as you know, I like coincidences, which brings me clumsily to the following.

You might find this interesting. It's an ode to Spellcheck.

I halve a spelling checker,
It came with my peasee.
It plainly marks four my review
Mistakes I dew knot sea
Eye strike a key and type a word
And weight four it two say
Weather eye am wrong oar write.
It shows me strait a weigh.
As soon as a mist ache is maid
It nose bee fore two long
And eye can put the era rite.
Its rarely ever wrong.
I've scent this message threw it,
And I'm shore your pleased too no
It's letter perfect in every weigh
My checker told me sew.

It was difficult for Maureen to type because her fingers knew the words were wrong and while we are feeling wordy, the words "listen" and "silent" use the same letters and "race car" spelt backwards still spells "race car".

See you tomorrow – sleep well.

It's tomorrow and it hasn't started well. I don't know, you just come down from boiling point, having turned on the BABC Breakfast TV, have a cup of tea, relax momentarily and then read the headlines of the paper. Today's first irritation is the news that the Home Office has spent £14 million over the past eighteen months in order to ferry would-be migrants back to their starting point/place of origin – whatever. £14 million! Wouldn't the money be better spent on training English nurses for English hospitals, Welsh for Welsh and Scottish lassies for Scottish? One flight, costing £250,000 (how on earth did it cost that much) was spent on returning one single Moroccan deportee. Other examples include the use of an airliner returning eleven Afghans and a 265-seat plane consisting of just 25 Nigerians. For goodness sake, we could have taken another 240 and just parachuted them anywhere, surely! But then, these faceless bastards who make these decisions are not spending their own money, only that which has been earned by poor buggers such as thee and me. What's that? You're boiling as well? Well, you would be, wouldn't you, I mean, you wouldn't have got this far through the book if you were a lily-livered Liberal Democratic. Oh, no, proper person you.

Oh, this is a hoot. Apparently, the C of E is suggesting that children receive lessons in ethics. A report entitled "The Fruits of the Spirit" recommends that teachers follow the lead of one of their number who "uses banana maths" in order to teach children about the moral value of Fair Trade bananas, whilst working out how much goes to the grower. Interesting the banana, I wonder if that is all they use it for. But that's just one fruit. In fact, the banana is the only fruit mentioned in the article. Anagram! Church of England equals Freudian thoughts. No, well, perhaps it should do.

As a footnote, it's worth commenting that this report comes from a religion that announces the following statistic. One in four parishes now have fewer than ten worshippers. The number of people attending C of E churches on an average Sunday (Songs of Praise venues excluded I imagine) is now 800,000, half the figure for the 1960's and yet they overpopulate the seats in the House of Lords. Why? What right have these people to pontificate on the course and social structure of this country? They are not elected. By the way, I've just checked my blood pressure – it's 186 over 69. At least the second number is one I can still recall with pleasure, though not action – not with my diabetes.

Never trust the motives of a man of the cloth. They speak with forked tongues and many a youngster has been on the end of it. Too much. The report also suggests that children should be praised for getting their sums wrong, providing that they have shewn improvement. This way, children can "encourage one another and learn to share in each other's learning." What tosh. It gets worse. Another scheme involves, wait for it, "badges of awsomeness" for displaying positive attitudes. Tosh 2, the sequel. Oh, and this next one really takes the biscuit or as we are talking about clerical innovations, should that be sweetie? Children should be encouraged to send in Twitter (Twatter) snaps of themselves … wait for it … with their family reading … yes, I assumed it was going somewhere else as well. The worrying aspect is the power these cults wield. Remember there are 4,500 C of E primary schools and 200 secondary schools, educating around 1 million children. That's a lot of namby-pamby, muddle-headed political correctness at best and skewed and lewd thoughts at worst.

Talking of religious schools, I do recall a classic example of learning for the future. There was an Irishman who wanted to become a priest. His bishop, whilst interviewing him for the post, said, "You must answer three (always three!) questions on the bible. First, who was born in the stable?" "Red Rum" replied the Irishman. "Second, what do you think of Damascus?" "It kills 99% of all known household germs" "Third, what happened when the disciples went to Mount Olive?" "Oh, that's easy," the Irishman's face beamed, "Popeye kicked the shit out of them!"

Whatever happened to the last few days? Visits to Basingstoke, Rainham (Kent), Stansted Mountfitchet, Hitchin, to give talks, plus five brewery tours later, I'm back at the pad. No keyboard for me still, every word handwritten and typed up later.

So, a few days' news to catch up on. Nice to see another benefit cheat has been caught and in his case, jailed. Vaughn Dodds, a 45-year-old former police officer and one-time guard to Tony Blair – remember his wife? – obtained more than £56,000 over a four year period in welfare handouts. After 14 years in the police force he claimed that nice old standby disability living allowance, income support and council tax benefit for himself and his wife. Apparently, the poor ex-plod claimed he suffered severe fatigue and depression, which left him housebound and occasionally suicidal. Obviously not that suicidal, which is a pity, as it would have cost us less. He also claimed his wife, Mandy, aged 47, suffered from a hearing condition which was so acute she couldn't even stand the noise of toilet paper rustling. I'd have thought that round your backside would have been far enough away, but never mind. Just a thought, it's difficult to rustle the quilted variety. I know, I've just tried! All the time, this pair of fraudsters was living a very noisy life, courtesy of me and thee. Fraud investigators revealed evidence of the couple sipping cocktails and dancing on their cabin beds (yes, that's what it says) on a luxury cruise liner, family holidays in Florida and Egypt, plus evidence of spending over £60,000 on restaurants and beauty salons. Mandy's noise problem appears to have come and gone as she was observed riding a motor-cycle and blowing someone's hair at the family owned beauty salon. Naturally, their generosity based on taxpayers' funding ensured that their children attended exclusive private schools – Durham High School for Girls and Durham Chorister School. They certainly were free with our money, one restaurant bill alone cost £6,781. How on earth can you spend that much on one family meal. It's obscene, I cannot imagine what they ate or drank, but I'll wager it wasn't ham, egg and chips. Just a stab in the dark. Oh, yes, just in case they turn up as your new next-door neighbours, remember they are Vaughn and Mandy Dodds.

The above appears insignificant however, as it is after all, only money and not malice, when reading of people, female usually, being victims of acid attacks. As I've questioned before, how can anyone carry out such a horrendous act. An amateur boxer has been jailed for life for attempting to destroy his ex-girlfriend's looks by hiring a friend to throw sulphuric acid over her while she stood at a bus stop. Her description of the shock, knowing as she was running and screaming, that her ear had melted beggars belief. After two months in hospital the lady has been left permanently scarred and partially blind. Anthony Riley, described as a small-time drug dealer, with whom the lady had an on-off relationship for seven years, hired a 39-year-old heroin addict two months before the acid attack to disfigure Adele Bellis by slashing her in the mouth, this assault did not take place fortunately. Riley however was not prepared for Miss Bellis to end their relationship and seek a new life. He tested the acid by dipping a live mouse into a jar of the substance and apparently laughed as the mouse died in agony. Words fail me. He then hired Jason Harrison, aged 27, to carry out the acid attack for the paltry fee of £500. What a small amount to ruin a person's life. Harrison received a four year discounted sentence, due to his guilty plea and evidence he gave for the prosecution. This is another instance of where an eye for an eye would benefit the crime, or in this case, plus an ear for an ear, and I say that without any sense of humour, merely a literal response to this barbaric deed. They would both get life sentences in my book. The mentality that sees rejection stretched to that degree of reprisal should not be trusted to ever be released into a society we wish to live in. Far too soft, far too soft.

If you've got a bucket of sand spare, can you drop it round as I need to bung my head in it for a while. Our elected daffy government are urging teachers to clamp down on sexist language displayed by children as young as five. There is a move, apparently, to drive out gender stereotyping in schools. The guidelines have been sent to every school in England advising heads to appoint experienced teachers as "gender champions." Some schools have already assembled squads of volunteer students to report any sexist language and behaviour to staff. We are in a new puritanical age and it's not good. Clare Thomson of the Institute of Physics stated, "Even low level comments are potentially an issue, with teachers using phrases such as 'man up'." Have you ever heard such tosh! Man up! At Fairfield High School in Bristol, the school's deputy head, Janice Callow, said that her school has a group of volunteer girls being assembled to spot sexist language. Phrases such as "don't be a girl" being said to a boy would be deemed unacceptable. For Christ's Sake, Ms Callow, grow up! I really worry about these people holding positions of power and influence. God or Allah knows what they are turning out at teacher training college.

Right, whilst I've got my head firmly entrenched in the metaphorical sand bucket, as nobody bothered to bring round a real one, let us think of nice things. And Carol Kirkwood will do very nicely. Once again, our Carol held her own and fights to smile another week. Daniel O'Donnell, a cheerful sort of chap it seems, got his marching orders. Right. Let's see what the week holds, the Inbox contains, and the post reveals within its envelopes. My head, by the way, is now out of the bucket.

It's an eye injection come 9.45 am, a talk in West Drayton at 8 pm, followed by a visit to Owlsmoor, near Sandhurst, tomorrow afternoon and a village outside Andover in the evening. Wednesday sees me visit Crayford in Kent during the morning, followed by a brewery tour at 6.30 pm. Thursday is without and Friday I am playing trains at my cousin's.

Well, the kettle has boiled, the semi-skimmed has been poured and the Yorkshire teabag dropped into my enamel mug. You know, it's the white mug with a blue painted lip and "Morning" painted in upper case – nice. There's enough water for two cups, if you would like one. Just say.

Okay, first the post. Bearing in mind it's Monday, crap, crap and more crap. Domino's leaflet again, a Donald Russell brochure and Saga, who always tenders the most expensive quote whenever I've rung them, are offering me the chance to purchase cheap motor insurance and once again I shall decline. Someone is in my area to give preferential quotes for replacement windows. I will, however, peruse the Donald Russell brochure. It's mouth-watering to view, even if you don't buy any of their produce, which we often do. Oh, and if you haven't sampled their wares, I can recommend the taste and texture of their meats and their afters – desserts to those outside sarf London – they are superb. The usual disclaimer applies, of course. I know nobody at the Donald Russell Company nor have I received one penny as a retainer to advertise its wares. I mention the above purely as a satisfied customer, signed A. Mann, Ash Vale. Other purveyors of fine fare are available.

Right, before we tackle the papers, the computer beckons as does another cuppa. Here we are, sat seated in front of the screen … click … mmmm … there's an offer to keep my garage warm all winter long. How does the sender know I have a garage – oh, probably my Surrey address gives that away. Some kind-hearted and community thoughtful soul has sent me a registered offenders map, which invites me to "click here" to see where they are living. Thank you, but if I really want to be abused I'll find my own paedophile, thank you. Moving sniffily on, water contamination reports are in and I can purchase a water purifier right now on the basis of this report. I think I'll leave it, but thanks for the offer. And finally, for today anyway, Dr. Dave is inviting me to reverse my blood pressure in only seven days. Oh, hang on, as we speak, another Spam has just arrived. I have actually opened this one to see a yellow backgrounded warning referring to the message as potential Spam. Well, all knowing Google, please let me be the judge of that, though they are not wrong. Somebody calling himself Gerald R says that he needs to verify my account so that I can start receiving commissions. Luckily for me there's also an access link. D'you know, I'm not sure if talk of my forthcoming commission is genuine. Gerald says, "See you on the inside, regards Gerald Reid." Where's that? The inside of Parkhurst? His address is actually given, if it's to be believed and that is 2775 Stark Hollow Road, Mountain View, Co82939. No, I've thought about it, I'm not going to take him up, you can never trust anyone with such a high numbered address, I mean, what sort of road must it be. If he lived at "The Manse" or "Prince of Wales Drive" or "Herriott Square" at least his scam would produce a modicum of respectability.

Sometimes there's a lighter story that makes you smile and as always, it's a wry smile, of course. I read that a couple has called their child Gary because they feel the name is in danger of dying out. Frankly, I'm surprised anyone would wish to keep the name alive. I know we have Gary's, both Lineker and Barlow, but usually Garys are fitters, artisans, manual labourers or salesmen with a very smarmy appearance and never to be trusted. And, as you know, I never generalise!

Do you remember those heady days of Liberal Democrat influence whilst in government? One of their more odious members, Chris Hulme, was found guilty of perverting the course of justice regarding a motoring offence some ten years previously. Yes, that's him. Well remembered. Anyway, he stated that it was his wife who was speeding when it was actually he. Both later got their just desserts. Well, here we have a couple from Cheshire who had visited Rhos-on-Sea in north Wales to assess a potential house purchase. Actually, it's a castle. There's posh. I won't let the fact that he is a property developer influence my view any more than I will the fact that he and his wife own a lurid green Lamborghini. No, I'll remain unmoved by my normal bias towards such occupation and crass display of wealth. The car was caught on camera exceeding the speed limit along the promenade. Neither Mr. Shenton, aged 68, nor Mrs. Shenton, aged 59, could remember who was driving at the time of the incident as both had driven along the promenade. They said they didn't want to lie and end up like Hulme and Price, so they requested camera evidence of their heinous crime. Now, I'm thinking as I'm reading this, they are hoping the court will dismiss the case on the grounds of lack of identification. But no, they have both been found guilty.

Due to the camera film being so grainy, the authorities were unable to identify the wrongdoer. Their fine ends up at £2,400, including costs. I read on in order to cackle at the speed this obvious show-off was driving at, when the article states that the camera showed them doing 35 miles an hour in a 30 mile an hour area. I have to say I find the whole case pathetic in the extreme and now feel extremely sorry for the pair of them. You get a much lesser fine for physical assault, displaying a knife or robbery. So, yes, they have a right to feel aggrieved. I do wonder, however, if the powers that be would have bothered with this obvious threat to civilisation as we know it if the perpetrator had been driving a Vauxhall Corsa. Just a thought.

From the light and the slightly unjust to the downright hypocritical – a chappie called David Walker is the Church of England's Bishop of Manchester. There is a picture of this complete arse sitting on a wall, dressed in a suit and bare-footed sandals (although Maureen has just corrected this to sandals without socks). He is wearing a dark pink shirt, dog collar and cross on chain. Balding and sporting a white/grey beard and moustache with glasses he looks for all the world your archetypal namby-pamby, limp-wristed, community spirited, socially skewed Liberal Democrat. All ideals and no reality. Actually, when you look at his face he could be a dead ringer as a sibling for Rowan Williams. Perhaps RW is DW's hero. His smile is as smug and sycophantic as that of a Guardian reader. His name was on a letter sent to Dave the Rave Cameron pressing him to accept more Syrian refugees into our greenery-depleted country. He urged ordinary people to welcome asylum seekers from Syria saying, it would be "a sad reflection" on society if they did not. Now, God's disciple in Manchester lives in a six-bedroomed house, free of charge, plus a salary of £42,000 per annum. What the hell does he contribute to this country or society for the greater good. His house was refurbished in 2013 and during this article David Walker explains how all the bedrooms are used for one thing or another and that whilst he and his arse Bishops encourage us poor sods to accommodate a Syrian family, he unfortunately can't do that himself. Bloody cheek! But then, hypocrisy has always been the by-word of religion since somebody thought "I'll write this novel about sex, fear and control. I'll call it 'The Bible', a sort of works manual for the world, then I'll just sit back and lead the meek who, by the way, will not inherit the earth."

Now, whilst Bishop Dave has offered a disused vicarage to Syrians – where is he when white British families are seeking housing? – he has stated that he couldn't have refugees staying with him or his wife in their six-bedroomed house. I mention this in case you have forgotten the number of bedrooms and I quote, "I have a smallish house by Bishop standards, a relatively modern house. It is adequate for our purposes, it allows us to entertain guests when we need to…". So good enough to entertain guests, but not quite right for practising what you preach to others. He goes on to say that refugees need self-contained accommodation, a place where they can be with their families, not try to share the breakfast table with a couple whose language they don't understand and where culture is alien to them. So it's all right for their culture to be alien to us, but not to this hypocritical cove. And he is right, there is a place for them to be by themselves with their own and not sharing our breakfast table. It's called Syria. Bugger off back there!

Now, whilst the following is a religious joke about another religious joke, or the Catholic Church as it's sometimes known, I like the principle of the story. Four Catholic men and a Catholic woman are having coffee. The first Catholic man says, "My son is a priest and when he walks into a room everyone calls him 'Father'." The second Catholic man adds chirpily, "My son is a bishop and when he walks into a room everyone addresses him as 'Your Grace'." The third Catholic man says, "My son is a cardinal and when he enters a room, everyone says, 'Your Eminence'." The fourth man, who by now has drunk his coffee and finished off his carrot cake, says, "My son is the Pope and wherever he walks, people refer to his as 'Your Holiness'." The Catholic lady looks up from her cup to see four sets of eyes upon her, their look inviting a response. She straightens herself and proudly announces, "I have a daughter, Maria. She is slim, double D bust, 24 inch waist, 34 hips and when she walks into a room everybody exclaims, 'Oh My God'."

What's that? You're off out for a while but would like a few more chortles before you go. This is most irregular, the reader telling the author what to write, but as you know, consideration is my by-word. Firstly, how the Internet started according to the Bible. In ancient Israel it came to pass that a trader by the name of Abraham Com did take unto himself a healthy young wife by the name of Dorothy. Dot

Com was a comely woman, large of breast, broad of shoulder and long of leg. Indeed, she was often referred to as Amazon Dot Com and she said to her husband, Abraham, "Why doest thou travel so far from town to town with thy goods when thou canst trade without ever leaving thy tent?" And Abraham did look at her as though she was several saddle bags short of a camel load, but simply asked, "How, dear?" And Dot replied, "I will place drums in all the towns and drums in between to send messages saying what you have for sale and they will reply telling you who hath the best price. The sale can be made on the drums and delivery made by Uriah's Pony Stable (UPS)." Abraham thought long and decided he would let Dot have her way with the drums and the drums rang out and were an immediate success.

Abraham sold all the goods he had at the top price without ever having to move from his tent. To prevent neighbouring countries from overhearing what the drums were saying Dot devised a system that only she and the drummers knew. It was known as Must Send Drum Over Sound (MSDOS) and she also developed a language to transmit ideas and pictures – Hebrew To The People (http). And the young men did take to Dot Com's trading as doth the greedy horsefly takes to camel dung. They were called Nomadic Ecclesiastical Rich Dominican Sybarites – or NERDS for short. And lo, the land was so feverish with joy at the new riches and the deafening sound of the drums that no-one noticed that the real riches were going to that enterprising drum dealer, brother William of Gates, who took over every drum maker in the land. Indeed, he did insist on drums to be made that would only work with Brother Gates drumheads and drumsticks and Dot did say, "Oh, Abraham, what we have started is being taken over by others," and Abraham looked out over the Bay of Ezekiel, or Ebay as it became known, and said, "We need a name that reflects who and what we are." Dot's eyes lit up as she enthusiastically said, "Young Ambitious Hebrew Owner Operators." "Yahoo", said Abraham, and because it was Dot's idea they named it "Yahoo Dot Com." Abraham's cousin, Joshua, being the Gregarious Energetic Educated Kid (Geek) that he was, soon started using Dot's drums to locate products around the countryside. It soon became known as God's Own Official Guide to Locating Everything (Google) and that, dear reader, is how it began. And that really is how it all started. This was sent to me by a friend of mine called Frank who lives in

Shepperton, so it is wry smile time, I hope. Thanks Frank.

Ready for another? Right. Mother Superior was on her way to late morning prayers when she passed two novices just leaving early morning prayers and now on their way to classes. As she passed the young ladies, Mother Superior said, "Good morning ladies." The novices replied, "Good morning, Mother Superior, may God be with you." But after she had passed, Mother Superior heard one say to the other, "I think she got out of the wrong side of the bed this morning." This startled the Mother Superior but she chose not to pursue the issue. A little further down the hall Mother Superior passed two of the sisters who had been teaching at the convent for several years. She greeted them with, "Good morning Sister Martha, Sister Jessica. May God give you wisdom for our students today." "Good morning, Mother Superior, thank you and may God be with you." But again, after passing, the Mother Superior overheard, "She got out of the wrong side of the bed today." Baffled she started to wonder if she had spoken harshly or with an irritated look on her face. She vowed to be more pleasant. Further down the hall Mother Superior espied retired Sister Mary approaching, step by step with her walker. As Sister Mary was rather deaf, Mother Superior had plenty of time to arrange a pleasant smile on her face before greeting Sister Mary. "Good Morning, Sister Mary. I am so happy to see you up and about. I pray God watches over you today and grants you a wonderful day." "Ah, good morning Mother Superior, I see you got out of the wrong side of bed this morning." Mother Superior was floored. "Sister Mary, what have I done wrong. I have tried to be pleasant but three times already today people have said that about me." Sister Mary stopped her walker and looked the Mother Superior straight in the face. "Oh, don't take it personally, it's just you are still wearing Father Murphy's slippers."

Here we go! A man walking along a Californian beach was deep in prayer. All of a sudden he called out loud, "Lord, I beseech thee, grant me just one wish." Suddenly the sky clouded above his head and in a booming voice (he'd taken lessons from Brian Blessed – an appropriate name at this point I feel) God replied, "Because you have tried to be faithful in all ways, I will grant you one wish!" The man asked, "Would you build me a bridge to Hawaii so that I can drive there whenever I want?" The Lord considered and then replied, "Your request is very materialistic. Think of the enormous challenges for that kind of undertaking. The supports required from the bottom of the Pacific, the amount of steel and concrete it would take. I can do it, but it is difficult for me to justify your desire for such worldly and frankly selfish things. Please take a little time and think of something more socially acceptable, more community spirited. Something that will benefit mankind as a whole and will honour and glorify me in doing so." As requested, the man continued walking along the beach considering other ideas. Finally, he stopped, looked up again and said, "Lord, I wish I could understand women. I want to know how they feel inside, what they are thinking when they give me the silent treatment, why they cry so readily, what they mean when they say nothing and how does one make a woman truly happy." The Lord replied, "So, this 'ere bridge, is it two lanes or four?"

You got time for one more then? Okay, just a quickie. A female CNN journalist heard about a very old Jewish man who had been going to the Wailing Wall in Jerusalem to pray twice a day, every day, for many years. So, to check out the story, she went to the wall and there he was, walking slowly up to the holy site. She watched him pray and after about 45 minutes as he turned to leave, using a cane and moving very slowly, she approached him for an interview. "Pardon me, sir, I'm Rebecca Smith from CNN, may I ask your name?" "Maurice Feinberg" came the reply. "And may I ask, sir, how long have you been coming to the wailing wall to pray?" "Over sixty years." "Sixty years, that's amazing. Tell me, what do you pray for?" "I pray for peace between the Christians, the Jews and the Muslims. I pray for all the wars and all the hatred to stop. I pray for all of our children to grow up safely as responsible adults and to love their fellow man." The reporter felt very humbled, "And how do you feel, sir, after doing this for sixty years?" The old man shook his head, "It's like talking to a f*****g brick wall."

Right, go, go, I'll see you later.

Ah, you're back before me, I see – which I literally still do after my monthly eye injection. Today's "allergy" when asked by the medical staff was given as David Walliams. I've no idea why I'm allergic to him more this morning than any other time, it's just the way it is. Never attempt to over-analyse anything in life, let alone an allergy.

Thought for the day: why do people believe you when you say that there are 4 billion stars in the sky but check when you tell them the paint's wet?

We have some time to write before my trip across the border to Middlesex. Many Tory MPs, it seems, are becoming anxious about the proposed welfare reforms that should – should – come into effect next year. I can understand their concerns. After all, it's very political but really, we are spending a fortune on welfare and benefits. The Tories do not need a repeat of the poll tax unrest. Let's be honest, it isn't good for votes. I do feel, however, that they should stick to their guns, hold their nerve and see it through. This country cannot afford the generosity it bestows on migrants, the feckless and the north, ie those who do not work but wish the state to contribute to the majority of their income. You know my feelings, if you want children, then pay for them. Don't expect the state to pick up the tab. I mean, let's be honest, why else would the world and its wife, families, in-laws, outlaws, etc. all attempt to travel from some far flung, feuding eyesore to Britain? That's right, it's our benefits and all are entitled, so stick to your guns.

Thinking about my journey to West Drayton, and I have been, I always travel up the M3 from Frimley to the M25, along the A4 and turn east towards London, or Mecca (there's more than a similarity) before turning off towards my destination. There have been roadworks on the M3 for well over a year now, widening the carriageway so as to enable the hard shoulder to become a fourth lane. All this does is to engender more traffic. Still, I'm sure the powers that be know best. At the same time, as housing and commercial premises are being squeezed into land bordering the motorway a literal forest of timber is being supplied from somewhere to provide very high fencing along the embankments. The effect is that of a twenty-mile long alley, a wide alley granted, but still an alley. How long will it be before authorities decide to bury motorways in tunnels, so to speak, by concreting over in order to build more houses and business parks. As space and land become even more of a premium this idea will surely find a developer. Of course, it has already happened in Hatfield where the Galleria has been built over the A1{M} and is a prime example of a small-scale development over a dual carriageway. There may be more, but I can see this form of development becoming a whole new area for expanding housing land.

The motorway now looks very much more hemmed in, whereas when built it stretched its tarmac path through relatively unspoilt countryside, but little by little, development by development....

You know, it's always the little things that can say so much. I think I must be feeling financially sound this morning as I forgot to mention we had another letter delivered bearing an unfranked stamp. Usually that would be my first and probably only joy of the day but today I haven't mentioned it until 2.30 pm. Oh, well …

Now here's a tit-bit to share with friends and family. Did you know that the actors Gretchen Franklin and Clive Dunn were cousins? No? Well, you do now.

Right! I've got some exercises, press-ups and paperwork to do before West Drayton, so I'll see you later.

I'm back from the urban sprawl that surrounds Heathrow to the urban sprawl that now spreads like a cancer in West Surrey. Kettle's on. I take it you're not going to bed just yet? No? Good. So, it's tea for two and we have a recorded "Midsomer Murders" to watch which, judging from the write-up, we appear to have seen no less than twenty-eight times, far less than the "Pudding Club" episode. I like the whimsical gentleness of it. Joyce is always joining a local history, archaeological, play-reading, brass-rubbing, music appreciation group, although ironically for one episode only! Cully is always up for an audition somewhere locally and just happens to say the right throwaway comment which gives dad the final piece of the jigsaw before he hastens away and solves the crime, leaving yet another of Joyce's culinary disasters sitting on the table. I told you earlier that I hate change and with "Midsomer Murders" there is certainly a lack of high-speed car chases. Actors and actresses in support of the main cast, many I know, others I have to look up on Wikipedia. I know it's sad, but I don't stay in much. Also, the scenery and architecture is nice and the people portrayed are … well … they're like us – no, I don't mean murderers. But proper people who take pride in their appearance and diction….

Now then, kettle's boiled. Sugar and milk are on the tray. I mean, some people do and some people don't, so I'll leave it to you to add to the cup that cheers.

Well, I've puffed up the cushion so let's settle down with Tom and Joyce and enjoy the title music as much as we once did with J Arthur Rank's gong. Oh, the anticipation of it all.

No, I didn't remember who had done it either. Incidentally, the consistency I seek in life continued to a degree after the retirement of Tom Barnaby some 13 series in and the arrival of John, his cousin, with his extremely attractive wife, Sarah, who is head of Causton Comprehensive School, which is nice for her. During Tom Barnaby's reign, he was accompanied by only three sergeants throughout that time. The last one, Jones, stayed on as John Barnaby's sidekick for series 14 and 15. The fourth and current sergeant is played by Gwilym Lee, who seems to be out of the same mould. Barry Jackson, who played Dr. George Bullard, the pathologist, from episode one with very few exceptions, right through to and including series 14 left and another pathologist appeared through that series, Dr. Kate Wilding, played by Tamzin Malleson. She remained through 15, 16 and 17 but – aah – she is to be replaced in series 18 by an Asian actress. Diversity triumphs, even in sleepy Midsomer.

I recall the awkwardness in the press when in March 2011 the series producer, Brian True-May, was suspended for telling Radio Times that the programme did not have any non-white characters, because the series was a bastion of Englishness. When confronted about the term "Englishness" and whether that should exclude certain ethnic minorities, Mr. True-May replied, "Well, it should do, and maybe I'm not politically correct." He later went on to say that he wanted to make a programme "that appeals to a certain audience, which seems to succeed." His comments were investigated by the production company and he was suspended. Later, being reinstated, having apologised, for that is what they have to do, I mean, there's no good having a view that's shared by the majority, the "certain audience" by the way is Me and many more like me. I reiterate a question I've asked before. How many white actors do they have on the BABC's Asian network? Mr. True-May stepped down as producer, having overseen eighty-nine episodes. Well done, sir. It hasn't gone unnoticed, however, that since series 15 more black and Asian actors have been employed – got to keep those targets achievable and the Race Relations lobby purring like mixed-race cats.

So where are we? Ah, yes, tablets (four) plus drink (elderflower and apple) before treading the boards to Bedfordshire. A quick-fire quad afore we go.

"My mate has just hired an eastern European cleaner, it took her 15 hours to hoover the house. Turns out she's a Slovak!"

"Just had my water bill for £175 drop on my mat. That's a lot of money. I read that Oxfam can supply a whole African village for just

£2 a month. Think it's time to change my supplier!"

"A mummy covered in chocolate and nuts has been discovered in Egypt. Archaeologists believe it may be Pharaoh Roche…".

And finally

"Little Billy asks his dad for a television in his room. Next day Billy comes downstairs and asks, 'Dad, what is love juice?' Dad looks horrified and at length tells Billy all about the facts of life. Billy sits with his mouth open and finally his dad asks, 'So, what were you watching, son?' Billy replies, 'Wimbledon'."

Good night.

I'm not saying anything yet as I'm still stretching. Oooh, that's better. And, yes, that was stretching and not scratching. Did that earlier! Thought for the day – "For every action there's an equal and opposite criticism." Well, talks this afternoon and evening. You know, the ones I mentioned earlier in Owlsmoor and later, a village near Andover. The papers are here, so let's see how quickly it takes for my temperature to reaching boiling point.

I'm on to page 6, and whilst I'm not boiling I am quietly simmering on Gas Mark 5. Last night more pressure was exerted on George Osborne to "rethink" (water-down) his tax credit cuts. Even Boris Johnson is worried about the effect it will have on the working poor. All this discontent from fellow ministers, the benches and especially the House of Lords does not bode well.

Perhaps the government would garner greater support from the public and softening from those opposing the act if they felt that the money saved was going to a cause they felt a kinship with. I note that one in five police forces are failing to provide a good service and that "bobbies on the beat" are becoming an endangered species due to the cuts. If I were able to use any leverage under the heading of "common sense" the police would be properly funded by immediately diverting overseas aid money. The NHS, libraries, community halls, village halls, recreation grounds and a whole host of extremely worthy causes would gain. Sadly, as we know, common sense died with the advent of health and safety, racial and sexual quality and that good old standby, human wrongs.

A quick note here, as I see the Daily Mail investigations unit has uncovered fraudsters in Australia obtaining health data from an online prescription service. I'm just surprised this is such a story. I've assumed for some years now that my personal details have been sold on by every organisation I've ever dealt with from the time that computers first went online.

Oh, this is interesting. There's an article by Bill Bryson on the National Trust. Basically, he is not a happy bunny when it comes to the costs of visiting their premises. He visited Avebury in Wiltshire, which is a stunning site, covering 28 acres, very atmospheric, very interesting – but the cost! As he points out, £25 for a family ticket which affords you entrance to Avebury Manor and garden, then there is Avebury museum, which is another £12.25. Before I go on I think we'd all agree that Mr. Bryson has probably got more than a modicum of common sense when it comes to finding his way round this country, but on this occasion, he couldn't, so he paid £9.99 for a map. In fairness, the National Trust states that free maps are available. What grates and not just for him but for me and most others is the price of a cuppa – £2.50! And to cap it all, having paid £37.25 to get in and walk about, there is also the car park charge of £7. I really do think the National Trust has to watch out. More than one supporter of that once fine establishment told me that they consider the National Trust is biting the hand that pays for the restorations. They should take heed while they still retain support and loyalty. Oh, and whilst I think of it, I do not like their two-tier payment option. They always quote the higher of the two admission prices – the higher is gift-aid included – but they fail to mention, unless you do, the lower price that can be paid if you do not wish to gift aid. I've had this out with staff on more than a few occasions and they always tell me that that is what they are told to say. I have filled in customers' comments forms, complete with name and address, but no-one has ever contacted me to discuss my views. I do feel that there is more than a whiff of arrogance in the historical air.

With regard to our American outlaws' problem with gun crime and gun possession, the following shows what an uphill struggle President Obama faces with opposition that is so blind to tragedy but fiercely protective of rights. A six-year-old shot and killed his three-year-old brother during a game of cops and robbers. It seems incredible to us in Blighty that the six-year-old was able to reach a handgun sitting on top of the fridge. The gun was loaded – naturally, this is America – their 25-year-old father was arrested on a child endangerment charge. The father apparently kept the gun wrapped in pyjamas atop the fridge for protection because he was a former gang member who had "snitched" on another former gang member during a trial. Keeping a gun for his own protection is bad enough, but telling your six-year-old where you keep it is unbelievable. This is where, in instances like this, you realise that America's culture really hasn't progressed very far. As we've said many times before, it is mainly a redneck country with just a sprinkling of acceptable society thrown in for good measure – that is rednecks in suits.

Just a thought, but do you know the difference between America and yoghurt? If you leave yoghurt for 200 years it develops a culture!

No post today. The post lady has just walked by and not even a spam on the computer, Chrissie barks the second the red GPO van trundles down the lane. She seems to think that all the post will be for her. Well, it's not, unless of course it's the Orvis dog catalogue that has been sent for her attention. Her barks are more incessant if we are about to have post delivered, rising to a crescendo when the letterbox flap is pushed open by the falling post. She then grunts begrudgingly until the van has departed but stays by the front door until Maureen or I have picked up the mail. Bless! Right! I'm off! See you this evening. Quite late, I'd imagine (missing you already!)

Right! I'm back and it's quite cold tonight. What's that? How's the new car? Very nice, I have to say. I really do appreciate the heated seat and steering wheel, although the gear knob and handbrake seem so cold in contrast. Now, as you know, I'm not a complete southern woose, but I think I'll ask my daughter, Deborah, to knit me a couple of covers for each, in colours suitable for a chap, naturally. Knowing her, she'll knit them in a shade of concrete, to match the interior walls of our house. She's like that!

Now, this is where boiling point will be easily achieved – animal welfare, or the lack of it. One hears every day about people traffickers, if only the same – or more – publicity could be brought to bear on this subject. It is alleged that foreign vets are working with eastern European and Irish traffickers to fake animal passports and vaccination records in order to help the smooth passage of dogs into the UK. The RSPCA speculates that there are nearly 100 criminal gangs operating throughout the country selling imported pets housed in dreadful conditions. Two countries known to be at the heart of this industry are Lithuania and Hungary. Do you not think this is yet another worrying feature of migration from the former eastern bloc. Their culture is entirely different from ours. We are, in this country, in the main a nation of animal lovers and the majority of us treat animals with the respect they richly deserve, but I would be surprised if the average foreign cove felt the same way. For them an animal is just a commodity. Look at the way they treat donkeys and horses. So, with the influx of more and more foreigners to these shores I fear for the longer term welfare of pets and wildlife. It's not as if we haven't got our own problems within. The Welsh have a very poor record when it comes to puppy farms. The last thing we need is more people getting in on a very lucrative trade that feeds the pocket but not the pet.

Well, we might as well get the painful stories over with in one fell swoop – until the next painful story that is. I'm looking at a picture in the Daily Mail of a dead elephant that is literally on its knees, tusks on the ground. A black man, dressed in a white shirt, blue shorts and sporting a peaked cap, is shaking hands with a German – note, German – who stands beside him. He is dressed in khaki shirt and shorts, a soft hat, dark glasses and carries a rifle. He has just killed one of the biggest elephants in Zimbabwe. The German, remember German, paid £40,000 to shoot the elephant which was aged around 60. There is unbelievably a Facebook page supporting African game hunting and it has been suggested that it was probably the largest elephant killed for fifty years. The writer of this Facebook page refers to the German, that's German, as a "lucky hunter". Well it certainly wasn't a "lucky" elephant. Apparently you can pay for a 21-day package hunting expedition where you get to kill, or murder, the "big five". That's an elephant, leopard, lion, buffalo and a rhinoceros. Why? I really don't get it. How can anyone take pleasure or be proud of shooting an animal, described either as magnificent or mundane. I remember in a previous book I wrote on a similar situation and how I commented that the picture would stay with me for months. And it did, as this one will do now. Is there not a test that can be deployed on all embryos to see if they are destined to become animal murderers when born? If so, the next step would be an instant abortion. Just a thought.

Oh how I cringe when I see gutless Dave and his old school batman, George Osborne, take on the Chinese. We want them as our new friends to provide money for projects that we should be paying towards ourselves, if only we didn't give it away in overseas aid and welfare payments. Not only is the government prepared to continue to roll over and have cheap steel dumped on our doorstep, losing thousands of British jobs in the process, they seek even greater companionship with the building of nuclear power stations. The Chinese will build, own and charge for the production of this form of energy. Their president is being courted in a manner not too dissimilar from Basil Fawlty and Lord Melbury. The grovelling, sycophantic way in which we have treated their visit, an audience in the House of Commons, an overnight stay at Buckingham Palace – oh – and now, the lowering of prices for visas so as to enable more of their fellow countrymen and women to come here and buy up our country – sorry, souvenirs.

The price of a two-year permit to visit the UK from China previously cost £324, but now, with our new-found funding it's a snip at £85. Oh, and we are also considering a ten-year unlimited visa for regular visitors. There isn't, however, likely to be a reciprocal deal for Brits. Why am I not surprised? The truly worrying aspect is that of the power China wields. Do we really want them being in control of our nuclear energy? We've sold everything from car marques – as opposed to Karl Marx – to steel and coal. We don't even keep the revenue from the Dartford toll. That's in foreign hands as well. It's a funny world.

The Daily Mail has named the German hunter who certainly isn't a gatherer, as being one Rainer Schorr, aged 53. He lives in Berlin and is an investment fund tycoon worth millions. Animal rights activists offered a reward to anyone who could identify him. The word "him" makes the arse sound human. This man – and I use the word extremely loosely – can only be described as total and utter scum, a disgrace to society and civilisation. I've just taken another look at the photograph. What on earth could possess someone, anyone, to contemplate murdering such a beautiful animal? Where, by the way, is the hunting aspect in all this? An elephant doesn't hide away, covered by undergrowth, something to flush out. It's a bloody great animal that doesn't possess a gun or any armoury. So how can that be a contest where the human aggressor feels satisfaction in his kill? I sit here, slumped in my chair, feeling totally disconsolate, no words, no one-liners can make me feel anything but despair and anger in equal measure. What I would like is a picture of Mr. Schorr on his knees, pleading for his life as someone in front of him stood there with a rifle cocked ready and the thought of it actually going off would fill me with great joy. What a bastard! See you later.

It's now Thursday, a day free from talks and tours. I feel better today, although that image will stay with me until Alzeimers sets in. But what's this? Aha, just to balance the nature books in a small way, it has been announced that a black rhino has been born in Howletts Zoo, Kent. It is the first example to be born in Howletts in their 40-year history. It's frightening to think that their numbers in the wild have dropped by over 90% since 1970. Oh, the greed of man. I also read that butterflies in Britain have suffered major losses with a specie called the White Letter Hairstreak, declining by 96% since 1976. Over that same 40-year period butterflies have dropped by 48%. Is it surprising, given the way we gladly consign our fields to the diggers in order to build more and more look-alike estates, affordable housing (if I hear that phrase once more I will have to ask what they mean by it) and business parks. And still we breed, and still we import the breeders.

Chapter 6

To Leave or Not to Leave – That is the Question!

It will be interesting to see how Dave's negotiations proceed with his European counterparts. I'm sure they will all smile warmly, shake hands enthusiastically but give away very little. But then, it's very little he's asked for and even less that he'll be given. The result will be a look of joy on Dave's face as he returns triumphant with a promise of change and total and utter humiliation behind that apparent joy. Remember, he said, "I will insist that in future those who want to claim tax credits and child benefit must live here and contribute to our country for a minimum of four years." He not surprisingly has since commented that he will naturally listen to alternative proposals. Why? But then, gutless is as gutless does.

Another aspect of the forthcoming vote will be the question of who gets to vote. With more than 1.5 million foreign nationals able to take part – and I can't imagine many would vote to leave – you wonder just how fair this vote will be. Will it represent the will of the native people of these islands, or will it be a catch-all to make sure we stay in? Remember, when Denmark voted against, they made them vote again until they got the answer they wanted. And will a vote to leave, if that is what happens, actually be binding? I have my doubts. Will a vote to stay be binding? Oh, yes, of that I have no doubt. The "leave lobby" must be united, singing from the same national anthem and focusing on this one chance we have to regain our freedom of sovereignty and freedom to chart our own course. It will be interesting. I just hope it's fair.

Never trust the French. One wonders why we bothered to save them seventy years ago. Looking back, we should have just left them to it. Their policy – and yes, there is one – in Calais is making life extremely difficult for our lorry drivers. The French show scant regard for people legally going about their business and I wonder why only 4% of asylum seekers have been returned from France to their country of ethnic origin. They must be laughing all the way to the port before smuggling their way out of it. Britain is such a soft touch. The French have never liked us. I don't know why we put up with the way they let migrants rule the roost. Every country needs leadership, especially France. Again, only when a bomb goes off and true French people are killed or seriously injured, will the French government start linking migrants to terrorism. At the moment they seem happy to act as an agency for migrants' final destination to the UK.

The years of beating up prisoners have gone. We are now in an age of beating up ourselves, although metaphorically speaking of course. It appears that four police forces do not employ a single black, Asian or Chinese policeman or policewoman. Who cares? Is it not the quality that matters? Perhaps these ethnic majorities simply do not want the job or perhaps they're not good enough if they do want the job. Who are these faceless and nameless people who spend their lives compiling statistics that frankly, just irritate the arse off the majority of white, middle-class natives who do not err, do not steal and do not abuse the system. Those in power should get out more, talk to ordinary taxpaying members of the public who are sick and tired of having race and sex equality forced upon them by government, the opposition and the media in general. Oh, for the days of the Sweeney....

I read today of a chap called Darren Kelly, aged 42, who was set upon by five youths as he walked along a street in Basildon. An argument ensued and he was stabbed in his side and arm. He staggered to a door, rang the bell and pleaded for help. He later died in hospital. Still, I'm sure Nick Clegg would have lectured the culprit for possessing a knife and then issued an Asbo for using it. If and when the police, be they white, black, Asian, Chinese or anybody else, apprehend ne'er-do-wells carrying a knife, they should be given a long sentence and if they use it, life. And for me, life means life.

There was an incident the other day when I was in Farnham. I parked my car in the Central Car Park and was walking along what is a narrow pavement at the start of West Street. A cyclist rode towards me on the pavement. I looked at him and pointed to the road, which is one-way at this point and opposite to his direction of travel. "This is a pavement" I exclaimed, adding, "and that's a road." He shouted, "F...k off" and sped past me, sadly without falling in the gutter, which was naturally very disappointing. The incident could, I suspect, have turned nasty but you have to stick up for your principles. Sadly, cyclists rarely have any.

Shock, horror! The group 'One Direction' have had to cancel a concert for one reason or another. Now why did I assume that was good news and apparently teenagers did not? I think it must be an age thing.

It's interesting to note that while gutless Dave jets around Europe attempting to garner support for his "please give me something to sell to the public" quest, Jeremy Corbyn is filling his boots and shadow cabinet with aides and advisors which bring a sharp intake of breath to the political arena. He has appointed Andrew Fisher, a man known for his foul-mouthed rants. He once described Tony Blair as "a scumbag for hire to scumbags". He rated the previous shadow cabinet as "the most abject collection of absolute shite" and referred to Jack Straw as a "vile git". So much for party loyalty and dignity then.

According to this Fisher character, Yvette Cooper was a pusher of "vile and racist welfare policies" when shadow Home Secretary. I bet he doesn't like the white middle-class either. He is a former Trade Unionist. I rest his card-carrying case.

Alongside this appointment is a chap called Seamus Milne who is Jeremy Corby's spin doctor. That's the newspaper's description, not mine. His views on the 9/11 attacks and British involvement in Iraq, can all be described as a personal view. But his assertion that the murder of PC Lee Rigby couldn't be seen as terrorism "in the normal sense" shows exactly where his swarthy colours are nailed to the mast. And they are certainly not red, white and blue. These people really hate the country they live in, I feel. Their anger always seems to be against those who contribute and cause no trouble, but defend those who would rail against what we stood for and would stand for, given half a chance. Mmmm....

Now, this isn't good news. I've just been looking in the mirror, no, not for vanity purposes, but in the hope that my previous look deceived me. Sadly, it didn't. I am losing my hair. I can see scalp where it used to be thick – well thicker. I've always had a thing about going bald. I may have mentioned this in previous tomes but when I was in my early teens I used to borrow my mum's linen tape measure and place the end against my eyebrows and measure the distance to the temples, and then repeat on the other side. Now, looking back, I know it wasn't scientific, let alone accurate, but it gave me a feeling of consistency so that every time I took a "reading" it differed very little. If, of course, you move the muscles in your forehead the distance can be less or more dependant upon whether you contract or stretch the skin. Yes, I know it's sad, but it worried me then and has continued to worry me for over fifty years. To be fair, if anyone at that time had shewn me a photograph of me aged 68 and said, "you'll have this much hair at this stage in your life" I would have been happy. More than happy, in fact. The problem is that it seems to be thinning all of a sudden. I have actually woken up in the night, most nights actually, and checked that I still have some left. I check the temples first, then my forehead, crown.... As you know, I rarely sleep well but this is an added burden. I know what you're thinking, if that's all you can worry about then life can't be that bad. But, let me tell you, that doesn't help a jot. You see, whatever way I look at it – and I have tried all ways – I do not possess the shape of head that suits baldness. I am beginning to think that I came out of the same batch of eggs as Peter Sissons. Perhaps it is just because I was caesarean. Do you think that could be it? Oh, well, hair watch is definitely on red alert.

Talking of sleep, you remember I dream a lot. Well, recently, I've had some very long, convoluted dreams that have involved "guest" appearances by people I don't know. Trevor Peacock, the actor, was in one recently, so was Sam Allardyce, the football manager, a little while ago John Alderton played quite a big part – and that for him was his second appearance in a dream – strange, isn't it?

Now, with regard to this next little story I am on the side of the National Trust. They are to ban the picking of mushrooms in certain parts of the New Forest. It is currently legal to take one-and-a-half kilograms (what's that in pounds?) per person per day providing it is for personal use. Yes, you've guessed it. Along come the greedy bastards who are extracting them from planet earth on a commercial basis and then selling them on for a profit. As ever, the few make it bad for the many. I agree with the National Trust's move but I don't know how they are going to make sure these people will abide by the principle.

What else have we got here of note? Oh, yes, I think the following story is indicative of many of this country's ills. A gentleman called

Richard Guest and a Mr. Adams heard the cries of two 13-year-old girls who appeared to be in trouble on the beach at Tywyn in west Wales. Mr. Adams said that he and Mr. Guest "locked eyes" and decided to help. They were about 50 yards apart on the beach. Mr. Adams managed to reach and then help back to the shore one of the girls. By that time a group of people had made their way into the sea to help. The other girl managed to make her own way back. Mr. Guest, aged 74, suffered a heart attack and drowned. Mr. Adams attempted to rescue him but was beaten back by the waves. Both men were extremely brave and it's nice to know that both the lasses from Shropshire survived. What a pity that Mr. Guest did not. The point here is that there were beach marshals on the water's edge who did absolutely nothing at all. The coroner, during the inquest in Aberystwyth, criticised them for dithering. "The beach patrol marshals did not seem to assist the rescue effort in any way and dithered on the coastline unsure of what to do." What an indictment. Who are these people? Who trains them? Do they actually receive training? I bet they have at least 20 A levels between them, including psychology, sports and media studies, sports sciences and Tai-Phoo, or whatever it's called. Mr. Guest lost his life needlessly. It really does show our systems for what they are when we tick boxes that say "fit for purpose" but are totally shallow and vacuous when push comes to shove. Sadly, with the onset of health & safety, nous, instinct and common sense all went out of the window. Just a thought, but when did lifeguards become "beach marshals"? And just how much did it cost to change names?

Right, my hand is hurting. I've had enough of writing and I'm hungry, so I'll be back with a couple of stories before bedtime so until then it's quiche, baked potato and "Not Going Out" across three episodes. No "Midsomer Murders" for me tonight, the residents of Badger's Drift, Midsomer Worthy and Midsomer Parva can all sleep safely. The foxes, of course, will still be barking and the owls will still be swooping and hooting in the woods as they have been in every episode since day one.

Well, that was nice. I had a bowl of cornflakes and tinned apricots for afters. Just thought you'd like to know. Okay, time for a couple of pre-bedtime stories. The first is called "The Wine Taster".

At a wine merchants warehouse the regular taster died and the director started looking for a new person to hire. He posted a sign at the entrance of the building that read, "Experienced wine taster needed, position starts immediately". A retired helicopter pilot named Tom, a drunk with a ragged dirty look and smelling of last night's rounds strolled by the building and saw the sign. Immediately he entered and applied for the position. Aghast at his appearance the director wondered how to send him away but thinking he was being fair he offered him a glass of wine to taste. The old pilot held the glass up to his left eye, tilted his head towards the incoming sunlight and studied the contents, whilst looking through the glass. He then took a sip and said, "It's a southern Californian Muscat, three years old, grown on a north slope, matured in steel containers, somewhat low grade but an acceptable tipple." The director was astounded. "That's absolutely correct." He glanced at his assistant and said, "Another more difficult test sample, please." The pilot took the newly filled goblet containing a deep, red liquid, stuck his nose into the glass, sniffed deeply and took a long slow sip. Rolling his eyeballs in a circle he then looked at the director and said, "It's a Cabernet Sauvignon, eight years old, south-western slope, oak barrels, matured at 8 degrees and I suspect requires four more years for the finest results." "Absolutely correct again," said the director. He beckoned forward the assistant to offer a third glass. The pilot eyed the liquid, took in a little of the aroma and sipped very softly. "It's a Pinot Blanc champagne, very high grade and very exclusive." The director was astonished and winked at the assistant to suggest a final test was imminent. She left the room and came back with a wine glass full of urine. The old helicopter pilot eyed it suspiciously. It was a colour he could not quite recall. He took a sip, swishing it over his tongue and across his teeth, musing upward for a while and then said, "It's a blonde, 26 years old, three months' pregnant and if I don't get the job I'll name the father!"

Right! Here's the second of the duo and it's called "A Lady's Reunion".

Jan, Sue and Mary haven't seen each other since leaving school. They discover each other via Facebook and arrange to meet for lunch. Jan arrives first wearing a beige Versace dress. She orders a bottle of Chardonnay with three glasses. Sue arrives shortly afterwards wearing a grey Chanel number. After the initial hugs and kisses she joins Jan in a glass of wine. Mary then walks in wearing a faded old T-shirt, blue jeans and boots. They all now hug and she too shares the wine. Jan explains that after leaving school and attending Oxford University she met and married Timothy with whom she has a beautiful daughter. Timothy is a partner in one of London's leading law firms. They live in a 4,000 square foot apartment in Park Lane and Anastasia their daughter attends drama school. They have a second home in the Algarve.

Sue relates that she graduated in medicine from Cambridge University and became a thoracic surgeon. Her husband, Clive, is a leading financial investment banker in the city. They live in Esher in the heart of the Surrey stockbroker belt and have a second home in Tuscany.

Mary explains that after she left school at 17 she ran off with her boyfriend, Darren. They live in Essex where they grow their own vegetables and run a tropical bird park. Darren can stand five parrots side by side on his erect penis. Several hours later and during the third bottle of Chardonnay Jan breaks down and blurts out that her husband is really a cashier in Tesco's and that they live in a small apartment in Bromley with a caravan parked on the communal drive.

Sue, chastened by Jan's honesty, bursts into tears herself and admits that she and Clive are actually nursing care assistants in an old people's home in Peckham. They live in a council house and take camping holidays in Kent.

Mary finally cracks and admits that the fifth parrot has to stand on one leg!

What's that? You're not tired yet? You want something to think about before you turn off the light? Mmmm, I think the following might just fit the bill. Someone sent this to me by email and I think it's very observant. So, here we go, it's the story of two cows.

SOCIALISM
You have two cows
You give one to your neighbour...

COMMUNISM
You have two cows
The state takes both and gives you some milk

FASCISM
You have two cows
The state takes both and sells you some milk

NAZIISM
You have two cows

The states takes both and shoots you

BUREAUCRATISM

You have two cows

The state takes both, shoots one, milks the other and then throws the milk away

TRADITIONAL CAPITALISM

You have two cows

You sell one and buy a bull

Your herd multiplies and the economy grows

You sell them and retire on the income

ROYAL BANK OF SCOTLAND VENTURE CAPITALISM

You have two cows

You sell three of them to your publicly listed company, using letters of credit opened by your brother-in-law at the bank then execute a debt/equity swap with an associated general offer so that you can get all four cows back with a tax exemption, the tax exemption being for five cows. The milk rights for six cows are transferred by an Intermediary to a Cayman Island company secretly owned by the majority shareholder who sells the rights to all seven cows back to your listed company. The annual report states that the company owns eight cows, with an option on one more. You sell one cow at a premium, leaving you with nine cows. No balance sheet is provided with the release and the public ends up paying for your bull.

AN AMERICAN CORPORATION

You have two cows

You sell one and force the other to produce the milk of four cows

Later, you hire a consultant to analyse why the cow has dropped dead.

A GREEK CORPORATION

You have two cows

You borrow lots of euros to build barns, milking sheds, hay stores, feed sheds, dairies, cold stores, an abattoir, cheese units and packing sheds.

But you still only have two cows

A FRENCH CORPORATION

You have two cows

You go on strike, organise a riot, block the roads and all because you want three cows.

A JAPANESE CORPORATION

You have two cows

You re-design them so that they are one tenth the size of an ordinary cow and produce twenty times the milk.

You then create a clever cow cartoon image called a Cowkimona and market it world-wide.

AN ITALIAN CORPORATION

You have two cows

But you don't know where they are so you decide to have lunch.

A SWISS CORPORATION

You have five thousand cows

None of them belong to you but you charge the owners for storing them.

A CHINESE CORPORATION

You have two cows

You have three hundred people milking them. You claim you have full employment and high bovine productivity.

You then arrest the journalist who reported the real situation.

AN INDIAN CORPORATION

You have two cows

You worship them

A BRITISH CORPORATION

You have two cows

Both are mad

AN IRAQI CORPORATION

Everyone thinks you have lots of cows

You tell them you have none

No-one believes you so they bomb the hell out of you and then invade your country

You still have no cows, but at least you are now a democracy

AN AUSTRALIAN CORPORATION

You have two cows

Business seems pretty good

You close the office and go for a few beers to celebrate.

A NEW ZEALAND CORPORATION

You have two cows

The one on the left looks very attractive

Nighty-night.

I'd like to say I had a good night's sleep, but sadly I did not.

Anyway, it's Friday and it's just after 9 am. I'll be heading up the A3 to Fetcham shortly where I will be picking up my mate, Mike, when we will then wend our way in a northerly direction to the far flung reaches of Surrey – or Epsom to be more precise where, along with my cousin, Simon, we'll be playing trains. No, it's not exactly a "train set" but it's fun for grown-ups anyway.

But first, let's take a look through the papers. Ah, yes, a little story, but one that could happen to any of us and did to Mr. Derek Sculthorpe, aged 77. He went to drop his brother off at Robin Hood Airport (what a ridiculous name) in Doncaster. The airport, by the way, used to be known as RAF Finningley, before emerging as a commercial enterprise. Why not just call it Finningley Airport? It's much more subtle and local but it's probably not the sort of name marketing boys and girls would want to have on their nameboards. It now has to be "zippy, full of pizzazz and...". Anyway, by now Mr. Sculthorpe, still aged 77, has dropped his brother off and decided to find a nearby aeroplane exhibition. He stopped at the side of the road to ask a passer-by if they knew how to get there. The man pointed the way and before our Mr. Sculthorpe could drive to the exhibition, he was pulled over by traffic wardens and issued with a ticket for parking. As he said in his defence, "I wasn't there for even a minute." The official time was recorded as 23 seconds. Is that not the most heinous crime you have ever heard committed? Mr. Sculthorpe continued, "I just stopped, opened the window and asked this chap for directions. I was not parking, I was not stopping. This feels like bullying, I'm really angry." And so he should be. Another case of "Greedy Bastards PLC" being legally able to extract every penny and in the process help achieve a financial target. A spokesman, or humanoid jobsworth as I think of him, for Robin Bastards Airport (RAF Finningley as was) explained, "Signage is prevalent all around the airport warning people not to stop, unfortunately we do hear lots of stories of people who do stop, even for a short period (like 23 seconds) and are then shocked when they receive a fine. We want to urge people to heed the signs." I'd like to urge the unsympathetic cove to chill out and give a bit of slack and then file the slack under the heading "Common Sense and Humility." Just for the record, Mr. Sculthorpe, probably now in his nineties, received a £60 fine, against which he appealed unsuccessfully, and it has now been increased to £100. Note for the future Mr. Sculthorpe, I suggest your brother flies from a proper airport next time.

I wonder how many people have called him Mr. Scunthorpe over the years? I'll probably never know!

Now, we haven't spoken much about football until now, but I read that Manchester City FC are facing a UEFA charge due to their fans booing the champions' league anthem. As the papers comment, it is, in essence, a curb on freedom of speech and protest. It's a bit rich when such a corrupt body attempts to bring its power and might against the very people who support the competition by paying an awful lot of money to watch the game, buy the jersey, buy the scarf, be fleeced by the price of the fleece.... Manchester City fans are not happy about their clubs treatment under UEFA's Fairplay Rules, which they do not consider to be overly fair. You could, of course, expand upon their criticism by asking if the payment to Mr. Platini of £1.3 million by Mr. Blatter was indeed fair play in itself. No doubt this will all come out in the dirty wash. Just let's hope it's not a whitewash. Any organisation that threatens sanctions or fines against a club for the verbal behaviour of its supporters should be looking at the cause of the protest and not get quite so prissy about it.

Right, it's nearly time to move on with the brushing of the teeth and then I'm off to Fetcham to fetch Mike – remember, we're playing trains today. What's that? You'd like to come to? Okay, but we have to get back by 6 pm as I'm taking a tour of the brewery. Oh, while we were talking of football, do you know what the difference is between the England football team and a teabag? The teabag stays in the cup for longer!

Right! Well, get your coat. Oh, you're wearing that, are you? No, it's fine. Let's go.

Well, I'll put the kettle on, shall I, as we're now back home. I hope you enjoyed the ride to Fetcham and then Epsom, the playing of trains, a trip to Ye Olde King's Head for ham, egg and chips. You won't know this, we always have the same meal, but we always scan the menu first. It's a sort of ritual.

The tour went down well, a good mix this evening and so it is a case of eating while I catch up with Teletext, or whatever they now call it, followed by an "Antiques Road Trip", followed by "New Tricks", although it's obviously an "Old Tricks" on Drama. What a wonderful series "New Tricks" was. Well, until the team departed at various stages. Some programmes transcend a change of personnel but "New Tricks" didn't. For my money the only actor who can hold his head up high as a seamless replacement was Dennis Lawson. A very good choice and the programme easily assimilated his character in exchange for James Bolam. Nicholas Lyndhurst never looked right physically in that long, grey coat and his persona and personal life was frankly too dour. Larry Lamb, who I think of as a very fine actor, appeared as a bully-boy with no empathy for the role whatsoever. They should have actually cut the series when Dennis Waterman left. He was the final member, in fact, the last man standing. Luckily, it's the sort of show that will be repeated for years. By the way, it's lamb Rogan Josh, accompanied by a bottle of chocolate lager from the Hog's Back Brewery. I've not tried it before, so this will be interesting and I have to tell you that it is only accompanying my meal for research purposes, you understand.

TV is turned off, I'm feeling replete, beer was very good considering I'm not a lover of chocolate or lager, but it contrasted very well with the curry. I poured it at room temperature, by the way, as it was stocked in the kitchen larder and not in the fridge. Cold beer equals no taste in my book.

Right, it's been a long day and those trains didn't run themselves, you know! Thought for the night – He who hesitates is probably right. Bye for now.

What's that? "Good morning?" Yes, I should have got in first, shouldn't I? So, good morning to you dear bedfellow and reader. I have a 1 pm brewery tour so wonder what the day holds other than Charlton losing or drawing at best, and then being on tenterhooks as to whether Carol survives for another week. I must say that Jeremy Vine is very good value as a contestant and to be fair, a good series so far.

As we finished with a thought for the night, we might as well start with a thought for the morning. So, here's this morning's thought. "Eagles may soar but weasels aren't sucked into jet engines". And you can't argue with that!

With cuppa in hand and yes, it's Yorkshire Gold of course, we'll start with today's papers. Oh, dear, oh dear, oh dear. There is a picture of an actor, well his head actually, made up to look like the living dead, or conversely, anyone you'd expect to see on a bus in Aldershot. Apparently, it's an actor called Tom Bateman who is in the latest TV adaptation of Jekyll and Hyde. It's on ITV and is being shewn at 6.30 pm. It's a 10-part drama beginning tomorrow and written by Charlie Higson. The programme contains gruesome monsters and displays violence towards various characters, well it is Jekyll and Hyde. I have no problem with any of the above, except the timing. It isn't just me, surely, that feels that this subject and content would be better broadcast after the 9 pm watershed. It really isn't a children's programme. When questioned about concerns from parents worried about the content being shewn so early in the evening, this Higson fellow retorted, "F..k them." Does this not show a complete disregard for the people you might hope to win over? What an arrogant sod. He's 57 years of age and should no better.

Well, here's an unexpected move. The government have made a decision with which I concur. Do you remember the name Kenneth Noye? It was he who stabbed a 31-tear-old electrician, Stephen Cameron, to death in a road rage attack. Noye had hoped he might be transferred to an open prison towards the end of his 16-year sentence, but Mr. Gove, the Justice Secretary, has vetoed the recommendation of the parole board that he should be moved from Wayland Prison in Norfolk. It will now be another two years before he can apply again. If it was down to me he could apply until he was blue in the face, but he would never be released. It was nice to read that Mr. Cameron's parents considered the decision to be a huge relief. I wonder if the parole board ever took their feelings into consideration.

I read that a convicted paedophile, Imran Khan, so not one of us, snatched a 6-year-old girl off the streets days after being released from prison on licence. He had previously been jailed for raping a 12-year-old girl. Khan drove around for some time in his car before luring the 6-year-old and then bundled her into the boot and drove off. Fortunately, he didn't assault her, but deposited her in a wheelie bin some time later. The judge at Burnley Crown Court sentenced Khan to life imprisonment adding that Khan should serve at least 6 years and 7 months behind bars. Hardly life, is it? What really bemuses the reader is trying to understand that Khan had only just completed a sex offenders' course before release. The court was told that the course "provided the defendant with the mechanisms of dealing with any sort of urges or intentions he may have had." What piffle. Who on earth dreamt up this psychological tosh? Who recommended him for release? These are the people who should be publicly apologising to the 6-year-old and her parents. They are responsible for their actions but are never brought to account. The best mechanism I can think of is castration. I bet that's against his human rights.

I'm always amused by those to the left of centre in politics who abhor dictatorships, capitalism and anything that smacks of a lack of freedom of expression (what a lot of 'ofs') and rights, yet seek to undermine all who oppose their own views in exactly the same manner. Who is it that teaches the teachers? Is there a secret code by which one achieves teacher status? I ask because of the left-wing leanings being nurtured in our schools, the political correctness which is being indoctrinated from the age of five when children start in their primary school. By the time pupils become students it appears to be endemic. Recently there have been moves to remove the statue of Cecil Rhodes at Oriol College, Oxford. Certain students feel that it serves only to glorify colonialism. Well, it certainly marks a period in our country's history where we did indeed colonise, but do they really wish to airbrush away our history? And who are these students? Are they British, you know, proper British with at least 500 years' heritage here? Or are they foreign students? Let's be honest, the country seems to be awash with them. In its own way it isn't a far cry from IS demolishing historic sites in the Middle East. The principle is the same, if it doesn't conform to your way of thinking – remove! Very dangerous, I say.

So, today, there is a report of police being called to confiscate magazines produced by students in Oxford. The magazine, entitled "No Offence" is, I read, quite offensive – to some. To others it is satirical, witty and barbed. And that's the point. It doesn't project the ideals of the students' union and that is apparently what matters. The magazine's editor, Jacob Williams, a politics, philosophy and economics student, was told by police that handing out the magazine may constitute a public offence. They seized the copies as a complaint had been made by the students' union. A union official, Kiran Benipal (mmmm) said the magazine was offensive and that she had alerted officials after a complaint from a female student. So no surprise there! Apparently, there is a "freshers fair" organised by the students' union from which the magazine was banned. The police thankfully decided that the magazine was not obscene and returned the copies for distribution by Mr. Williams. The old adage stands, if you don't like someone's argument or view, then come up with a better one, ie put up or shut up.

I know what I was going to say, were you aware of just how many fireworks went off last night? Firework night seems to start on New Year's Eve and continues through any date or birthday deemed necessary by some thoughtless arse until mid-October, when it becomes an almost nightly occurrence. It builds to a crescendo on Hallowe'en and then continues unabated until the third week in November when it subsides with only sporadic interventions until starting again Christmas week.

Right! Well, I'm going to get ready for the tour, then I'm going to Farnham to get fuel at Sainsbury's and then will check to see how many Charlton have lost by. I have two "New Tricks" to watch this evening and a "Not Going Out." "Match of the Day" will be with tomorrow's breakfast. Isn't life exciting. I'll see you on Monday.

It's Monday and it's 6.32 am precisely. Last Saturday Charlton lost 3-0 at home to Brentford. This follows the 3-0 loss to Preston North End last Tuesday and the 1-0 loss to Reading last Saturday. The week before, we drew 2-2 with Fulham and this set of results so far has mirrored those achieved during September when we drew the first match of the month and lost the three following games. The two goals against Fulham, by the way, were the only two scored all month. I wonder how we will fare against Middlesbrough next week. My breath is one thing I will not be holding. Football and acquisition seem to be the hobby of the rich. Now in Mr. Abramovich's case he is very rich and Chelsea have prospered under his ownership but clubs like Charlton, owned by a Belgian, has not. The current owner is a Flemish cove called Roland Duchatelet (there should be an upturned whatsit over the 'a' but Maureen can't find it on the computer settings so it was easier to tell you!). This Belgian also owns a team called Sint-Truiden, a side based 40 miles east of Brussels and until this year he also owned Standard Liege. Managers and players appear to hop on and off a merry-go-round of clubs within his ownership. The result is a total lack of stability, quality managers or players. The state of the pitch has suffered greatly over recent years, the morale and enthusiasm of staff and players is sadly very much the same. I have always said that no-one should own more than one football team. It is bound to cause a conflict of interest. Once again, it is showing a total lack of respect to all concerned, especially the fans that pay the wages of those who appear hell-bent on destroying the history, the principles and the good name of once proud clubs. If there is an investor, preferably English, with south-east London roots, who would like to help, please contact the club, preferably before our forthcoming game at Middlesbrough, it might give us hope!

Thought for the day, because there isn't going to be one tonight – I hate predictability.

"Experience is something you don't get until after you needed it."

A few questions that need answering, I feel. Why are they called stairs inside a house and steps on the outside? Why is there a light in the fridge but not in the freezer? And why do psychics always have to ask your name?

It's now 7.14 am and I am on my second cuppa, having written the above and completed the 2 x 50 press-ups and various other exercises designed to do absolutely nothing for my physique or weight. It just makes me feel better about myself – although I am still fretting over the loss of my hair. I mean, it never goes from your chest, armpits or nether regions, does it. Why not? I could lose it from any of these places without any fuss, regret or angst but oh no, mankind loses it from the one place they cherish. As we all know, life's not fair but if it was, America would never have been discovered.

So, to the papers. The government's plan for welfare reform continues to divide and scatter. The opposition opposes because that is what oppositions do, but dissent, hesitation, a wavering from within, now that is not a good sign. Today's papers are full of the latest battles as the lords are expected to defeat the government over tax credits. Nicky Morgan, the Education Secretary, in whom I have very little faith, informed anyone who wished to know that George Osborne was "listening". That is not a good sign. It usually means they have not got the confidence in their own convictions or policies. If the lords do defeat the government it brings into question why these lords have so much power and leverage. We vote for a party to govern, we do not vote for any of the lords. Where is the democracy in that?

There is a lovely photograph in the Daily Mail of Anton du Beke lightly clasping Katy Derham's bottom as they dance the salsa – badly, according to the judges. Only Jeremy Vine received a lesser score. Carol wasn't in the bottom two, despite Bruno Tonioli describing her waltz as having "all the romance of a cleaning session." To be fair, he wasn't far wrong, but our Carol lives to clean another dance floor. The dance-off was between Jamelia and Ainsley Harriott. I have to say that as neither of them were in the bottom two on the "scores on the door" and that both participating dancers were black, I'm surprised there haven't been any suggestions or accusations of racism but as you know, I do not subscribe to Twatter or Fastbuck so maybe there were some comments on the media vine. So, it's RIP Ainsley Harriott who I feel I know very well as I once ate his couscous. I know it was his because his face was on the packet.

Slightly darker is the news article alongside which informs us that Scouts and Girl Guides have been banned from marching in Biggleswade's Remembrance Parade for, and I quote, "health and safety reasons". The British Legion said it made the decision in case the event is disrupted by protest groups that could put the children at risk. Youngsters in the town have joined with members of the British Legion for the past 35 years. I'd like to know just who it is that the Legion expects may protest. If they are referring to Muslims then they should say so. If they are pacifists, members of some student union in some far flung bastion of communism such as Oxford or Cambridge, then say so and then stand up to them. No-one has the right to intimidate a native of this country going about a lawful activity in order to honour the fallen. Gutlessness has become endemic and common sense has flown out of the window.

Mmmm, that Jekyll & Hyde programme was aired for the first time last night. Not only is the writer, Charlie Higson, showing himself to be nothing more than a foul-mouthed yob and one displaying a total lack of respect for viewers' concerns, but he attempts to justify the decision to air his programme at 6.30 pm by arguing that "because children are now exposed to so much graphic content on the internet, TV has to become more extreme to keep up." Now that is a worrying conclusion if it's applied by all programme makers. To me, it's just another part of the continuing decline in television standards. Indeed, standards throughout life. I see no problem with the drama itself, it was probably very good, but not at tea-time. What an arrogant sod!

Am I glad that I'm self-employed and over the age of retirement. I would hate to be an employer. I would just want to employ the person I felt most fitted the job vacancy that I was seeking to fill. David, the misguided one, Cameron will announce today that job applications will no longer have names on them so as to stop discrimination. I retain the old fashioned view that you employ the person you want to and yes, I would want to know if they were white, black or any mix in-between, English, British, foreign, their age and if female, whether they were of child-bearing age and whether they intended starting a family. I would also want to know if they had started life as a male or female and then transmuted into another sex and possibly, transmuted back again. Who knows? I mean, you need to know about toilets for a start if they're going through that transitional period. It can have an effect on other members of staff. I bet in this politically correct age that you cannot ask if they are straight, homosexual or lesbian – and no, I can't see why one cannot enquire. They're always harping on about how normal it is. So, don't hide your bush, your Brazilian or your shaved patch, under a laurel leaf, dearie.

Time for some humour, methinks! Irish humour this time, or more precisely, jokes concerning the Irish. Old hat I know, but tried and tested. Still bet you smile.

Are you sitting comfortably? Then I'll open the biscuit barrel and please help yourself.

So, Paddy caught his wife having an affair and decided to kill her and himself. He put the gun to his head, looked at his wife and said, "Don't laugh, you're next!"

Paddy calls Ryanair to book a flight. The operator asks, "How many people will be flying with you?" Paddy replies, "How the hell do I know, it's your fecking plane."

Two Irish couples decide to swap partners for the night. After three hours of amazing sex Paddy says, "I wonder how the girls are getting on?"

Paddy takes his new wife to bed on their wedding night. She undresses, lies on the bed spread-eagled and says, "You know what I want, don't you?" "Oh, yes," says Paddy, "the whole fecking bed by the looks of it."

Paddy, the electrician, was sacked from the US Prison Service for not servicing the electric chair. His defence was based on the fact that in his professional opinion it was a death trap!

Paddy, the Irish boyfriend of a woman whose head was found on Arbroath beach was asked to identify her. A detective held up the head, at which point Paddy said, "I don't think that's her. She wasn't that tall."

Fifty-three thousand Irishmen meet in Dublin for an "Irishmen are not stupid" convention. The Irish Prime Minister addresses the crowd. "We are all here today to prove to the world that Irishmen are not stupid, so can I have a volunteer please?" Paddy McGinty gingerly works his way through the crowd and steps up to the stage. The Prime Minister asks Paddy, "What is 15 plus 15?" Some 20 seconds later Paddy replies, "Forty!" Obviously everyone is a little disappointed. Then, a dozen or so Irishmen start chanting, "Give him another chance, give him another chance." The Prime Minister responds, "Well, since we have a capacity crowd, worldwide press and global broadcasting media here, I think it's fair to give Paddy another chance." He then asks, "What is 5 plus 5?" After nearly 30 seconds Paddy eventually says, "Twelve." The Prime Minister looks crestfallen and lets out a dejected sigh. Everyone in the crowd is disheartened and Paddy starts to cry. But then a hundred or so Irishmen begin to yell and wave their hands, shouting, "Give him another chance, give him another chance." The Prime Minister, unsure whether he is going to do more harm than good, eventually says, "Ok, then, Paddy, listen carefully and think, man, think. What is 2 plus 2?" Silence hangs over the stadium. Paddy closes his eyes and after a whole minute exclaims, "Four." Pandemonium breaks out throughout the stadium as the Irish crowd stand to a man. Waving their arms, they stomp their feet and scream, "Give him another chance, give him another chance."

Now, the term "feminazis" is new this year, well, it is to me anyway. A very appropriate word I have to say. An article by Ruth Dudley Edwards in the Daily Mail asks questions that worryingly as yet have no answer, as the path the feminazis take is long and their journey unrelenting. The word was first witnessed by me with regard to an extremely pretty, nay, beautiful barrister, one Charlotte Proudman. Yes, the name is almost forgotten now, unless you are in legal circles, but it was she who complained most vehemently and publicly when a male barrister complimented her on a photo of herself that she had put on a networking website. Now, I recall the shot of the barrister and to be fair, it was very well taken and she did, indeed, look very pretty. It is unlikely, I would have thought, that anyone attempting to attract business would put up a mugshot of oneself in rollers, dressing gown, whilst sporting a fag! Oh, no, this photo was designed to attract, although she strongly denies this. So I have to ask, why put up a photo in the first place if the idea is not to attract? I found her comments harsh, unnecessary and disingenuous, but then, she has rights and she felt the need to go public with them. I am surprised she hasn't changed her name to Proudwoman, or Proudperson, or maybe when people call themselves a Chair, as opposed to a Chairman or Chairwoman, perhaps she could just be a "Proud". I have to ask, what is wrong with a member of the opposite sex commenting that you look pretty? For God's sake, get over it and just be thankful that you are pretty.

Getting back to Ruth Dudley Edwards and her article, she cites the changing face of feminism and the fact that Germaine Greer, once considered to be at the very heart of the feminist cause is now considered too "establishment" and "middle of the road", not radical enough for today's left of centre young females "wot's got rights". There is a young lady by the name of Rachel Melhuish who glories in the title of Women's Officer at Cardiff University Students' Union. Ms Melhuish describes herself on her Twatter account as "a lover of intersectional feminism and food." I hope that gives you a clue. I did understand the reference to food, obviously, but the inter-whatever was lost on me. Germaine Greer was due to speak at Cardiff University on "Women and power … the lessons of the 20th century." Ms Melhuish and a band of like-minded lefties have pleaded with the authorities not to allow Germaine Greer to air time, due to the fact that Ms Greer has "demonstrated time and time again her misogynistic views towards transwomen, including continually misgendering transwomen and denying the existence of transphobia altogether. Since trans-exclusionary views should have no place in feminism or society, universities should prioritise the voices of the most vulnerable on their campuses and not invite speakers who seek to further marginalise." So, what she's saying is that there is no place in her life to acquire first-hand knowledge of a different point of view and if it is at all possible, she'll stop anyone else from listening as well. Asking the authorities to cancel a speaker is no different from burning books in Germany before the Second World War. Very short-sighted and with very dangerous implications. Ruth Dudley Edwards ends her article by asking if Ms Melhuish could be given some George Orwell to read. I'd like her to be given a bath, so that she could scrub some of those chips off her shoulder and then be issued with a book printed by Mills &

Boon. You know, so that she can learn what a proper relationship is all about!

On a lighter, but still feminist, theme I read that women bishops are proposing to call God "she", but then they would, wouldn't they! You can't see the wry smile on my face, but it's there. The very thought that for men, their God is a he, and for women it's a she, seems more than faintly ridiculous. As a devout and practising atheist someone really ought to tell these poor saps that their bible is, at the end of the day, only a novel and that they shouldn't believe all they read – as readable as I believe some people find the Bible to be. It is merely fanciful tosh with one or two pointers towards a fairly mundane life-style thrown in as cliff-hangers.

Incidentally, I've just received an appointment through the post from Frimley Park Hospital. On the back it gives my address, although still listing Ash Vale as Aldershot, Hants. They certainly know how to rile me. My religion is noted as atheist but ethnic group … British White. I am not an ethnic group or any part of one. It should, in my book, say English … Native. It then wouldn't need to add "white" as it would come under the heading of bloody obvious. Plus, it would hopefully really upset the race-aholics. I always circle "white" and add the word "very."

Question: What has London got that Iraq, Ruanda and Eritrea struggled to achieve? No, well, it's a high rate of TB. To put it in perspective, London has 107 cases per 100,000 people. Iraq has 45, Ruanda 69 and Eritrea 92 – all per 100,000. London had 2,500 new cases last year alone. The cost to the NHS, or us, is phenomenal. Migrants, refugees, difficult to tell them apart I know, the homeless (them again) and drug takers (so, self-inflicted in their case) are all cited as being responsible for this appalling statistic and still we take them in, and at what cost to the NHS?

I don't know what's happened to the week. Chelmsford, Ewell, St. Alban's have all been visited and now it's Friday. Time to catch up, methinks.

These clerical paedophiles continue worming their way out of the woodwork, as opposed to out of a child! Remember Bishop Ball, friend to Prince Charles, well, he has another friend, a vicar by the name of Vickery House. Sounds like a mews premises in Richmond, doesn't it. Oh, I've just read on – he's American – so that explains it. This House man was yesterday found guilty of a string of sexual attacks against boys in the seventies and eighties. One boy complained to Bishop Ball about House groping him and received a letter saying it was being dealt with and it wouldn't happen again. Not surprisingly, it has come to light that a number of the victims were being groomed by the bad Bishop as well. Both were targeting novice monks. House will be sentenced tomorrow. I just wonder what percentage of genuine religion there is with these people when they become "men of the cloth" and what percentage is an "opportunity for abuse". Which of their chosen lifestyles has the greater motivation because there is a hell of a lot of them within the various cults.

Ye Gods! Oh, this is rich. A Southend locksmith is having to pay compensation to a homosexual named only as "Tim" who was the victim of a staff member's gestures. There had been a dispute over a refund apparently and "Tim" had visited the locksmith's on a number of occasions over a ten-month period in order to sort out the problem. He counted more than twenty homophobic gestures over these months. These gestures ranged from a "sarcastic kiss" to winking and "vile and vulgar gesturing." I'm intrigued. The accusations were denied but "Timbo" won the day – so there was no surprise there – and the locksmith is having to pay him £7,500 in compensation. How much I hear you ask! That's right, £7,500, far more than that received by a victim of assault or fraud but then we are dealing with the delicate.

This case reminds me of that couple I wrote or spoke about a few years ago. This concerned a boarding house in Cornwall where the owners refused to allow a pair of homosexuals to sleep in the same room. They were vilified by the Rights Lobby, taken to court and ordered to pay £3,600 in compensation. They were subjected to vandalism, abuse and threats of violence and all because they had principles. I can remember when an Englishman's home was his detached Guest House.

Okay, with cuppa in hand I am now sitting at the computer. We've had a couple of new talks booked since I last wrote my notes and the confirmation of a provisional visit to Shenfield. But, let's see what the email has to offer. Aah, well, there are details of a venue for a golf club talk in deepest Surrey, an invitation to attend a WI's birthday party the year after next, so let's hope I'm still alive, and the following uninvited offers that once again I can turn down without any pangs of conscience. "Probiotic America" is suggesting that "fatigue, stress and being overweight could be a culprit in me not feeling myself." Well, I haven't felt the need to feel myself since I got married! Oh, I'm not sure that's what they mean. "Peak Life" is recommending that I stay well rested with surprising sleep solutions. And there was me assuming "Peak Life" was a monthly magazine for Buxton, Bakewell and Matlock. There's another chance for me to claim a $50 gift card from Walgreen's and there's a very pleasant chap in Nigeria who is asking for my bank details so that he can check my balance. They don't actually mention the word "Nigeria". We just know.

I'd never heard of the charity Kids Co until its recent demise. I had observed its colourful leader, Camilla Batmanghelidjh, being interviewed on Breakfast television, but lost interest attempting to get past the Batman bit of her name. Lorded by Dave "I'll give your money to anyone" Cameron and his wife, who appears to be very taken with the lady, it looks very much like a spectacular fall from grace and a heck of a lot of missing money. Many charities struggle to attract the low thousands of pounds in grants. This Kids Co lot has attracted millions in funding, to be imprecise some £46 million over thirteen years. That's an awful lot of taxpayers' money. What a charmer Camilla appears to be having extracted that amount of cash from our elected worthies. It will all come out in the work-shy wash, I 'm sure, a wash that will take one hell of a rinsing before all is clear.

Knowing me by now, as you do, you will be only too well aware of my aversion and distrust of anything genetically modified, especially crops. I have no doubt that dirty tricks will be used and also no doubt that they have already been used by bio-tech companies attempting to get us to eat food produced by this method. I will never knowingly eat anything grown in this manner for as long as I live. I've never doubted the motive for their introduction to our farms. Forget feeding the world, this is all about maximising profit. Michael Meacher, who died recently, was a great sceptic and campaigner where such crops were concerned. I always admired him for his stand on this issue. It comes as no surprise to read that oilseed rape growing in the UK is to be destroyed as it was found to be contaminated by GM seed from France – where GM crops are ironically banned. The seed was found within a batch of conventional rape that was sown in a number of small, unidentified, experimental sites in England and Scotland.

These sites were used as trial areas for the official registration of new plant varieties. Whilst affected plants will be destroyed by the seed company, one has to ask how the GM seeds came to be within that batch. Sabotage? To be fair to the French and I suppose occasionally one has to be, it's nice to know that they are baulking at the introduction and cultivation of genetically modified crops. Long may that stance continue.

Okay – time for a little story. This one is called "The Singing Frog". Are you sitting comfortably? Good, then I'll begin.

A man enters his local bar holding a frog and an iguana. He sits them down on the bar and says to the barman "I bet you £1000 that my frog here can sing any song you care to mention." "Okay." Says the barman, "how about 'Blue Moon'?" The man whispers something to the frog and the frog starts crooning "Blue Moon." "That's amazing," says the barman as he slaps down £1000 in notes. The man looks at the barman and says, "Okay, now I'll bet you that my iguana here can do that too." "Well, I can believe a frog but not an iguana. You're on. Have him sing 'God Save the Queen'." The man whispers something to the iguana and it sings "God Save the Queen." As the barman hands over another £1000 a businessman walks up to the bar and says, "I just saw what happened and I am amazed. I'd like to buy your iguana for £100,000." The man says, "Okay" and exchanges the iguana for the money and the businessman leaves. The barman says, "Are you off your rocker? You could have made millions with that iguana." The man replies, "Oh, the iguana can't sing, the frog's a ventriloquist."

Oh, right, you've time for another then? Two! Okay, well, this one involves a newly wed couple and it's called, "The First Time".

Two newly weds went on their honeymoon and were getting undressed together for the first time. The groom took off his shoes and socks and his toes were all twisted and discoloured. "What happened to your feet?" his wife asked. "I suffered from a childhood disease called tolio." "Don't you mean polio." "No, tolio, it only affects my toes." He then removed his trousers, only for his wife to gawp as her eyes centred on his odd looking pair of knees. "What happened to your knees?" she asked. "Well, I also suffered from kneesles." "Don't you mean measles?" "No, kneesles, it only affects the knees." As he removed his pants his wife gasped and exclaimed, "Don't tell me, you also suffered from smallcocks!".

And lastly, "A little old man". A little old man shuffled slowly into an ice cream parlour and pulled himself gently and painfully up onto a stool. After catching his breath he ordered a banana split. The waitress looked at him kindly and asked, "Crushed nuts?" "No", he replied, "arthritis." I know, I know....

Memory Lane time now and no, I'm not referring to Brian in New Tricks. When my paternal grandfather died in Aberdare my father cleared out a cupboard high in the kitchen/scullery area. It contained much that I do not remember and was subsequently thrown out. It would probably make a fortune now on Antiques Road Trip but back in the early sixties it was considered worthless. What we did keep were some twenty copies of the Great Western Railway magazine, which ranged in date from 1931 to 1939. These would have been collected by granddad who, as some of you will know, worked as an engine driver for the Taff Vale Railway and latterly the GWR. He worked out of Aberdare shed, where I spent many an hour as a child, sitting on a buffer beam at the end of one of the roads in the shed, watching the engines move in and out awaiting their turn of duty. Heaven, pure heaven. In front of me are some of these magazines. As well as being interesting to read for railway buffs, especially aficionados of the greatest railway ever constructed – God's Wonderful Railway – and yes, in this case God is definitely worth a capital! The GWR deserves nothing less. But it is the adverts that are so interesting. On the cover of this particular magazine, dated March 1936, price 2d, a full-page advert has been paid for by Whiteleys, the Department Store in London. Their punchline, alongside a pen drawing of the store, declares, "Buy your car the wisest way – the Whiteley way." The wording underneath gives a prospective purchaser an assurance about the company, free from gaudy colours or a celebrity endorsing the product and without an invitation to "check out our website". It states, "Whiteleys have been famous for motor car sales and service since their advent and were first to offer reasonable deferred payment facilities. Furthermore, the reputation of this renowned business house stands behind every sale and ensures satisfactory service."

The advert then lists the manufacturers for whom they are dealers. Austin, Rover, Morris, Wolseley, Humber, Hillman, Vauxhall, Ford, Standard, etc. etc. Interest charge is 5% per annum. Any make supplied. It then goes on to quote, "An example of our convenient terms:- New Series II Morris ten four Sun saloon £182.10s. Or cash down £15. 9s.

154

5d. and the balance payable in 11 equal monthly payments of £15 .9s. 7d. It is so easy to read and interesting how the reader gleans so much information with a telephone number to ring as well, a number that I'm sure would have been answered immediately from a member of staff who you just know would have diction and grammar matching that of a BBC continuity announcer of the day, either in the store or sales room, not by an Indian, whose grasp of English at best would be acceptable and at worst, unfathomable. Just for the record, the telephone number was WELbeck 5326.... Ahhh....

Oh, yes, that was for car sales only. Their main switchboard number for the store was BAYswater 1234. Now that was marketing! Incidentally, our telephone number at home in Clapham Junction where I lived was BATtersea 0237.

Turn the page and Henry Pooley and Sons of Birmingham and London are advertising their weighbridges. J. Compton Sons and Webb are extolling the virtues of their uniform clothing, helmets and caps. They were situated in Old Ford Road, London E3 and Swindon, Wilts. Their phone number, by the way was ADVance 1940 – three lines. Alongside is an advert for "The Thames Steam Tug and Lighterage Company Ltd – Lightermen Tug and Barge Owners and Shipping Agents." There's pride in them there words, you can almost smell the Thames. On another page Dunlop are advertising their "Dunlop 90 Giant Tyres".

Now, this is a corker, an advert in the form of a testimony from a doctor. The advert is headed

To the

SLEEPLESS

Read the personal experience of a doctor

Many thousands of personal letters have been received by the proprietors of "Ovaltine" testifying to the supreme value of "Ovaltine" for inducing sound, natural sleep. The following letter from a doctor is a further spontaneous tribute to "the world's best nightcap."

Dear Sirs,

I have great pleasure in testifying to the excellent qualities of "Ovaltine" as experienced by myself.

For some few years I have suffered from a mild degree of insomnia, my sleep at night averaging three to three-and-a-half hours. Although I have prescribed "Ovaltine" for my patients for a number of years on account of its energising and soothing effects, I did not make a personal trial until about three weeks ago, when I sampled it for the first time, on the advice of my daughter, who has taken "Ovaltine" for several months.

I took a breakfast-cupful on retiring, and I had the best sleep I have had for some considerable time. I thought this might merely be a coincidence and repeated the experiment the following night with the same happy results.

Needless to say, I have not missed my "night-cap" since, and I shall have the greatest pleasure in continuing to prescribe a preparation which I have personally found of such inestimable benefit. My general health has improved, and I now sleep six to seven hours every night, and feel much more able to face the duties of the morrow than heretofore.

Yours very truly,

(Signed) .... MB

Note:- the name and address are withheld in accordance with medical etiquette – but the original letter can be seen at the offices of the proprietors of "Ovaltine". Isn't that wonderful?

Winegartens, the jewellers, seem to have held the monopoly for advertising on the back page, where GWR employees were given a 20% discount on all purchases. Quite substantial, I must say.

So, back to the papers and the modern world. It's not always plain-sailing for believers as god moves in mysterious ways, doesn't he? Or, in this case, Allah! There is a Muslim male by the name of Mohammed Salim who says he doesn't believe in contraception and believes it's his god's will to go forth and multiply – and has he! Eleven children, no responsibility and all rights. This 58-year-old, who appears proud to state that he is better off on the dole than working, is married to a female called Noreen, who is aged 40. They receive £27,000 a year in child tax credit and job avoiders (sorry, Seekers) allowance, which is a bit of a joke. If ever there was a reason for the government not to lose its collective nerve and push through their welfare legislation it's because of instances like this. What a wastrel. The man should be sterilised, although naturally, not on the NHS.

As well as the imbalance of white, Asian and black presenters on the BABC I still attempt to support them because as I said previously, they represent our country on the world stage. Its reputation (tarnished though it may be) its history and many of its programmes, and all without advertising, is what I hold dear to my licence fee. The support dissipates, however, when you read of the fees and expenses paid in claims. Alan Yentob – him, again – spent nearly £1,500 of public money gallivanting around in taxis in just three months. The man is paid £330,000 a year, don't forget, by the Beeb, plus his time spent as Chairman of Kids Company. Between April 2009 and now he has also been paid £85,000 in expenses by the BABC. Polly Hill, their Head of Drama, spent nearly £5000 on fares and hotel bills for a four-night stay in Beverley Hills for the Golden Globe Awards in Los Angeles. These executives don't come cheap, do they.

Tomorrow is Saturday and therefore Strictly. Will Carol stay? We will know by the end of the weekend.

Some questions before we go. How important does a person have to be before they are described as assassinated as opposed to murdered? How is it that we put man on the moon before we worked out that it would be a good idea to put wheels on luggage? Why is "bra" singular and "panties" plural? By the way, the word "breasts" is an anagram of "bra sets". Why do they bother to use sterilised needles for death by lethal injection? Whose idea was it to use the letter S in the word lisp? Why do people constantly return to the refrigerator with hopes that something new to eat will materialise? And, finally, why do people keep running over string a dozen times with their vacuum cleaners, then reach down, pick it up, examine it and then put it down to give the vacuum one more chance? And Tony's money-saving tip for the day, for those of you on metered water, always make sure you go to the loo when visiting someone else's house and that way you save on your own water bill.

Good morning. It's now the day I really object to each year, well, along with all the other days I object to, but this one is due to its hijacking by the Americans – Hallowe'en. As it is now a ritual for this most irritating of "celebrations", having extracted a sign from the garage, dusted it down and erected it once more upon the gate, it will remain until tomorrow morning when we thankfully move into November and we're free of this annual onslaught for another year. The sign reads, "Sod off, you little bastards!" I think any parent or parents with sprogs eager to attract free sweets will hopefully think twice about entering. Of course, I can do little about the fireworks, which is a great pity but they have been revving up the audio waves and lighting up the sky for a number of days in practice, so 31st

October is no more than a build-up to the 5th November and then, Christmas – aaaghh!

It's a busy day today, three tours of the brewery, followed by two tomorrow.

Thought for the morning: Success always occurs in private, whilst failure is always in full view!

Tea, toast and McKay's marmalade, let's see what the news has to offer. Well, in the Lords the Lib-Dems are leading the bid to defeat the draft bill over surveillance powers. Is it a "snooper's charter" or a necessary evil in today's society where we need to control, if not exterminate, the enemy within and for that matter, without. I've generally been on the side of "if you haven't got anything to hide then why kick up a fuss". There is, however, always the nagging doubt over one important word in this issue – "trust". Can you trust the powers to be, to be only interested in signs of terrorist activities or will they be looking for any signs of "abnormal activities" such as listening to Michael Buble on Youtube, watching Magic Roundabout from 1958, when narrators spoke crisp BBC English, along with very acceptable diction, or will they be monitoring those who log into the Signpost Restoration Society's website? I mean, Angela does Accrington has been downloaded by everyone – hasn't she? I think I'm now on Noreen from Nottingham.

This Kids Company rumpus looks set to continue. Six figure payments to children, a £50,000 donation towards the cost of a Ph.D for the child of an Iranian diplomat – how poor was he? One of the Kid's Company's adult clients received £47,000 in tax-free support during one year alone. I'm sure we could all do with that. It also appears that two children, registered as clients and both of whom had a parent on the pay-roll, benefited from almost £135,000 of spending since 2009. These payments covered the cost of designer shoes, which were signed off as "therapy costs" among other areas of expenses. What a rip off! What a total disregard for taxpayers' money. There is more than a whiff of arrogance here.

A busy weekend was had by one and all, me included. Hallowe'en and the ensuing fireworks came and went with no unrequested visitors, so the sign worked then. Carol survived, whilst Kirsty Gallagher did not. Oh, and Charlton lost 3-0 for the third consecutive game to Middlesbrough. All the way up to the north-east for those very loyal fans, but at least we are becoming consistent.

When Nicky Morgan was appointed Education Secretary I did wonder whether it was due to her outstanding capabilities or whether it was because she was female. Well, you never know – targets are all. And, yes, you do become cynical. Whatever you might think of Michael Gove, at least he appeared to have a desire to achieve higher standards. The proof of that pudding, is that when you hear a teachers' union bleating, you can be fairly certain that the idea put to them would improve education. Nicky Morgan, however, has shewn her true lack of metaphorical balls by caving in to the unions and ordering a review of tough new tests for primary school children. Mr. Gove suggested that heads should make erring pupils do laps of the school grounds. That's not going to happen under Nicky Morgan. She has stated that she wants a "partnership with teachers, not a war on ideas". I find this strange as it implies teachers are capable of ideas. Mr. Gove allowed universities a say over the content of A Level courses and that has now been overturned. In 2013 Mr. Gove told striking teachers that they'd never had it so good. Nicky Morgan later told them that they are "working far too hard, for far too long, and promised to slash teachers' workload."

It will be interesting to see Russia's response to one of their airliners being blown up on its way from the Egyptian resort of Sharm el Sheikh to St. Petersburg. Two hundred and twenty four passengers and crew on board and all killed. When will countries wake up to the Muslim problem? Because, don't fool yourself into thinking that this is IS overseas, this problem is on our doorstep. It's been knocking on France's door for some time and it literally knocked on a cartoon character's door and killed a number of workers, but still no mass uprising from the French people. Perhaps they'll respond when the regional elections take place in the New Year. Then, again, perhaps they won't. No-one in the west appears to want to acknowledge the grave choices it faces, although I suspect the Russians might. We shall await with interest.

Mmmm, in line with my doubts about those in charge of programming at the BABC, it has just been announced that they are breaking with tradition for their scheduling of the Festival of Remembrance broadcast this year. The service has always started with the parade of Royal British Legion flags. This entails the National Standard being carried by its bearer, followed by over 100 flags from local branches. The broadcast producers have, in their infinite lack of wisdom and no doubt inexperience, decided to remove this section of the proceedings, in order to make it – wait for it – "contemporary and exciting". Instead, the flags will already be in place and the event will start with the arrival of the Queen and other members of the royal family. I wonder just how much excitement one can take for what is, let's not forget, a Remembrance Day service. Why can't these people just leave things as they are. I very much doubt if those responsible are vaguely over the age of consent and if they are, then they're most definitely Oxbridge educated, or should that be indoctrinated?

We are just two months shy of that odious time of the year when Honours are meted out to those who don't deserve them, but they are an actor-luvvie who has never won a Bafta or a lord who never achieved much as an MP, a hanger on or even worse, a private secretary. The army of Sir Humphrey's lives on, governments come and governments go.

In today's Daily Mail there are six photographs of an Exmoor pony in various stages of its life, from rescue to contentment. It's all down to a lady called Dawn Westcott. She had been told by a walker that there was an undernourished foal struggling to survive. When she got there it was days away from death, just four months old and abandoned. He was stranded in a deep, wooded valley, weak and struggling to stand up. The pictures show this pitiful little fellow, sodden, muddy and very unhappy – eyes tell you everything. Mrs. Westcott managed to lead him to her trailer. He was apparently too weak to argue. Whilst in transit to the vet's he collapsed eight times. The vet feared she may be too late. Mrs. Westcott runs the Moorland Exmoor Foal Project that looks after the breed and currently has twenty-five other Exmoor ponies on her farm. She is known locally as the "pony whisperer" due to her patience and knowledge in handling the breed. The top three photos show the pony in "being rescued" state, whilst the lower three show him running in fine fettle and being cosseted by Mrs. W. Well done that lady – and will she be up for an award of some sort – I can't imagine so for one moment. To be fair, I can't imagine that she'd want one but I like to see recognition where it's due. What a pity we cannot compel Messrs. Cameron and Osborne to divert some of the taxpayers' money currently sent to India, Nigeria, etc. to charities in this country. Oh, look – did you see that? That's right, it was a flying pony.

On p29 of the Daily Mail there is a photograph of a lollipop lady resplendent in her hi-viz lime green/yellow coat bearing white chevrons and hood, whilst proudly holding her pole – no, not another migrant but one displaying the STOP on black outline of a young girl holding the hand of a younger male sibling. The lollipop lady is smiling, though she has every right not to be as she has been banned for waving at children in cars. The ban is not surprisingly on the grounds of health and safety. The lady in question, Mrs. Dixon, is 74 years old and was born in an age when common sense was common place. This all came to the notice of the council when a member – a single member – of the public complained about her waving. Of course, it isn't the local council who enforce rules these days. Oh, no, it's a contracted outfit. In this case a company called "Cordia" – I expect someone was paid a fortune to sort through letters to come up with this nonentity of a name – like Montego, Arriva, Aviva – all pointless and meaningless. Still, Cordia did swing into action fairly quickly. The day after the complaint was lodged they sent another lollipop man to be with Mrs. Dixon to make sure that no waving motions were enacted, as it really does conflict with the company's health and safety policy. A spokesman for Cordia stated, somewhat cynically I feel, "A member of the public expressed concern about the behaviour of one of our school crossing patrollers. We had a chat and they were provided with further training (brainwashing or blackmailing I say). We are satisfied the issue is now resolved." Pompous arse! And since when have they been called 'patrollers'?

I have a talk to a U3A in Surrey this afternoon and should be back, M25 willing, by 5-ish – and will there be crumpets for tea? No, probably not, but maybe ravioli – BFN.

Chapter 7

Fois Gras Or Sandwich Spread?

I'm back! A quick sandwich … mmm…. Sandwich Spread (Heinz) and sliced tomatoes on thick white bread spread with a liberal amount of Lurpak unsalted butter. Mouthwatering, or what! You can keep your foie gras and your ravioli. Give me a Sandwich Spread sandwich, a sugar sandwich, a dripping sandwich or a "Fussels" condensed milk sandwich and I'm a happy bunny. Incidentally, "Fussels" is no longer a brand, having been brought within the Nestles range and marketed as "Carnation Light Condensed Milk". While I've been making it, Flog It has been on TV. It always intrigues me when an expert says to the expectant punter, "I feel that it's worth two to three hundred but to make sure we sell, we should put a reserve of £200 on. How does that sound to you?" "Oh, yes," they say, never previously thinking it was worth the square root of bugger-all when Aunt Mona gave it to them on one of their rare visits to see the old girl, holed up in Eastbourne. You then get to the auction and it is revealed to Paul Martin that in between the valuation date and now the owners have contacted the auction house and told the staff that they feel it was under-valued and they will now increase their reserve to £300. I always smile (a wry one, naturally) as it seems that neither Paul Martin, the expert nor the auctioneer have had any experience of the object d'art in question but for the couple who own the item, their mate Brian down the pub knows everything there is to know about nothing and convinces them that it's worth a lot more than it really is. What a pity people become so greedy. I hate it. Be content. The joy for me is when the item that has had its reserve raised to £300 only nudges its way up to £210 and therefore doesn't sell and the greedy couple have to travel back home with their tails and their object of hopeful greed sitting between their legs. Display smug smile now!

It's now later and I've enjoyed a feast of "Would I Lie To You?",

"New Tricks" and "Not Going Out." I'm off to bed, so I'll leave you with the following to smile over.

Firstly, this one is called "Female Medical." During a lady's medical examination, the doctor says, "Your heart, lungs, pulse and blood pressure are all fine. Now then, let me see the bit that gets you ladies into all kinds of trouble." The lady starts to take off her underwear but is interrupted by the doctor. "No, no," he said, "don't remove your clothes, just stick out your tongue!"

Secondly, "Snowploughing". On a bitterly cold winter morning a husband and wife in Dublin were listening to the radio over breakfast. They heard the announcer say, "Today we are going to have between 8 and 10 inches of snow. Therefore, you must park your car on the even numbered side of the street so that the snow ploughs can get through." On hearing the news, the wife went out and moved her car. A week later, again whilst eating breakfast, the presenter announced, "Today we are expecting 10 to 12 inches of snow and this week you must park your car on the odd numbered side of the street so that the snow ploughs can get through." Once again, the wife went out and moved the car. The following week they are once again halfway through their eggs and bacon when the radio announcer said, "We are now expecting between 12 and 14 inches of snow to fall today. Therefore, you must park…". At that point the electricity went off. The wife became very upset and with a worried look on her face said, "I don't know what to do. Which side of the street do you think I need to park on so that the snow ploughs can get through. I'm really worried." Then, with all the love and understanding in the voice that all men who are married to blondes exhibit, the husband replied gently, "Why don't you just leave the bloody car in the garage this time."

I know, I like that one as well.

It's been another busy few days and there have been a few of these, looking back through the diary. I was going to say "hello" yesterday but time got in the way. Three talks and four brewery tours later it is now time to have a review of the recent editions of the newspapers.

Oh, here's a surprise. Apparently up to half of our tax, which has been given away under the heading of "foreign aid" for Syrian refugees has been squandered on United Nation's red tape. What's that? No, you're right, it's not really a surprise. We taxpayers have contributed £1 billion to "help" these people, whatever that means in reality. Around £600 million has been given over to 3 UN bodies, the World Food Programme, Unicef and a refugee agency called UNHCR. Interestingly, Unicef cannot or will not give a breakdown of where its contribution has been spent, while the UNHCR has diverted £7 million to funding its press office. I cannot imagine these "charities" having bosses that will work for the same peanuts that they appear to be handing out to refugees – and I'm being overly generous with the use of the word "refugees" because we don't know how many terrorists and would-be terrorists we are feeding under the name of refugees. It's difficult to tell them apart until they blow themselves up, sadly taking innocent people with them.

When you think that government policy is to waste 0.7% of our national income abroad it is, to be honest, a bloody scandal. You might think that somebody would be employed to check where our money is going, but then that would come under the banner of responsible government. What you do know is that from the moment it leaves our banks everyone in the chain will be doing very nicely thank you, until it comes down to those who arguably need it and I'm convinced that that is where the charity stops. The Radio 4 programme "File on Four" stated that it was extremely difficult to discover how much was spent on what as there was a total lack of transparency at the UN. I suggest the UN should be twinned with FIFA, they would make good bedfellows and would no doubt garner even more money to swash around in their already overly-bloated bellies. These overly-bloated bellies being matched only by the overly-bloated bellies of the malnourished Oomygooly tribe who mis-guided charities would argue is a far more worthy contender for aid than a day centre in Droylsdon. No doubt as I write, another British care home is closing down due to lack of funding, another library will be closing its doors and another post office…. The price of everything, the value of nothing.

Now, I have seen a trailer for Citizen Khan, a situation comedy aired over three series and I understand about to play out a fourth. It doesn't appeal to me, not because the characters are mainly Asian, but having seen the trailers, which are presumably highlighting the series, I can honestly say I've never found it funny. Raucous, manic, yes, but not qualities that induce me to watch a comedy. What I did find interesting, however, was that the main character, played by a Muslim Pakistani called Adil Ray said he thought that any negative comments would be outweighed by pride that a Muslim Pakistani family was at the forefront of a BBC sitcom. Apparently, Mr. Ray was wrong. The first series received over 700 complaints, accusing the show and all associated with it of making fun of Islam and stereotyping Asians. The poor chap has even endured death threats over the three series and suffered online abuse via social media. If you don't like the comedy that the Beeb offers in an attempt to up its minority content and you're not in favour of our freedom of speech, then as I've always said, leave. You don't have to stay in a country so generous of spirit. So, rearrange the following words into a well-known suggestion – "Off sod!".

Now, here's a subject close to my heart, or more precisely, my ears. I read that the Culture Minister, Ed Vaizey, is suggesting that FM Radio could be switched off permanently as DAB spreads its listening power across the airways. He enthusiastically states that "More than 30 million of us are tuning in every week, with digital listening hours increasing every year." Is it? Are we? I don't know anyone who listens to DAB. Perhaps they do and the subject just never comes up over dinner. Radio 4 is on FM. Everyone I know listens to Radio 4 when they're driving, with over 25% of all new cars still being fitted with analogue radios. I've listened to programmes where the subject of DAB has been discussed and there appears to be a high number of listeners not happy due to the poor quality signal and programmes cutting out. Not the sort of thing you need when Rob is about to manipulate and control poor Helen once again – and he will – he's like that. Funny how listeners to the "Archers" know what he's like and yet the cast still seem to be blissfully unaware.

Mr. Vaizey says that FM will be switched off when a "certain target" of digital listeners has been achieved, although the government would be "led by the listener." Really? Well, that's a first. Imagine a government listening to the population at large.

The teaching industry is back in the spotlight today but as ever, for all the wrong reasons. There are schools, according to a new report, that are failing the white working classes. They needed a report for that? Nicky Morgan, in whom I have absolutely no faith whatsoever, will be "parachuting" 1500 teachers, described as "elite", into weak schools in an effort to increase the standards. Or, as they say in modern parlance, "drive up standards." I just drive up the road, but never mind, although there are people like Ms Morgan who continually drive me round the bend.

The National Teachers Service will target poor performing schools, many being in white working class areas, which is encouraging as I didn't know we still had any, with a team of talented teachers and heads. If we have 1500 spare teachers who can be parachuted in, what has this elite force been doing in the past? Waiting in disused bunkers? It doesn't make sense. The aims, according to Ms Morgan, will be for all 14-year-olds to study "key" academic subjects. There are many areas where the majority of pupils still do not achieve any good GCSE's in any subject. Shock, horror! I thought all pupils attained at least 25 GCSE's. I mean, surely it is much harder these days to fail than pass?

My previous comments regarding the poor quality of teachers are not without support from this article either. It comments that semi-literate teachers are hampering attempts to improve children's grammar and vocabulary. Trained teachers (who trains them?) struggle with the basics and a lack of confidence to teach youngsters about the proper use of English, including punctuation and spelling. The National Curriculum expects teachers of all subjects to develop pupils' ability to use English. A survey by the National Literary Trust worryingly discovered that 21% of teachers admitted to not being confident that they had enough "subject knowledge" to do this. Unbelievable. The Trust surveyed 2,376 teachers and found that 63.3% felt that that "their colleagues could benefit from improving their own literacy, while 45.1% commented that the quality of teaching and learning was a barrier to children's overall literacy attainment." Not surprisingly, when asked, the Department for Education stated that the quality of teachers in our classrooms is now at an all time high. I wonder just how close to a classroom – and I don't mean Eton and Harrow – any of the mandarins from the DoE have felt it necessary to attend, when making these observations and judgements.

Just a point in passing, but it might help with the groceries, a survey has revealed that butter is becoming popular once more and red meat isn't as bad for you than first thought. Or was it red wine? It doesn't really matter, as there will be another survey published next week, contradicting the survey of last week.

Here we go again, another 93-year-old German has been brought out of his metaphorical bunker to stand trial as an accessory to over

170,000 murders. To be fair, that's an awful lot for one man. The chap in question was a guard in Birkenau for two and a half years from January 1942 to June 1944. For goodness sake, it was over 70 years ago. He was one of thousands of guards. At his age, he is no doubt one of the last ones left. What does anyone get from trying a man of his age? Revenge? Justice? It was a war – unpleasant though it may have been – it's over. Let it and those who suffered rest. Mind you, I'll never forgive the Japanese – which is, I believe, an anagram of bastard!

I do wish the public would vote with their feet, or in this case, their choice of chocolate bar. I remember the furore when Cadbury's were bought out by that ghastly American dynasty, Kraft. Within months of the takeover, they closed the factory in Keynsham, near Bristol, and have since moved production to Poland, as it's cheaper. There is probably some deal between government to import 1 million Poles to Britain in exchange for the production of chocolate to Poland. Probably not, but I just felt like saying it. Kraft is not endearing itself to the British chocolate buying public. Having discontinued using the Dairy Milk chocolate for the outer shell of its traditional cream eggs, it is now adding sultanas to its Fruit and Nut bar. They can't leave anything alone, can they, so to all you chocoholics out there, boycott Kraft products in their entirety. After all, I never did take to their cheese slices.

Oh, how society changes – and as we know, rarely for the better. Students were the educated ones, the clever ones, the ones parents were proud of. Now, the subjects appertaining to their progression through the workplace seem to come a poor second to political correctness, race awareness, gender awareness and a berating of anyone possessing a view unworthy of their rigid ideals. Who elects these student union officers? There's an example here, a young lady by the name of Bahar Nustafa, who has escaped prosecution after charges were dropped because there was not sufficient evidence to provide a realistic prospect of conviction. This 28-year-old Asian is not fussed on the colour of the country's natives, ie white. She was accused of labelling somebody "white trash" after she asked white students and men specifically, "not to come" to a diversity event at Goldsmith's College, London. A row ensued with fellow students complaining that she was making some sections of the community feel excluded. She was alleged to have written, "Kill all white men" on Twatter. This was denied. She wrote on a website, "I never actually Tweeted it, but I don't condemn it either." What a nasty young lady. If these officers are genuinely voted in, then who the hell votes for them? Why do I get the feeling that if it were a white person labelling another student "black trash", there most definitely would be enough evidence for a prosecution?

Following neatly on is an apparently "bitter sexism row." Britain's new passports are to be issued shortly. The 34 pages contain icons of British history and include nine people from our glorious past. Not surprisingly this is where the problem starts. Seven are men and only two are women. Does it matter? As a chap it wouldn't upset me if there were seven women and two men, or indeed nine women and no men. Now, ladies will say that that is the point, it isn't going to happen. I have to say, I wish they'd attempt to put pressure on government appertaining to issues of a more general nature, issues that affect all of us. Either that or make a brew and re-do the shopping list. Or, maybe they could change the bed linen – or crochet a vest. Calm down, dear, it's only a man!

There are many down sides to immigration that remain below the radar. They are not overly obvious, yet eat away at our native society's idea of what is acceptable and what is not. In some Asian countries a female life is not considered as worthy as that of a male. Fine, if that's what they feel, it is their culture but where you have increasing numbers of migrants their draconian traditions transcend continents. From female genital mutilation to aborting foetuses just because the child-to-be is female. These practices are illegal in this country and make a mockery of "real" rights. We have a case in the newspapers today of an Asian doctor who, whilst working at a private clinic in Birmingham, agreed to provide an abortion on the grounds that the foetus was female but recorded that the reason for the abortion was that the mother was "too young for pregnancy". A Daily Telegraph investigation led to the General Medical Council reviewing the doctor's actions and that of a second doctor who was filmed allegedly making a similar offer. The GMC has suspended the doctor mentioned in the first case for three months but dropped its investigation into the second. Interestingly, the first case was dropped by the Crown Prosecution Service some time ago due to them considering it "not in the public interest." Why not? Too racial, too awkward, too ethnically incorrect? The Medical Practitioners'

Tribunal Service has now ruled that the doctor acted dishonestly in agreeing to the abortion and then recording a false reason for it. It amazes me that he should ever be allowed to work in this country again. Still, he has rights and Allah has a will, I suppose.

Sticking with stories of foreigners what err, these IS chappies and chapesses do not appear to be endearing themselves to the Russians either. It now appears that a bomb smuggled onto the airliner at Sharm el Sheikh Airport was to blame for its demise. We now have 20,000 Brits stranded there. Frankly, I cannot imagine for the life of me why anyone would want to spend any time in that part of the world. Have they never holidayed in Cleethorpes? What's that? You have – and that's why you go to Egypt? Oh, well … it takes all sorts….

Now, I am tired, my wrist is aching and it's late. Don't look like that, it's only aching due to the excessive writing – mucky pup. Time for a short story before I lock up. Tomorrow is the 5th November and an excuse to light up the sky and test the eardrums of every canine in the land. From the fireworks let off locally tonight you'd think the little bastards had got the wrong date, so gawd knows what tomorrow will be like.

Right! A little story. A Texan stopped off at a local restaurant after a long day roaming the streets of a town in Spain. Whilst sipping his wine he noticed a sizzling, scrumptious looking platter being served at the next table. Not only did it look good but the smell was mouth-watering. He enquired of the waiter, "What is that you've just served?" The waiter replied, "Si, senor, you have excellent taste! These are called Cojones de Torro, bull's testicles from the bullfight this morning. It is a local delicacy?" The cowboy was impressed. "What the heck, bring me a plate of those." The waiter replied, "I am so sorry, senor, there is only one serving per day because there is only one bullfight each morning. If you come here early tomorrow and place your order, we will be sure to save you this delicacy." The next morning, the cowboy returned, placed his order and that evening was served the one and only delicacy of the day. After a few bites, and having inspected his platter, he called the waiter and enquired, "These are delicious but they are so much smaller than the ones I saw you serve yesterday." The waiter shrugged his shoulders and replied humbly, "Si, senor, sometimes the bull, he wins!"

Well, I didn't die during the night, not that I expected to, it's just … well, I didn't, anyhow. So, a new day beckons and later tonight

Midsomer Murders will be turned up high enough to drown out most of that offending noise from the fireworks that will permeate until the small hours descend.

Thought for the day, and appropriate to breakfast I feel – the hardness of the butter is proportional to the softness of the bread.

Now, here's a story that makes you smile, bet you're glad it's not your own mum. An 82-year-old lady called Sheila Fitzgerald went shopping for a new dress. She left her home in St. Helen's, Lancashire, in order to drive to Ormskirk, which is some 6 miles away. Whilst driving back from her shopping expedition the fog set in and she drove in the opposite direction for eight hours, ending up in the town of Gisburn. Mrs. Fitzgerald had travelled via Southport and the M65 bypassing both Blackburn and Burnley, which to be fair, is undoubtedly the best way to see them, before being stopped by the police at 2.30 in the morning. Apparently her 49-year-old daughter had driven down from Cumbria and was surprised not to find her mother at home. Having reported her as a missing person, the police acted very swiftly and located her car travelling northwards at several points on her journey, before a police car managed to block her attempt at a U-turn some 50 miles from home. Nice to read a story where all's well that ends well. Sad to report, however, that it turned out to be a wasted journey as Mrs. Fitzgerald never did find a dress she liked.

Mmmh, I'm finding it hard to take to Benedict Cumberbatch. I cannot understand any actor who feels the need to use the stage to plea, confront and involve an audience about any subject that has absolutely nothing to do with the play either he or she is in. The foul-mouthed yob, Cumberbatch, is currently berating this country's immigration policies and cursing all politicians. His exact phrase was, "F... the politicians" which is always nice to hear at the end of a play when it's not part of the script. This oik picks up a CBE this week. Why? What has he done for society that deserves such an award? Maybe in his case it stands for "Cannot Be Educated." Just a thought, but his local town twinning committee might consider him to be an equal match for Charlie Higson.

Talking of arses, I see that our odious Speaker, John Bercow, has no thought for the public purse any more than the previous MPs who excelled with their expenses claims. He, and one of his staff members, cost taxpayers just short of £10,000 for a three-day trip to

Japan. Eight thousand, three hundred and fifty three pounds went on flights, £1,436 for staying at the 5-star Shangri-La Hotel in Tokyo, well, he would never have stayed at Mrs. Hiroshima's B & B, would he. One hundred and forty eight pounds went on "subsistence and taxis". What was he doing there in the first place, one may ask? Well, he visited Japan during August in order to represent our parliament. We have also funded his trips to South Africa, New Zealand and India. I am sure that these countries have gained a lot from his visits, as ours did from his overseas escapades.

There are a couple of disturbing photographs in the Daily Mail today of students and anarchists clashing with the Metropolitan Police in London. It's strange when one agrees 100% with the aims and principles of the protestors yet finds oneself poles apart due to their lack of subtlety and disregard for the law and property. I've never understood why one penny should be paid by a student in exchange for a university or college education. We, the taxpayers, should fund the fees of our offspring as part of the education budget. There are, however, provisos that I have never veered from. All students receiving free education must be born here to British parents and complete the course, be it one-year, two-year, four-year, etc. If a student decides it is not for him or her and they quit the course at any stage, then every penny should be paid back to the institution concerned. Students have a responsibility for their education as well. The disgusting scenes of yobs, for that is what these photos depict, squaring up to lines of police outside government offices in Westminster, show just how far to the radical left they are. Not surprisingly, the Shadow Chancellor, John McDonnell, was on hand to address the rabble. Students held aloft placards on poles to be used in an aggressive act if necessary, masks, hoods, flares, all aspects of protest designed to be confrontational and violent. Remember Mr. McDonnell said three years ago, "whatever means should be used to bring this government down". He referred to it as "an elected dictatorship". It's strange that, as to many a person in the street that is exactly the description one could use to describe the Shadow Cabinet but then, there's democracy and there's communist democracy.

Our generosity to failed asylum seeking rapists knows no bounds. Another court case, another judge totally out of touch with native feelings along with any sense of fairness or reality. The judge in this case is a naïve chappie called Michael Kent. The case concerns an

Iranian cove who has, like so many, abused our hospitality, so no new story so far. He was not named in the press as he is challenging his deportation order. This would-be migrant has so far cost our country a small fortune. He arrived on our shores in 2004 but 3 months later his asylum application was refused. He appealed and the appeal failed. But do we send him back? Oh, no. We let him stay. Why?

Five years later the migrant was found guilty of rape and sentenced to five years in prison, that is probably a year for every year he was here. On his release, not surprisingly, he was allowed to stay and goes to live in Brighton. In March 2012, (so he never served his full five years, did he?) he strikes up a relationship with a British woman (yes, I know, British can mean anything) but he does. And, guess what? He gets her up the duff. At the time of the sprog's birth he is back in prison for the possession of drugs. We come to the present and Judge Michael Kent feels that despite this foreigner costing us a fortune over eleven years and certainly one lady an awful lot of unnecessary distress, he can continue to rob us blind – or as literally as one can without being blind. He has even given the Iranian his return fare from his latest home in Cosham, Hampshire, to Canterbury where his now ex-girlfriend lives with their child.

The judge stated that he should be handed the costs of fortnightly trips to visit the child, therefore overriding the Home Secretary's ruling that he should pay for them himself. He smokes 35 cigarettes a day and to add insult to our financial injury Judge Michael Kent said the man needed the extra money because he was addicted to cigarettes and had already cut down on food to support his habit. He added that by not paying his travel expenses he would be in breach of Article 8 of the European Convention on Human Rights that protects private and family life. Unbelievable. What about the human rights of the lady he raped? The people who should be brought to account are those responsible who, over the past eleven years, have failed to remove this unwanted foreigner. If he had been deported in the beginning, the lady would not have been subjected to the assault. Why are these bureaucrats let off so lightly, why so unaccountable? Just another example of the gutlessness and lack of leadership at all levels that this country has had to come to terms with.

Do you remember when we had Gulf War Syndrome? If I recollect, shortly after it became widely known, we all suffered from it, including those who had never been to the Gulf and those who had never been to war but felt in need of a syndrome. Well, it does make you special! Recently, we've been alerted to the damages caused by Seasonal Affective Disorder. Have you ever heard such tosh? Not surprisingly, SAD, as its initials tell you, is fairly sad and to be diagnosed with such bull can apparently result in a vast myriad of symptoms – depression, overeating, anxiety, loss of libido – the list goes on and on. The SAD Association (there had to be one) estimates that one in five Britons suffer from the various symptoms. Well, they will. You give some sad sap an excuse for feeling "off" and they'll lap it up. They will officially be seeking a cure and secretly hoping there isn't one. They love the attention. Well, help for those who want it is apparently at hand. A light box offers relief by emitting bright lights intended to simulate the sun's rays. These light boxes can cost upwards of £200. Listen up you SAD people, this is Britain. We have seasons that means warmer weather in the summer and colder in the winter, longer days in the summer and shorter days in the winter. You see, that's how it works, year in, year out. It's been that way for some time now, so get used to it. It's called seasons. They change – so can you, if you have the will, get out of bed and work like everyone else. (Sits back in smug contentment).

Hey-up, can you hear that? Yes, they've started. The fireworks are off and I'm about to turn up Barnaby. Oh, Joyce has just found that the meal she prepared isn't tasting exactly how she assumed it would. No-one has said anything but I can see the look on Tom's face. Strange that Joyce hasn't. I'm just going to put Joyce on hold for the moment. It's quite funny, really, because Tom has cutlery in his hands that is almost to the mouth but hasn't quite got there. Well, I think it's funny, anyway.

I'm going to say goodnight now, because as soon as I turn off the television I am not going to start writing, so it's appropriate to finish by telling you a little trio of appropriate comments as I'm all fired up.

"You won't see me sitting on the top of a bonfire tonight, I'm not that sort of guy."

"This is definitely not the best night to send up a distress flare."

"It's Bonfire Night tonight – or as they call it in Liverpool – Natural Selection Evening.

Night, night.

Good morning, you find me in Orpington, sitting in my car in a car park in anticipation of a talk in the adjacent church hall. I've been to this club on three previous occasions and what a lovely group they are. So, whilst I await the witching hour I think we'll have a quick perusal, shall we.

The first thing to note is that gender-agenda laden protesters were out in force last night. As we know, these are not protesters with peaceful intent, this scum is hell-bent on creating chaos. For them, it is a war against anyone who is not one of them. Why would you want to take lasers that can be used to blind police horses? Why arm yourself with fireworks to throw at police horses? I thought these people – I use the word loosely – might at some stage in their lives have been animal lovers, or at least animal acceptors. There is a photograph of a burning police car. These anarchists are costing the country a fortune. What a pity their parents didn't consider them worthy of abortion.

Ah, I see a female master of a hunt has died aged 44. She fell from her horse and suffered brain injuries. Well, that's one less with a rabid desire to kill foxes then.

People wonder why there is such antipathy shewn towards local councils. In the north Wales town of Ruthin, a pensioner has recently been fined for dropping litter. Her heinous crime was to drop a receipt. Now, she says she was attempting to put it in her purse. As she walked from the shop from where the receipt was issued, along with her purchases, she was stopped by a council warden. Now, the Daily Mail describes these employees as "Litter Stasi", which is not only humorous but a very descriptive term for these pointless arses. Now, I hate litter and have absolutely no problem at all with the fining of those who blatantly discard litter. The rub is that these litter wardens are not employed by either Ruthin Council or Denbighshire County Council. Oh, no, these Stasi are contracted arses, their employers being a faceless company called "Kingdom Security". A fund was initiated on behalf of local people wishing to donate in order to pay Mrs. Coleman's fine of £75. She appealed to the council, but they dismissed her appeal, adding that she could always challenge the fixed penalty notice through the courts. These contractors are armed with a body camera in order to garner evidence for their money-grabbing bosses. I wonder if they would have confronted a youth throwing a McDonald's bag out of the window of a Suburu Impreza or a souped-up Ford Focus. Would they question a tattoo-sporting multi-ringed smoker stubbing out their cigarette or indeed, throwing away a butt?

I doubt it and let's be honest, a 74-year-old pensioner is fair game. Even a local councillor has donated to the fund. It buggers belief, as we say. Still, it all contributes to the salaries of those unworthy of employment in the real world.

Right! It's time to exit the car and enter the hall. See you later.

It is now much later, the M25 was relatively kind to me, there being only a slight delay between Junctions 6 and 5. The main irritation on the way home was some cove on Radio 4 using that dreadful phrase "downplay" and then just as I drove through Wimbledon thinking all would be well, someone else commented on an "upcoming" programme. I know shouting at the wireless doesn't change things, but just for that moment.... Oh, yes, just the other day someone used the word "argumentation". Where are these people educated? Indeed, are they educated, other than attending a five day seminar at a marketing school. I'll be visiting the post office shortly to post a book and then Lloyds the Chemist to pick up a prescription – that's if it's ready, of course. I've never witnessed a less-organised chemist than the one we have here in Ash Vale. They've never got your prescription ready. It's not just me. You stand alongside other customers who discover that theirs isn't ready either. You then form a club of "tutters" who roam, prowl or stand dejectedly within the floor space not taken up by those queuing at the counter only to be told the very same thing. The counter staff is always very pleasant. It is just there doesn't appear to be any real leadership. Still, I'm sure it's cheap to staff.

Right, as I've been prattling on, the book has now been packed, the address written so I'm off. In the words of Oates, "I'm going out now, I may be some time".

Some short while later.... Only queued for seven minutes. Now that is pretty damn good. Book posted without hassle, although I was asked by the lady behind the counter what was in the package. "Why?" I queried. "We have to ask," she replied. "It's a book," I answered. "Thank you," she said. "Mmm," I thought, whilst handing over my £2.80, which is the current cost of sending a book (yes, just one book, it's unbelievable, really). It's two pounds and sixteen shillings if you think about it. That should put it in perspective for those of us slightly under the age of dead!

I'm spending the rest of the afternoon reading and relaxing. BFN

It's 10.45 pm and I've just awoken, having slept through the whole of New Tricks and Would I Lie To You. Still, it means I have two more episodes for another day.

What's that? You can't go to bed until I tell you a story. Oh, all right then. Now, let's see....

Ah, yes, the fleeing Taliban. A fleeing Taliban, desperate for water, was plodding through the Afghan desert when he espied something far off in the distance. Hoping to find water he hurried towards the oasis, only to find a British officer selling regimental ties. The Taliban asked, "Do you have water?" The soldier replied, "No, there is no water here, the well is dry but you could buy a tie instead. They are only £10 each." The Taliban shouted, "You idiot infidel. I do not need one off your over-priced ties, I need water. I should kill you but I must find water first." "Oh, okay," said the soldier in a remarkably composed manner, "it does not matter that you do not wish to buy a tie and that you hate me, for I will show you that I am bigger than that and that I'm a much better human being than you. Now, if you continue over that hill to the east for about two miles you will find our sergeants' mess. It has all the ice cold water that you could wish for." "Inshallah," cursed the Taliban as he staggered his way over the hill. Several hours later he staggered back, and collapsed through dehydration. Looking up towards the British officer, he gasped, "They wouldn't let me in without a f.....g tie!"

Yes, I like that one too. See you tomorrow, sweet dreams (if you're female and well.... Dreams, nightmares, whatever if you're male).

And good morning to you. Didn't expect you'd be up this early. You're not usually up at 5.30 are you? Cuppa? Lots of exercises to do and I'm taking three tours of the brewery today. You really ought to book yourself onto one, you know. I'm sure you'd enjoy it. You never know, you might get a really knowledgeable guide or if you're really unlucky, me!

As I write this paragraph, it is with a complete mix of feelings. Yesterday's tours went well, I'd like to think. The evening meal went well and today's tour went well. Sadly, however, a cloud without a silver lining emerged earlier this evening as Carol was ejected. She kept her poise (non-dancing poise, obviously) and decorum in a manner we have come to expect over the previous weeks. She was, let's be honest, on borrowed time. In fact, it's arguable that she should have departed prior to Kirsty Gallagher and Ainsley Harriott. This feeling of loss conflicts with the one of joy I feel after last Tuesday's loss by 1-0 to Milton Keynes Dons as Charlton actually won, 3-1 at home to Sheffield Wednesday. There's a rarity.

There is a photograph of a horse, one of six harmed through the action of the protesting scum. You remember, the ones throwing fireworks, cones, etc. at horses. This isn't protesting, this is pure thuggery. One of the horses was poked in the eye with a stick. As I also mentioned previously, lasers were used in order to dazzle both rider and horse. These thoughtless bastards can cause permanent blindness to both. Another aspect of Sharia law I would bring in and it would literally be an eye for an eye.

What adds salt to the wounds is that three suspects walked free from court, having refused to give their names. The magistrate told them that they could all go, but they could "come back next year". Unbelievable. A retired Metropolitan Police detective and a Tory MP, Mr. Peter Bone, both found it incomprehensible that they could laugh in the face of the law by acting in this manner. I'd have them locked up until they gave the details required. Where is the backing for the police or law and order in general? It's another slap in the face for justice. Apparently, anyone not revealing their identity to a police officer can be fined £1000, so why was this flotsam not fined or jailed for their assault on animals. The whole thing is laughable.

Talking of laughable, there is an advert in the far right corner of the Daily Mail. It's a "Remembrance Day Appeal". Well, that's fine. It then goes on to add, "For brave Gurkha veterans". The advert continues, "They were, and there are, and those of the future will also be". Of that I have no doubt but I really feel that the last charity I would ever contribute to is one helping the local Gurkha population which has expanded to such a ridiculous extent and has had such a huge social impact on one relatively small town. There are thousands of them now in the Aldershot area, ever since Joanna Lumley's plea to the government, that time she assumed the role of Immigration Minister (without portfolio, or if you are dyslexic – without Fort Polio). Try sitting on a seat in Aldershot or Camberley town centres. From dawn until dusk ageing Gurkhas wander aimlessly around the towns, men in front, women some 20 to 30 feet behind, no talking, no social inclusion, just a meandering that is costing our social services, NHS and housing benefits a small fortune. Ultimately, housing itself needs to be addressed as yet another field falls foul of the developers and not for children from this country.

I'll be witnessing this spectacle on Monday week as I travel across the border into Hampshire and be subjected to the monthly eye scan and probable injection. They will be there like smaller Lowry characters, aimlessly, slowly traipsing along the roads. Aldershot, or as it is now known by even its own residents, Aldershit, was once a proud, buzzing market town. Interestingly, the page after the advert I have been referring to has an advert in exactly the same place and exactly the same size, only this one is seeking funds in order to help donkeys that are ill-treated in Africa. I know which I would rather save. There is a sign in Ash, just before you cross the border into Aldershot, which reads, "Welcome to Aldershot, newly twinned with Switzerland". It's not because it's an area of outstanding natural beauty, but it's where you go to commit suicide!" Only joking.

I read that a young girl, aged 18, has been raped by a gang of Syrian migrants – I refrain from using the word "refugees". True refugees should just be bloody grateful they've been allowed into the first country that would have them. These chancers, like many before them aim for this country due to the luxury of Human Rights laws and lawyers, benefits and the freedom to abuse. This girl was attacked at a "supervised facility" – or care home, to thee and me. She alleges that five Syrians raped her. These young men have been housed in this location by Kent County Council who is beleaguered by the aforementioned chancers seeking a new life on our benefits. Four of those arrested claim they are under 18. Now, this is another impediment to fair policing. How does anyone know their age? They do not carry documents but they certainly know their rights. They can always hide behind an indefinable age as easily as they appear to hide behind a spare wheel under a lorry. No doubt refugee agencies, Liberty, the Green Party and all the lame Liberals will feel sorry for them and support their rights to stay here and reoffend here again and again. Well, every little helps! Let's be fair, they might have had it rough. Sadly, not as rough as the young lady in question and as sure as eggs are eggs, she will never have the same rights as they do.

Now, this is not a surprise. Dr. Who's ratings have dropped to their lowest level since returning to our screens ten years ago. Peter Capaldi, the present Dr. Who, claims it's down to BBC bosses who moved the programme from 7.30 pm to 8.35 pm in order to accommodate "Strictly". May I suggest that the cause could be Peter Capaldi. I have never taken to his interpretation of the role. I appreciate that every Dr. is different from the last and whilst I never took to Matt Smith, I always felt David Tennant was up there with the best of them. I cannot take or warm to Mr. Capaldi. Right! We've sorted out that one. Next!

And next it is – education to be precise. Interesting to read that whilst a grammar school in Sevenoaks, Kent, is hoping to open a 450 pupil satellite school close by, there is an organisation called "Comprehensive Future" which appears determined to undermine the proposal. Their challenge could cost the taxpayer millions of pounds in court costs. It is the first grammar school planned for fifty years and could well set a precedent for others to follow. This group, Comprehensive Future, is backed by Nic Dakin, Jeremy Corbyn's schools' spokesman – so we all know where this is going. He wishes to abolish all grammar schools and end selection by ability in publicly funded schools. I, along with many others, really have a problem with that. Selection sorts the wheat from the chaff. Although the creation of new grammar schools is currently illegal, expansion of existing ones is permitted. The argument by the anti's is whether or not it is an expansion or a new school. The group's patrons include the Lib-Dem peer Baroness Williams, who attended St. Paul's School in London, Caroline Lucas of the Green Party, who was schooled at the fee-paying Malvern's Girls College and Lord Kinnock. Chairman of its Steering Committee is Melissa Benn, daughter of Tony Benn, whilst its Vice Chairman is Fiona Millar, who attended Camden School for Girls, which when she attended was, surprise, surprise, a grammar school. She, by the way, is the other half of Alistair Campbell. Very cliquey, isn't it.

Why do the Left always wish to bring everything down to the lowest common denominator when they have benefited so greatly from the very education they attempt to dismantle? Those in government rarely send their offspring to a comprehensive but many of us would support grammar schools for the populus should they ever to be increased in number. I never have a problem with principles but have a problem with hypocrisy. Admittedly, Tony Blair sent his children to a so-called "normal" school but let's be honest, the Oratory is as close to grammar as you can get. Ruth Kelly, erstwhile Education Secretary sent her offspring to a private school, as did Diane Abbot, although in her case it was her son who chose the school, apparently, which she feels lets her off the hook. Doesn't fool us though. Harriet

Harman sent hers to a selective grammar school, Tristram Hunt, Shadow Education Secretary, who looks for all the world like a Tory, stated that he "Wouldn't rule out sending his children to private school". Polly Toynbee, she of BABC TV and Radio 4 left-wing social conscience, also sent her children to a private school. Nick Clegg, ever the fence sitter, said he would "Not let his children be hostage to a game of political football". If I had young children now I would work day and night so that they never, ever had to soil their shoes on the front steps of a comprehensive. At least with a prep school they are going to be mixing with "stock" from likeminded people who actually want their children to receive an education. And, of course, with the increasing problem of multiculturalism, migrants and refugees I would never countenance sending my offspring to a school where 64 languages were commonplace and white faces were in the minority. You know, the sort of school that is favoured by the BABC whenever they wish to extol the virtues of integration.

No, I'm all right, I'm just going to go and take one of my pills.

What's that? How are the children? Oh, well, Glynn, my eldest, is now 44 and living just outside Farnham that is, as you know, much better than living just outside Aldershot. He's a gardener and a very happy bunny, I'm glad to say. He is currently working for a landscape gardening business owned by a very young chap who has been privately educated, speaks nicely and appears to be going places. Does that sound awful? Oh, goody!

Debbie is now 42, alive and well and living in Alton, a mother of three boys. Oh, by the way, they were married two years before their first child was born. Thought you'd like to know…. The eldest two are at the stage where they grunt between 8-hour bouts of computer gaming, broken only by school and a desire to visit the kitchen to pig out. The youngest one, who is 9, enjoys Lego, Scalextric and eating but with reduced bouts of grunting. So there is hope. My son-in-law (yes, they're still married) is a graphic designer and their mutual ambition is to be able to pay off their mortgage before their children retire.

William is now a taxpaying member of society and no, I never saw that one coming either. He is currently a valeter during the week, whilst retaining his gardening customers through the winter and at weekends, on an as-and-when required basis, although I suspect he will be back into full time gardening once spring comes around.

He could easily end up like me, having 38 jobs since he left school, which is what I've had to date – although some of them have been like a prison sentence, they've run concurrently.

Ah, the post has arrived. Good God! What have we here on the doormat? I'll just sort this lot out. You can't believe it, actually you probably can, there's a plea from the St. Mungo Charity – bin – another plea relating to Syrian refugees – burn – Donald Russell's Christmas offers – to be read, savoured, ordered and then savoured for real. There is apparently a half-price sale at Reclinamatic. How do they know my age? Now here is an envelope with a window. The wording of the enclosed when gleaned through the window reads, "A message from China" as if that would entice me to actually open the letter. There's another one here from a charity called Crisis inviting me to consider "What it's like to be homeless at Christmas". I have, work and you won't be! Next! I'm not uncharitable, as you know, but really....

There's a flyer from Domino's inviting me to purchase a "Big Night In Deal" for £24.99. Twenty-four pounds and ninety nine pence! I could buy a coach for my model railway for less than that. Oh, yes, and finally, BT are offering me an introductory Broadband deal. I bet it's cheaper than the Broadband deal they introduced me to some months ago. These deals always are.

So, it's another cuppa and a peek at Donald Russell. Oh, no, hang on, there's a postcard that has slipped through the net, so to speak, but not the doormat. So, who is this from? There's a colour picture of a child – white, which is unusual – writing. He or she, I can't tell which, probably best to be non-gender specific, is dressed in a post-box red polo shirt with a lit Christmas tree behind. How very seasonal. The wording reads, "Deliver the most important letter". Underneath is a web address and below that a slogan which they will have undoubtedly spent a fortune on designing and finding the correct words. It reads, "Much more than mail". Yes, well, that got the juices flowing. I turned the card over. It's actually an invitation to work for the Royal Mail. It starts by telling the reader just what a busy time of year Christmas is for deliveries and how they are looking to recruit people from the local community – that over-used word again. Why don't they just say "local people". It continues that they are in a "fast-paced environment where you will need to be flexible and adaptable, changing from one role to another".

No previous experience is necessary as full training is provided. I can only apply by going on-line at a website they provide and then entering the letters TW in the location filter. What the hell is all that about? Ah, now we have the politically correct employment notes. "We are an inclusive employer and welcome applications from people of all different backgrounds, beliefs and circumstances". Does that mean foreign, Muslim and non-English speaking.... Or ... surely not ... they're not looking to interview those from 'The North'?

I know there's a lot of walking involved but I'd still wager that a one-armed, dyslexic, pregnant, Marxist, black lesbian, having recently been declared free from morning sickness and club foot, would still get preference over a white, healthy, heterosexual native from down the road. Well, it's a thought.

And while we're on thoughts, here's one for the day. "If you must choose between two evils, always pick the one you've never tried before."

It's second cuppa time. Mmmm, yes, it'll be the East Stirling FC mug that I purchased a couple of years ago. Oh, how time flies. I've just looked at the date on the cup and it's actually for the 2007/8 season. That's the year they won their last match of the season 3-1 against Montrose. The significance of that win is that it took them off the bottom of the table, thus avoiding having their status reduced from Full Membership of the Scottish League to that of Associate Member. That can lead to a vote in order to decide a team's continuation of league status or relegation to a lower league. So having ended their season in bottom place for five consecutive years it was with a great sigh of relief that the last league match ever to be played at Firs Park was a home win. Not being bottom at the end of the season was a feat equal to that of an English premiership team avoiding relegation to the championship on the final day. Sadly, East Stirling moved out of their traditional home. With little money in the coffers, they were unable to invest in the ground improvements required by the Scottish football authorities. They now ground share with local team Stenhousemuir. There are hopes that a new stadium can be built which they can call their own. I raise my ESFC cup to that. Out of interest, they were so broke at the turn of this century that their manager was unpaid at one time and the players were on £10 per week. Why wouldn't someone wish to support even from an armchair such a plucky team, even if it is another country.

I rarely get to see Charlton play these days as weekend brewery tours have taken over most of my life and I certainly have never visited East Stirling, either the club or the area but I bought a mug and a polo shirt in order to show solidarity. Good luck to them, I say!

Today's headlines are full of salaries, expenses and treats willingly accepted by public sector leaders. No wonder us poor tax and ratepayers find these industry leaders so greedy and grabbing. We are distrustful with reason. The Daily Mail has placed on its website a very interesting list of those who should never be allowed anywhere near the public coffers. Who sanctions their salaries? The chief executive of Cumbria Council was paid £411,025 in 2014. Kieran Stigent, Chief Executive of West Sussex Council, received £396,143. Some chap by the name of Peter Duxbury received £382,392 over the same period. He works in Birmingham and revels in the overblown title of "Strategic Director (Children, Young People and Families). In Wandsworth, Paul Robinson is paid £354,452 as Director of Children's Services, and in Fareham, Hampshire, a chap who goes by the name of Garry White obtains a salary of £327,984 as Director of Regulatory and Democratic Services. You never imagine anyone called Garry – or even Gary – earning that sort of money, do you? What the hell do these people do to justify such incomes? The last named cove seems to have a title plucked from an episode of "Yes, Minister". The article includes a photograph of a middle-aged blonde lady holding up a glass whilst smiling in a very self-satisfied manner. And so she should! Her name is Tricia Hart. She was, presumably, Patricia when born but this is probably her contribution to the NHS cutbacks by reducing the length of her name. This lady glories in the title of Chief Executive of South Tees Hospitals NHS Foundation Trust. Now, her total salary package is a staggering £1.26 million. A sum not to be sniffed at. Steve Allen, Deputy Chief Constable of Police Scotland, earned £737,500 last year. Again, not a bad little earner when considering the ever-decreasing number of officers he actually has on his books, and even less on the beat.

It's not as if these monies spent are purely on individuals. Essex County Council spent £874,640 on private medical insurance for its bosses over the past three years. Surely that money could have saved a community centre or two? The list goes on. Do go online and check the Daily Mail list of high earners. It's under the heading "Daily Mail investigation reveals deals for councils, police and...". It's a depressing sight and a depressing site.

Also depressing is reading of more hand-wringing from Jeremy Corbyn regarding the pressing of the nuclear button. He has publicly stated that he wouldn't if push came to shove, which is telling you that he really will not push when shoved. It makes any full-bloodied Englishman feel that his castle is more akin to a cardboard box with this "wet week" of a leader. To be fair to many Labour MPs, and I suspect supporters, a large number of them support Britain's nuclear deterrent but with no cohesive policy what sort of potential government would one be voting for. They have to get their collective act together. Let's be honest, no-one wants to go to war but I'm sure we'd feel safer knowing that our leader would be strong if there had to be an option to retaliate. The idea of having a button that will forever remain untouched because our democratically elected leader doesn't feel "committed", leaves me feeling somewhat uneasy. It's akin to being led by a lemming.

As you know, I've never taken to John Bercow, the current Speaker of the House of Commons. The man seems so far up his own backside I am surprised he can see over his own ego. He has commissioned research to see if "gender neutral" or "transgender toilets" should be provided. Also under review is the possibility of replacing works of art depicting historic battles of men in suits, with pieces featuring women. Mr. Bercow is apparently attempting to create a "gender sensitive parliament". Sarah Childs, who is ... wait for it ... a professor of gender and politics at the University of Bristol (so it's not a proper job) will provide the analysis after interviews with staff and MPs. Jane Fae, an equalities campaigner, commented that this all sounds like a "fairly sensible step by Mr. Bercow". Well, she would, wouldn't she.

The sad aspect of all this invective is that intelligent women who have genuine claims regarding gender disparity appear to lose the plot with their feminist tunnel vision, one that isn't pink with bunnies and heffalumps, but one that is bland in colour, whilst sporting aggressive anti-male slogans, alongside ones of sisterly support. If they concentrated their collective bile where it matters to women across the workplace, especially regarding the equality of all, then I cannot think of a male who would disagree.

Do you remember that female barrister, Charlotte Proudman, who we discussed a while ago? Oh, that's good, you do. Well done. Well, her fizzog – and a very pretty fizzog at that – is back in the Daily Mail today. She says that since that incident when that senior solicitor, Alexander Carter-Silk, commented that she was the subject of a "stunning picture" and was subsequently castigated by every left-thinking female, several women have not unsurprisingly revealed to her their own experiences of sexual harassment. But then they would do, wouldn't they. The Mail has dubbed her "the feminazi lawyer". It really is an inspired nomenclature. I find it a pity that these women are so bitter and driven by areas of life that in the round are fairly insignificant and lacking in consequence. Why make such a big deal out of a man complimenting you on your looks? Be grateful it wasn't critical. As we've previously discussed, Charlotte Proudman placed a photograph of herself on Linked-In, the website chosen to entice customers. Yes, for business no doubt, but it was there because whether she cares to admit it or not, a pretty face sells far more than an ugly one! It's as simple as that. Accept it dearie!

On an entirely different subject, I was disappointed to read of a new book co-authored by Till Zimmermann and Nikolas Durr, entitled "Faces of Evil .. Crimes and Criminals". These two chaps have compiled what is, in their opinion, a list of the 20th century's most evil men. Note – not women. Shouldn't I be suffering from palpitations at this disclosure? Apparently, Pol Pot, Joseph Stalin and Mr. Hitler have all been included but so has Lord Kitchener and, I find this inclusion very disturbing and insulting, it is the name Sir Arthur "Bomber" Harris. What a bloody cheek! I shall nail my colours, red, white and blue, to the mast. This misguided duo has included Mr. Harris because his fight against the Nazi tyranny involved bombings that killed half a million civilians and made many more homeless. Shouldn't this pair of authors stand back with a cup of Yorkshire tea each and cogitate over their inclusion of one of Britain's finest? For a start, look at the inclusion of the German Mr. H. I mean, to be fair, he started it. He took his country to war and we responded. What about those killed or made homeless in London, Coventry, Portsmouth, Plymouth, etc? It was a war, civilians are casualties of war. Frankly, I'm sick to death of the apparent embarrassment and hand-wringing we witness in this country every time Bomber Command is mentioned. We don't have to gloat, we don't have to make regular, triumphant soundings but never forget that this was us against them – a battle we had to win and Bomber Command played their part.

Mmmm, this story concerns a complete arse called Aaron Halstead. He is 24-years-of-age and should know better. He is facing jail for illegally trading in endangered species. Sadly, he hasn't learnt from previous experiences. In 2011 he was cautioned by the police for selling stuffed endangered birds. This time police have found stuffed giraffes, a tiger's head, a cheetah's skull, sperm whale teeth, whilst in the boot of his car lay a stuffed bear! The possibility of a prison sentence doesn't seem to do him or his revolting trade justice. I would have him put down, although not stuffed, obviously.

Now, here's a story that should be an advert. A couple living in Ipswich have experienced problems with their neighbour's children. Well, to be fair, it is Ipswich. As they say, children laughing and playing is one thing, screaming for prolonged periods is another misery entirely. As we both know and have no doubt witnessed, parents and children have rights, but very few responsibilities. Apparently, these children were so bad in the summer with their screeching that the couple had to resort to spending their time indoors, unable to enjoy their own garden, with doors and windows closed. The retired couple thought they had found the answer to their woes by purchasing a black box which fits on the outside wall and emits a sound inaudible to adults, but extremely audible to little sods (sorry, children). Apparently the frequency used is at a pitch only heard by children and likened to nails being dragged down a blackboard – I can hear the shouts of racism now – why not a whiteboard! Anyway, the children's mother complained that her nameless and blameless were fleeing inside every time it was switched on for periods of up to ten minutes at a time. Good news so far! Mummy contacts Ipswich Council, who despatch Environmental Health Officers. They, unsurprisingly, side with Mummy and screechers and the retired couple are faced with the threat of court action and a possible fine of up to £2,500. What a cheek! Now, whose side would you be on, a retired couple in their sixties, he being a retired science teacher, or a 36-year-old Miss or Ms with four offspring under ten years of age. I think I know where my sympathies lie.

Oh, yes, better tell you this before I forget, the 8 inch black box costs £130 and is marketed as an "Ultrasonic Teen Deterrent". They should be fitted as standard in public houses with gardens and walls of houses bordering pre-school nurseries. Do you know, if I was a young rep looking for a product to help calm society I could sell these with total confidence and empathy with would-be users. Of course, for the really bad examples of children's vocal excesses nothing beats a Taser!

Right! I'm going to paint – or rather "weather" – some locomotives that I have recently purchased. For those of you who are interested, there are two "Duke Dogs" and two recently purchased "64XX" Pannier Tanks. Their number plates and smoke box plates have arrived, so they can be affixed after the weathering. I enjoy this aspect of railway modelling, from light weathering to work-a-day grime dependent upon the photographs of the real engine taken during the period that I wish to model. I then apply paint to the whole of the locomotive body, below the footplate, sandboxes, etc. All aspects are examined and the colours mixed and application made. Some modellers swear by acrylics but I've always preferred enamels. Paints, thinners, turps, brushes of every size known to man sit alongside cloth, mixing bowls, toilet roll, glasses, magnifying glass with holding tabs and not forgetting the most important aspect of all modelling, a cuppa. See you later.

What's that? You're going out while I'm attempting to turn a princess into a frog? Oh, all right. To be honest, you won't get much out of me for the next couple of hours. Byee.

Oh, you're back. Two Duke Dogs down and two 64XXs to go. I'll break off for a while to tell you a little story. Then it's back to the paint and I'll see you tomorrow.

Are you sitting comfortably? Then I'll begin. A duck walks into a pub and orders a pint of beer and a ham sandwich. The barman looks at him and says, "Hang on, you're a duck." The duck replies, "There's nothing wrong with your eyesight." "And you can talk," exclaims the barman. "Hearing's up to scratch, too," says the duck, "now if you don't mind, can I have my beer and sandwich, please." "Certainly, sir, sorry about that," says the barman as he pulls the duck's pint, "it's just that we don't get too many ducks in this pub. What are you doing around this way?" "I'm working on the building site across the road," explains the duck, "I'm a plasterer." The flabbergasted barman cannot believe the duck and wants to learn more but takes the hint when the duck pulls out a newspaper from his bag and proceeds to read it. Eventually, having read his paper, drunk his beer and eaten his sandwich, he bids the barman goodnight and leaves. The same thing happens for the next two weeks, then one day the circus comes to town. The ringmaster walks into the pub for a pint and the barman says to him, "You're with the circus, aren't you, because I know this duck and he would be just brilliant in your circus. He talks, drinks beer, eats sandwiches, he reads the paper and everything." The ringmaster is impressed. He hands over his business card and says, "Sounds just the sort of act we could do with. Get him to give me a call." So, the next day when the duck comes into the pub the barman says, "Hey, Mr. Duck, I reckon I can line you up with a really top job, paying really good money." "Really," says the duck, "in my business you're always looking for the next job, where is it?" "At the circus," beams the barman. "The circus?" repeats the duck. "That's right," replies the barman enthusiastically." "The circus?" the duck asks again, "with the big tent?" "Yeah, you've got it," the barman replies. The duck frowns. "With all the animals that live in cages and performers who live in caravans?" "Of course," the barman replies. "And the tent, with its canvas sides and a big canvas roof, with a hole in the middle?" persists the duck. "Yes!!" says the barman. The duck shakes his head in amazement and exclaims, "What the bloody hell would they want with a plasterer?"

Yes, I like that one as well! It's one you can build up like a really good shaggy dog story and with a very credible punch-line. Kettle's boiling, d'you fancy a cuppa?

Thought for the day, and one practiced in Aldershot, Portsmouth and Southampton....

"Money can't buy you love, but it can rent you a very close imitation."

Here's yours, no sugar for you. Ah, that hit the spot.

While you're sitting enjoying that biccie, I'll see what's in the emails. Oh, that's good, a ladies' club in Wokingham have confirmed a booking for an enquiry they made last week. Mind you, the year after next seems a long way away. Oh, it's downhill from here on in. A Mr. D. Trump is revealing ground-breaking secrets in order to triple my income over the next year, which is nice for him! Delete!! The Divorce.Attorney Data Line is offering the right divorce for me. We've had this lot before, haven't we? Delete!! Jessamine O. Plympton is inviting me to see what love and pussies are all about.

Delete!! Adrian Smith has informed me that my Internet activity report is now ready. Delete!! My "gift card" from McDonalds is expiring – thank Christ for that! Adrian has told me that my life is at stake. Mmmm, I wonder if that's the same Adrian who compiled my Internet activity report. What a coincidence that would be. There's another one here, End Day's Survival … the bible warns Mr. Obama will not finish his second term. And lastly, Neighbourhood Alerts are warning me that child predators are in my area. What does it want me to do? Go out and ask them in for tea and biscuits? Take them down to the cinema? Or, probably bore them to death by showing them my still tacky Duke Dogs. Delete!!

Hello, and gruntings from Aylesbury. I'm here to give a talk to a local Women's Institute. They meet in a hall that is set in a lovely park. I've arrived in good time as the hall is used by various groups. It's easy to find the car park so it's my sort of venue. Brewery tour tonight, so whilst we have a bit of time to spare, let's have a quick perusal of the papers.

No surprises here. There are more high-profile public figures cashing in on every just-about-legal money-making, expense-raking avenue of income that they can get their grubby little publicly funded mitts upon. From chief constables claiming between £39,000 and £55,000 just to move house to a former chief executive of Dyfed-Powys PCC, who was paid £169,751 for nineteen days' work within one year in office. His actual salary was £41,381, but when the powers-that-be decided he wasn't value for money they had to pay him £126,117 just to be shot of him and his role. For me, the question is, who decided on the role in the beginning?

Oh, now here's a surprise. It appears that white, British pupils are less likely to go to university than ethnic minority children, so it's also unsurprising that ethnic teenagers are winning top places at higher education institutions. One of the researchers of this finding (how much did we pay for this survey?) described it as "staggering". Why? All education resources appear to be funnelled towards black, Asian and Middle Eastern offspring. Since when has it been fashionable to place time, effort and money into children from families native to these islands. Still, the survey did give work to those who would otherwise be unemployed – or working on another survey. They sound the sort of people who will install a gamut of "applications" on their personal telephones and use words like "pod" and "hub".

I see "our Dave" is setting out and about throughout Europe, charging hither and thither on the near and distant continent on his white charger, brandishing the Union flag in order to set out his demands for the UK's continued membership of the EU. What a farce. His original proposals were weak and never far-reaching enough. As he travels between countries attempting to garner support from his fellow European leaders and more importantly, those who hold the real EU power but have never been elected by the European populus, you know damn well that his demands will forever be watered down. Negotiation, renegotiation, compromise and final acceptance means that he will eventually raise in arms in triumph, stating that he recommends our continual ball and chain as the preferred option. Angular Merkel et al will say they have bent over backwards (which is not a pretty thought) to accede to our "demands","" and the Remain vote will be recommended to all and the various sundry. Off camera and microphone, the French, German and those with the most to lose, ie those having to harbour migrants instead of sending them here, will be laughing all the way to their grand dinners. I have no doubt they are closing ranks in secret meetings as I write. By the time you read this, however, the vote will have taken place and our immediate future known – if not assured. David Cameron is the wet seeking to water down the watered down.

He never stops, does he? I read that the foul-mouthed Cumberbatch has now received his CBE for services to charity. It certainly wouldn't be for services to verbal respect. Why should theatre-goers be subjected to his continual requests for money for migrants? When I go to the theatre in future I'll have to find out if one of our luvvie actors is going to start touting on behalf of one of their causes and embarrassing the audience in order to extract their hard-earned cash. It's bad enough attempting to blackmail people, or at least make them feel awkward, but why the foul language. I can only assume that he is impressed by that patriarch of all foul-mouthed yobbery, Rob, the slob, Geldorf. I gave not one iota to Ethiopian famine victims then, any more than I care about migrants now. They are all a drain on our society. If you want to ask for money, at least choose a cause that could really help itself without human intervention. Any donkey sanctuary, PETA, WWF, etc. Save one donkey, not 5 million humans. Where is his priority, the man's an arse!

I see that another "survey" has found that an increasingly warped sense of humour could be an early sign of dementia! I wonder if I'll make it to the end of this…!

Well, that's the light relief over with. Brief, wasn't it. I say that because we have a familiar story of rape and abuse upon a 13-year-old white girl by fourteen Asian men. Familiar story, huh? White child, Asian men. The young girl was "on the system." That is, known to social workers and the police, sadly in the end no-one actually stepped in to put an end to the violent abuse. It's strange but not for the first time, or as we know the last time, the "racist" attack "element" of the crime is not mentioned. If it were fourteen white men and one black minor – oh! I think I can read the headlines now. One rule for the indigenous population and one for coloured incomers.

Wry smile time. Interesting to note that Cherie Blair has just purchased another three flats. This takes the family property portfolio to 34 homes, ten flats in Manchester, plus these three new ones in Stockport, plus another fourteen in the same town plus two London properties, one worth £3.65 million and the other, £800,000. Oh, of course, that's not including the Grade 1 listed house they own in Bucks, which is worth a cool £5.75 million. Then, of course, you have the other London houses purchased for their offspring. Oh, to be a socialist!

Right, well the doors are open, the ladies are entering the hall and I must away. See you later.

It is now 9.35 pm. Aylesbury went well, a joyful group with a good sense of humour. The brewery tour was jolly, with one or two big personalities with whom you could banter. Good craic, as they say in Ireland and Moldova – well, they will when the Irish arrive.

Excuse me while I eat my take-away and watch QI. I'll be with you shortly.

It's now 11.10 pm and I'm just taking my tablets. What? Oh, no, not because of the take-away, that was fine, these are for the diabetes and high blood pressure. Interestingly, a doctor at the quack's said that she could save me 730 blood pressure tablets a year by not reading the Daily Mail! Yes, I found that amusing as well.

Just so as you know, the take-away was Chinese, sweet and sour pork (Hong Kong style) egg fried rice and a spring roll (large). This was all washed down with a rhubarb and apple juice, courtesy of

Copello. It's always the same meal from the same take-away in Ash Vale. I always peruse the menu, um and ah, and then select the same. There's a very pleasant lady behind the counter, she actually has it written down before I make up my mind and tell her – it's a sort of ritual – very similar to the ham, egg and chips Mike and I have at the Olde King's Head in Epsom when we play trains. We always look at the menu but end up having the same. Sad, but true.

Right, a quick dose of Father Ted, then to beddy-byes. A little story before I go. This is called "Are you a pilot?".

You think you have lived to be 80 years of age and know who you are then along comes someone and blows all that assumption to smithereens. An old marine pilot sat in Starbucks still wearing his old USMC flight suit and leather jacket and ordered a cup of coffee. As he sipped the coffee a young woman sat down next to him. She turned and asked, "Are you a real pilot?" He replied, "Well, I have spent my whole life flying planes. First Stearmans, then the early Grummans, then I flew Wild Cats and Corsairs in World War 2, later on in the Korean conflict, Banshees and Cougars. I've taught more than 260 people to fly and given rides to hundreds, so I guess you could call me a pilot and you, what are you?" She said, "I'm a lesbian, I spend my whole day thinking about naked women, as soon as I get up in the morning I think about naked women and when I shower I think about naked women. When I watch TV, I think about naked women. It seems that everything in life makes me think of naked women." The two of them sat sipping their coffees in silence. A little while later a young man, who had overheard the conversation whilst sitting close-by asked, "So, are you really a pilot?" The old man looked and said, "I always thought I was, but I've just found out I'm a lesbian."

Sleep well.

Chapter 8

A Roaring Fire And A Donald Russell Brochure

I'm busy with talks in Frimley, Maidstone and Reading, plus a tour or two so will see you on Friday afternoon, before the weekend's tours.

Friday is here. I surprised Reading, which is a feat in itself, no Carol and no match for Charlton, so at least by not playing they won't lose. It's just putting off the inevitable, I suppose.

So, what's been happening over the past few days? Well, the Daily Mail have commendably outed university chancellors and heads of school that if not failing are not exactly setting the academic world alight. It really does appear that success in one's supposed field of expertise is no indication of the salary to be commended. It's not just salaries, which can be justified by a means of student success, although that in itself is arguable, but it's the expenses, medical packages, pension contributions and then, of course, the pay-off when all else has failed. Again, do log in to the Daily Mail website and discover for yourself just how much these greedy bastards are making, not earning, out of the public purse. It's an absolute disgrace. Sadly, as in policing, the idea of a service to the public has lost its importance. It's all about money.

Figures released show that instead of the government successfully lowering the number of migrants, in the first nine months of the year the workforce has risen by 430,000, 325,000 of which have come from within the EU. These figures are unsustainable. How is it that you talk to anyone "in the street" and they can all see it, but sadly not David Cameron and his ill-informed ilk, grrrr.

The following story shows just how soft this country has become. I find the phrase "happy slapping" to be totally distasteful. It is assault, it's intimidating and it hurts. In Wath-upon-Dearne in Yorkshire, a 12-year-old lad was wrestled to the ground by a 14-year-old and hit twenty-three times. The incident was filmed by a 12-year-old girl on her mobile phone and then downloaded onto her Fastbuck page. What sort of girl of twelve would want to do that? What sort of mind-sets are we instilling into our offspring? A still photo in the Daily Mail shows the lad covering his head with his hands while the apprentice thug bends over and hits him. The completely pointless police did get involved but stated that the attack wasn't violent enough in order to take the incident to court. The 12-year-old lad was treated in hospital for bruising and concussion. The attacker, who goes to the same school as the victim, was given an equally pointless "youth caution." I bet that scared him. This form of "punishment" was introduced two years ago as a formal out- of-court method for dealing with crimes whereby the youth admits responsibility. The victim's mother, a midwife, not unreasonably criticised the police for their soft approach, but the CPS responded by commenting, "This matter was handled by South Yorkshire Police who dealt with it by way of a youth caution." That's it, cold and stark. Doesn't give you a lot of confidence. Would the same have happened if the victim had been black, or blackish?

Oh, dear, how sad, never mind. I see that a Eurostar train was delayed by 8 hours after a wild boar was hit and killed. The incident – even I can hardly call it murder – occurred on the line as it passes through forests near Calais. So few boar, yet so many migrants, life isn't fair, is it?

Now, it's lunch time, a packet soup I feel would be conducive, not to mention warming. Mmmm, yes, it's an Ainsley Harriott Sweet and Sour Something, with added croutons. They are added by me, by the way, not Mr. H. I need to build up my strength, reserve, fortitude and stiffness of upper lip for a journey I am to make mid-afternoon, but more anon.

Whilst the kettle is boiling I shall continue. The "thought police" are really on the up, aren't they. New officers are likely to require a "degree in policing" before being let loose on a suspecting public. It appears that some forces accept applicants who possess no academic exams, whilst others require an equivalent of five GCSE's. Call me suspicious or cynical, but I'd always assumed the latitude was there to make sure that the target level of black, Asian, lesbian, homosexual and transwhatevers would forever be achieved and boxes ticked. Fix the intelligent levels too high and … well … you never know what you could achieve! Standing back and looking at the bigger picture, as they say, I'm just agog that the police are still taking on new recruits, where do they end up, certainly not as a bobby beating his or her way around our urban sprawl.

If there was a competition to find the face exuding the smuggest look of all, it would surely go to that dreadful Batmangheligjh woman, she of Kids Co fame. As we've said before, she must be good at selling herself. Successive government ministers have flocked, nay, tripped over themselves, in order to get her to take our money. Remember, Kids Co was given £42 million in funding. It's one hell of a lot of dosh with no return and little evidence of accounting. Who looks after our money that goes to all these charities, not just hers? Are there accountants designated to protect our lack of investment or are they part of the cutbacks as well? As with everything else in this country, when it goes pear shaped no-one is accountable but as ever, we will learn from it.

Interesting comment from the Sports Minister, Tracey Couch – never thought a few years ago we'd ever have a minister called Tracey. Anyway, she has commented on tax credit cuts by saying that complaining workers should cancel their pay TV subscriptions and so say I, our Trace! Most of these whingers on benefit certainly benefit from our involuntary contributions. Cigarettes, lager, lottery tickets, Sky, Netflix, mobile phone (top of the range and one for each member of the family), plus all the apps appropriate, and for the kiddiwops inappropriate. Then, there's holidays, theme parks, McDonald's burgers, Burger King burgers, sugary drinks, take-aways, both Indian and Chinese, Kentucky Fried Chicken, kebabs – I'm sick to death of these people on benefits who are so well off.

Naturally, the Shadow Treasury Secretary said, "It's outrageous for a serving minister to claim that working families need to 'go without' in order to make ends meet." Even more naturally, poor Tracey has had to apologise for causing any offence. "I'm sorry for giving the impression of a lack of understanding of the financial pressures many families face – nothing could be further from the truth." So, the usual apology spiel when pressure is brought to bear. No-one sticks to their guns any more – totally gutless.

I've supped while I've written this. It is now time to drive to Frimley to the Midland Bank (as was, HSBC as is) for what will be the very last time – ironic to think that my bank will be closing today, Friday 13th. Still, I need to be there at this sad time to say my farewells to the gals behind the counter and thus draw a close to years of coming to this lovely little branch where parking was easy (across the road in Waitrose) and service was always with a smile. Apparently no-one is being made redundant. The two ladies who work at the bank on a fairly full-time basis are moving to the Camberley branch, as I may have mentioned previously, but I'm not looking back through my notes just in case I haven't. So, if it's news, it's news. If you already know, then at least you're not suffering from Alzeimers. The HSBC head office in their infinite lack of wisdom asked me if I could change my branch to their one in Camberley, but that's as bad as Aldershot, so I will be moving my paying-ins to Farnham. At least I'll be more in tune with the language, ie English and any preference that irritates Jeremy Hardy makes the move smugly satisfying.

I remember receiving a letter from the Midland Bank in August headed "Important changes to your bank." In small print in the top right hand corner it says, "What's happening?" Underneath it explains, "Frimley branch is closing." It was downhill all the way from there.

Well, I'm back home. I popped into Waitrose and purchased four boxes of chocolates to give to the girls. One each for the two regulars and one each for the two ladies who deputise each week for high days and holidays. End of an era, another branch closes and another piece of the social jigsaw fades into oblivion.

Oh, dear, some people do have a skewed sense of proportion, propriety and ego. The former head of Scotland Yard investigating alleged sex crimes carried out by celebrities and personalities is becoming slightly deluded, I feel. Peter Spindler, a retired Metropolitan police commander, has described the force's "Operation Yewtree" as having "embedded itself in the national psyche" and "empowering" victims to come forward. He actually said their investigation was now a "global brand". Let us unpick the above comments. "Embedded in the national psyche"? I think he means we are all wondering who was next and whether or not it was true, or just a witch-hunt. One can never be sure. You never know really if it's a cast iron case or a chance to retaliate as the suspect never bought a raffle ticket for the Secret Policemen's Ball. The police have very long memories. As to "empowering victims" everyone is being empowered, not just victims. It all started with that outdoor bondage exponent, Mrs. Pankhurst. It fell away a bit until Germaine Greer and has now made its way to the universities and Woman's Hour. As for being a "global brand", I actually do think that is a bit trite and slightly dismissive of the victims of such abuse. Manchester United Football Club calls itself a world brand, so delusion is not just the preserve of the police in relationship to this phrase. Manchester United is nothing more than a football team and they should never forget that. Sadly, everything is a brand these days. I remember someone referring to the NHS as a brand. It's not, it's a system whereby people pay by way of contribution, in order not to be charged per visit, operation or every time they are ill. It is free at the point of treatment. It comprises doctors, nurses, clinics, health centres and hospitals. It's a lot of things but a brand – never!

Migration is never far away from the front page of the papers. I could comment on it every day but it's all too depressing. It's bad enough constantly reading the names of those synonymous with the human flotsam, like Cumberbatch and Geldorf and the other luvvies who have become cause celebres and require sating on a performance basis. One who has got her back slightly more to the wall currently is Angular Merkel. A leading German politician described her open door policy of recent weeks as being akin to a careless skier who triggers an avalanche. He's not wrong. The enthusiastic, sometimes comically rapturous welcome now being shewn on TV to migrants of various countries has dissipated somewhat, with violence against the incomers being increasingly common in Europe. There is a picture in today's Daily Mail showing a Slovenian soldier patrolling a razor wire fence, erected to stop the masses from massing and ultimately messing on their border with Croatia.

At least one of these countries is showing some sense. A coloured map in the paper shows the flow currently trudging relentlessly through Turkey, Greece, Bulgaria and Slovenia until the advent of the barbed wire – they do not like it up 'em. They then mass in Hungary and Germany where they dispense towards Britain, the Netherlands and France. There is, of course, that other favoured destination, Sweden. Poor Sweden, as we previously mentioned, what the hell have they ever done to deserve such upheaval to their social structure. Still, it's sobering to read that David Cameron has offered £275 million in aid to Turkey (we would see it as a backhander) in order to stem the flow. How doesn't that work? Do we hand over our money before it gets pocketed by ministers and flunkies and others within the hierarchal system, with the mass still continuing their north African exodus? No, I don't understand it either.

Well, not a lot to be said. It's Sunday and the world is coming to terms with a series of suicide bombers who have devastated families and society in Paris. It's not a question of "I told you so" but definitely a question of "when us?" Nearly 130 people have been killed, many injured. Will this invasion of our democratic western culture do anything to really stir those who have the power to make a difference regarding terrorism. I sadly doubt it. Questions, debate, rhetoric, and evermore debate.... The west's best chance is to align with Russia who do not take prisoners – literally – and make an impact where it counts. I feel that NATO and the "allied forces" are acting in a manner not too dissimilar to a bunch of Liberal Democrats – woolly, indecisive and policy-less. In my very humble opinion, the west should support that very nicely dressed Mr. Assad and the Russian forces. They should mount a full-scale military assault with ground troops bringing to heel IS and any other insurgent based, democratically opposed group of mercenaries who are waging a war indiscriminately on decent law-abiding people.

What sort of person fires into a crowded bar and shouts, "God is great". Slightly disillusioned, I feel. The wholesale desire to allow "freedom of movement" between countries in the EU, along with the lack of border controls for terrorists masquerading as migrants/refugees lays the west open and vulnerable to a world of increasing terrorism. Label the mass as you wish for we have collectively created a recipe for violent acts, which can manifest swift and efficient mayhem wherever and whenever the perpetrators choose.

Back to the Kids Co debacle and the missing millions. As if it wasn't bad enough linking Camilla Batmanwhatever and the odious Alan Yentob within the same sentence, we now discover that Tory minister, Oliver Letwin, a man I wouldn't trust to walk my dog let along invest my money, has had a lot to answer for with this enquiry. It was he who overruled civil servants in order to hand over yet another £3 million just three months after his department had authorised a further £4.3 million grant. I know of charities that metaphorically have to jump through hoops of fire when applying for Lottery funding or indeed grants from any authority, but Kids Co ask and it shall be received! I note that as far back as 2002, when in opposition, Mr. Letwin was there, supporting government grants for Batman and Co. Letwin is both a trustee and a governor of Sherborne Girls' School. Now, Sherborne allows free places to children that are helped by the Kids Co. It's no surprise, therefore, to also learn that Batman attended Sherborne in the 70's. Small world, isn't it?

How nice it is to see someone standing up against that grand old whipping horse of bitterness – racism! A black/coloured (delete as inappropriate) MP by the name of Clive Lewis (Labour, naturally) accused the BBC of sacking him for racist reasons. His old boss, Tim Bishop, former head of BBC East, said he fired the Lewis character because as a "political reporter he was expected to know about politics". He didn't. With Mr. Lewis's consent his boss sent him a simple, political test concerning a local MP and his background. The test consisted of three questions – he got them all wrong, apparently. Mr. Lewis agreed afterwards that he had guessed the answers. My surprise is that anyone in Norwich would vote for a Labour candidate and that there would then be enough of them to elect him as MP. Well, you get what you vote for, I say.

My head is metaphorically in my hands, as always. Please save me from marketing managers and anyone inviting me to "enjoy the experience". Not only are we still on course to waste billions on the HS2 project linking the beautiful south with the pointless north, but it appears that those in charge have announced a 46 strong "independent design panel". They will be paid £200 a time for monthly meetings. Among those appointed are characters (probably without character) who work for Barclay's Bank and have a background in "customer experience". Also in the mix is a special and cultural strategist. It's a bloody train service!

A lady who goes by the name of Sadie Morgan is to chair this new panel. Who is she, you ask. Well, it seems our Sadie is a leading architect and states that the panel represents "great value for money". Surely it should read, "great money for value". I assume she is dyslexic. It gets worse, there was a recruitment advert for membership to this very special club – sorry – panel. It actually asked for "philosophers", "thinkers" and "champions". Have you ever heard such bull? Oh, you'll love the profiles of some of the other lucky money-makers. A chap called Reuben Arnold is on the panel. Now, he is Senior Vice President of Marketing and Customer Experience (that word again) at Virgin Atlantic. Lucy Musgrave is a design consultant described as a "leading practitioner in the fields of urbanism and the public realm". No, I can't believe it either! May I suggest that the only fields she is practiced in are those that her urbanism is sadly building over. We then have Greg Nugent. Now, he was the Chief Marketing Officer for the London Olympics. On a sober and serious note, could you imagine Mr. Brunel requiring all these hangers-on to be around him as he masterminded the railway line from Paddington to Bristol? As you will probably remember from my past musings, the best committee is that which comprises two people of which one never turns up for a meeting.

Now, below this article in the paper is a half-page advert for the public's chance to buy the complete series of Downton Abbey. I always liked Penelope Wilton's role in the programme – mind you, I've always liked Penelope Wilton, especially as Ann in Ever Decreasing Circles. I think it was her voice, precise, slightly commanding, classy and very sexy. Now, here is a little story sent to me by a friend about Downton Abbey, so allow me to share it with you.

The story is entitled "Downton Abbey Aplomb".

His Lordship was in the study at Downton Abbey when the butler approached and coughed discreetly. "May I ask you a question, my Lord?" His Lordship looked up from his newspaper and responded, "Go ahead, Carson." "I am doing the crossword in The Times and I have found a word that I am not too clear on." "And what word is that?" asked his Lordship. "The word, sir, is 'aplomb'." "Now, that's a difficult one to explain. I would say that it is self-assurance or complete composure." "Thank you, my Lord, but I am still a little confused." His Lordship tapped his lip and said, "Well, let me give you an example to make it clearer. Do you remember a few months ago when the Duke and Duchess arrived to spend the weekend with us?" "I remember the occasion very well, my Lord. It gave the staff and myself much pleasure in looking after them." "Also." Continued the Earl of Grantham, "do you remember when Wills plucked a rose for Kate in the rose garden?" "Ah, I was present on that occasion, my Lord, ministering to their needs." "So, you probably remember the rose and the thorn that embedded itself in his thumb very deeply." "I witnessed the incident, my Lord, and saw the Duchess remove the thorn and subsequently bandage his thumb with her own dainty handkerchief." "Well, that evening the prick on his thumb was extremely sore and Kate had to cut up his venison from our own estate, even though it was naturally very tender." "Yes, my Lord, I did see everything that transpired that evening." "The next morning, while you were pouring coffee for her Ladyship, Kate enquired of

Wills in a loud voice, 'Darling, does your prick still throb?' and you, Carson, did not spill one drop of coffee. Now that is aplomb."

Oh, and Jeremy Vine has just been eliminated from Strictly. Good night.

We awake to news that one of the Paris suicide bombers was "waved into Europe posing as a Syrian refugee" and that another terrorist was stopped by police but later released. More pictures, both on TV and in the newspapers, show the resultant carnage, shock, disbelief and fear that expresses itself so well through these captured moments. Naturally, it's the time for rhetoric to move up a level. Mr. Hollande, the French President, is reinforcing his country's determination to defeat terrorism. Our own Maggie May – or in truth, Theresa May – has also declared that terrorism will be defeated. In fact, most of the western world has nodded in collective agreement. Ironic, therefore, that Messrs. Cumberbatch, Geldorf, Bishops whatever and wherever, plus Yvette Cooper and the other supporting wets are creaming themselves in the knowledge that the first planeload of Syrian refugees will be landing on our soil tomorrow. What folly, what cost!

With the exception of one or two stories of Muslims in Britain, as opposed to the ridiculous term "British Muslims", little is being done in the way of verbal and written opposition from those who could do more to allay native fears of just how many are democratic and just how many are either terrorists or wannabe and gunnarbee terrorists. The Muslim population in European countries is frightening – literally frightening. Germany and France have nearly 5 million each and you know that by the time you read this, the figure will have exceeded that bench mark and the next million will be well on its way and that's published figures, of course, not real ones. In Germany's case it equates to nearly 6% of the population, France 7.5% and Great Britain has nearly 3 million, or 4.8%, Italy 2.25 million or 3.7% – lucky them! Bulgaria, with their newly found right to roam, or should that be right to Roma, has over 1 million but that equates to nearly 14% of their population. The Dutch have 1 million also, but equals 6%. The Spanish have just under 1 million, which equates to 2.1% – even luckier them. Belgium and Greece each have over 600,000 that represents 5.9 % and 5.3% respectively. And, lastly, Austria has received 450,000, or 4.5%. And the numbers grows day by day, month by month. What was it Mr. Nostradamus said about the East, and needing to be aware of it? We never see published the percentages of Muslim babies born here in contrast to those of the native population. Perhaps there should be a list of Catholic children being born here as well. Christ, we're being controlled by both sides of the social and religious spectrum.

Mmmm, yes, I know, I do a lot of mmmm-ing. Sad to report that further erosion to our native practices has been taking place in that once capital of the tobacco manufacturing industry – Nottingham. Portland Primary Academy in Bilborough is from Monday serving only chicken killed the "halal" way. Many parents are unhappy about this. Not surprising, really. I would be if I had a child forced to eat meat from animals slaughtered in this manner. As one parent succinctly put it, "Muslim children would never be forced to eat non-halal meat so why are my children being forced to eat halal?" I'll tell you why, Mrs. Leanne Poxon, because there is one rule for the Christian-ish native and one for religion-toting (and very often bomb and gun-toting) incomers from the east.

I remember early this year when Islington Council took pork chops, sausages and bacon off the menu in primary schools in order to sate the culinary desires of both Jews and Muslims. Standing back, taking a deep breath, staying calm and metaphorically unclenching my fists, I ask the question again, "whose bloody country is it?" And not for the first time, I reply, "Well, it's not ours, pal!"

With regard to halal produced meat I remember back in 2014 when this subject reared its throat-slit head in the newspapers, I rang Waitrose's head office, which is in Bracknell – most unfortunate. A head office in Farnham, Guildford or Reigate would certainly add gravitas to their commercial bearing and let's be honest, Bracknell is on a par with Milton Keynes, Staines (sorry, Staines-upon-Thames) and Harlow. Nice people, pity about the towns. Anyway, I spoke to the head meat buyer at Waitrose – a very nice man – who told me that basically their meat has greater markets if killed by the halal method, as meat is retrieved for sale to other outlets that results in less waste. Waitrose actually offered me a pre-prepared statement, which was issued free to people like me who asked. And it did explain that all the animals supplied under their own label are stunned before slaughter, meaning that the animals are unconscious and (hopefully) not subjected to pain.

UK law currently permits slaughter both with stunning and without – a requirement of some faiths. However, to maintain Red Tractor assurance scheme standards all animals must be pre-stunned. It goes on to say that all Waitrose meat and poultry achieves this standard and if your lamb is coming from New Zealand their laws require animals to be pre-stunned. Interestingly, it goes on to comment that "to give our customers a choice, our Duchy Originals from Waitrose lamb and the English, West Country and Dorset lamb sold on our service counters is not slaughtered with a halal blessing". The explanations are easy to follow and I understand the business end. I just feel that at the end of the day it is still a sop to minorities.

I do object to the fact that meat prepared to halal law is not being labelled by other retailers as you are not necessarily buying what you assume to be the case in a country that apparently only has 5% of its population following the Muslim faith. Yet another case of tail, dog and wagging?

The Daily Mail invited responses from major supermarkets and they varied considerably. Tesco's stated that some of their animals were pre-stunned, Asda replied that they all were, which is a much better response than that from Tesco. As you know, I still wouldn't be seen dead or alive, halal or non-halal in either – Tesco's, for reasons of buying up land just to stop other retailers from moving in and Asda, because of the quality of their customers, not their food. Many of the females trudging aimlessly around their store appear vaguely under the age of consent, whilst pushing prams containing offspring sporting names such as Chardonnay, Tyler, Roxanne and Kylie. Physically, many of them appear to have been bit-part players in the film "Deliverance" or possibly outcasts newly arrived from Norfolk. The one thing they all have in common is their obesity, never conducive to making you feel comfortable on a Friday morning.... Now, Sainsbury's also reported "some animals" as being pre-stunned, whilst Morrison's response was the most worrying, as they commented that they "didn't know". I wonder if they do now?

As you are aware, all of our meat is obtained from either Donald Russell from Sutherland – as opposed to Donald Sutherland from Russell – Waitrose or Farmer's Choice. I rang both last year and was assured that they supply only British reared beef, genuinely free range and killed in a manner acceptable to animal welfare societies. Both firms said they had received similar phone calls from concerned folk such as myself. Interestingly, the chappie I spoke to at Donald Russell (Scottish, naturally) said that someone rang the day before the furore erupted. The caller was told that none of the meat was halal and he seemed very disappointed. I asked if he thought the caller might have been a journalist somewhat galled by the fact that he was unable to get a scoop on a company priding itself on quality, integrity and welfare. "It's a point," he said, "I never thought of that." Nice chap, I felt, as were the ones I spoke to at Farmer's Choice. And, joy of joys, no music, no-one telling me my call was important to them and how I'd be responded to shortly before I died waiting. No, proper people to a man and they were representatives, both displaying all the courtesy and accent of those born here with lineage going back at least 500 years!

Just getting back to the school that started all this debate, can someone tell me what the difference is between a primary school and a primary academy? Is the latter crowd-funded, community based, and independent of local council control? More importantly, do they employ a higher standard of teachers, you know, ones who are genuinely qualified in a subject they are teaching, as opposed to those who obtained a certificate from the University of Inner-Congo or Outer Mongolia.

As you know, I've never been a fan of local councils and even less of those who serve on them. The only time I've ever contacted the parish council was to enquire as to who was responsible for the grass verge along the Vale Road close to where I live, as motorists were parking on a daily basis, turning it into barren earth. There has been no change over the years and not helped by the fishing fraternity when fish mutilators, murderers and mercenaries take to the Basingstoke Canal in order to bugger up the tow path by camping all over it so proper people who just wish to walk and take in the beauty, end up tripping over rods placed in order for the hapless walker to circumnavigate or hop over the offending tackle. Getting back to the grass verge, the parish council informed me that it was a Guildford Borough Council issue, who subsequently passed me on to the Highways at Surrey County Council. Guess what? They suggested I rang Guildford Borough Council! And, so I rang our local councillor, an amiable cove called Nigel Manning, who incidentally took up with another councillor, Mrs. Marsha Moseley, some years since. They both share the same telephone number, which is nice for them! Mr. Manning sympathised and told me he felt the same way and he would see what he could do. To be honest, I never felt convinced of his ability to actually get something done at the time and years on, the verge is still grass free where the residents of the offending properties still park and where, come the season of rod waving, the selfish bastards in vans and 4x4's still dig ruddy great track marks in the soil. Still, what do they care? They've caught a sprat from the canal and in many cases have left lager cans, fag packets and other assorted wrappers, in a manner not dissimilar from a dog leaving its scent.

The original point of this piece was actually bugger all to do with fishing and much more to do with the ineptitude of councils and councillors in general. As you also know, I've always been of the opinion that the main reason anyone gets into local politics is because it will (a) help their business, (b) allow them to socially network, (c) for the expenses one can claim and (d) the ultimate – being elected chairman of the Cemeteries and Lighting Committee.

Have you ever been to Dunster in Somerset? It's a nice little town, slightly less so now. Some of the walkways possessed Bronze Age stone sets that were attractive and appreciated by the locals and visitors alike. It's small things like this that give a place its personality, its history, its social appreciation. Sadly, Somerset County Council thinks nothing of this. Earlier this year they ripped up many of the stones and replaced them with slabs, the sort you'll find in any town. Locals complained about the new paving slabs being too "blue" in hue and out of character. They were also considered too smooth and made paths look as if they were on a new housing estate. Somerset County Council is now to spend £45,000 on replacing the offending slabs with Brecon grey slabs. Villagers have accused the council of vandalism and Historic England are not best pleased that they weren't consulted before work to destroy the stones commenced. SCC stated their removal was down to – wait for it – health and safety! Small-minded men usually along with small-minded women who possess absolutely no idea of heritage, tradition and ultimately the best use of taxpayers' money are always those allowed to open the purse strings. I bet that £45,000, on top of what it cost first time round, could have probably saved a care assistant's job for a couple of years, or maybe a library from closing. Just another thought.

I'm just reading a recent copy of "Ash Matters". That's the 8-page, high quality glossy paper newsletter that wings its way throughout the parish three, maybe four, times a year. Mr. Manning, the chappie I was just telling you about, is Chairman of Ash Parish Council and we residents cannot wait for the newsletter to fall upon our porch floor (that's if you have one) or hall floor, if you can afford one. I understand there are those living in houses that possess neither porch nor hall and that their post drops directly onto the floor of their sitting room/diner/kitchen, but that's social housing for you.... But, anyway, it appears through one's letterbox and Mr. Manning's "Chairman's bit" as he amusingly entitles his tattle, tells us of vandalism within the parish which has caused damage to two street lights in Manfield Road. I don't know it personally, so I can only assume it's on an estate. As the perpetrators of this crime have not been caught, we, the taxpayers, will be picking up the tab and in this case, the cost for repair to these two lampposts is £3,000. What on earth did they do to them? It never ceases to amaze me how council repairs can cost so much, but then how many councillors does it take to change a light bulb!

Dog walkers who allow their mutt to foul and not pick it up will be subject to a £50 fine for a first offence – I'd make it £300. Magistrates can issue fines of up to £1000 – now, that is more like it. Oh, I've just read on. There is also a £50 fine for leaving a bag of dog's doings by the verge, on it, under bushes and possibly a fine of up to £2,500 if it goes to court. Now, that's more like it.

There is very little else of interest within the 8 pages, unless you are attending the "Picnic in the Park" or you wish to listen to the Guildford Friary Brass Band. I am pronouncing it internally as Brass, not brarss, as one considers it to be such a northern pastime. There's going to be a Christmas Fantasia at Ash Wharf and you can also become a "Good Neighbour" which is nice for someone, I'm sure. Turn to page 8 and with a heavy heart I see we have a list of telephone numbers for various councillors – all very local and all very white by name. Jeremy Hardy please take note! Oh yes, and at the top of the page there is a badge and Surrey Police alongside with the motto – because they must have just made it up for a box of crackers – "Surrey Police – with you, making Surrey safer". How would they know? There are never any police to be seen on the beat. There's the occasional police car in Normandy, but they're just sitting with speed cameras (bastards!). You never see any policeman walking round. Still, the article does add that you can dial 999, 112 or 101. I just wonder if anyone would answer, what with all the cutbacks!

Talking of the village, we used to have three pubs, the Admiral Napier, now more trendily named Napiers, the Bridge House, which became the Wharfinger – no, I agree, certainly not an improvement and which in turn, was subsequently demolished with the land becoming part of Vale Furnishers. Next door but one, past the erstwhile Tolley's Garage, which sold Burmah fuels and was also a British Leyland dealership, still stands the Standard of England. Closed some years ago, this has been the subject of an application by Morrison's, who would either rebuild or convert into a retail store. Nothing has happened, except the letters spelling the pub name continue to fall off the wall, recently it read 'andard o ngland'. Budgen's, by the way, just around the corner is now the Co-op. If only it had been purchased by Waitrose, an improvement of that magnitude would have helped house prices enormously.

Oh no, I'm just perusing a recent edition of "In Touch". It's the Tory leaflet that comes out just prior to an election and mentions all the good works perpetrated and encouraged by "Your local Tory councillor". There is going to be a pedestrian crossing in Manor Road for use by school students (pupils to me) who arrive and depart from Ash Manor School. Councillor Marsha Moseley (in bold letters) insisted, "this crossing was a condition of any planning permission being granted to Taylor Wimpey" (or Greedy Bastard plc) for new homes off Manor Road. Morrison's was asked by Councillor Moseley's other half, Councillor Nigel Manning (in bold letters on flyer) to hold an exhibition showing revised proposals before they submitted them, but they refused. Well, you got the pedestrian lights, don't think too badly of yourselves.

Now, what other good news are they imparting? Ah, yes, the council tax has been held down and Councillor Moseley has backed local groups by making a series of financial allocations from her (her?) yearly local allowance. Is that her personal allowance or our taxpayers' money? This really is quite self indulgent, Councillors really do find it easy to be pleased with themselves.

Wry smile time, I'm afraid. Just turned back to the top of the front page and noticed that mothers with toddlers are asking for a pedestrian crossing to be built in Ash Hill Road so that they can gain access more readily to Victoria Hall for the nursery held there. Remember Victoria Hall? Yes, that's the hall where the next door neighbour complained about the clock striking and disturbing his sleep. Now, to be fair to Mr. Manning, he has been extremely tactful in his little bit about the hall on page 2. Headed "We are not amused" (good use of Victorian pun), there is a picture of Victoria Hall and underneath one of the splendid clock tower. He writes, "The Victoria Hall's management charity is having to divert vital funds raised by local people to fit a new mechanism to silence the clock chimes after a nearby newly-arrived resident complained. The clock has chimed day and night since the end of the reign of Queen Victoria – until now!" Very subtle. He didn't mention that this was due to the "unreasonable attitude of a cove of foreign extraction, or an 'incomer'". Perhaps that is why Mr. Manning is in politics and I'm just a freelance scribe.

Meanwhile, back on page 1 with the nursery mothers, a petition to the Guildford Local Committee (who they?) asks for action to be taken. The leading light in this campaign is Councillor Murray Grubb Junior. That wry smile has just re-emerged. Murray Grubb Junior! What is he – American? A Grubb Senior is bad enough, but to inflict another Grubb upon the world and then add Junior certainly doesn't help the situation. I'm just trying to work out if Grubb Junior is an anagram of Arse! Which reminds me, "Leonardo da Vinci" is actually an anagram of "Vindaloo and Rice". Bet you didn't know that.

I feel like a joke. So you play the part of Polly and put the kettle on as I'm parched and while it's boiling, how about this, a little story passed to me by my very good friend, Mike. You know, the one who resides in Fetcham, near Leatherhead, you know the one I play trains with. Yes, that's the one.

Anyway, the story is called Fifty Shades of Chocolate:

Mr. Cadbury met Miss Rowntree on a Double Decker. It was just After Eight. They got off at Quality Street. He asked her name. "Polo, I'm the one with the hole", she said in a Wispa. "I'm Marathon, the one with the nuts", he replied. He touched her Crème Eggs, which was a Kinder Surprise for her. Then he slipped his hand into her Snickers, which made her Ripple. He fondled her Jelly Babies while she rubbed his Tic Tacs. Very soon they were Hearthrobs, it was a Fab moment as she screamed in Turkish Delight. Three days later, his Sherbet Dip-Dab started to itch. It turns out Miss Rowntree had been with dirty Bertie Bassett and he had Allsorts!

Silly I know, but it amused me, and that's the main thing.

And to follow, the blame game: A woman in a hot air balloon realised she was lost. She reduced altitude and spotted a man below. She descended a little more and shouted, "Excuse me, can you help me? I promised a friend I would meet her an hour ago but I don't know where I am." The man below replied, "You're in a hot air balloon, hovering approximately thirty feet above the ground and you are between 40 and 41 degrees north latitude and between 59 and 60 degrees west latitude." "You must be an engineer," exclaimed the balloonist. "I am," replied the man, "how did you know?" "Well," answered the balloonist, "everything you have told me is probably technically correct but I've no idea what to make of your information and the fact is, I'm still lost. Frankly, you've not been much help at all and if anything, by talking in this manner you've probably delayed my trip even further." The man responded, "You must be in management." The balloonist replied, "I am but how did you know?" "Well," said the man, "you don't know where you are or where you are going, you have risen to where you are due to a large quantity of hot air, you made a promise which you've no idea how to keep and you expect people beneath you to solve your problems. The fact is, you are in exactly the same position you were in before we met but now, somehow, it's my bloody fault!"….More than an element of truth in that story, methinks!

I'm off to Hove, actually, to give a talk to a ladies' club so an early start, as I have to be there at 10.15 am. The speaker's secretary has reserved me a space in a private car park opposite the church, which is always appreciated. My natural courtesy, charm, bonhomie and all-round hale-fellow-well-met personality is always severely tested the second that I sniff out that most odious and feral example of humanity – the traffic warden! So it's easier to park where invited and not have to search local streets within unfamiliar surroundings.

Well, I survived the M25, M23 and the A27, arriving at my destination shortly after 10 am. A lovely chatty group of ladies, so a few hours now to read the papers, a snack to eat and maybe a few minutes shut-eye and then it's off to St. Alban's for a talk to a group of residents at a care home.

Okay, then, I'll make the tea. It's only fair, you made it earlier this morning. What's that? Custard creams, no thanks, still trying to cut down on the biccies and crisps.

I noted in the papers that the weak Labour-lack-of-leader stated that with regard to terrorism our police should not be allowed a shoot-to-kill policy. His comments come just three days after the Paris attacks. Principles are one thing, safety is entirely another. What does he expect the police to do? Talk to them? Offer them counselling? Free holidays? Or possibly tuition fees to pay for a course of their own choice? Gutless, absolutely gutless! To be fair, many of his fellow party MPs are not overly enthused by his stance. We none of us want to see armed police on our once quiet streets, but that was then and this is multi-cultural now. We cannot stand by and tolerate a "well, you shoot first and I'll try to capture your aggressive stance on my head camera before I return any fire on the grounds of Health and Safety and legal restrictions."

What is sickening is that in Bedford a meeting took place last Friday that really sums up what this country is facing. Attended by approximately 240 Muslims, those present listened to a panel of preachers arguing for an Islamic state. They criticised our education system for applying our values in our schools to Muslim pupils. The organisers planned to take their meetings on tour. One of the panel, a certain Mr. Mustafah, said, "The government want to decide what is taught in Islamic schools … you think that makes people welcome". Let me tell you Sunshine, and this may come as a bit of a surprise, but actually you and your views are not welcome. The old rules still apply, if you don't like our values, our democracy and the way we live our lives generally, ie treating our women as equals, then sod off!

Richard Littlejohn put it well in the headlines to his column, entitled "Our Policy On Islamic State". He said, "Clueless at best, spineless at worst". Here we go again, if it's not the Muslims attempting to change our future life, then it's protestors campaigning to air brush it out. In this case it's a school in Bristol. Colston Girls' School was founded in 1891 and funded by a legacy given them by William Colston, a merchant and MP. He traded in cloth, wine and sugar and amassed a fortune from the slave trade. So? That was then … and you know the rest. It is certainly not fair on the girls as they walk home from school being harangued by protestors, attempting to talk to them about the schools history. After a commemorative service for Colston School at Bristol Cathedral the girls had to leave via a rear entrance to avoid protesters. Why should they be treated in this manner? I would love to know what the protestors think they are going to achieve, other than division. You cannot turn the clock back. He didn't squander his ill-gotten gains, he left them to his city to further the education for many generations to come. Accept it, move on. And, anyway, just a thought, but how do these protestors have so much time to protest. Do any of them work? You know, contribute to the general good of the country, or are they heading straight back to Oxford to continue protesting against the Cecil Rhodes statue? Mealy-mouthed sods and sodesses, I say.

Crikey! Is it that time already? I'd better get dressed before wending my way in a northerly direction. I wonder if the M3 and M25 will be as kind as the motoring system was earlier. I'll see you later.

As is often the case it is now much later. In fact, St. Alban's seems but a distant memory. Yes, it was only yesterday but earlier today I travelled to Horsham and then to Crowthorne.

Coincidences are funny things. During a recent conversation a lady mentioned a fashion house called Hermes. I only knew of an aircraft carrier of that name and here in today's papers there is a photo of a singer called Josh Stone who is campaigning to help put a stop to the hideous crocodile handbag industry. It takes three crocodiles to make one handbag, apparently, as Hermes use the tender, soft parts, ie lower jaw, throat and belly. These bags are not surprisingly purchased only by the richest and therefore most vacuous of people. According to the article, Victoria Beckham owns many, as does a lady called Petra Eccleston. The photo of her shows a lady looking young enough to be Bernie Eccleston's daughter, so it's probably his wife. The Eccleston females bag cost £30,000, while the Beckham woman's is estimated to be worth an obscene £280,000. This is because it is studded in diamonds. So much money, so much vanity. That money could have been spent on a brain cell or more usefully for the world, donated to PETA and helped alleviate the suffering of these crocodiles at farms. Animal welfare comes a very poor second to the purchaser's glamour and vanity.

Meanwhile, back in the world of terrorism I read that the Belgian authorities have lost one of their canine companions after a sniffer dog died in a hail of bullets. Diesel, a Belgian Shepherd, was sent in to a terrorists' lair ahead of its handlers in an effort to locate explosives. Sadly, the 7-year-old was killed in action. This raises once again the question as to whether animals should ever be used by humans during acts of warfare and conflict. I have never had a problem with dogs being used to sniff out drugs or explosives at airports, on planes, wherever, but active combat is a contentious matter. Readers of previous tomes will know of my sorrow that hundreds of thousands of horses have died over centuries during battle. They never sought to take part in man's power struggles. Whether they be sea mammals or pigeons, it does not sit comfortably with me. It was reported that Diesel may have been wearing a camera, or cameras, in order to flush out resisting terrorists. This really isn't fair on any animal. Send in captured terrorists, mouths taped and then, when the enemy starts firing you'll know there are other terrorists within and you are not putting at risk one of your own.

Sorry? Has someone from Liberty got a problem with that? Perhaps there should be a slogan, "Save a dog, kill a jackal!". Or maybe a Facebook campaign headed, "Canines matter, terrorists do not".

Wry, jaundiced smile time now. It appears that the Muslim Council of Britain has taken out an advert denouncing terrorism and violence – which is nice for them. The problem is that for British people – and I mean real British people – the proof is in the pork-free pudding. How do you trust these people to actually mean what they say? Fine words do not a democracy make! I have and always will work on the basis that they are all guilty until proven innocent and that way you won't be disappointed – or hopefully killed!

You know, the longer I write this book, the more I realise just what power the Supreme Court wields, just how anti-British the judges are and how totally out of touch with the views of the poor sods who pay their wages. The same name keeps rearing its very provocative head. Their president, Lord Neuberger, is concerned that Theresa May's attempt to ensure migrants speak a proficient standard of English could be breaching the Human Rights Act. Now, there's a surprise. Any attempt to improve the standard of those wishing to partake of our over-generous hospitality is continually met with a wall of left-wing, pro-refugee, migrant, incomer-of-any-sort argument in order to let the buggers in. Why should there be this continued collision course between the government, inept as it is, trying to raise the standard of applicant and the judiciary who should be supporting the government. Time and time again Neuberger and his questionable ilk are at odds with those elected on our behalf. The very fact that they wish to consult with lawyers from Pakistan and Yemen, the Home Office and ... that dreadful refugee support outfit Liberty ... sends shivers down the spine of those who remember England when it really was quite nice.

Right! It's anagram time. I always find these oddities interesting so I have collated some well known and not so well known examples, designed to amaze, surprise, wow or possibly just encourage you to mutter, "Well, I never".

Elvis = Lives

Madam Curie = radium came

A telephone girl = repeating hello

Western Union = no wire unsent

The countryside = no city dust here

The centenarians = I can hear ten tens

Clint Eastwood = old west action

Dictionary = indicatory

The Morse Code = here come dots

Slot machines = cash lost in me

Astronomer = moon starer (it also spells, 'no more stars')

Postmaster = stamp store

Desperation = a rope ends it

The eyes = they see

Television programming = permeating living rooms

Debit card = bad credit

Church of Scientology = rich chosen goofy cult

Laxative = exit lava

Semolina = is no meal

A gentleman = elegant man

The public art galleries = large picture halls I bet

Funeral = real fun

Catherine of Aragon = a nag to force an heir

A domesticated animal = docile as a man tamed it

A shoplifter = has to pilfer

Father in law = near half wit

Benson and Hedges = NHS been a godsend

Statue of Liberty = built to stay free

And lastly, very prophetic

Princess Diana = end is a car spin

Finished? There, I told you that you would be, well, vaguely interested.

It's precisely 9.18 pm. I spent the afternoon in Bexhill, well, Little Common actually. It's a very friendly village with extremely sociable people. There must be more clubs per head of population than anywhere else. I appear to be here close to the Sussex coast about every three months on average. I took the 6.30 brewery tour and not for the first time I'm about to devour a sweet & sour pork (Hong Kong style) with egg fried rice and a pancake roll. It's my monthly treat so I will be back with you soon.

It's now 10.05, I'm finished and very nice it was too.

Interesting to read that the Uni-stazi as I now think of them are continuing their relentless drive in order to stifle freedom of speech. This time Cambridge University has removed Dr. David Starkey from its £2 billion fund raising campaign, as he is – and I quote – "a man who has a well documented and undeniable history of racism and sexism". Dr. Starkey was one of three well-known folk at the forefront of a three minute video raising awareness of the University's aims, the other two being Dr. Stephen Hawking and Ian McKellen. I mean, call me cynical, but as one's disabled and the other's homosexual they appear to tick all the right boxes and, both male! Naturally, an open letter signed by student union officials and lecturers called for Dr. Starkey to be edited out of the video. Their letter went on to say, "Any institution making this choice of representative would seem to care very little about its appearance in the eyes of black and minority ethnic students and staff, current and in the future". These people really should get out more, talk to ordinary people and see what's happened with multiculturalism in their own town, then stand back, remove their blinkers and take in the bigger picture instead. Noteworthy is the fact that Dr. Starkey commented that he had not put himself forward for inclusion and had been asked to contribute. He's probably too polite to even think of sticking up two fingers but I'll be there should he require a proxy gesture.

Much as I still love the Beeb, it's bad enough defending it, what with the likes of Alan Yentob's costly association but it doesn't help itself when I read that despite "cutbacks" they are still employing 129 press officers. What on earth do all these people do? ITV employ 35 and Channel 4, 27. BABC employ 305 staff in finance, 2034 in technology and 2089 in other "support function roles". It now employs 74 senior managers who are on a higher salary than the £142,500 enjoyed by our Prime Minister. Yet, still they support their paymasters and accept without argument the closing down of the Red Button service.

Now, I do hope that you are going to join me in raising a glass, or cup in my case, to a couple who have just tied the knot. George Kirby, aged 103, has just married Doreen Luckey – and I'm sure she is – aged 91. George is almost a cradle snatcher. The pair met back in 1988, so well done to them both. I do love a happy ending. Appropriate thought, I feel – "You know you're getting older when the person you fantasise about is the one you are living with!".

You're not tired yet? Okay, how about we both have a glass of Glava? I've never been partial to whisky but this tipple with honey is very acceptable. Yes? Okay, I'll pour and you relax. Oh, you've got out a One Foot in the Grave DVD, have you? Fine, well, I'm up for it. Cue theme tune and....

Two episodes later – you never get a bad episode or even a substandard one. Every one is a veritable gem. Oh, I see you like the Glava – yes, I did notice, twice you've put Victor on hold whilst you went to the loo and twice you came back with a refilled glass. You thought I hadn't noticed! I'm just looking at the bottle and what's left of the contents. It's described as "a smooth and unique taste experience. A subtle blend of spices, the finest Scotch whisky and just a hint of citrus, best enjoyed over ice". Now, that's what it says on the front. On the rear label it expands by referring to the Scotch whisky as being "selected" and then "married carefully with a rich variety of natural herbs, honeys and flavourings to achieve the distinctive and original taste". I have to say that I am now feeling as mellow as the Glava, and in the words of Victor Meldrew, "Coming over all tickety".

No jokes or thoughts, other than to get to bed without stumbling. Good night.

Now, today, Friday, has started off in a similar vein to where yesterday left off. Certainly in relation to Cambridge University. Fortunately, we still possess educated people holding the view that freedom of speech and thought are precious enough to hang onto. Regarding Dr. Starkey's removal from their promotional video due to his alleged controversial and racist views, Frank Furedi, Professor of Sociology at Kent University, commented that the University's actions were very cowardly, adding that it indicates that if you have controversial views you risk being marginalised and shut down. Alan Smithers, Professor of Education at the University of Buckingham, made a very telling statement. He said, "We want people who will clearly speak the truth as they see it. David Starkey is one of those people. There is a weakness now in intellectual life where people are always looking out to take offence. The point about higher education is to be able to assess the truth of statements and if they are wrong, defeat them by argument, not seek to ban the person". Hear, hear.

You remember those thin wedges that turn into very thick ones, well, be warned. Regulators in the USA have now approved the country's first genetically modified fish for human consumption. It sounds ghastly and I really hope it tastes the same. Apparently, an Atlantic salmon is injected with a gene from the Pacific Chinook salmon, which makes it grow faster. The marketing name for this profit-making little exercise is AquAdvantage salmon. Doesn't exactly roll off the tongue, does it? Developed by a company called "Aqua Bounty Technologies" of Massachusetts these salmon reach maturity in sixteen to eighteen weeks, as opposed to the more natural thirty months of an Atlantic salmon. I really do hope it does not become another American import we have to endure, either by the front door or with another marketing blanket to hide its origins. They will probably market the real name in small print just before the box that states, "Warning this salmon contains fish." I would add, "sort of."

Page 17 of the Daily Mail has a photograph of whingeing left-wing students protesting in Cardiff last week. They hold above them banners proclaiming, "transphobia kills", "why all the bigotry?" and "bigotry rewarded here". This shower of non-democratically minded oiks was protesting against the appearance of Germaine Greer. Can you imagine what the humourless ticks would be like if and when they are ever employed by someone at some stage during their miserable lives – a life enmeshed in continuous campaigning and complaining. They really are sores on the face of society.

Ah, oh to read of higher standards being tried out on a new estate for once. The Westwood Park Development in Beverley, Yorkshire, is on the site of a former Victorian hospital with Grade II listed status. It is being converted into twenty-five luxury apartments, the four-bedroomed variety selling for a not insignificant £450,000, which for the north must be positively palatial. PJ Livesey, the developers, is drawing up contracts with potential owners in order not to lower the value of the estate. Buyers will not be able to hang out any washing in a manner that may "detract from the visual enjoyment of the building". Caravans and trailers will also be banned from being parked on driveways for prolonged periods. Mmmm, a little too weak on that last point, methinks. I'd ban caravans and mobile homes from all drives, they are, quite frankly, a bloody eyesore, look common and reflect very badly on the owner. From what I've witnessed over the years most caravan owners are indeed common but, as you know, I never generalise!

The power of advertising; In graphic colour, spread over two pages are the "advertised take-away products", which took hours to photograph and probably photo-shop afterwards. And the real thing? Nothing like. It really comes home to roost when you see just how far removed your burger is from the glossy, mouth-watering, fully-stuffed to overly-stuffed example shewn in the advert. Burger King's Whoppa appears to be totally the opposite, a very deflated apology-rating of 2 out of 10 on the Daily Mail's Richter Scale. McDonald's Big Mac rated a 3 out of 10, with the real burger described as looking "chaotic" – they're not wrong. KFC's Original Chicken Rice Box didn't fare too badly with 6 out of 10 and Yo! Sushi gained an admirable 7 out of 10. As you are aware, even if they all achieved 11 out of 10, it still wouldn't induce me to soil my well-trodden Marks & Spencer shoes over their unfortunately well-trodden doorsteps.

From the mildly heady heights of relative success by the previously mentioned outlets it's all downhill from here-on-in. Nando's grilled chicken wrap appeared to be all lettuce and no substance, although the reviewer, in fairness, did describe the chicken as "scrumptious". Was it free range, I wonder? Leon (who are they?) sells a haloumi wrap, which garnered a 4 out of 10, with the cheese being labelled as an "amorphous lump". Going down! Costa Coffee received 2 out of 10 for their mozzarella and tomato sourdough panini. It does look awful. To be honest, compared to the advertised product it looks as if a staff member (a very fat staff member) has sat upon the example sold to the reviewer. Starbucks all-day breakfast panini is also appalling. The advertised example, rich in content, the egg, free range apparently, bacon, mushrooms and all served in a stone-baked ciabatta sandwich. Well, really, it looks like the flattest, meanest looking, limp bacon effort and their rating of 3 out of 10 seems overly generous. The daddy of them all, or for those in Oxbridge, the mummy, the transgendered partner, the lesbian partner or the homosexually challenged, has to be Subway's steak cheese melt, at £3.99. To be fair, the marketing people have done a terrific job as the advert shows a very mouth-watering example. The reality appears to be almost steak-free. They actually received nil points. (Note: interestingly, Maureen has just typed nil points correctly. I asked her how it was spelt. In my written notes I've spelt it "pwar" with two question marks because I wasn't sure, so in my mind there was always a possibility that this spelling was incorrect. There, you can't be more honest than that!) Anyway, getting back to their steak cheese melt, which has by now melted, obviously, it did look hideous. Oh, how smug I feel, having never frequented any of their over-priced establishments. Give me the café in Woodbridge Road, Guildford, (just by the cricket ground) any day. You will struggle to find a better breakfast.

Meanwhile, back in the world of rabid feminism I read that plans are afoot to reduce the breadth of feminist content from the A-Level politics syllabus. Only one female – Mary Woolstencroft – would remain and the suffragette movement mentioned only in despatches under the section on pressure groups. My smile is wry. I have no problem with the feminist movement being explained when it comes to equality regarding pay and conditions but they just never stop their bleeding heart whingeing. Naturally, there has been an online petition to ensure women are not "erased out of history", unlike the rest of the country's heritage, and I couldn't agree more. The trouble is that those signatories to openness and enlightenment are not prepared for others to have a differing view on matters and are quite happy to erase or airbrush any colonial past altogether. It might make them and their ethnic brethren feel cleansed, but as we know and have said before, it's always dangerous to attempt to rewrite history. So, with that in mind and feeling just slightly chipper, though I can't think for the life of me why, I will leave the following, dedicated to all students, lecturers, grand dames, both male and female, Guardian readers and the usual caveats that include all those suffering from a humour by-pass.

"Met a beautiful girl at the park today. Sparks flew. She fell at my feet and we ended up having sex there and then. I really do love my new Taser."

"Now on sale at Ikea – beds for lesbians. No nuts or screwing involved, it's all tongue and groove."

"Medical Association Researchers have found that patients needing blood transfusions may benefit from receiving chicken blood rather than human blood. It tends to make the men cocky and the women lay better."

"I received an email from Screwfix Direct thanking me for my interest but explaining that they were not a dating agency."

"I was devastated to learn that my wife was having an affair but by turning to religion I was soon able to come to terms with the whole dreadful experience. I converted to Islam, and we're stoning her in the morning!"

"My wife suggested I get myself one of those penis enlargers so I have. She's nineteen and her name's Cathy."

"The cost of living has become so bad that my wife is having sex with me now that she can't afford the price of batteries."

"A man dials 999 and says, 'I think my wife is dead.' The operator says, 'how do you know?' The man replies, 'Well, the sex is the same but the ironing's piling up.'"

"I was explaining to my wife last night that when you die you are reincarnated and must come back as a different creature. She said she would like to come back as a cow. I said, 'you obviously haven't been listening.'"

"My wife has been missing for over a week now. The police have told me to expect the worst, so tomorrow I'll have to trot back down to the charity shop to get her clothes back."

"A woman is standing nude in front of a mirror and she says to her husband, 'I look horrible, I feel fat and ugly, pay me a compliment.' He replied, 'well, at least your eyesight's good.'"

"While next door, a similar scenario was being played out and the wife, when naked and disillusioned asked, 'What turns you on more, my pretty face or my sexy body?' Her husband became very thoughtful, looked her up and down, then replied, 'Oh, it's your sense of humour.'"

"After years of research scientists have discovered what really makes women happy – NOTHING!"

Last thought:

"Hell hath no fury like the lawyer of a woman scorned."

Do you know, re-reading the above, I feel that there could, just could, be examples of humanity out there who may feel slightly affronted by those jokes – I really do hope so!

Chapter 9

Ham, Egg And Chips Please

A quick perusal through the pages, a look at the breakfast news and, may I say, Carol is looking as lovely as ever! On to the Red Button service – no, nothing of note there either. So, it's downstairs to exercise, then over to Worplesdon to pick up my accountant, who is also a railway enthusiast and modeller. He is driving from his home in Woking to his mate, the one who lives in Worplesdon, who happens to be a paid employee of the Mid Hants Railway. I'm then driving the pair of them to my cousin's, so we can all play trains. What's that? What about Mike? Oh, yes, well I'm picking him up, naturally, from his house in Fetcham. Changes are afoot in Fetcham by the way, as Sainsbury's has replaced Budgen's. The journey will, no doubt, be incident free, although we will gloat as we mingle with the local populus through Ashtead High Street when we will espy the strip of land that Tesco's wanted to build on in the High Street but the threat of a store appears to have receded since their poor results last year. They have announced that certain stores would close and that newly planned developments would not take place. A lot of people were against Tesco's moving into Ashtead as it would do what they've done everywhere else, totally destroy the local butcher, baker and candle-stick maker. Joy, sheer joy.

We will partake of lunch across the road at Ye Olde King's Head. That's right, you remember – ham, egg and chips for Mike and myself. Won't it be exciting! Even more exciting of course, seeing how our two guests peruse the menu and possibly choose something completely alien and untried, such as Cumberland sausage and mashed potato, with onion gravy of course, or maybe hit the heady heights of international cuisine and go for lasagne. Still, before our culinary choices are made we will be playing trains. I promise not to shout out "all aboard" as I open the doors for my fellow intrepid enthusiasts in Worplesdon. I have to have everyone back by 6 pm as

I have a tour at 6.30 pm. Now, I know we are not traipsing off to the North Pole, but it is Epsom, and it all needs organising! See you later.

It's now a lot later, Sunday evening to be precise. Two more tours of the brewery yesterday and one today have brought us up to now. As usual, interesting people on the tours. It really is a pleasure taking visitors around something you believe in. It's local, privately owned, real ale and five minutes from home which always helps! We will look through the papers shortly, but first the Strictly elimination. This week it was Jamelia who played her part through the well-trodden path of the dance-offs and on this occasion did not do enough to stay for next week's round. More of a surprise was Charlton's 1-0 win away at Birmingham. Only one goal, but three points. I wonder how important this win may be come the season's conclusion.

Looking through the papers I've just noted another example of the way our country is descending into social chaos. Chaos that, as ever, comes at a price regarding the law of this country and its equally law-abiding citizens. Kent is a county taking in more than its fair share of migrants, refugees, migrants masquerading as refugees, terrorists masquerading as refugees.... The Crown Court in Maidstone tried two rapists who were definitely Syrian refugees. You and I have history in this country that can be traced back to our birth due to the fact that we have birth certificates to prove it. We also have National Insurance numbers and tax reference numbers. This court case was notable because the age of the two Syrians could not be verified. Therefore, the police refused to give the press information regarding their names. The judge had to tell them not to speak out of turn in the dock. Really? No manners, no social etiquette and presumably no passports. This pair were among a group of Syrian chancers (refugees, is by the way, an anagram of chancer) who are being housed at our expense at a hostel in Gillingham. What the hell has this town ever done to deserve this ungrateful, morally-starved free-loading baggage? And still they are welcomed by our government.

The money we are paying out for "services to the unwelcome" could go towards the printing cost of tax discs for road vehicles. Rarely have I witnessed such an ill-conceived money-saving idea. The tax disc itself provided immediate evidence that the car was legally entitled to be on the road. We, the public, could always help by informing the authorities of a suspicious vehicle. I wonder how much we have truly saved as we all know from things governmental and locally governmental, the accountant's pen will tell you one thing whilst reality will tell you another.

Mmmm, it seems that the "intolerable cancer" permeating Oxbridge has expanded its poisonous cells to Warwick University. They are holding "consent workshops". One student, 19-year-old George Lawlor, wrote on his blog that he felt that the overwhelming majority of people don't have to be taught "not to be a rapist". I would have thought this to be a not unreasonable comment. Sadly, Mr. Lawlor's challenge to the student elite has made him public enemy number one. Jeered at, hounded, intimidated in a public house and the names "rapist" and "racist" added when you look up his name on search engines. The poor sod!

And just to return to Oxford, there is a row going on over the theme of this year's summer balls. The idea was to base them on a New Orleans theme, ie F Scott Fitzgerald's Great Gatsby of 1926, but students are concerned (aren't they always) that – wait for it – women and ethnic minority students may be upset. Somebody called Arushi Garg, not surprisingly a law student, said it would force people to remember "a college devoid of women and people of colour". Slight hint of bitterness, maybe? I've just read on and it's a "she". Well, hard to know with that sort of name. I mean it could be anyone of the two – no three – or it is now four genders currently available through the NHS, with more options on the way, no doubt.

The Garg woman added "1926 at Magdalen was a time when people of colour and women were entirely absent from college spaces". Get over it, dearie, grow up and read up on your law. You'll need all the guile and wit you can muster when you stand there in court defending refugees, migrants and migrant ref....

And just to finish this tale of those I would rather not be a parent of, I see that sombreros and false moustaches were banned from a University of Birmingham fancy dress party as they were deemed racist. Who are these people? Mind you, I remember a friend of mine being invited to a party where the host told him to go "dressed to kill". Apparently, sporting a turban, beard and a backpack wasn't what they had in mind! For myself, I always recall attending a Muslim birthday party and let me tell you, you've never seen me play pass the parcel so quickly in all my life!

Right! On that note, I'm off, but not before the tablets have been consumed. Fancy a cuppa before we go? Okay, milk's in the jug, jug's in the fridge. I'll get the Yorkshire tea bags. Good night all.

It's now Tuesday and I've just returned from Carterton in Oxfordshire where I gave a talk to a mixed group. Nice afternoon, pleasant journey there and back.

I read that the BBC's "lack of humour police" is fully employed today. Jimmy Carr, not one of my favourite people, was engaged to appear on the "One Show". He commented that he had come up with a two-word gag. It is, "Dwarf shortage". Having told the studio audience and viewers his joke he then added, "if you're a dwarf and you are offended by that, grow up". Two viewers have complained to Ofcom. I would love to know if either of the complainants are, or possibly were, dwarfs because if they are, they most definitely need to grow up. I've no doubt that they also read the Guardian and vote Liberal Democrat.

Naturally, with one or more complainants Ofcom are investigating as to whether potentially discriminatory comments in the programme met generally accepted standards. How can this throw-away line spark such outrage and then galvanise such action? It's a pity that Ofcom do not have anything better to do with their time and our money.

Also interesting to read that a Jewish group in Germany has called for a limit on the number of migrants coming to the Motherland due to the problems with integrating the mostly Muslim arrivals. What goes round comes round – and then goes round all over again.

With all the cuts to police funding I see that a poll reveals that seven out of ten of us rarely see a policeman. Mmmm, that means that three out of ten of us have! It must be the same policeman, surely.

A furore has erupted in the cinema world over the decision by DCM, an advertising group, to ban a 60-second advert featuring "the Lord's Prayer" stating that it did not run adverts linked to "personal beliefs". I have no problem with that but if I see an advert shewn on behalf of Catholicism, Wesleyism, Calvinism, Baptism or any other ism, plus of course that accepted alternative, Islam, I really will be … well, not best pleased. A spoke for the National Secular Society said the church was "arrogant to imagine it could foist its opinion on a captive cinema audience". He's not wrong. I just hope that the policy is fair and appropriate to all cults.

Now I know you and I both hate injustice and there is no greater effrontery to society that I can think of, having read the following.

Two young women accepted a lift home from the bouncer of a club they had visited, the bouncer had been drinking. He crashes his car through a barrier on the M62. One of the ladies was so badly injured she is still in hospital 16 months on, having received such horrendous head injuries. These were so severe that her two children, aged 8 and 10, were not allowed to visit her for 7 months for fear of the distress it might cause. The other lady is paralysed from the chest down and will never walk again. The bouncer, one Jon Morton, aged 32, pleaded guilty to a charge of drink driving and driving without care and attention. He received a 3-year driving ban, a fine and a twenty week overnight curfew. Three weeks after his court appearance he asked for the curfew to be lifted so that he could join friends on a stag do. Unbelievably the court agreed and he was allowed to "jet off" as they reported it in the Daily Mail. It really does bugger belief. It's a punishment, or should be, not a negotiable timescale to be discussed when something better comes along. Irrespective of his conviction, he doesn't seem an overly nice chap. He has since been fined £500 for possession of pornography and an indecent image of a child on his mobile phone. One drink driver and two lives ruined, three years doesn't seem much to pay.

Okay, time to check the emails. That's good, two invitations to speak at clubs, one in Bucks and one in Kent. There's a confirmation of a talk. Ah, one from Orvis with their latest range of offerings, another from Hatton's of Liverpool and Aviva with whom I insure the cars and house. Now, what's this? Oh, no, this is not good news. I must act immediately. It's from a lady called Eileen, upon whom some dreadful luck has befallen. Her email reads, "I am writing this with tears in my eyes. I came down to Istanbul, Turkey, for a short holiday. Unfortunately, I was mugged at the park of the hotel where I stayed, all cash and credit card were stolen off me but luckily for me I still have my passport with me. I have been to the police here but they're not helping issues at all and my return flight leaves in few hours from now but I'm having problems settling the hotel bills and the hotel manager won't let me leave until I settle the bills. Well I really need your financial assistance. Please let me know if you can help me out and I need you to keep checking your email because it's the only way I can reach you. I'm freaked out at the moment. Eileen."

The surname is also written and I do actually know the lady concerned as she is the speaker's secretary of a club, but having met her I cannot imagine her ever lowering her standards to publicly admit that she is "freaked out at the moment". We're stoic here in the south, we don't freak out at any moment.

Now, what else is there? Ah, yes, a lady called Olga is one of many "exotic Russian women waiting for me now. Pics inside". Another email is encouraging me to seek the help of an attorney to "help me win my case". I am informed by another email that I can attend nursing school – day or night – and receive an online nursing degree. Strange, as I assumed all degrees were just downloaded anyway in order for the recipient to work as an agency nurse for the NHS.

Next! Oh, there are amazingly priced Costa Rica holidays available online. Denise Wilson is offering me an Asda gift card. She obviously doesn't know me or she wouldn't dream of insulting me with such a pointless waste of plastic. Nicoli B Cradel is inviting me to "take my time and get to know Nicoli better". Why? And lastly, the Outback Steakhouse is offering me a complimentary dinner for four if I bother to open up their email. And I won't! Delete!

I'm going to relax with an episode or two of "One Foot in the Grave". Do you fancy joining me? Okay, I'll budge over, but while the DVD is settling in and the preamble plays, I think a quickie is in order. No, not that sort of quickie! A quick story of two Texans.

Two Texans were out on the range talking about their favourite sex positions. One said, "I think I enjoy the rodeo position best." "I've never heard of that one," said the cowboy. "What is it?" "Well, it's where you get your wife down on all fours and mount her from behind, then reach around and cup each of her breasts in your hands. You then whisper in her ear, 'these feel just like your sister's' and then you try to stay on for eight seconds."

Right: Shoosh up, the tortoise is on the move.

Another day and another trip to north Kent. Always a relaxed audience in this part of the world, hopefully to be followed by a "quick nip" back around the M25 as I have a brewery tour at 6.30 pm and I can feel a Chinese coming on. Just a quick thought, "Two wrongs are only the beginning" which brings me to a follow-up thought – "No-one is listening until you make a mistake."

To the papers and not a good start for animals and their welfare. China is building the world's largest animal cloning factory. It will produce dogs, horses and up to one million cattle per year. Some of the dogs are to be bred as pets, some as police dogs. The horses are to race and the cattle bred for food. I am just waiting for Panorama to announce its investigation into the import of banned Chinese meat and how we will "learn from this...."

I see we have a new breed of Stazi – the Litterstazi. These enforcement officers are contracted by local councils from profit-making agencies with whom, no doubt, they are in partnership with and let's be honest, these days everyone has a partner. I have no qualms with the fining of litter-louts, but do have reservations when the enforcement officers are not directly employed by the council as one's thoughts are immediately directed to targets, which will be the only measure of success and that common sense will automatically go out of the window. In the incident I have just read about a man's bookmark fell out of his book. A lady enforcement officer apprehended the instigator of this heinous act and informed him that he had breached the council's "zero tolerance" litter policy. Despite all protestations a fixed penalty notice was issued, although later, I am glad to say, rescinded as the council, when on viewing evidence from the enforcement officer's body worn camera, concluded that there was insufficient evidence to prove that the chap concerned had deliberately dropped the bookmark. Now this lady enforcement officer should be issued with two options – either agree to be put down for the greater good of society or be trained, as she obviously has potential, to work in border control!

Right! Kent and the brewery beckon. By-eee.

We have missed a day – it's now Friday and I'm home. It was during my journey to Kent that I heard George Osborne shirk our nation's responsibilities by telling all and sundry that tax revenues are likely to be so much better than previously thought that he doesn't have to implement the welfare reforms after all. Isn't that good news for claimants!

From nowhere that any analyst can find convincing proof, guileless George has apparently found £27 billion. When you read the small print, of course, we haven't actually found that sum, it's what is expected to come in over and above that which was originally anticipated, so it's now filed under the heading of complete bollocks. Doesn't it tell you everything you need to know about Mr. Osborne being totally out of touch with the majority of people who still think in terms of fairness and common sense when you realise that at £16 billion the overseas aid budget is higher than that of the Home Office. More money goes to nebulous schemes abroad than on our police and immigration services. When Clueless Dave came into office the overseas aid bill was £8 billion. Over the past few years we have lost 17,000 police officers to the government accountants' knife. We have lost thousands of jobs at our borders' lack of control. Meanwhile, we give the Nigerians £230 million to help raise their school standards, £15 million went to the Columbians in an effort to reduce cattle flatulence, which in turn was to help climate change. For Christ's sake, some of that could be spent at home, surely. They mismanage our money but are never brought to account, merely removed by the whim of the electors at an election and then the baton of plenty passes to the next incumbent.

Still, the main thing is that irrespective of whether it is a diktat from either Dave the Brave or Georgie Porgie, all you know is that our rates will go up again next year, but it's nice to know that the government are always looking out for "hard working people". I know, because I'm one of them.

Of course, he could have been taught economics by young Paddy. Young Paddy bought a donkey from a farmer for £100. The farmer agreed to deliver the donkey the next day. However, the farmer arrived and said, "Sorry, son, but I have some bad news. The donkey has died." Paddy, slightly distressed, replied, "Well, then, just give me my money back." The farmer, shuffling from foot to foot nervously said, "I can't do that, I've already spent it." Paddy said, "Okay, then, just bring me the dead donkey." The farmer looked confused. "What are you going to do with him?" Paddy beamed, "I'm going to raffle him off." The farmer replied, "You can't raffle a dead donkey." Paddy was now very enthusiastic. "Sure, I can, watch me, I just won't tell anybody that he's dead." A month later the farmer met up with Paddy and asked, "Whatever happened to that dead donkey?" Paddy replied, "I raffled him off. I sold 500 tickets at £2 each and made a profit of £898." The farmer looked incredulous. "But didn't anyone complain?" Paddy said, "Only the chap who won, so I gave him back his £2!" Paddy is now doing ever so well at the Royal Bank of Scotland!

I read that it will be Black Friday tomorrow. Well, it's started a day early. The Budget is one thing but Tim Wonnacott leaving "Bargain

Hunt" only made inside reading in the pages of the Daily Mail. I suspect that over the long term his departure will affect me far more than George Osborne's proclamations. The financial cost of his policies may be more but the psychological effect of not knowing who will be presenting the next series is disturbing. I hate change. Mmmm, I think I have just self-diagnosed as having Asperger's or possibly OCD. Could it be ADHD or could I just be normal?

Right, time to celebrate any newly acquired ism with a joke.

This is called Star Trek. The Iranian ambassador to the UN had just finished giving a speech and walked out into the lobby of the Convention Centre where he was introduced to a US marine general. As they talked the Iranian said, "I have just one question about what I have witnessed in America." The general replied, "Well, if there's anything I can do to help." The Iranian whispered, "My son watches this show of yours called 'Star Trek' and in it there are various characters – Captain Kirk, who is Canadian, Chekov who is Russian, Scotty, who is Scottish, Uhura, who is black and Sulu, who is Japanese. But there are no Muslims and my son is very upset and doesn't understand why there aren't any Iranians, Iraqis, Afghans, Egyptians, Palestinians, Saudis, Syrians or Pakistanis in Star Trek?" The general leaned towards the Iranian ambassador and whispered in his ear, "That's because it all takes place in the future...."

I'm just off to the hairdressers which I hate as the lights are not conducive to the thinning process. Ageing, some people call it, though stress I know it to be.

Talks in Newbury Park, East London, this afternoon and Basingstoke this evening take up most of my thinking day, so I'll see you later.

Well, it's nice to see that both reality and common sense have made a return appearance to society, although I suspect only briefly. A high court ruling has meant that the current Education Secretary, Nicky Morgan, was wrong not to force schools to include "non-religious beliefs" in religious studies classes. The judge ruled that Nicky Morgan's failure was an "error in law". I suspect it's a bit like a mother-in-law but never going to provide as much inspiration for the likes of Les Dawson. Anyway, the point was, that Ms or Mrs M should review the curriculum as there was a "duty of care" that information was conveyed in a "pluralistic" manner. Well, they're not wrong. I've commented in previous tomes that I always felt cheated in school during RE when the master discussed religion, Christ, God, Holy Ghost, etc. but not once was the supposition raised that it could all be complete bollocks, which not surprisingly reminds me of a joke. This one combines both aspects of our last topic.

Lie clocks: A man died and went to Heaven. As he stood in front of the Pearly Gates he observed a huge wall of clocks behind him. He asked St. Peter, "So, what are all those clocks?" St. Peter answered, "Those are lie clocks, everyone who has ever been on earth has a lie clock. Every time you lie the hands on the clock move." "Oh," said the man," very interested. He pointed to a particular clock, "Whose clock is that?" "Ah, that's Mother Teresa's," replied St. Peter, "the hands have never moved indicating that she never, ever told a lie." "That's incredible," said the man and pointing along the wall asked, "And whose clock is that one?" St. Peter responded, "Well, that one is Abraham Lincoln's clock. The hands moved twice, telling us that Abraham Lincoln told only two lies in his entire life." The man was now cottoning on. "So where's Tony Blair's clock?" St. Peter looked above them, "We're using that one as a ceiling fan."

Telling, wasn't it?

You know, justice really doesn't live up to its name any longer. It says in the papers that a couple, both aged 86, suffering from dementia but wishing to remain in their own home, had a carer from an agency who befriended and ultimately defrauded them. The carer, one Frankie Yeoman, apparently manipulated them, treated them to cakes until the point was reached where they disclosed their bank pin number to her. She then used their credit cards for her own gain. One of the couple's daughters noticed regular withdrawals from her parents' bank account and the alarm was raised. She, the Yeoman character, obtained £1,750. How could she do that? The couple were unable to stay in their home of 45 years and were then split up by Social Services as they suffered from different forms of illnesses. Sadly, the husband died on the day of the trial, having not seen his wife for over a year. Having destroyed the last years of this couple's life the "Yeoman of the Card" was found guilty of theft and 12 counts of fraud. Naturally, the judge said he would be merciful as she had a 5-year-old daughter. Unbelievable! They should take the child into care. She really should have a better start than with a parent like that. Yeoman received a suspended sentence and then walked free. If I was a family member I would be bloody livid. Yeoman has to complete

300 hours of unpaid work, be under supervision for two years and abide by a 9 pm -5 am curfew for nine months. How much is all this costing the taxpayer to oversee?

Oh, this is good. I see the HSBC is to pander to the "gender patrol" and blank out the names of candidates in order that women are given a better chance of promotion to senior positions. Mmmm, the article doesn't consider that by not declaring the name it also means that you will not be aware if the applicant is British or foreign. Still, I'm sure at some stage the applicant would be able to show his or her face when all interviews, up to and including selection, are not completely cyber-based. You do get the feeling that human involvement in interviewing is nearing the end of its passage and that every aspect of applying, interviewing and ultimate selection will all be done by computer and when it shows that the percentages are not exactly 50% male/female, black/white, then the computer will, no doubt, be accused of bias. Oh, what a prospect to look forward to. Hang on, there's someone at the door. I do wish they wouldn't call when I'm writing!

You know, I recently met a lady representing a charity who asked me if I wanted to contribute to the floods in Pakistan. I said that I'd love to but our garden hose only reaches to the end of the drive!

This reminds me of a member of an audience last week who told me that she was asked to buy a raffle ticket for an Afghan orphan. She said, "Good God, no, with my luck I'd end up winning one of the buggers." We did laugh.

Well, it's Saturday and I have a talk today in Bexhill. As before, not quite Bexhill but Little Common, actually. I'm looking forward to the visit, although this means no brewery tours today. I do, however, have two tomorrow. Yesterday, Friday, was unusual. I've never been issued with an ASBO before. Now, it's not an official ASBO but I've been informed that I am persona non whatever at a local post office. It's not the regular post office I use but one that happened to be convenient on my journey.

I think I mentioned that Budgen's has now become the Co-op and we no longer possess a post office in our urban sprawl, so I usually pop into the one in Frimley Green. I take books for posting, the Asian chappie behind the counter takes the books, me having placed the parcel on the scale beforehand. He affixes the pre-gummed paper label, takes my money and I bugger off. At this particular post office, however, the lady behind the counter, white of hue and given her general lack of humour, demeanour and dress sense, would wager her to be a Liberal Democrat. Anyway, she asked what was within the cardboard packaging as I laid the parcel upon the scales. "Why do you want to know?" I asked. "Because we have to think of staff safety," came the reply. Her attitude and haughtiness were not endearing. "In what way?" I queried. "We have to," she advised vaguely. "It's for security, isn't it?" I suggested. She reiterated that GPO staff, or whatever their current "brand", is now required to be protected. I asked if she was going to open my parcel and see what was within before it was sent. Grimly she said, "No, but I need to know." By now there was a queue forming and I was not going to let this go lightly. "So, I could tell you anything within reason and you would be happy with that, would you?" I asked. She hesitated before answering. "Well, yes." "And that's my point." I continued. "Asking me what's in the package and then not checking but going by my word doesn't seem very safe to me. It proves nothing. It's all about terrorism, isn't it?" By now I could feel she was becoming more than slightly agitated whilst I was beginning to feel a certain futility in the situation. I then came to the point and said, "It's a book, it's not a bomb, look at me, I'm white, middle-class and possess a GU postcode. Do I look like a bloody terrorist?" It was at this point she exclaimed, "That's racist, that is," and called the Asian manager who, after another fifteen minutes of discussion, decided she didn't want to accept my "bomb", sorry book. I left with my head held high and my parcel still under my arm and a queue of tutting customers. Later that morning I travelled via Frimley Green on my way to Waitrose. The Frimley Green Asian chappie took my book, issued the usual receipt, having placed his seal of approval and post paid upon my innocent parcel and I duly buggered off without him ever asking what was in it. What is the point in pursuing a pointless policy at one branch and not at another? Perhaps they expect bombs to be sent from certain hotspots. I don't know! What's that? A cuppa to calm the nerves? All right, but no biccies, I'm on a diet, remember.

So, what's happened of note in the world of, well, the world actually. Apparently we're going to bomb the hell out of Syria, that'll be nice. If they need to practise before going abroad they could always drop a few on Milton Keynes, Telford, Wolverhampton … the north.…

Aha, what were we saying about the scrapping of the tax disc? I see that car tax evasion has increased in the last two years from 210,000 to 560,000 cases. Not an insignificant number. That amounts to nearly one and a half percent of all vehicles on our roads being unlicenced. Interesting to note, of course, that the sum expected to be saved by withdrawing the paper licence was £10 million. The sum now expected to be lost in revenue this year is thought to be £80 million, as opposed to the £35 million before the arse-in-charge of policy persuaded the chief arse-in-charge of implementation of policy to go for gold – or in this case, broke. Still, I expect the government's accountants will deem it to be another rip-roaring savings success.

On reading the smaller print in the Chancellor's budget I note that the Queen is to receive an increase in her Sovereign Grant. Another £2.8 million is to be added to the glittering trough, making a not inconsiderable sum of £42.8 million available. Cut backs never seem to stretch to Buckingham Palace or the others who have so much but always seem to get so much more. What was it about "Animal Farm" that I found so illuminating? Oink, oink!

No-one is more aware than me (bold statement or total bull) that taste is in the eyes of the beholder. Anyone who has visited Waddesden Manor in Buckinghamshire cannot fail to be impressed with the splendour of the buildings. Described as being built by Baron Ferdinand de Rothschild in the French Renaissance style in 1874 it is simply stunning.

So far, so beautiful. The house was bequeathed to the National Trust by his nephew in 1957. The property is still managed, however, by the Rothschild Foundation, chaired by the present Lord Rothschild. He has commissioned a new building on land within the estate. Talk about chalk and cheese. Well, actually, it's more like beauty and the most hideous beast. In the vernacular of Loyd Grossman, "Who would build a house like this?". It's called Flint House and looks like a door wedge, as that is its shape. Go on line and see for yourself. Flint faced and built in a stepped fashion, it gives the impression of being a staircase to nowhere. It is truly awful. Naturally, it has won "House of the Year" by the Royal Institute of British Architects, or RIBA. They described it as "An intriguing and intelligent mixed application of roof tops, terraces and recesses that continue to deliver a stunning piece of liveable, provoking modern architecture". I am sure there are some who will like it. It is modern. It was designed by an architect, or architects in this case, some firm or outfit called Skene Catling de la Pena and this is the rub. The whole design is as pretentious as the architect's name. It's like so many buildings that have been erected in London since the 1960's, totally out of keeping with their surroundings. Again, there will be those who would wish to live in a building like this and it does "provoke" but mainly for me, it's words like "pointless", "hideous" and built by those for those who have more money than design sense or aesthetic appreciation. It is a statement that says, "Look at me and look at how much money I have". Frankly, I wouldn't be seen alive in it!

You may recall the case of the poppy seller, one Olive Cooke, aged 92, who took her own life after being depressed and having sleepless nights. A lot of this depression was brought upon her by the constant requests for donations to charities. Her details were amongst thousands sold from one charity to another. Some sixty-nine charities hounded this poor lady for money. The Fundraising Standards Board has been reporting on the lengths that some of these organisations will go to in order to extract money without menaces but with an awful lot of emotional blackmail and some of their tactics are really not that healthy. People like Miss Cooke are at the extreme end of the spectrum when it comes to taking things to heart, extremely sensitive and vulnerable to others' needs. Not everyone gets depressed by other people's suffering so it's good to know that in the main, we do not take it all to heart like this lady. From my point of view any charity that posts unsolicited envelopes, letters, bags requesting donations through my letterbox, can rest assured that absolutely no notice will be taken of any attempt to extract one penny from me. Poor Miss Cooke received up to 270 begging letters each month. It really isn't right. Charity is big business with chief executives on salaries approaching that received by those heading corporations, local councils and universities, oh, and the Police. There is an awful lot of money swishing around in these funds. I would dearly love to know what the true percentage is of that which gets handed over to the end user. No-one, I suspect, will ever really know. Honesty and charitable money do not seem to be good bedfellows. Temptation will always out, just look at the continuing revelations concerning Kids Co.

Oh, now, this is good news. That bastion of legal support for those naively described as "oppressed, repressed and generally needy", the Court of Human Rights, actively came down on the side of proper people yesterday. France's ban on the wearing of veils was actually upheld by the court. A female by the name of Christiane Ebrahimian, aged 64, a Muslim social worker, was informed in 2000 that her contract at a psychiatric hospital in the Paris suburbs would not be renewed. Not surprisingly, patients had complained about her refusal to remove her veil. At great cost to the public at large she lost her case in the French courts. Not content with that decision she continued her whinging all the way to the European Court of Human Rights in Strasbourg, citing that it "breaches her right to manifest her religion". It might be her religion, but fortunately, at the present time at least, it's not everybody else's. The court has now countered that France's decision did not breach her human rights. It's a very telling judgement, timely and necessary. Thank Christ someone has actually shewn some common sense and more importantly, guts. Not something you associate with courts, high or low, here or abroad – France in particular!

Oh, dear, oh, dear, oh, dear, oh, dear. Here we have an example of why cyclists are getting quite such a bad name. As you know, I have always felt that a goodly number of them are no better than arrogant arses and the following just emphasises what bitter, chip-on-shoulder and generally nasty coves they have turned out to be.

Here we have the case of a cyclist, henceforth referred to as an LCA (lycra-clad arse). Whether the arse was lycra-clad at the time, I know not, but it always helps in my dislike of him. Anyway, said LCA was thrown from his bike when a dog lead became entangled in his wheels. The cyclist's name is Anthony Steele, and he is aged 59. There is a colour picture of the cove, accompanying the article. He is standing, leaning on his two-wheeled steed. White trainers, dark jogging bottoms, bright yellow top and yellow helmet. Now, it could be just my interpretation, but the man looks smug. He has the self-satisfied look of an LCA who has just been paid out £65,000 in compensation. As a result of his encounter with the dog's lead and yes, there was a dog at the end of the extendable lead, his ride along the promenade at Morecombe in Lancashire was prematurely curtailed. The incident left him unconscious. He suffered from a fractured skull, permanent hearing damage and broken ribs. So, his name might be "Steele" but he certainly isn't made of it. Most people would put it down to bad luck and get over it. Not this chap – oh, no, he and his solicitor traipsed around in "wind and rain, combing the promenade for clues" for three years! Can you believe it? Three years! All that traipsing must surely have aggravated his discomfort. He eventually found the culprit, a little old lady in her seventies who had been walking the dog for a friend while the friend was on holiday. The LCA filed a claim at Manchester County Court in order to seek financial help for his rehabilitation and raise awareness of how dangerous retractable leads can be. What a paragon of virtue this man is. Instead of facing a lengthy and costly court case, the pensioner has settled out of court. He may have spent 7 weeks off work, but how all these other injuries took place after falling off his bike is quite extraordinary. At what sort of speed was he cycling, one has to ask? He cites a major, not a minor fracture to the right side of his skull, hearing damage in his right ear and fractures to his clavicle and ribs, as well as cuts and bruises. Oh, yes, and during his 7 week lay-off he required specialist physiotherapy and cognitive rehab. I'm reading on and as I do, a whole orchestra of violins is playing the most eye-watering music in the background. He says, "The experience has left me with permanent hearing loss (so you probably can't hear the violins then), dizziness, headaches, balancing issues and pain in my right shoulder." Well, he's certainly given me a pain in the arse. Still, as he says, "All I wanted out of this was to get the financial support I need for rehabilitation and raise awareness, etc." What a pity he doesn't wish to make aware how dangerous arrogant LCA's can be when they ignore traffic lights, ride the wrong way down a one-way street, ride on the pavements, with no lights on the front or rear of their bike, whilst conversing on their mobile phone.... Need I go on? But then, when you've just won a cool £65,000 as a cyclist I probably wouldn't give a monkey's either and yes, I do feel very sorry for the pensioner. I don't know what dog she had on the lead but she's been bitten financially by a very tenacious terrier.

Alongside this article is a study that has come to the conclusion that men with beards are more like to be sexist and hostile, which is interesting, as I've come to exactly the same conclusion about women with beards!

A very worrying, "oh dear" now. A judge in South Africa has decided to lift a ban on the sale of rhino horn. Two game breeders, John Hume and Johan Kruger, are claiming it is their "constitutional right" to sell rhino horn. The pair of them describe the horn as a renewable resource. I smell "constitutional rights" as a cover for "short-term unsustainable profit". Jason Bell of the International Fund for Animal Welfare described the move as dangerous. He's not wrong. Eighty per cent of the world's population of 20,000 rhino is in South Africa. They need protecting, not poaching. Sadly, so much is sold as body parts to the Chinese – the price of everything....

Right! It's time for my trip to Bexhill – all right, Little Common. Well, at least you were listening. I'll see you later for dinner, maybe.

What a lovely afternoon that was – such hospitable and welcoming people. The return journey was slightly marred when listening to Radio 5 Live as I learned that Charlton had succumbed 3-0 to Ipswich and at home too! So, after two consecutive wins we are back down to earth. Ipswich are quite a free scoring side with a manager in Mick McCarthy who I've always admired. I put him in the same category as Neil Warnock. Honest, outspoken and both will call a spade a bleeding shovel, although not in a racial way, obviously! Christ, you can't say anything these days.

Okay, so as the microwave is counting down and the lamb rogan josh is bubbling beneath its pierced plastic covering, time for a joke or two before Strictly. Who will be in the bottom two tonight? The tension mounts, which is more than you can say for me, what with my diabetes.

What's that? You liked the Irish ones from several pages ago? Okay, let's see what we've got.

Yup, the first one concerns Murphy, a furniture dealer from Dublin.

Murphy, a furniture dealer from Dublin, decided to expand the line of furniture in his store, so he arranged to travel to Paris and see what he could find. After arriving in Paris he visited some manufacturers and selected a line that he thought would sell well back home. To celebrate the new acquisition he spent a little time in a small bistro and had a glass of wine. As he sat enjoying his tipple, he noticed that the area was becoming quite crowded and that the other chair at his table was the only vacant seat in the house. Before long a very beautiful Parisian girl came and asked him something in French. Murphy couldn't understand her so he motioned to the vacant chair and invited her to sit down. He tried speaking to her in English but to no avail. After a couple of minutes he took a napkin and drew a picture of a wine glass and then showed it to her. She nodded so he ordered a glass of wine for her. After sitting together at the table for a while he took another napkin and drew a picture of a plate of food. Again, she nodded. They left the bistro together and found a quiet café that featured a small group of musicians playing romantic music. They ordered dinner, after which he took another napkin and drew a picture of a couple dancing. They danced until the café closed and the band began to pack up for the evening. Back at the table the young lady now took a napkin and drew a picture of a four-poster bed. And to this day, Murphy still has no idea how she guessed he was in the furniture business!

Again?

Three dead bodies turn up in a Dublin mortuary, all with very big smiles on their faces. The coroner calls the police to tell them what has happened. "The first body," he says, "Pierre Dubois, Frenchman, 60, died of heart failure while making love to his 20-year-old mistress. Hence the enormous smile, Inspector," says the coroner. "Second body, Hamish Campbell, a Scotsman, aged 25, won £50,000 on the Lottery, spent it all on whisky – died of alcohol poisoning, hence the smile." "Sad," said the Inspector, "what about the third body?" "Ah," says the coroner, "this is a most unusual case. Paddy Murphy, Irish, 30, struck by lightning." The Inspector looks perplexed. "Why is he smiling, then?" "Oh, he thought he was having his picture taken."

And lastly,

Murphy applied for a fork-lift truck operator post at a famous Irish firm based in Dublin. A Norwegian applied for the same job and since both applicants appeared to have similar qualifications they were asked to take a test and led by the manager to a quiet room with no interruptions. When the results were in, both men had scored 19 out of 20. The manager went to Murphy and said, "Thank you for coming for the interview but we've decided to give the job to the Norwegian." Murphy said, "And why would you be doing that? We both got 19 questions correct. What with this being Ireland and me being Irish, surely I should get the job?" The manager replied, "We have made our decision, not on the correct answers but on the question you got wrong." Murphy said, "And just how would one incorrect answer be better than another?" "Very simple," said the manager, "to question 7 the Norwegian wrote 'I don't know' and you put 'neither do I'."

Right, settle down, settle down. Strictly is about to start.

Strictly has come and Strictly has gone, so let's browse the papers.

I don't know what gets into some people, I really don't. Fairly close to home, Fleet actually, a 16-year-old oik, set fire to a church causing £4 million's worth of damage. All Saints Church is a Grade II listed building. Apparently he sprayed a cross on the wall with deodorant and then set fire to it. At an earlier time he had left a burning bible on the altar. Surprise, surprise, he suffered from a "difficult upbringing", so the court was told. Suffering also from attention deficit, hyperactivity disorder he took cannabis, methadone and consumed alcohol from the age of 15. I think it's fair to say that it is now the church that is suffering, but don't worry, it's society's fault.

Are we learning? The photographs of this year's "Black Friday" bears no comparison to the scenes witnessed only a year ago. The snaps of empty floors, escalators and tills with little activity between 5 am and 9.30 am at shopping centres throughout the country show that there has been a lessening of interest. Last year saw scenes of marauding hordes, hell bent on getting there first, wherever "there" was and I'm not sure many of the sad creatures knew themselves. If it looked cheap then it was a bargain. If it was a bargain they'd want to buy it. No finesse, no dignity and basically no class. They genuinely are the sort of people who should stay in their rented accommodation or affordable housing for much longer periods. There, I feel much better for that!

The aspirations of those with a politically correct bent – and I do find them "bent" – knows know bounds. Kerry McCarthy, at the time of writing, the Labour Party's Environment, Food and Rural Affairs Spokesman, went on the computer and via the pages of something called Social Media invited suggestions for a less sexist word for "fishermen". She commented, "Shouldn't say fishermen, but 'fishers' sounds wrong as a gender neutral alternative". Why, I ask, does one require a gender neutral alternative? You would think that with all the environmental food and rural affairs issues that she could tackle, is a new word for fishermen really that high on the agenda? Well, obviously, because that's what it's about. Gender! I could just call her a fishwife!

The BABC shove political correctness down our collective throats in a manner not dissimilar from ducks being force-fed prior to turning up on a plate of foie gras. You have to have a spoke, a chair – I mean, what's wrong with chairlady, or heaven forfend – actress. Everyone is now an actor. Can someone remind me exactly when that one was changed?

Getting back to "Fisher People" and the like, I note that one of Andy Burnham's former members of staff came up with a suggestion of "fisherfolk". This, however, was rejected as being "too twee". You may remember Miss McCarthy as being the one who suggested that meat be subjected to tobacco-style health warnings. No surprise that the lady is a vegan. I have no problem with veggies, vegans or anyone with a principle but I do wish they would stop trying to make everyone else feel guilty about their own choice of nosh. She pointed out that what we affectionately referred to as "firemen" are now "firefighters". Not to me they're not, they're still firemen. It's the same with signalmen at railway stations. When referred to on the BABC they call them "signallers". The reference to the firefighter caused suggestions of "fishfighters" and "codbotherers", which I did like. Someone suggested, bearing in mind her vegan views, that "fish murderers" would be appropriate and that's what I like about our nation, even when those around us are being absurd and pointless, we can still find a way of laughing at the situation.

Talking of fishing, another waste of our overseas aid I see is that £5 million is going to Bermuda, Jamaica, the Maldives, the Seychelles, St. Lucia, Tobago and Trinidad. This not insignificant sum is to help the countries with their "maritime economies". David Cameron said he wanted to ensure countries "make the most of their natural maritime advantages". The total package of help to the Caribbean is £26 million. It is all so unspecified, there is no substance to this contribution. We're there for disasters, climate change and that good old standby, waste recycling. £26 million? We could have saved a library in Lewisham, a hostel in Halifax or a community hall in Cambridge. Oh, no, not Cambridge – the National Union of Students would be demonstrating, demanding that it be renamed the Mandela Centre. But it's nice to see that at £26 million we can state categorically we are still funding the pirates of the Caribbean.

Right, I'm off to bed now. I'll just check the computer afore I call it a day.

That's interesting, there's one from Orvis informing me of their latest buy two, pay for three offer. Well, it's something like that. And one from a lady called Marion Gibson, which begins, "How are you?" I think we'll just delete her, don't you.

I'm tired now, too tired even for a joke, although maybe a thought

– "we could all take a lesson from the weather, it pays no attention to criticism."

Well, we've skipped Sunday, a day of two brewery tours and Peter Andre's dismissal from Strictly and it's now Monday, the start of the working week. So, let's have a quick perusal as work is heavy this week.

Oh, this is good. There is a 62-year-old man, Roland Frankel, who obviously basked in the glory by being entitled "Villager of the Year". The village in question is Theydon Bois in Essex. I have to say that his CV has everything to bring about a wry smile. Last week at Chelmsford Crown Court he pleaded guilty to two counts of making or downloading indecent photos of children over a ten-year period. He had amassed 18,385 indecent photos and 390 videos. He has been handed a 36-month community order (whatever that is) and put on the Sex Offender Register for five years and banned from contacting any girl under the age of sixteen. Mr. Frankel – and this is where the smile becomes a self-satisfied beam – runs a printing business, has sung in the local church choir (how did I know that already?) and he used to sell candy-floss at the local fete! Oh, joy, all the ingredients of a suspect but wait, it gets better! He is also a former Liberal Democrat councillor. I'm now smugly rubbing my hands with glee. A paedophilic Liberal Democrat. I just had to write that for the sheer satisfaction of seeing the words together, in print! I wonder if he knew Cyril Smith? How about this? Mr. Frankel told the police he looked at photos of naked girls because he was interested in the "body shapes" of children as an "art form". Did he honestly expect the authorities to believe that lily-livered drivel? Well, possibly, I mean, he was an ex-Liberal Democrat Theydon Bois parish councillor. Oh, how the local hero became the local paedophile – ooops – sorry, villain, and all due to his interest in body shapes!

You'd be forgiven for thinking that this next piece was written on the 1st April. It would seem that the Ministry of Justice, or whatever private company is now running the system under contract, is hell-bent on making offenders' current cushy life even cushier. This Christmas, up to 100 prisoners serving life sentences will be allowed out in order to spend a five-day break with their families. Why? They committed a crime, in most cases a fairly heinous crime, why should they be given anything at Christmas other than an early day from breaking rocks in a quarry. Last year 1,387 prisoners, including 93 serving life terms, were allowed home. Of these 300 were convicted of violent crime, 202 for robbery or burglary and 9 for sexual offences. Over 550 were for drug related crimes. The Prisons Minister, one Andrew Selous (shouldn't that be changed to Zealous) naturally defended the decision, describing temporary release as helping prisoners' rehabilitation and encouraging them to take responsibility for their actions and taking control of their lives. Gutless and presumably cheaper.

It gets worse, just under 130 prisoners took driving lessons or tests last year. Among those were 30 convicted of drug offences. Well, at least they'll now be able to travel with more road knowledge between clients in future. I just hope they indicate before pulling over. I cannot abide bad motoring manners, as you know. Interestingly, our "new to the road" offenders include 21 robbers, 4 burglars and a sex offender. I expect he was offered a free sat-nav in order to help him search more quickly for local schools. Fortunately for the taxpayer, who part funds this little jolly, the inmates are "thoroughly risk assessed". No, it doesn't give me a lot of confidence either. What I would love to know is how many of these mollycoddled prisoners have reoffended whilst they have been out and about. The trouble is, you cannot trust any figures offered by a politician these days.

What's that? You're away for a couple of days? Where? Ahhh, the west country to see your old school friend. That's right, north Devon, I remember now. Okay, well, I'm pretty busy myself, as I said, so we'll catch up after the weekend for another round of fun and frolics. By then we'll know the fate of the latest dismissal from Strictly, drive safely now, and no speeding!

Chapter 10

Speaking English Would Be A Start

(Some three days later).

Ah, nice to see you back. Have a nice time? Good, a weekend nattering, long walks with the dogs and pub lunches, can't go wrong!

What's happened while you've been away? Mmmm, I remember commenting on this way back in the last book, or maybe it was the last CD, concerning our country's most popular names. I read that with girls the most popular is Olivia, followed by Sophia, Lily, Emily, Amelia, Chloe, Isobel, Sophie, Ella and finally, Isabella, which is quite a tight-knit group with variations on a very limited theme. With boys it's much more telling. Muhammed and all its derivative spellings is in pole position at No. 1. Shouldn't this fact send shivers down the spines of politicians who fail to see what is happening in and to this country? The rest are the usual suspects, Oliver, Jack, Noah (poor sods) Jacob, Harry, Charlie, Ethan (which always sounds like an American Baptist to me) James and Thomas. I can't imagine too many observers of these statistics betting 30 years ago that Britain's immigration open door policy would have a foreign religious name as the most popular in our country. It will end in tears, it's just a question of time.

The government is feeling a little queasy about the amount of information that is now available to the public under the Freedom of Information Act. The cat can be very embarrassing now that it is out of a politician's bag. Statistics, finances, salaries and expenses can be viewed, perused, commented upon and the perpetrators of public finance indiscretion called to account. Government now says that this freedom is "too costly" to administer. Not a problem, transfer money from overseas aid in order to fund it. Sorry, I'm just hesitating while a flying pig passes overhead.

Luckily, a number of politicians of all party colours are vowing to inflict a defeat on the government, David Davies, being one of the most vociferous among the Conservatives on this matter. Openness and transparency are two of the flagship policies waved in the public's face by any party in power but they are hated by them when it happens. The potential for embarrassment is great. I really do hope the government lose the vote on this one as it would be a real slap in the face for democratic openness and literally freedom of information.

When I harp on about the gradual, but persistent, erosion of our freedom of speech and basic equalities, along comes another example and not surprisingly, it's Muslim related. A Labour Party rally in Oldham, ahead of the by-election for the Oldham West and Royton seat shows the seating layout at this rally. Men to the left, women to the right, that's if you're standing in front of the audience – or the other way round if you're behind them. On suggestion that this was a possible case of segregation, a Muslim Labour MP refuted the idea commenting that it was all down to young women's cultural sensitivities. About a fifth of voters in this constituency are from an ethnic minority, with 17% being Muslim. This segregation is an echo of a previous meeting in Birmingham prior to the last General Election. So, whilst Labour claim to be the party of equality, they will always turn a blind eye to this lack of equality when it involves Muslims, colour or race. All the ingredients for mustering a retreat from the high moral ground they would seek to impose, should the protagonists be white.

On another subject – sorry? Yes, I'll have a cuppa, please. You'll find the Yorkshire teabags on the top shelf of the larder (I keep them separately from the Red Label which are given to visitors from outside the county). Where was I? Oh, yes, why do actors and actresses feel the need to use expletives and think those listening will be happy or comfortable with their foul-mouth outbursts. The latest in a lengthening line of miscreants is Helen Mirren, who frankly, behaves nothing like a dame. A fine actress, revered by her peers and audiences alike, so why does she feel the necessity to use four letter words? I mean, she's seventy for Christ's sake, she should know better. Having read the article about her it appears that she has been effiing and blinding for years and was told not to use expletives at the 2007 Bafta's, as it was going out live. It didn't stop her. Perhaps she is just arrogant or basically not a very nice person. Put it this way, she won't be joining us for afternoon tea, will she.

If ever we need to curtail the indiscriminate acceptance of everyone from anywhere coming to these shores, the following acts as another example of our weak and yellow-belly response to EU rules – and it does! In short, four men burst into a home in Wimbledon where a father was playing a board game with his wife and daughter. He was "beaten to a pulp". He suffered a broken jaw and a fractured eye socket amongst many other injuries. Having a photograph accompanying the article depicts him still sporting extreme bruising, even though he smiles whilst hugging two of his three daughters. One of the four aggressors was more lenient and the victim has since visited him in prison, along with his wife and the daughter who happened to be in the home at the time of the attack. What a show of forgiveness. I couldn't do it. His aggressor has been given 19 years but the victim felt his aggressor to be worth saving, so to speak. All but one of the gang had long criminal records, with thirty-two convictions between them. The one visited in prison had eleven convictions, including four cases of burglary whilst in his home country of Poland. I feel that Wimbledon Man has more faith than I do. The irony in all this is that the victim was not the one intended for the acts of violence. They had actually targeted the wrong house. Another member of the gang received 19 years and the remaining two, 13. All are Polish, all are thugs and we've allowed them into our country to continue their nefarious ways and when caught, we'll be supporting them with our food, bedding, re-education, rehabilitation, welfare, health and social support. Bread, water and never-ending misery would be my recipe, whilst a treadmill would be my suggestion regarding 24 hour exercise, and that's on the basis that we couldn't send the buggers back!

Talking of arses of a non-British nature, I read that a young lady, aged 21, was run down and killed in Birmingham last year. She and her friend were waiting at a bus stop when two Asians decided to race each other in their respective wheels of death. The scene was described by a witness as being akin to a scene from the film "The Fast and the Furious". The killer, one Sukvinder Mannan, aged 33, so old enough to know better, was at the wheel of a Mitsubishi car whilst his opponent, one Inderjit Singh, aged 31, drove a BMW M3 sports car. As the arrogant pair sparred with each other at speeds of up to 100 mph in a 30 mph area, the Mannan hit Rebecca McMannis and Harriet Barnsley, also 21. Mannan admitted causing death by dangerous driving, causing serious injury by dangerous driving and failing to provide a blood sample following the crash. He was sentenced to 8 years, with Singh being jailed for 1. The sentences are totally inadequate. For me, Mannan should never be allowed onto the streets of our country again. The other lady, Miss Barnsley, was left in a coma for three months and has undergone over 50 operations. Why should these two gutless, thoughtless specimens of something not yet approaching humanity be given second chances? They showed scant respect to anyone else on the road – or pavement – that day. What are the chances of their reforming their ways? Personally, I would never give them the opportunity to do so.

Thanks, by the way, that cup of tea went down a treat.

I see that in an everyday story of gun-toting folk, a masked gang has shot dead fourteen people at a disabled centre in San Bernadino, California. Still, it is the American way. Strange principles with guns.

Okay, time for a little light-hearted interlude – or in other words, a joke or two.

A woman in a supermarket is following a grandfather and his badly behaved grandson around the isles. He has his hands full with the child screaming for sweets, and everything else that his eyes rest upon. The grandfather says in a controlled manner, "Easy, William, we won't be long." Another outburst and she hears the grandfather calmly stating, "It's okay, William, just a few more minutes and we'll be out of here." At the checkout the little horror starts throwing items out of the shopping trolley. The grandfather again says in a controlled voice, "William, try not to get upset, we'll be home in five minutes. There, there, William." Very impressed the woman goes outside to where the grandfather is loading his groceries and the boy into the car. She taps him on the shoulder and says, "It's none of my business but you were amazing back there. I don't know how you did it. The whole time you kept your composure and no matter how loud and disruptive he got, you just calmly kept saying things that made him feel it was okay. William is very lucky to have you as his grandfather." "Well, thank you," replies the man, "that's very kind of you but I'm William, this little bastard's name is Kevin."

JOKE NO 2 – ARE YOU INSURED FOR SEX?

Make sure you get the correct insurance for the sex you are having. Please find below the company that most caters for your taste.

Sex with your wife – Legal & General

Sex on the telephone – Direct Line

Sex with your partner – Standard Life

Sex with someone different – Go Compare

Sex with a lady of generous proportions – Morethan

Sex on the back seat of a car – Sheila's Wheels

Sex with a posh bird – Privileged

Sex with a prostitute – Commercial Union

Sex with your maid – Employers' Liability

Sex with an OAP – Saga

Sex resulting in pregnancy – General Accident

And finally

Sex with a transvestite – Confused.com

What's that? You like statistics. Okay. The Civil Aviation Authority disclosed the following airport screening results for December last year. Statistics on the full body screening are as follows:

Terrorists discovered – nil. Transvestites – 133. Hernias – 1485. Haemorrhoid cases – 3172. Enlarged prostates – 8249. Breast implants – 59350. Natural blondes – 3. It was also discovered that 650 politicians had no balls. You might like to know that this was an increase from 648 the previous December!

Okay, we've got three minutes so one more.

Fred and Fiona were making passionate love in Fred's transit van when suddenly Fiona, being a bit on the kinky side, yells out, "Come on, Fat Boy, whip me, whip me." Fred, not wanting to pass up this unique opportunity, sadly did not have any whips to hand but in a flash of inspiration opened the window, snapped the antenna off the van and proceeded to whip Fiona until they both collapsed in masochistic ecstasy. About a week later Fiona noticed that the marks left by the whipping session were not healing but instead were starting to fester, so off she goes to the doctor. The doctor, taking one look at the wounds, asks, "Did you get these marks having sex?" Fiona, a little too embarrassed that she'd even slept with Fred, let alone allowed him to indulge in her own kinky desires, eventually admitted, "Yes, I did." Nodding his head knowingly the doctor explained (wait for it) "I thought so because in all my years as a doctor you've got the worst case of Van Aerial disease I've ever seen!"

Right! Onward and maybe not upward, but onward anyway. Oh, this is interesting. I read that researchers have found that the increasing numbers of overseas nurses are aligned to the significant increase in the number of complaints by patients. Frankly, it didn't require a research study to confirm what everyone knows and feels but it's also good to know you're not wrong. The study states that for every 10% increase in the number of overseas nurses in a hospital, there is a 12% drop in patients' satisfaction levels. It transpires that patients consider that they are not always respected by those allegedly caring for them and that they lack confidence in their skills and are therefore more likely to complain. There's a surprise. The report cites nurses' language difficulties, differences in medical training and a lack of cultural awareness. Did I say there's a surprise? There are now 98,200 registered overseas nurses at work here – that's 1 in 7 of the workforce. There are those who will raise their hands in frustration and shout, "But where would we be without them?" I tell you where we'd be, we'd be training our own. We could, but it's all about cost and that's the last thing this country wants to do, spend money on long-term benefits. Wherever there is a seemingly cheaper option, this country will go for it. Never forget, we know the price of everything and the value of nothing. Don't tell me that 98,200 ladies and gents couldn't be found among the 1.8 million unemployed who, with a bit of incentive and lack of benefit, might find a career away from that lifetime work-shy culture of benefit or bust to be slightly more rewarding.

Aaah, how refreshing to see that many students are now showing a leaning towards hating everybody, irrespective of colour, race or gender. The overriding focal point is that their hatred is towards anyone who holds a view differing from their own. They are all the same and boringly so. As we know from previous examples, they demand freedom of speech and action for themselves, with tacit silence at best and forced silence at worst for all others. This time the incident involves an Iranian human rights activist and her attempt to give a talk at London's Goldsmiths College. The lady concerned, Maryan Namazie, is a former Muslim who had to flee Iran and was speaking as an atheist. Certain Muslim students were not happy about this. Within Goldsmiths College there is an Islamic Society (Isoc) – where isn't there one! Anyway, her talk to The Atheist Secularist and Humanist Society was not one these hard-lined single religion humourless saps were going to allow without a modicum of bully-boy tactics. Miss Namazie, aged 49, received death threats on Twatter, one of them charmingly advising her to "talk about Islam again and

I'll have your f......g head chopped off". So, nothing like a well-reasoned argument then. During her speech the Islamists concerned apparently banged on the door of the hall before entering. One turned off the projector that the lady was using and then repeatedly walked up and down in front of her. The audience was scared and very quiet apparently. This feudal group has a president who wrote to the talk's hosts saying, "We feel her presence will be a violation to our safe space. All she will do is incite hatred and bigotry". Isn't that strange, because to most people their philosophy could easily be considered slightly skewed, worryingly hypocritical and a violation of all of our spaces, safe or public, but still we stand by and do nothing. Trust me, it will end in tears.

Just a small statistic, but just to remind you that it was announced today that the UK aid budget to India will increase by £11 million to £279 million a year. Another library, another community hall....

And the good news? Yes, there is some. Alan Yentob resigned as a BBC executive yesterday. The BABC will save the grand sum of £183,000. This has all come about due to his links with that dubious charity Kids Company. Sadly, with good news there generally follows bad and in this case the man I wouldn't trust with a new car, let alone a second hand motor, will still be paid £150,000 per annum as editor and presenter of an arts programme. Damn!

Here we have another case of "If you are well known you are more than likely to get off with it". Yaya Toure, who plays football for Manchester City, was caught on camera driving his Porsche at 101 mph on the northbound carriageway of the M6. He received 6 points on his licence and was fined £1,665, plus costs of £85, a victim surcharge of £120 and criminal court charges of £150. It's small beer when your salary is £220,000 a week. Now, that is criminal. His mitigating circumstances that helped his case so that he wasn't banned was that he mistook the miles for kilometres – yawn, yawn, yawn! If you don't know our laws and our measurements, then don't drive in our country. You could always bugger off back to the continent and play for Paris St Germain.

According to an advert in today's Daily Mail it's going to be a "magical Christmas at Morrison's". That's nice for it.

There are two pictures of life jackets abandoned on the Island of Lesbos by migrants having successfully crossed the seas to obtain a new life at our joint European expense. They've just left them on the beaches. No attempt to dispose of them responsibly, no thought about the possible danger to sea life or even a hint at recycling, no indication that anybody has asked, "Can you tell me where we are to dispose of these?" No, bugger all, just left them for someone else to remove. Doesn't say much for their lack of social skills when they reach Rochdale or Rotherham, does it.

Today's papers also give the results of the Oldham West and Royton by-election. Labour obtained 17,209 votes, or 62.1% of the vote. UKIP, a very disappointing 6,487, or 23.4% of the vote. The Tories, meanwhile, slipped to just 9.4%, with 2,596 votes. The mealy-mouthed, limp-wristed coves, or Liberal Democrats as they are officially known, received 3.7%, or 1,024 votes. Tell me, how on earth could you find 1,024 Lib-Dems in one constituency. They must have bussed them in for weeks beforehand so that they could register for a vote. Unbelievable! Just to complete the list of candidates, the Greens took 0.9%, or 249 votes, whilst the Monster Raving Looney Party, whose candidate stood under the name of Sir Oink-a-lot garnered a not unreasonable 141 votes, or half a percent. Twenty per cent of the constituents are Asian so where were all the white voters with only a 40% turnout. Whilst the Labour candidate was white, very few Asians will vote for UKIP so the indigenous population need to wake up to the situation staring us all in the face and make the effort before our society has changed forever.

Right, well, as we've been discussing the world and its left-wing partner, Strictly's results have been announced and this time it is the turn of Helen George to depart the glitter-strewn set and return to her role in "Call the Midwife" which, by the way I've never seen. Oh, you have ... well, that's nice for you. And, by the way, Charlton lost 3-2 to Brighton & Hove Albion last night. It looks like being a very hard winter at The Valley. Still, we're now owned by a foreigner – and Belgium is very foreign. I don't see a lot of passion around the ground notwithstanding the passion from our loyal fans who seem lost as to what to do for the best. As I've pleaded before, surely there's a local boy made good who can ride to the rescue – someone – anyone – hello!

It's been a long day and I'm off to bed, so a joke or three before I go.

A man had just boarded the aircraft and settled into his seat next to the window when another man sat down in the aisle seat and put his black Labrador on the middle seat next to the man. The first man looked very quizzically at the dog and asked the owner why the dog was allowed on the plane. The second man explained that he was from the Police Drugs Enforcement Agency and that the dog was a "sniffing dog" and for that reason his name was "Sniffer" and in his experience was the best he'd ever seen. "I'll show you once we get airborne. I'll put him to work." The plane took off and once it had levelled out, the policeman said, "Watch this." He told Sniffer to "search." Sniffer jumped down, walked along the aisle and finally sat very purposefully next to a woman for several seconds. Sniffer then returned to his seat and put one paw on the policeman's arm. The policeman said, "Good boy," turned to the man by the window and said, "that woman is in possession of marijuana. I'll make a note of her seat number and the authorities will apprehend her when we land." "That's amazing," replied the first man. Once again, the policeman dispatched Sniffer to search the aisles. The lab sniffed about, sat alongside a man for a few seconds, returned to its seat and this time placed two paws on the agent's arm. The policeman whispered, "Two paws means that the man is carrying cocaine, so once again I will note his seat number and give it to the police and he'll be arrested on arrival." "I'm finding this very exciting," said the man by the window. Once more Sniffer was dispatched, walked up and down the aisles, sat for a moment, raced back to the agent, jumped onto the middle seat and emptied his bowels all over the place. The man by the window was quite disgusted by its actions and couldn't figure out how such a well-trained dog could behave in such a manner. "What's going on?" he asked the policeman. The policeman replied nervously, "It's not good news, he only does that when found a bomb!!"

Next! A Yorkshire rugby league player is drinking in a local bar when he gets a call on his mobile phone. He hangs up, grins from ear to ear and orders a round of drinks for everyone in the bar, announcing that his wife has just given birth to a typical Yorkshire baby boy, weighing in at 25 pounds. No-one can believe that any newborn baby can weigh in at 25 pounds. The rugby player just shrugs his shoulders and replies, "Think you'll find that's about average in Yorkshire, like I say, my boy's a typical Yorkshire baby and is going to make a grand rugby league player." Congratulations showered him from all around. There were many exclamations of "Wow" and "Hey-oop" with one woman actually fainting due to sympathy pains.

Two weeks later the father returns to the bar, the barman says, "I remember you, you're the father of that typical Yorkshire baby that weighed in at 25 pounds? Everyone's been making bets about how big he would be in two weeks, so tell me, how much does he weigh now?" The proud father looks around at all assembled. "Twenty pounds." The barman is puzzled. Others looked concerned and not a little suspicious. "I don't get it," said the barman, "he weighed 25 pounds the day he was born." The Yorkshireman takes a few gulps of his Tetley's Best Bitter, wipes his lips on his shirt sleeve, turns round towards the crowd and proudly announces, "Aye, well, we've just had him circumcised."

One more for the road? Anna lost her husband almost four years ago, since when her daughter was constantly calling her and urging her to get back into the world. Finally, Anna said she would go out but she didn't know anyone. Her daughter immediately replied, "Don't worry, mum, I have someone for you to meet." Well, it was an immediate hit, they took to one another like ducks to a village pond and after dating for six weeks he asked her to join him for a weekend in the country. Their first night there, she undressed as he did and there she stood nude except for a pair of black lacy panties. He was in his birthday suit. Looking over her he asked, "Why the black panties?" She replied, "My breasts you can fondle, my body is yours to explore but down there I am still in mourning." He knew he wasn't going to get lucky that night and the following night followed the same pattern. She stood there wearing her black panties and he was in his birthday suit again but this time he was wearing a black condom. She looked at him and asked, "And what's with the black condom?" He replied, "I'm hoping you'll accept my deepest condolences."

The following is a perfect example of why we need a new political party in power who will put our country first, one who thinks outside of the Westminster bubble and sees the real world for what it is. That calm, erudite but pointless Jeremy Hunt has just arrived at the conclusion that foreigners do not pay enough for medical services. This is a conclusion that all proper people have been aware of for years. Foreigners are obliged to pay for all non-urgent treatments but apparently we are not overly good at collecting their payments. Is it me, or us, but surely if the treatment is non-urgent and therefore a planned procedure, shouldn't a system be in place whereby we charge at that point before the operation or whatever treatment required is actually administered? Under new proposals every time a foreign Johnny, or Jenny, calls an ambulance they will be required to pay for the service. Quite right, too. It just seems so blatantly obvious so why does it take this long for fair play to take place. For Johnny Foreigner read "anyone outside of the EU". As ever, there are caveats, beneficial to them and detrimental to us. Any non-EU citizen who is resident within our shores will be exempt from payment, as are those who require emergency care. He is hoping to save some £500 million per year. This could have been saved years ago. I'd tell those responsible for collection to treat Johnny Foreigner as traffic wardens and councils treat British motorists, ie dealt with immediately, without compassion, mitigating circumstances or bribery – which as we know, is a very foreign way of settling any account.

If you think for one second I am exaggerating about the drive (excuse the pun) the determination and sheer bloody-mindedness of all those involved in traffic penalties, it hasn't gone unnoticed that this year was a record for council fees and fines. Seven hundred million pounds! Not a bad little earner, is it. That's £33 million up on last year. Westminster Council brought in £46.4 million in parking fines that equates to £126,000 per day. Chelsea & Kensington were in second place with £33 million and Camden, third, swelling their coffers by £24.5 million. Outside of London Brighton topped the provincials with £18.6 million. At least you know the places to avoid.

Hmmm, now this is interesting. Apparently, there are those out there in the real world who consider fines to be used just to increase councils' incomes. You know, pay for those who have flashy titles but contribute the square root of bugger-all to council services. The local government association's environment spokesman, one Peter Box, which is ironical really, as I once had a hedge named after him – anyway, PB, as I think we can call him, said the income from fines is spent on running parking services and any surplus is only spent on essential transport projects. Really? I can think of many hundreds of potholes and cracks that need repairing. Still, I'm sure he knows best....

It's going to be another busy week with talks in Fleet, Bagshot, Chelmsford, St. Alban's and Wigmore in Kent, followed by a tour of the brewery on Wednesday evening, so I'll probably see you then. What's that? What am I doing on Thursday and Friday? Well, as you ask, it's Leyton Cross in Kent on Thursday, followed by a visit to Tring in Herts on Friday, which in turn is followed by another brewery tour in the evening. I have tours on Saturday and Sunday. Look, wouldn't it be better if I just handed over the diary to you, then you wouldn't have to keep asking.

I had occasion to travel to Waterloo Station by train recently, the graffiti on the approach to London is appalling. This is where Sharia Law should be introduced with the little buggers' hands being cut off. They certainly wouldn't be able to deface property – private or public – again! The number of people sleeping in underground stations is staggering and interestingly, the number uttering "Please" with foreign accents gives an indication as to their lack of origin. I have no doubt many are serial scroungers. I know there will be those out there reading and thinking, "It's all right for you, pal, sitting in a warm house (with a porch), pontificating over those less fortunate" etc, etc. Let me say that I have absolutely no sympathy whatsoever for those blocking doorways and thoroughfares. They look awful, they give a dreadful impression of our society and frankly, if it wasn't for benefits, handouts, soup kitchens, care-workers, core workers, the church, the do-gooders … these drains on society would actually be contributing by working for a living. The will to survive is in the genes but the will to survive for them is in the pockets of somebody else's jeans. They drink, smoke, inject drugs, inhale drugs and all made possible because of those who continue to support them and their dog. I wouldn't be surprised if an intravenous drug-drip wasn't available through some taxpayer-funded agency. Not with a penny from me, oh no! 'Save a donkey, not a down-and-out." I quite like that. Anyone out there looking to buy a slogan? I say, … hello….

Talking about Sharia Law, as we nearly were, I see that a 91-year-old grandmother was walking home after collecting her pension when a youngster approached her with a sob story. Sadly, the lady stopped to listen. In a voice quoted in the newspaper article as being a "little voice" the boy said, "Excuse me, madam, I am very worried, can you help me?" Frankly, if I had been approached by a youngster speaking like that, I would have been very suspicious. For a start I would think he was suffering from Aspergers. He went on to tell the lady, "My father has shut me out of the home and I want to get back to my mother who lives in Carlton." (I understand it's in Nottinghamshire, which is unfortunate in itself). Actually, just saying the north would have sufficed and at the same time, aroused suspicion. The very nice lady thought he looked presentable and nicely spoken so she extracted her purse at which point the little sod took off with it. This all happened at 11.30 am last Thursday. Good fortune played its hand as Honor Avis, the lady concerned, had secreted her £150 pension within her handbag and the little love, all right, little shit, escaped with £30. Her description was of a young boy aged between 10 and 13. It's not known if he was black, swarthy or white. It would be nice to know as it all affects ones level of expectancy.

As with all the information I extract from newspapers, I physically cut out each article for evidence should anyone wish to take issue with anything we've discussed here. So, as I cut out a photograph of Helen Mirren, let me tell you that it will be laid arrogant face down. What is wrong with the woman? Why does she feel the need to behave so badly? She may be a dame but I suspect she earned that title for her acting performances and never for her pantomime performances when in mufti. As previously commented upon, she certainly didn't get the gong for dignity. She is a great actress, a veritable success, an icon to many and probably every other soubriquet that can be bestowed upon her, but here she is in the photo sticking out her fairly long tongue whilst raising two fingers, topped by dark red painted nails, displaying all the finesse of a drunken skunk. She has the face that says, "Sod you, I am who I am…." Yes, luckily, I suspect there is very little chance of us meeting so it's good news for me and it's smug mug down for her.

It was reassuring to read Richard Littlejohn berating the BBC for its Euro stance on millimetres of rain, kilometres and Centigrade when discussing depths, distances and temperatures. I will always measure in Imperial, as do many of us and as Mr. L says, miles and yards are still the official measurements on roads so why sell us short. Because they can, I suppose. I will still swelter at 80 in the shade, 25 degrees in foreign means absolutely nothing to me. Good on you, sir.

That Donald Trump, he does make you laugh. I've never been impressed as to what he has done in Scotland with his land grabbing, his lack of style and his arrogance but I will laugh my socks off, that's black ones which match suits and dark trousers, obviously, if he is elected as President. Currently there are other nominees in the frame but as their voting system grinds to its conclusions, it will be very interesting to see an America led by this rather brash chap who is not a politician but a business man used to getting his own way. Of course, he will have to receive the nomination to represent his party and then take on most probably Hilary Clinton. Will he win? I'm not sure but his involvement is certainly brightening up what would otherwise be a bland series of primaries, with frankly very uninspiring and predictable candidates. If he does become Mr. O's successor I feel confident in sitting back contentedly and reflecting that America and he, on balance, probably deserve each other. He is on the front cover of today's paper after his comments that parts of the UK are so full of Islamic extremists that the police fear for their lives. He has also stated that the USA should close their borders to all Muslim migrants. Now, that's an interesting proposition! Still, one's concentration on this subject was averted by the photograph to the right of the article on the front page of the Daily Mail. The Duchess of Cambridge is pictured side profile, wearing Princess Diana's tiara. And I have to say, what a lovely shaped nose she has. It really is as perfect as you can get and again, for those who know me, I am a nose person. They matter a lot. If the nose isn't right, then the rest can never be! I know, I know but I'm sure there's an "ism" for it.

A fund has been set up to raise money for those affected by the floods in Lancashire and Cumbria. I wonder how many donations will arrive from Pakistan, India, Nepal, Nigeria … I really could go on, no, I really could!

Here we go again – I read that the Football Association is hoping to stop newspapers from publishing match results for under-eleven teams as losing could be a disincentive for kiddiwops. It considers that reports should be more "child centred and less results orientated". You just know that the perpetrators of this action will be voting Liberal Democrat. One succeeds in life, one fails in life, it's how you handle both ends of the emotions and scale that is important. You cannot prepare children for life, which is a very competitive world, without experiencing elation and despair. Talk about mollycoddling. As ever, it will end in tears before bedtime.

As you know, I'm not the country's greatest supporter of teachers or the industry as a "hole" but I'm nothing, if not fair-ish. I read that a teacher in south Wales – and by the way, that's the original one in Wales, as opposed to the "new" one in Australia – was accused of cuffing an unruly pupil around the head with a book. Regina Hungerford (lovely name!) aged 54, has won her appeal and is free to continue teaching her classes at Merthyr Tydfil College. To be honest, I would have thought Merthyr Tydfil would welcome any teacher it could find, as I commented earlier it really is frankly, a ghastly place. The "unruly pupil", one Shane Jenkins, accused Mrs. Hungerford of hitting him on the side of the face with a hard-covered book. Mrs. H says she slammed the book down on the desk in frustration and two witnesses agreed that the book was an A5 spiral notebook. Not quite the hard-covered book one would be led to believe. The consequences of her failure at appeal would have meant loss of her job and her ability to lead the local Guides. The ramifications of these yobs getting heard and believed are enormous for others. Bear in mind, Mrs. H only lost her rag because the ill-mannered little tick refused, despite many requests, to turn off his music video he was watching and listening to in class. What total disrespect. She did throw his phone out of the window, but little seems to have been made of this. After her successful appeal against conviction, which the yob failed to attend in person, preferring to give evidence by video link (probably felt more secure in front of a TV screen) it was revealed that in a separate incident he is currently charged with sexual assault and intimidation of a witness. Sounds like a nice boy. There is a colour photo of Jenkins sporting a yellow and blue top and blue baseball cap. That alone would warrant three years' imprisonment in my book! Let us hope he grows up to be less arse-like. One can but hope.

I remember a teacher who suffered from being cross-eyed. Some commented that she had very wayward pupils!

Not that he needed to nail his red colours to the mast but Jeremy Corbyn is not making it easy on himself and is currently playing straight into the hands of the Tories. The man actually wrote a letter to be used by a lawyer in order to support a fraudster from going to jail over Christmas. The fraudster is named Mohamed Dahir, so not one of us. He is accused of funding IS. For Allah's sake, Jeremy Corbyn wants to make sure he's home (wherever that is) for Christmas. It fairs beggers belief. "Can he have bail, please?" I'd give him gruel and then only when accompanied by a confession. It's still a funny world.

Okay, let's take a break for a cuppa and a nut-based gooey bar which includes berries and well, more berries, I think. Healthy-ish eating! Probably better than custard creams or chocolate hobnobs

– although just the one bar usually, you understand. The radio is on in the background and I've just caught the sound of someone saying they have been "upskilling" themselves. Do they mean learning or training? Upskilling their English, as opposed to American, might be a start. Really!

I've taken this opportunity to look at the emails. One book order, one confirmation of a talk and the following, which will shortly be deleted. There's one here headed "Your bonus – claim your free giveaways every day." Can't think that I will. It all seems innocent enough, of course, until you read the next wording which adds, "This message contains graphic images…". Mmmm, something called "Congalotto" is imploring me "not to miss the chance." I think I will. Michelle McManus has a proposal, if only I would email her. Can't think I will do this either. I can receive "life cover for less AND protect my family for 17p a day." I do take issue with the assumption that my family's worth that much. Joke, honest. Pauline is asking, "How's it going?" I suppose she could be referring to the now half-eaten muesli bar. The last offering, before deletion, is advising me not to take a cruise but to hire a chartered yacht. Can't see that one coming off.

The arrogance and greed of the … words fail me, so read on. The killer of Fusilier Lee Rigby is currently suing for compensation. This human flotsam is claiming that he should receive financial reimbursement for losing two teeth during an altercation. Officers were escorting him from his prison cell when he lashed out at the five warders. He wants £20,000 of our money – bastard! The good news is that he's been refused Legal Aid. A recent change in the law prevents him from using public funds. The bad news is that he is privately seeking restitution. The really sad aspect of this case is that there is a solicitor in this country who is prepared to lower himself and in my very humble opinion divorce himself from dignity by taking up this lack of case. The solicitor concerned is Julian Coningham of Coningham Solicitors and are located in London. Not surprisingly, the Coningham character has refused a request for an interview with the Daily Mail. How could he, or anyone in his "profession", act on behalf on such a vile, cowardly waste of space? I'm just amazed as to how restrained our prison officers were. If it were down to me, the perpetrators of the murder of Lee Rigby would have been hung at a public gathering. There would be no mercy for either Michael Adebolajo or his accomplice, Michael Adebowale. I wish the pair of them all the bad luck in the world. You know, pain, suffering, pestilence, a day in Crewe. I'm not won to forgive easily you know....

Right! Time to cleanse the air from the smell of killers and profit, never a savoury mix, so a joke or three.

I was in a pet shop when I noticed a Muslim girl with a most amazingly coloured parrot perched on her shoulder. "Where did you get that from?" I asked. "Germany, there's bloody thousands of them," replied the parrot.

Next! A devout Arab Muslim entered a black cab in London. He curtly asked the cabbie to turn off the radio because as decreed by his religious teaching he must not listen to music because at the time of the Prophet there was no music and this is western music, which is the music of the infidel. The cab driver politely switched off the radio, stopped the cab and opened the door. The Arab Muslim asked, "What are you doing?" The cabbie replied, "In the time of the Prophet there were no taxis, so sod off and wait for a camel."

And finally – I forgot to tell you but a Muslim man in a local shop was bragging that he had the Koran on DVD. Being interested, I asked if he could burn me a copy and that's when it all kicked off.

Aaah, feeling so much better now.

Just to add to the comments earlier regarding Donald Trump and his views about Muslim Britain, the BBC has been very vocal in its news of the online petition to stop him from visiting Britain. Again, very dangerous. I come back to the principle that the best way to counter an opposing argument or view is to come up with a better one, not stop the alternative being heard. Nearly half a million signatures have been added to the list of those stating their desire to see Donald Trump barred from these shores. To be fair, at least he speaks a form of English. What the BABC didn't bother to tell us was that nearly half a million signatures to "stop all immigration and close UK borders until ISIS is defeated" was also an online petition. No, that little nugget of news was sorely lacking.

Another record has been broken, no, not in the world of sport so I won't be mentioning Charlton, but in the potentially more competitive 90,000 GCSE and A Level results that have been "changed on appeal". Of that figure 99% were given a higher mark. Ofqual, the exam's regulator, stated that "Teacher anxiety" has fuelled a 27% increase in grade queries in comparison with a year earlier. They appear to be just as precious as the pupils who can't cope with failure. My advice to both is "work harder?" There, simple.

The Rotherham child sex trials are continuing. Three Asian brothers, their uncle and two white women are on trial. Leaving aside the racial aspect that no Lib-Dem wishes to acknowledge or discuss, the aspect about the case that sickens me most is the lack of support these girls received from the homes that should have been there to protect them. The apparent ring-leader, a drugs dealer called Arshid Basharat, would blatantly pick up under-age girls from their care homes. According to one victim, he checked that it was "all right with a member of staff to bring them back before 11 pm that night". What sort of carer allows vulnerable girls to just go off in someone else's car – be they Asian, black, white, mixed or swarthy? It matters not. What sort of people is the care system attracting? Who employs these people? Who employs the employers? The profession, or lack of it, seems woeful in its ability to show the slightest flicker of common sense or to "read" the obvious warnings. These girls are vulnerable, without close family and under-age. It appears that despite some of these girls returning "bloodied" the situation was never considered worthy of comment or investigation. To add insult to assault, one of the girls, aged 14, was allegedly told by the accused to perform a certain sexual act because "Asian women don't do it as it's against their religion". Interesting that, because whatever the sexual act is, or was, children shouldn't be involved as they are under-age! It appears that religion has precedence over law, and rape over consent. If down to me, they'd be castrated and forcibly removed from these islands and no, I wouldn't care if they had been born here to first, second or umpteenth generation incomers. They would be deported to their place of origin. As for the two white women, they obviously see money as being more important than a child's wellbeing, so a sentence of 20 years each I think would be appropriate and a course whereby they learn maternal instincts wouldn't go amiss either, would it.

Oh, I like this. A police inspector named Zoe Hallam, that's Zoe Hallam, aged 48, attempted to retire on medical grounds in order to secure an enhanced pension. She was apparently injured in a car crash. She claimed that injuries suffered by her in 2011 left her unable to drive for more than 15 minutes and needed a stick to walk. Fifteen minutes, huh! I bet that's a bit of a bugger if stuck in traffic. What would she do if that happened? Ask a passer-by to drive her home? Her bosses became suspicious of her intentions when she appeared disinterested in returning to work but overly interested in her insurance policy. They ordered a "medical surveillance". Oh, joy, Zoe Hallam was observed driving her motor-home for several hours at a time through France and Jersey during two family holidays. Swimming in the sea, cycling, rowing and sailing a dinghy were all activities witnessed by the surveillance officer. She didn't see him/ her or it coming, did she, which makes you wonder just how good she was at her job. "He's behind you!". She has now been sacked after a 5-day hearing found her guilty of gross misconduct. Twenty-five years she served in the police force – what a way to end a career. The article doesn't state if this decision affects her pension but I obviously hope it does.

Donald Trump is providing the press with an awful lot of material they could only have dreamt of prior to the American primaries. He claims that more Muslims join IS than the British Army. Thinking about that for not more than a nanosecond, he's probably not wrong. It's all a question of percentages and figures that can be massaged.

Right! Cuppa. Fair enough, my turn to put on the kettle. While we're waiting for it to boil, who do you think will leave the "Strictly journey" tonight? I guess it will be between the remaining dancers. Christ, even I'm hedging my bets, or lack of them but at this stage it could be anyone's guess. The tension mounts. Whilst thinking of Strictly my mind turned to the Radio Times. We had it on subscription for a year. They sent a letter stating that we had now come to the end of the discounted period but a new one-year deal could be had with the benefit of a 10% reduction. I wasn't overly impressed so they were contacted to cancel any extension that they may feel like imposing to the contract, due to my not reading any small print at the time and not for the first time a proposal to withdraw one's patronage was greeted with a smarmy offer to increase the discount to 25% from 10% as "you are a valued customer". That really pigs me off. Obviously not that valued, otherwise they would have offered us 25% in the first place. Oh, no, that offer is to be left on the shelf as a sop, should the buggers decline the original offer. And yes, I did decline. Aviva have also done that in the past with their insurance. I really don't want to haggle, I just want someone to give me their best price and stick to it.

What's that? You've made the tea whilst I was talking and mine's getting cold. Sarky sod!

Yes, I will have a Hobnob, dark chocolate, please. Right, shoosh up, the Strictly theme tune is playing.

That went quickly, didn't it? Anita Rani went this week. I thought she had done extremely well for someone who had never danced before. Seems like a nice girl. Oh, and our lot drew 0-0 at home to Leeds.

Early night tonight, well, definitely before midnight anyway. Busy week again this week, I've just looked in my diary and there's a talk every day until Saturday. Doesn't time fly when you're a sad git! I think a joke is in order before I turn in.

This one is entitled "Dear John". A soldier was stationed abroad and received a "Dear John" letter from his girlfriend back home. It read, "Dear Dave, I can no longer continue our relationship. The distance between us is just too great and I must admit that I have cheated twice since you've been gone and it's not fair to either of us. I'm sorry, please return the picture of me that I sent you. Love, Kim." The solder, with hurt feelings, asked his fellow soldiers for any snapshots they could spare of their girlfriends, sisters, ex-girlfriends, aunts, cousins, etc. In addition to the picture of Kim, Dave included all the other pictures of pretty girls he'd collected from his army friends. There were 43 photographs that made their way into the envelope, along with a note that read, "Dear Kim, I am so sorry but I can't quite remember who you are. Please take your picture from this pile and send the rest back to me. Take care, Dave."

Night night.

A new dawn and a joke before we turn to the papers.

Breakfast: She was standing in the kitchen preparing the usual soft-boiled eggs and toast for breakfast, wearing only the T-shirt that she normally slept in. As I walked in, just awake, she turned to me and said softly, "You've got to make love to me this very moment." My eyes lit up and I thought, "I'm either still dreaming or this is going to be my lucky day." Not wanting to lose that moment I embraced her and then gave it my all, right there over the kitchen table. After we had finished she said, "Thanks," and returned to the stove, her T-shirt still around her neck. Happy, satisfied, but now a little puzzled, I asked, "What was all that about." She wanly replied, "The egg timer's broken!"

Just so as you know and you're not thinking of us spending time somewhere today like the zoo, British Museum or a mosque or any other sightseeing trip, that sort of thing, I've got to tell you that I'm going off to the wilds of West Wickham in Kent for a talk and thence to Otford to have dinner with my oldest chum. My namesake, in fact. I think I might have mentioned it several years ago in books 1 or 2, although it could be in 3 or 4, but we grew up together in Battersea. Me, in the newsagents at 107 Falcon Road and he in the dairy, at 85. In 2014 we dined at the Running Horse, Mickleham, in leafiest Surrey in order to celebrate our 60th. Acquaintances we possess in numbers, true friends on the fingers of one hand.

What is it about prisoners demanding compensation? They shouldn't even be allowed to submit a claim form. This time we have the case of a 44-year-old murderer who strangled a female teacher, aged 31. He had become obsessed with violent pornography. This warped cove, called Graham Coutts, watched footage of simulated strangulation before embarking on turning his fetish into murder. Having strangled the victim, one Jane Longhurst, with a pair of tights, he hid her body in a cardboard box in a storage facility in Brighton. He then returned "every few days". Staff became aware of a smell so he took the box to woodland and set fire to it. He is claiming compensation of up to £40,000 after an anxiety attack in prison. Can you believe it? He argues that prison guards delayed his journey to hospital after he complained of chest pains. Apparently this Coutts cove is miffed that staff made him change into his prison uniform prior to his hospital visit. He also claims not to have been issued with an apology from the deputy governor of Wakefield Prison over this "distressing incident". So for that he is suing the Ministry of Justice. There there, diddums.... I couldn't be a prison guard, knowing what crime he'd committed. If he'd told me he was suffering from chest pains I'd be tempted to respond dismissively, "Yeah, whatever" and walk away. The cheapest option for the taxpayer is for him to suffer the same fate that his victim did. Bearing in mind that since 2013 those wishing to claim for personal injuries are unable to use taxpayers' money to fund their cases through free legal support, it's unclear as to how this murderous case is being funded. He could apparently be paying out of his own pocket – which would probably be a first – or more likely, resorting to the ambulance chasers, lawyers who work for free. What I find adds to the already incredulous scenario we witness as law-abiding members of society, is that this murdering bastard is allowed to "update" all the events of the system he's playing by informing the public via his blog. How the hell are these inmates allowed access, either directly or by third parties to the public media? I expect we have the human rights lobby to blame, certainly not thank for that little sop to what should be the prisoners self-inflicted social restrictions.

Oh, controversy, controversy. There has been a BBC backlash from viewers angry that Katy Derham has made it to the final showdown. The social media was awash with text, Fastbuck and Twatter messages from disgruntled aficionados. Words like "pathetic" and "dreadful" were used. Now, this is heady stuff. Actually, you'll probably discover that 80% of Strictly viewers are also listeners of the Archers.

Just a thought, but as a further note on overseas aid and its pointlessness, we hand £300 million to India, whilst they purchase 200 mph bullet trains from Japan. If overseas aid was linked to exports one might feel more sympathetic to our money's dispersal.

Right! I'm off to the wilds of West Wickham, Kent, then dinner at the Running Horse so no, the venue hasn't been changed. I'll see you later.

Aaah, it's just before 11 pm. It was nice to see matey, lovely meal, always is. Not cheap but a good atmosphere and surroundings. Two talks tomorrow, one on Wednesday, two on Thursday and then a pre-Christmas lunch with all my model railway friends. Well, there will be three of us there, anyway. I feel a joke coming on. What's that? Am I about to look in the mirror? How cruel can you get. Right, here we go.

The blonde mortician: A man who had just died was delivered to a local mortuary wearing an expensive, expertly tailored black suit. The female asked the deceased's wife how she would like the body dressed, pointing out that the man looked good in the black suit he was already wearing. The widow, however, said that she always thought her husband looked best in blue and that she wanted him in a blue suit. She gave the blonde mortician a blank cheque and said, "I don't care what it costs, but please have my husband in a blue suit for the viewing." The woman returned the following day for the wake and to her relief found her husband dressed in a gorgeous blue suit, with a subtle chalk stripe. The suit fitted him perfectly. She said to the mortician, "I am very satisfied. You did an excellent job and I'm very grateful. How much do I owe you?" To her astonishment, the blonde mortician said, "There is no charge." "No charge, really? But I must compensate you for the cost of that exquisite blue suit." "Honestly, m'am," the blonde said, "it's nothing. You see, a deceased gentleman of about your husband's size was brought in shortly after you left yesterday and he was wearing a very attractive blue suit. I asked his wife if she minded him going to his grave wearing a black suit instead and she said it made no difference so long as he looked nice – so I just switched the heads!"

Thought for the night: "A conscience is what hurts when all your other parts feel good." See you tomorrow – or possibly the day after.

Chapter 11

The Strange Case Of Mother Teresa's Miracles

Well, it's actually the day after the day after – or Thursday as some people would call it. Tuesday's talks to a local U3A and a Middlesex Townswomen's Guild went well, or at least I'd like to think they did. Charlton drew for the second match in succession, the improvement over last Saturday's draw with Leeds is that this time we actually scored two goals. What a pity Bolton did as well. Still, it's better than losing again! What's that? You're out and won't be back till late, okay, bye for now.

Sainsbury's took out a full-page colour advert in the Daily Mail yesterday, advising us that Christmas is for sharing. The picture is of a rustic table with a semi cut pair of joints, I mean ham and beef, not – oh, you know. There is a bag of something on a tray, plus two bowls of vegetables, two halves of what I assume is an orange and a jar of possibly pepper seeds. All rather artisan, as they say – don't they? But the label sitting in the middle of these culinary delights states, "Half price". For me, that totally takes away the desire to buy anything shewn in the advert. We are over a week away from Christmas. This isn't stock that's been left on the shelf and needs to be moved on quickly. Are Waitrose and M & S selling joints with a 50% discount? I sincerely hope not – even after Christmas!

Mmmm, interesting to note that in the battle for pro EU minds the government has handed out 1.9 million national insurance numbers to EU citizens over the past four years, but only logged 751,000 arrivals for statistical purposes. Well, there's one foreigner who, whilst out of work, won't be crying his way to the Job Centre. Chelsea have dispensed with the services of Jose Mourinho. The Daily Mail estimates he's leaving with £10 million. So, even if the true figure is only £5 million, I'm allowing for press excess, it's still a very reasonable half-season's work.

While I am not on the subject, can anyone explain why telephone numbers are now delivered orally with a different emphasis. People used to give you their telephone number and say, "0208-999-999." Now, they say,"020-8999-999." Why? Who decided to change the accepted norm? It was always four figures, three figures, three figures? Why change it to three-four-three? Is this yet another American influence? A move to align it with football positions, or the product of one of our own think-tanks? Anyway, I thought I would just share my discontent with you.

I'm off shortly to a U3A meeting in Aylesbury and then a Ladies' Group in Banstead, so had better check the emails before I go.

Ah, ha. A lady is seeking details of my talks for a club she runs in Bedford, a gentleman is confirming all the details for a Probus lunch in January and sadly, it all goes downhill after that. There is an offer from something called "Red Lobster" inviting me to dinner for three. Funny number, isn't it – two or four I could understand. Do you go as a couple and pick up a vagrant en route as part of David Cameron's big society? Or are these people just loitering without intent? Who knows, who cares. A cove by the name of Reg Anderson is saying, "Hell O??" Why? Emily Davis has left two messages advising me of an upcoming revolution in handbags. Does she know something about my psyche that I didn't know about myself? There is "Health cover for less." It goes on to offer me an alternative to queuing on the NHS but then also informs me that the message contains graphic images. I think not! Car Finance 247 tells me that they have an offer on No Deposit Finance. There is notice of approval at 0% APR representative on a Sure-Card £2,500 facility – and apparently, "Poor credit is not a showstopper." Delete! And, lastly, someone by the name of Lucinda Agnew is attempting to contact me. Well, I assume it's me as it says my name. Apparently, Lucinda says she is searching for an Anthony Mann living in Aldershot – so that's not me then. The email goes on to say that "This person have [sic] been specially selected to get a chance to get the keys to a brand new family car – you can choose whatever model you like." There then follows a list of five names, in which mine is included. Three, it appears, have already confirmed their interest in this complete load of bollocks, two (me included) have yet to confirm. Really? Do people actually respond to these emails? All gone – clear screen! I'm going to get ready, Aylesbury beckons – as opposed to Aylesbury ducks.

Where does the time go? I certainly subscribe to the view that the older one gets the faster it flies, especially just before Christmas. Only last month it was, well, a month away, now it's this week.

Just as an aside and another irritation brought about by the young generation's continual over-hyping of words requiring a tad of substance before use, I had to make an enquiry regarding insurance cover for the house. Having negotiated the hurdles set before me with regard to the robotic voice informing one that one is a valued customer and that someone will take your call at some stage shortly before one's death, I listened to some asinine drivel regarding Data Protection, the sharing of information and every other reason for their not paying out in the event of a claim. The young lady who eventually answered was pleasant, chirpy but sadly sported a Black Country accent. As if this verbal assault/intrusion on one's hearing wasn't bad enough, she asked my address and when I gave it replied, "Cool". "It's an address," I said, "that's all it is." My tone was, I have to say, one of slight irritation, not helped by her propensity to raise the pitch of her voice at the end of a sentence. My enquiry that she may be Australian or a Neighbours devotee brought a nonplussed response, one you could read down the phone. She never cottoned on that her use of modern jargon was not only inappropriate, but vacuous and lazy. My email address was greeted by the reply, "Amazing" and my telephone number with "Magic". I was tempted to respond that my telephone number had nothing to do with magic but had, in the distant past, been provided by the erstwhile GPO as part of a series issued to folk such as myself when receiving a telephone landline. There is only much "nonplussedness" that one can cope with so I thought better of it and just grunted, "Really". I will be obtaining other quotes but you have to pluck up the courage to deal with people at the other end, and that's assuming you ever get through. I'll probably leave it until I have a spare year or the policy expires, whichever is the soonest.

Right, I'm off to the delights of Buckinghamshire. In case you were thinking of going on a tour of the brewery they're all on hold now until the New Year. Just thought I'd mention it.

I'm back! And not just from Aylesbury and Banstead but also from our railway Christmas lunch at Ye Olde King's Head in Epsom. 'Tis nearly Saturday evening, Charlton have lost 4-0 to Burnley and Strictly has been won by Jay McGuinness and Aliona Vilani. I have to say I, like others I understand, felt Kelly Bright should have won it. I was never overly-fussed on the girl but fair's fair, she was the best on the evening but never underestimate the public's ability to put sentiment and passion before talent. What's that? Did I vote? Good God, no. I've never ever considered doing such a thing. Criticise when the vote goes against, is what I say.

By the by, I haven't seen much of you since your day out, where did you go? Really! I went there a few years ago, vowed I'd never go back again. Do you have relatives there? No! You just went there on a whim, extraordinary! At least that explains why you didn't look … well … quite right on your return. No wonder you looked tired and hungry, humanity has trudged through war torn continents and fared better than you, but then they've not been to where you've been, still you're back now. Lesson learned is all I've got to say on the matter.…

So, after all that excitement and before I go to bed, a story or two, methinks.

Birth and pain: A married couple went to the hospital in order to have their baby delivered. Upon their arrival the doctor said that the hospital was testing an amazing new high-tech machine that would transfer a portion of the mother's labour pain to the baby's father. The doctor asked if they were interested. Both said they were very much in favour of it. The doctor set the pain transfer to 10% for starters, explaining that even 10% was probably more pain than the father had ever experienced before. But as the labour progressed, the husband felt fine and invited the doctor to go ahead and increase it a notch. The doctor then adjusted the machine to a 20% pain transfer. The husband was still feeling fine. The doctor then checked the husband's blood pressure and was amazed at how well he was doing. At this point they decided to try for 50%. The husband continued to feel quite well and since the pain transfer was obviously helping his wife considerably, the husband encouraged the doctor to transfer all the pain to him. The wife delivered a healthy baby with virtually no pain and the husband had experienced none. She and her husband were ecstatic. It was only when they got home that they found the milkman dead in the porch!

A, B, C, D, E, F, G, H, I, J, K   After being married for thirty years a wife asked her husband to describe her. He looked at her for a while and then said, "You're A, B, C, D, E, F, G, H, I, J, K." Puzzled, she asked, "What does that mean?" He looked at her lovingly and said,

"Adorable, Beautiful, Cute, Delightful, Elegant, Foxy, Gorgeous, Hot." She smiled happily and said, "Oh, that's so lovely, but what about the I, J and K?" He sat back and replied, "I'm just kidding." The swelling in his eye is now going down and the doctor is fairly optimistic that he can save his testicles!

According to the news it looks as if David Cameron is fighting a losing battle with the EU over his "demands" to curb benefits from migrants until they have been here for four years. I use the phrase "fighting a losing battle". Sadly he has never really fought for this country and he was always going to lose this battle. We all know that the deal offered and accepted by our lack of esteemed leader will not cut the mustard with our British electorate. We have to realise that when push comes to shove the Euro buggers dislike the UK intensely and will go out of their way to punish us in any way they see fit.

Interesting to read Richard Littlejohn's little piece regarding the cancer-like growth in collecting for a fashionable cause célèbre in theatres. The musical "Wicked" is currently playing to audiences in Gravesend, among many other towns no doubt. At the end of the performance, according to one attendee, a leading actress (she won't like that description) launched into a speech about homophobia and urged the theatre-goers to donate to that bastion of homosexual rights, Stonewall. Why do I always think they're called Pinkwall. So, as the audience left the theatre, they passed volunteers rattling buckets. It seems even worse than Christmas at the entrance to Sainsbury's when jolly men of a certain age and dressed in seasonal apparel stand there inviting you to give to the local poor. Bugger them, I say. Nobody should have to "run the gauntlet" as John Littlerichard commented when attending a theatrical performance. It's not what you go to the theatre for. This Stonewall lot recently received £2 million in order to help tackle "homophobic bullying". What a dreadful waste of money. Any animal sanctuary would have been more deserving than that cold shower of limp-wristed buggers.

On the subject of "odd" it's interesting to read that children could have as many as 32 parents, such is the advance in DNA and genetics. The name for this futuristic mixed heritage is "multi-plexed parenting". For futuristic, by the way, read "not far off" as it is already being tried on mice and appears to be successful. A law professor, one Sonia Suter, from the George Washington University, is of the opinion that "clans" of large numbers of people could be linked through their shared offspring. The name of this genetically modified form of creation is known as "in-vitro gametogenesis, or ICG". Do you know, I've now read the article twice but I'm still unsure of any real advantage to man or humankind. I understand that infertile couples will no longer require someone else's egg and that instead of a mummy bear and a daddy bear you will be able to have up to thirty two parental bears all contributing their best assets to the resultant child through their genes, but please tell me where the advantages are over the possible side effects, psychological misgivings as to "Who am I?" and "Where did I really come from?" The article concludes by saying that IVG would allow same sex couples to reproduce in a manner similar to straight couples (that's a mummy bear and a daddy bear). Let's just hope that these experiments go hideously wrong before their transfer to an expectant "gang of 32".

As if I wasn't convinced that Christmas had been with us or upon us since the end of July, I see that H Samuel are offering 3 for 2 on all Chamilia! No, I haven't a clue what it is either. Is it the plural for chameleon, but then they'd be in the pet shop wouldn't they. Anyway, they're three for two. Another look at the red and green coloured seasonal advert also states that H Samuel are "at the heart of Christmas", so is Bernard Matthews! Oh, the advert also depicts a green tree bauble displaying the phrase "as seen on TV", a phrase that induces the viewer from ever watching a commercial station.

And while we're in festering mode, Delia is still the top chef for Christmas, which is nice for her.

On a serious note, I see the erosion of justice in this country continues, even at Christmas and it sends a very poor message to those disposed towards a just society and an invitation to ne'er-do-wells to, well, ne'er do well! You remember those suspected rioters who refused to reveal their identities? Surprise, surprise, they had the charges against them dropped. Unbelievable. What sort of signal does that send out to the offending fraternity? They were ordered to stand trial in the New Year but, hey-ho, Christmas comes early for this flotsam. Solicitors who accrue their ill-gotten gain by defending the indefensible will be rubbing their hands. No mitigating circumstances, no plea to the judge or jury about bias, colour or sex, no disabling lack of capacity, no aunt in Abergavenny who needs regular tending – or trending – oh, no, bugger all. You just refuse to open your mouth and wait for the CPS, otherwise known as the

Completely Pointless Service, to tell you it's all off and you're free to carry on causing mayhem and havoc whenever and wherever you wish. It really does make a mockery of the law and justice in this country. Another nibble at the edge of the plate called democracy.

And if that wasn't bad enough, the Daily Mail has just advertised its "Free inside" guide (14 days that is!) to all the Christmas and New Year TV. The guide, which they describe as brilliant, with a Dickensian Christmas scene, displaying a bevy of period costumed chaps and chapesses. Mmmm, the lad on the left of the picture is black. Is that a true Dickens character, I wonder, or the selective addition to Victorian life as decreed by the BABC's ethnic and equality division, which I can imagine fielding the largest number of staff and gaining the biggest budget to go with it. Seriously, was there a black lad in Dickens's novels? I am aware Shakespeare had a sprinkling in his but as you know, the Beeb's desire to re-define Guinevere in the Merlin series as black did not go down well with yours truly. Apart from that, Merlin was a cracking series and sadly missed. Atlantis was a very poor and seemingly hastily screened follow-up, containing characters I felt absolutely no rapport with. I felt exactly the same regarding Saving Private Ryan. Never gave a monkey's whether he was saved or not in that film's case – pure American pap.

Talking of scum, which we do all too frequently, I read that dog owners who incite their four-legged friend to fight other dogs, badgers and foxes, have taken to social media to brag about their activity. How can these people take pleasure in seeing two animals tear each other to shreds? There is something extremely warped about these people. Now, if those in charge of DNA and genes could find one that affects this sub-specie of humanity, the gene in question could be isolated and hopefully the vermin aborted. The League Against Cruel Sports is doing its best, but with limited resources and an ever-decreasing number of police officers for real police work, we really do need stiffer sentences. I would recommend ten years for even owning a banned breed, twenty years for encouraging it to fight and a continuous extension depending on the severity of the injuries and possible subsequent death of an animal – domesticated or wild. I'd bring back the birch tomorrow if I could. Oh, how these bastards would suffer. Bread, water and a true Dickensian experience for the duration of their sentence, back to the treadmill. If it's good enough for the Poles, it's good enough for dog bleeders. There – feeling better now!

And as I write the sun has just appeared over the garden. It's obviously come out in sympathy!

David Cameron has back-tracked on migrants' benefit reform as the Eastern European leaders, led by the Polish, rejected a call for restricted benefits for their countrymen – and women. Still, I'm sure David Cameron got something out of his latest rounds of talks, even if it was only a good dinner or two. And just to make a point, the number of foreigners now living here has topped 5 million. Now, you could say "But there are millions of Brits abroad". Absolutely right, but given the choice, who would you rather have here – someone who hailed originally from Horsham or Esher or someone who hailed from Bucharest or Budapest? I know there are nice Poles, Hungarians, Latvians and Lithuanians. It is just that we don't quite have the space for them all. Our social services and NHS facilities are at breaking point in no small way due to their ever-increasing breeding programme. If they're not Muslim they're Catholic. Still, I'm sure Dave the Brave knows best.

Talking of Davids, I've never been a fan of that Dimbleby fellow. I always see him as full of self-importance, arrogance and frankly, not overly nice. His invitation on question time to "That woman at the back" or "The one in red, yes, you" always makes me feel uncomfortable. I really do dislike his lack of courtesy for he never uses the word "lady" and I always consider his manner to be condescending at best, so it was nice to see the chap get a little comeuppance when he pointed out to the audience that the Conservative MP, Jacob Rees Mogg, had been educated at Eton. His only reason could be a cheap laugh at someone else's expense and to jump on the bandwagon regarding educational privilege for the children of the wealthy. Apparently, and with perfect timing, having allowed the laughter to subside, Mr. Rees Mogg replied that he was at Eton alongside David Dimbleby's son, Henry. What I also learned was that Henry is a restaurateur and yesterday received an MBE at Buckingham Palace for his work on improving state school dinners. Did you know that? I thought all that improvement was down to Jamie Oliver. I mean, his name appears in print or on television every time a healthy option is placed in front of you. And now we have this Dimbleby fellow getting in on the improving act. Gongs for tarts, huh!

Yesterday we witnessed the end of an era. Britain's last remaining deep coal pit closed and 450 miners found themselves above ground and looking for work. It is a sad end to what Britain was built upon. Men had worked at Kellingley Colliery in North Yorkshire for many years, some since they left school. Margaret Thatcher has a lot to answer for with regard to our now extinct deep pit mining industry. I never thought the time would come when the National Union of Mineworkers represented only 100 souls. Drax Power Station, which is only seven miles away, was powered by Kellingley Coal. It will now be driven by coal delivered by ship from Columbia for £13 a ton less. The accountants and politicians will, as ever, tell you it is good business, greener no doubt, saving on taxpayers' money, everything to dot the i's and cross the t's, as if they really cared. But no mention is made of the industry and the jobs lost. A sad day and no mistake.

I love jokes and this one is good!

Mother Teresa is to be made a saint by someone in Rome, a chap called Pope Francis. Apparently the do-gooder performed a second miracle (didn't know she'd performed a first but some people never know when to quit} on a seriously ill man in Brazil. The hoot is that she performed the "miracle" eleven years after she died. Have you ever heard such complete tosh. Probably not since the time that they discovered a priest that didn't have a history of sex abuse! So, a truly rare event. Anyway, to qualify for sainthood you have to have performed two miracles, both of which need to be recognised by the Catholic Church. You really can't take this seriously, can you. I've read on and this canonisation is set to take place in about 10 months time, as it coincides with the anniversary of her passing in 1997. It is also the period of Pope Francis's holy year of mercy. A spoke for Mother Teresa's Missionaries of Charity Religious Order said the nuns were "over the moon" – an oft-used phrase. Mrs. Kumar (wonder if she ever lived at number 42) sycophantically drooled "we thought her whole life was a miracle." Oh, please, will someone fetch the sick bucket. It gets better. Thomas D'Souza, the arse Bishop of Calcutta, said the news was "The best Christmas gift one can get." Mmmm, has he never heard of a Hog's Back Brewery T-shirt? He eulogised, "We are grateful to God and extremely happy". Meanwhile, back at Catholic HQ, the Vatican announced "The Holy Father has authorised the congregation for the causes of saints to proclaim the decree concerning the miracle attributed to the intersession of blessed Mother Teresa". Yes, I got lost through that as well.

What about the miracles, I hear you say? Well, her first centred on a Bengali female who was suffering from a cancerous abdominal tumour in 1998, but was apparently "cured" when a locket containing a picture of Mother Teresa's face was placed upon her stomach. Church officials and Mrs. Besra, the cancer sufferer, claimed that a beam of light came out of the locket and killed the tumour. It was probably a beam of light shining through a hospital window. In England we call it the sun! All a bit spurious, I say. Talk about believing in what you want to believe. In 2002 Pope John Paul II described Mrs. Besra's good health as being down to "supernatural intervention." However, Mrs. Besra's doctor told of how he had prescribed medicine that cured a cyst, not a tumour. Mother Teresa, herself, had been dead for a year when the above happened. The second "inexplicable healing" of an unnamed Brazilian chappie centred upon his viral brain infection. Said to be in a coma and dying and about to undergo surgery, he suddenly awoke symptom free. His wife said he had been continuously praying to old ma Theresa. So there you have it. Another pointless sucking-up to a false god.

I remember this next piece happened a couple of years ago over one of the nailing weekends. Apparently huge crowds gathered in the Vatican City to witness a historic ceremony where two popes, not one but two, John Paul II and John XIII were declared saints, which must have been nice for both of them. The mass co-celebrated by Pope Francis and his predecessor, Pope Benedict, was watched by and listened live by one million pilgrims (who counted?) and a large TV and radio audience. Royal dignitaries, heads of states and foreign delegates swarmed in order to attend. Apparently it is the first time that two popes have been canonised at the same time, presumably as opposed to being sodomised at the same time, which I understand is fairly typical, especially if it's late night opening! Such joy! The only real miracle is just how many hapless souls can be fooled so easily for so long a time. Unbelievable. All this, not unnaturally, leads me to a joke or two, but these are real jokes, not real life, starring a mass of deluded souls.

A young couple wanted to join the Church. The priest told them that there is a special requirement for new member couples. "You must abstain from sex for one whole month." The couple agreed, but after two and a half weeks returned to the church. When the priest ushered them into the office the wife started crying and her husband became very distressed. "You are back so soon, is there a problem?" the priest enquired. "We are terribly ashamed to admit that we did not manage to abstain from sex for the required month," the young man replied sadly. The young priest asked what had happened. "Well, the first week was difficult ... however, we managed to abstain through sheer willpower and faith. The second week was terrible but with the use of prayer we managed to see the week through. By the time we came into the third week our desire was unbearable. We tried cold showers, more prayer, reading the bible – anything to keep our minds from carnal thoughts. One afternoon, however, my wife reached for a tin and dropped it. As she bent over to pick up the tin, I was overcome with lust and seeing her in that position I had my way with her right then and there. I tell you, Father, it was lustful, loud, passionate sex. It lasted for over an hour and when we were done we were both drenched in sweat." The man looked shamefaced. The priest said sternly, "You understand this means you will not be welcome in our church." "We know," said the young man, hanging his head, "And we're not that welcome in Homebase either."

Ready for the second?

A little boy got on the bus and sat next to a man reading a book. The boy noticed that the man had his collar on backwards. The little boy asked why he wore the collar backwards and the man, who was a priest, said "I am a Father." The little boy replied, "My daddy doesn't wear his collar like that." The priest looked up from his book, smiled and answered, "I am the father of many." The little boy persisted. "Well, my dad has four boys, four girls and two grandchildren and he still doesn't wear his collar that way." The priest, getting slightly impatient, replied, "I am the father of hundreds." He went back to reading his book. The little boy sat quietly thinking for a while, then leaned across and said, "I've just been thinking, maybe you should wear a condom and put your pants on back to front instead of your collar."

It's 21st December, four days to go before – well, you must remember from last year, surely! The Post Office has conducted a survey. The big surprise for me is that they still have enough staff left in their service in order to conduct one in the beginning. It appears from that survey that for one in six, or 16% of Brits, it takes until the end of Christmas Day to get into the festive spirit, whilst 17% prefer Boxing Day to Christmas Day. I prefer the day after when the whole farce is over, but that's me! A third of the sample of 2000 people said that putting up the decorations was the single most enjoyable aspect. Thirteen per cent preferred a glass of mulled wine to a smooch under the mistletoe – who said alcoholism was dead? Apparently, 11% start planning for Christmas during the summer. Now, these people are sad. Eighteen per cent of women think about Christmas three months in advance, as opposed to 10% of men. I bet that 10% are homosexual, it's the sort of thing they'd do. Oh, and not that this will affect you, what with you reading it "in the now" or in the future really, but as I write, today is the GPO's last posting day for first class mail. First class, with four days to go? Christ knows when the last day was for second class, probably during the reign of Henry Tudor. Still, what with technology most of mine go by email via some lady called Jacquie Lawson – I think that's her name. This way, of course, it's all nicely sanitised, everyone gives the same card and later receives the same one back. I like continuity. (My wife says there are hundreds to choose from and the likelihood is they would get a different card, and as she's typing this I suppose she better have her opinion stated!) I would still like to think they get the same one.

Anyway, before I was interrupted, I like continuity and the great thing about email is that it doesn't cost over twelve shillings to send the bugger in the first place. Half the time you have only sent someone a card because they sent you one last Christmas. It's not a sense of friendship but a form of obligation. Thank Christ it only comes once a year.

Nice to see the Bank of England admit that migration to Britain has depressed wages for the low skilled of this country. This isn't news and it certainly isn't a surprise but don't expect to find this "news" being bandied about once the referendum starts. The Bank of England will foretell all manner of storms and pestilence should we be brave enough to leave.

Aha, the contentious policy of charging for parking your car at an English hospital is raising its costly head once again. I am sympathetic to the need to protect parking spaces. To be fair to the hospitals, some are situated near railway stations and I am well aware that commuters, given half a chance, would park freely all day if they thought they could get away with it. There are always those who make it bad for the many, but sadly, necessity very quickly becomes a cash cow. I note that the University Hospital, Southampton, raked in £3.87 million,

East Kent Hospital, £3.25 million and Sheffield Teaching Hospital, £3.16 million. What riles the punter is that so much of this money is not going to medical use but to parking companies contracted to govern the car parks. If it were all profit for the hospital with maybe a board within reception displaying where the fees went and what additional revenue streams it brought to various departments, the public's anger would probably be quelled. It is agencies, contractors, those in it for profit that stinks. It is our NHS and our parking fees. Use them for our benefit. There! That feels better.

Oh, dear, just when I said I felt better I have espied on page 13 of the Daily Mail a photograph so eerie in content, so sickening in format. It is a visual nightmare that should see the newspaper issuing warning notices on the front cover. I am struggling to tell you this, it is a ghastly vision of Elton John and his other half, David Furnish, laughingly described as his "husband". The article concerns Elton John's decision to part company with his long term PR chief, Gary Farrow. Basically, having read the article, it appears that close friends, both personal and working, have departed from the Elton John empire. Even his own mother hasn't spoken to him for over seven years. The finger seems to be pointed at David Furnish who appears to be furnishing Elton John with all his needs and services. It's not a pretty picture. What's that? A cuppa? About time, any more of this pair and I can feel the smelling salts will need to make an appearance out of the larder. It's not often you'll find me turning a cutting upside down in order to conceal something distasteful, but really. Oh, yes, it says, "Mr. Furnish, who is never far from his partner's side at glitzy events, and Sir Elton have two sons, Zachary, aged 4, and Elizah, 2". With names like that, they should follow the suggestion I made regarding Bear Grylls and have them taken into care. Thank God the smelling salts have arrived. So, EJ and DF, you join Helen Mirren face down and no, that's not an invitation.

Just in case you needed to know or be reminded, a half-page advertisement in today's Daily Mail informs the reader that one can "make it a magic Christmas at Morrison's". I take it that it is the same magical Christmas they promised us in an advert yesterday and on several other occasions in the past month. This time the "magic" refers to alcohol. There are two bottles of wine for £8 (normally £5 each). What I find distasteful is that the caveat under the bottles states "max 36 bottles of each". Who on earth wants to buy 72 bottles of wine in one purchase. There is a chianti wine on offer for £6 instead of £10 and again, the instruction to purchase a maximum of 36. Sadly, the beer and lager offerings are as predictable as Carol Kirkwood's loveliness, but not half so pleasing. Stella Artois, Carlsberg, Budweiser, Foster's, John Smith's and Strongbow Cider are offered at two packs for £20, with either 18 or 20 cans per case. This time the proviso is "max 12 cases in total". It's obscene that so much corporate, gassy crap can be offered so cheaply but even more criminal is the fact that there are arses out there in the street that will consume these apologies for beer, lager or cider.

Now, here's a statistic you wouldn't have come up with knowingly. Due to our ever-changing eating habits, we are now spending £9 million more on avocados than we spend on oranges. Or, to put it in spending terms, £142 million on avocados and a smidgeon less than £133 million on oranges, which are obviously not the only fruit. And just in case you care to know, avocado sales were up 26% last year, while oranges plunged by 4.3%, so avocados are now No. 8 in the annual fresh fruit top ten. Apples remain at No. 1, with grapes and bananas taking up positions 2 and 3. Not surprisingly, Waitrose saw sales of avocados rise by 30% after Nigella Lawson made avocado on toast during her BBC 2 programme, "Simply Nigella". This little piece really ticks all the right boxes for me, classy fruit, classy store and classy lady! Ahhh!

You remember what we were saying about agency nursing staff? I'm sure we did, – oh, perhaps it wasn't you. Anyway, I read that these agencies make up to 50% profit on the hourly rates they charge and these rates are not insignificant, Medicare charges between £43 and £69 per hour for a general nurse and £76 for an A & E nurse. Everything is short term, as we've discussed over the course of this book and sadly, in previous tomes. If only the money spent on placing metaphorical sticking plaster over the nursing crisis was spent on training home grown nurses, who at least speak English as a first language, that would be a start. I would even accept those nurses whose speech pattern "goes up at the end". At least they can be re-programmed. I mean, there's a therapy for everyone.

Well, we're a day nearer the witching hour of Christmas Eve and today Morrison's half-page advert involves even more of a magic Christmas. There are selected Gammon Joints (smoked and unsmoked) at £3 per kilo (whatever that is), a British Beef Roasting

Joint at £4 per kilo (still no idea) although it's "max 2 in total" and a British Turkey Crown at £7 per foreign measurement, to which is added the word "large" and serves nine to twelve people. Who on earth has that many friends? The offer on the latter two "ends Christmas Eve – or, while promotional stocks last. I think it's appropriate now to tell you a little shopping story.

A couple were in a busy shopping centre just before Christmas. The husband wandered off as the woman was standing in queue, saying something about being back a little later. After getting through the queue the husband still wasn't back and since they had more shopping to do, the wife called him on the mobile phone. "Where are you?" He said, "You remember the jewellers we went to about ten years ago and you fell in love with that diamond necklace and I couldn't afford it at the time, and I said that one day I would go and get it for you." Tears started to flow down her cheeks and she became all choked up. "Yes," she said, "I do remember that shop." "Ah, that's good," he said, "because I'm in the pub next door to it."

You remember the phrase "the right hand doesn't know what the left hand is doing", although it may be vice versa for equality purposes. Anyway, an award-winning headmistress has had to resign after 23 teachers at her school left following allegations of bullying. The head, one Pepe Hart (funny name!) and her two deputies have all stepped down after the school became so short staffed that complaints were being received from parents. This has all happened a year after she won "Manager of the Year" in a competition by the recruitment company, Reid International. Pepe, and I'm sure I can call her that, after all, she needs all the friends she can get, was even named "Teacher of the Year" by her own staff in 2008's "Pride of Britain" awards. Parents have been apparently clashing with staff over a lack of permanent teachers and the continual drafting in of supply staff. When you read of senior staff making life difficult for pregnant teachers, newly qualified teachers, with allegations of harassment and bullying, it really does beg the question, did Pepe get a little bit too big for her job? Some people just never know their limitations.

I remember Eric Sykes once said, "I'd like to think I got to the top of my profession, but I'd hate to think that I trod on anyone on the way up". Well said, Mr. Sykes.

If ever you wanted a basic, one-off reason for leaving the EU, irrespective of economical arguments for and against, it is the fact that we are unable to deport criminals. Ne'er-do-wells have to meet "deportation requirements". Since April 2013 only 13,250 have met that requirement. Sadly, 13,000 more haven't! This is at a cost to the taxpayer of £40,000 per inmate per year. What a waste of our money – another large amount that could go towards the recruitment of British nurses, British policeman and British teachers. I could go on, but I will. Some of these criminals we fail to deport include rapists and murderers. How on earth can they fail to meet the criteria for deportation? UKIP's immigration spokesman, Steven Woolfe, MEP, hit the right note when he said: "These numbers are evidence that our immigration system is plagued with lawlessness. The only thing worse than the lack of enforcement of deportation orders is when those who are deported sneak back into the UK, and that is what is happening because the Home Office Border Control information technology systems at ports and airports is deemed not fit for purpose in counting who comes in and who leaves. On the one hand, we have a growing 'human rights industry' which clogs Britain's courts with facile legal challenges to allow criminals and bogus asylum seekers to stay, and on the other, we have no way of knowing who comes in or out of the country." Couldn't have put it better myself, and I didn't!

Chapter 12

'Tis Christmas Eve, I Must Buy Some Presents!

Well, it's Christmas Eve and it's just been revealed that to date, 4.5 million 999 calls have been made so far, give or take, obviously. Among the less important calls were the following:

A woman rang because her kebab was cold.

Another woman rang asking where she could obtain the best bacon sandwich.

A man informed the operator that he'd got 50p (ten shillings) stuck in a washing machine

Another caller stated that as his family had overslept and would therefore be late for their flight, could the police use their sirens and lights to escort them to the airport.

I can only assume the callers were once pupils at a comprehensive school!

What did amuse me was the news that demand for goose this Christmas has increased enormously. According to farmers, this is all down, apparently, to a storyline in The Archers.

The arrival of goose breeders, Rex and Toby Fairbrother, in the Radio 4 soap opera has seen families switch from turkey, as the brothers ruffle feathers by providing competition for the turkey business run by the Grundy family. A lady who rears 100 geese has seen just ten of her flock unsold weeks ahead of last year's figures. She said that they are receiving lots of orders from "names I had never heard of before. I started asking customers and they said they'd heard it on 'The Archers'". That little piece was reported in the Daily Mail earlier this month. Oh, the power of a 60 plus year old soap!

Well, that's it before tomorrow, that big build up, close to the end of yet another year. I was going to say another pointless year, but we'll wait and see. David Cameron has urged people to reflect on Christian values in his Christmas message. He said that the country's "important religious roots" made it a "successful home to people of all faiths and none." Jeremy Corbyn used a newspaper article to highlight homelessness and praise emergency services. Green Party leader, Natalie Bennett (that Australian woman) called for a "different sort of society", whatever that means, while Tim Farron, Liberal Democrats, said the world was "in need of hope". Well, certainly hope that they don't retain many seats in the next election!

If I remember correctly, you're off home for a couple of days, aren't you? Ah, yes, well, your cases are by the door, that should have been a giveaway. What's that, time for a cuppa before you go? Well, okay with me. As ever they are Yorkshire teabags. Yes, whatever cup you like and I'll have mine, you know, the one with the green engines on it. You'll find it on the top shelf. Biccies? So, I haven't asked, what are you expecting from Santa this year? Really? Well, I'm sure it will look good on you. They are going to be all the rage with low income families. No, I'm joking, it'll be fine. Heads will turn – or roll.

I'll just check the computer, I'm not expecting any book orders or new talks this late in the day. Morrison's have now closed for Christmas, by the way. Amongst this festive eve's email crap is an offer to "get a bonus today", followed by the now worryingly regular wording "this message contains graphic images." They all seem to do that. Why? Bissell Direct News is advising me that I can save over 40% on carpet shampoo and to be fair, that is without graphic images, whilst Windownice is offering a 30GBP welcome package, with graphic images. Anne Bennett says "Hello me" and salutations, followed by a long mixture of letters and numbers. Crap, complete crap. And finally, I have received, subject to downloading the full spiel, a Vanquis application. If downloaded I can "apply today for the card that has said 'yes' to over 3 million people in the UK". This is followed by the usual caveat regarding one's graphic images. Well, that's all deleted, kettle has boiled, biccies to the ready and a seasonal joke or two, methinks.

A little boy gets home from school and says, "Dad, I've got a part in the school Christmas play as a man who's been married for 25 years." His father replies, "Never mind, son, maybe next time you'll get a speaking part."

Sam decided to propose to Julie, but prior to her acceptance Julie felt she had to confess to her man about her childhood illness. She informed Sam that she suffered from a disease that left her breasts at the maturity of a 12-year-old. He stated that it was perfectly okay as he loved her so much. However, Sam felt it was the appropriate moment to open up and admit that he had a deformity as well. He looked Julie in the eyes and said, "I, too, have a problem. My willy is the same size as that of an infant and I hope you'll be able to cope with that once we are married." "Yes," she said, "I will marry you and learn to live with your infant-sized willy." Well, the pair of them got married and couldn't wait for the honeymoon. Sam whisked Julie off to their hotel suite and they started touching, teasing and holding one another close. As Julie put her hands in Sam's pants she began to scream, backed off and ran out of the room. Sam ran after her to find out what was wrong. When he caught up with her at the end of the corridor she said, "You told me your willy was the size of an infant." "It is," he said, "I told you the truth. Six pounds ten ounces and nineteen inches long!"

A family is sitting at the Christmas dinner table, the son asks his father, "Dad, how many kinds of boobs are there?" The father leans back, somewhat surprised, and answers, "Well, son, there are three kinds of boobs. In her 20's a woman's are like melons, round and firm, in her 30's to 40's they are like pears, still nice but hanging a bit and after 50, they are like onions." "Onions?" "Oh, yes, you see them and it makes you want to cry." This infuriated his wife and daughter who were also sitting at the table and the daughter asked, "Mum, how many kinds of willies are there?" Her mother, though surprised, smiled and answered, "Well, dear, a man goes through three phases. In his 20's his willy is like an oak tree, mighty and hard. In his 30's and 40's it's like a birch, flexible, but reliable. After his 50's it's like a Christmas tree." "A Christmas tree!" exclaims the daughter. "Oh, yes," replies the mother, "the tree is dead and the balls are just for decoration!"

And to finish off, a couple of very short Irish jokes.

Paddy says to Mick, "I see that Christmas is on a Friday this year." Mick looked shocked. " Well, just let's hope it's not the 13th."

And lastly, Paddy thought his new girlfriend might be the one, but after looking through her knicker-drawer and finding a nurse's uniform, a French maid's uniform and a policewoman's uniform he finally decided that if she couldn't hold down a job, then she really wasn't the girl for him!

Right! Well, you're off now. Safe journey, see you on the 27th. Sorry, what was that? What do I want for Christmas? Mmmm, a broken drum, I suppose. You just can't beat it! Good night.

So, Happy Christmas, lots to do and plenty of time to do it in. I'll leave you in peace until tomorrow or the day after – we'll see, but first I'll pull a cracker or two and I'm not referring to Carol Kirkwood or Lorraine Kelly.

Two snowmen in a field, one turns to the other and says, "I don't know about you, but I can smell carrots."

What do you call a youngster who doesn't believe in Santa? A rebel without a Claus.

And just a thought, but if my surname was Massey, I think I'd call my daughter Chris.

Lastly, were you aware that Christmas is an anagram of "trims cash"? No, really!

Enjoy your dinner.

It's Boxing Day, hope your turkey didn't stuff you too much. I can't resist noting the following:

Apparently, some boys and girls' names that years ago were commonplace are now as rare as a pale face in Bradford, Slough and East London. Only nine Dereks were born in the last year (that many!) two Rodneys, very few Terrys, Ians, Donalds and Darrens. It is really not surprising, I mean other than Ian, they are all pretty, well, common and names you used to associate with comprehensives, estates and social housing. Mind you, who are the parents who have replaced these traditional names with Nimrod, Jester, Boden, Lion, Lovie (Lovie?!) Lomond or Golden and yes, these were all boys' names. They should all be taken into care, it's really not fair on the poor little sods – and they probably will be. With the girls there are now very few Helens, Claires, Sallys, Karens or Susans. I've always liked Susan and Helen. They are names that transcend time for me. They've been replaced in similar vein with Venus (we know where that one came from, probably very popular in certain areas of South East London), Delphie, Oceana, Tulip, Arya (a character in Game of Thrones, apparently – never seen the series) and three Lexus's. Were they named after the car? If so, why? I mean, at least Bentley would have some gravitas.

Interesting to note once again that we are to send £123 million to Somalia, £197 million to Afghanistan, £129 million to Syria and countless millions to other pointless enterprises. Sadly, we still cannot afford to provide lasting flood protection in Lancashire, Yorkshire and Cumbria, where residents have once again suffered from horrendous levels of flooding. But, never mind, this is England, the country that provides the taxes enabling those elected to spend it on those who have never contributed.

Oh, and while we're at it, Britain is more reliant on overseas doctors than any other major EU nation, whereas Poland has only 2.7% of foreign doctors and Italy 5%. The UK has 35.4%. Many are not fit to practise in a western state but they are available, instant and cheap, although a need to speak English is not a major requirement.

At last, the government is to pass legislation stopping fraudulent claims for whiplash allegedly caused during a traffic accident. This panacea for all ills – or rather the lack of them – is costing some £2 billion a year. With a bit of luck, common sense and the change becoming law, victims will be able to have their rehabilitation paid for but not compensation for the accident.

Nice to know that sexual abuse in the church isn't confined just to Catholicism and the Anglican Church. No, it's spreading its angel wings much more widely now. Today we read of a Jehovah's Witness who abused girls by choking them for sexual pleasure. At the time he worked as a church librarian. There are various children identified who were subjected to his fantasies. The most worrying aspect is the response from the parents of a 14-year-old girl who the abuser, one Ian Pheasey, grabbed around the neck and threw on the floor before straddling her and squeezing her throat. She fell into a state of unconsciousness. He told her that he would kill her if she told anyone, adding that if she grew up to have female children he would rape them. What a nasty piece of work he is. The young girl ran home screaming and crying and very bravely told her mother what had happened. Her mother told her to "clean herself up" before she was taken to hospital for bruising on her neck. Mr. Taplow, the prosecutor, told the court that "Sadly, her parents chose to conceal the sexual nature of the incident and told their daughter not to say anything about it. They continued to understate the seriousness of the assault and the matter was swept under the carpet by the church". Now, where have I heard that before? Bastards!

And now for something completely similar, the New Year's Honours List. It's the last day of the year and happy bunnies of both sexes are rubbing their mucky little paws in glee at the addition to their title, or in some cases, the uplifting of their status, as they ascend the greasy sycophantic pole. Lin Homer, who was in charge of the failing immigration service and now runs the deficient UK tax office has been awarded a Damehood. I'd anoint her with a "Couldn't Give a Toss Hood". As well as luvvies in political circles, Tory party officials, David Cameron's Australian election campaign manager, Ed Davey, the former MP receives a Knighthood, an Asian called Zameer Choudrey, who is the owner of Bestway Cash and Carry, receives a CBE, but to be fair, he did donate nearly half a million pounds to the Tory party. The acting luvvies have also made their mark. Barbara Windsor is now a Dame, Imelda Staunton has been upgraded from an OBE to a CBE (why?) and Sian Phillips also becomes a Dame. Martyn Lewis, the ex-BBC news anchorman is to be handed a knighthood for charity work. It really is a joke. All these people are just doing their job like everyone else, be they politicians, actors – oh, and actresses, "pop stars" and civil servants. At least Jaqueline Gold, who founded the Ann Summers sex shop chain brought a respectability and lightness to a subject discussed behind closed doors but never viewed from the High Street. Probably the most deserving recipient I'd say, Jaqueline Gold was made a CBE.

Morrison's is inviting you to have a Happy New Year with a 10-pack Tempora prawns or 10-pack melting cheeseburger. There is also a 10-pack cheese bauble selection or a similar number of mini posh dogs, whatever they are. Still, it's a thought. And all at £3.50 per pack.

I think I told you that Charlton lost 4-0 at Burnley on the 19th, well we finished off the year with a 1-1 draw at Bristol City on Boxing Day and then lost 2-0 at home to Wolves. The season doesn't bode well. Just two more cuttings from the newspapers, to whom I thank, and have supplied me with a wealth of stories on which to comment over the past four months. Regarding humour, well certainly a wry smile, I read that a learner driver careered through a police cordon and was found to be positive for drugs, whilst his instructor was nearly four times over the drink/drive limit. This incident occurred not far from where I live in the parish of Worplesdon. Incidentally, the cordon was protecting an overturned and abandoned van. The police traced the owner to a home less than 3 miles away where he was also tested positive for alcohol. These three must have helped the police targets for the day. The "I never thought this would ever happen" story relates to the fact that 2,000 armed police officers have had their leave cancelled tonight due to security fears that terrorists could strike on New Year's Eve. How sad is that.

And so we come to the end of the year and towards the end of the book. I remember commenting in previous tomes that despite promises, rhetoric, threats even, nothing really changes. Most change is generally for the worse. I really do fear for this country, it is not in a good place and if we vote to stay in the EU the future will be even bleaker. Despite words of supposed comfort from David Cameron regarding "UK rights" over the "import" of Turks and Serbs and anyone else who joins the muddy paws club, just look at what happened once we allowed that second influx of Bulgarians and Romanians. The government think that the public at large are fairly stupid and do not see through their manipulation of figures. The point is not to trust anyone from any party. Work on the basis that they are, in the main, lying bastards and here for their own furtherance. There is a saying that 99% of all lawyers give the rest a bad name. That analogy applies equally to politicians.

Everyone appears to be on the fiddle, from VW attempting to dupe the purchaser over the omissions rigging scandal, to figures issued over migration. I would love to be told the truth with regard to just what percentage of non-British flotsam occupies our prisons. What is the percentage of murder, rape, assault, fraud, etc. being perpetrated by foreigners? I'd love to know the number of blacks and Asians responsible within each category compared to the native white population. Perhaps an analysis should be developed according to religion. A sort of cross-reference, in order to build up a more complete picture – an honest picture, so that the British public may know just what previous government policies have created and future ones have in store.

I come back to the amount of Green Belt land we are building over. Only when Buckingham Palace is deemed necessary for conversion to flats and affordable housing will those in power wake up. The problem is that politicians are never subjected to the effects of their policies. Their everyday life is divorced from libraries, post offices, community centres, public toilets, comprehensive schools. There is no money, apparently, but then if politicians don't use them, why should they even think about them? Over 46,000 pensioners have seen their meals-on-wheels service discontinued over the past three years. Taxes rise whilst services shrink. Something has to give.

On a global scale half of the world's primates are under threat from man's intervention, expansion or destruction. Birds, reptiles, mammals, fish, vertebrates, invertebrates are all in danger but still we carry on logging, drilling, extracting, procreating.

With regard to birds, more than a quarter of the UK's species are on the "at risk" register. Who would ever have thought, years ago when we had self respect and a more caring society, that starlings would be on the list of conservation concern. Again, something has to give.

If you stand back and look at our country as a whole, as opposed to a "hole", which is all too easy and far too obvious, obviously, everything is stretched to breaking point and the common denominator is people. The population is out of control and I mean that in a wider sense than just plain birth rate. We don't know who is coming in, who has come in, who has been sent back and then come back in again. We've cut the border force at the sharp end, prisons are struggling, we release murderers, rapists, armed robbers, each month by "mistake". The good news, of course, is that we are always "learning" from it. No, it doesn't fill me with a lot of confidence either. Every government department appears to have been learning something for years. How can it be deemed fair for migrants to be able to claim child benefit when their offspring are not even in this country? I read that under new EU rules thousands of European doctors and nurses will be able to work here without vital checks on their qualifications and ability, as they will be handed electronic "passports" which automatically allows them to practise in hospitals and surgeries. Everything this country has built up over the centuries is now being eroded from within and without.

Irrespective of the economic or political manoeuvring by either the Remain or the Leave campaigners, immigration and its damaging effect upon our society is what will unite many thousands of ordinary people who have seen their town, village and countryside transformed by those from an alien society or culture. It is quite possible that the UK population could swell to 70 million plus. It's not difficult, those that come here breed! They have children, who have children. It also swells their race and their religion. They care not a jot for the indigenous population who have been brought up in a socially democratic and mainly law-abiding society. No better an example was an interview with a Romanian now living with his family in

England. He said, "I don't do bad things any more because I am not poor and live on your benefits. I arrived in the UK three years ago and went to the Job Centre to get a National Insurance number." He added, "Your benefit system is crazy. Of course Romanians will settle in Britain if they get this kind of money. I have never been told to look for work by the Job Centre. Why would I want a boss when I get £300 put into my account every week for nothing?" He also commented that in other European countries where he lived he "never got benefits". Unbelievable! In the article there is a photograph of him with his other half and enormous brood of extended family by the door of their red brick terraced house somewhere in a street formerly occupied by people who either worked or didn't get a penny. Is it any wonder that in the past year to September, 206,000 Romanian and Bulgarian nationals have been issued with NI numbers. With net increase in immigration running at 336,000 over the past twelve months, David Cameron is going to have to pull out all the stops in order to cut his self-imposed target to 100,000. Because if he doesn't, he could just find that this single issue, the one that makes such a difference to our everyday lives, could come back to haunt him, his political career and this country's destiny.

The EU buggers about with the shape and dimensions of cucumbers but sits back and accepts that 185,000 animals are tested in labs every year in this country alone. What hell-holes in Eastern Europe one asks are animals confined to. We should be ashamed of ourselves. Five hundred animals a day are put through what is described as "unbearable pain", just so a scientist can attempt to find a cure for some human ailment or cosmetic transformation. I sometimes wonder if, as in the church where paedophiles enter under a cloak of goodness, these animal torturers enter the world of science for their own perverted ends. It wouldn't surprise me.

The police bring a lot of public suspicion upon themselves, but no profession can function properly unless it is funded and staff employed in all roles feels supported. Sadly, the divisive nature of government and politics leaves the police with a morale twinned with that of workers in the NHS, education and virtually all other government departments that are interfered with by politicians. Cuts equal cutting corners, cutting corners leads to a decrease in services and the ability to do the job properly, whatever the profession. The downward spiral continues and a malaise sets in. Who would have thought even a few years ago that towns would be starting up their own protection force as there were no police visible on the streets. The days of properly trained police, the recruits that succeeded at Hendon are but a distant memory in some reaches of our islands. The Independent ran a very interesting series on the effects that cuts to the police force are having. In Gainsborough, Lincolnshire, the report highlighted the example of one Kevin Burnett, who had been recruited to the grand order of volunteer PCSO's, which in full reads, Police and Community Support Officer. He is, as they report, recruited, put in uniform and then sent out on patrol. He does not receive the same degree of training as a fully paid up member of the PCSO's, whose salary is £27,000 per annum. No, this volunteer is actually paid £1 per hour. As the newspaper remarks, he looks the same as the fully paid up members but has a small silver "V" for volunteer which sits neatly upon his uniformed shoulder. He is part of Theresa May's grand plan for the police's future. God help them and us.

As commented upon in an article in the Daily Mail, Frinton-on-Sea is a "genteel" town, but sadly, bereft of its previous police presence. So worried are the townsfolk at the lack of visual policing they have actually clubbed together to pay for a private company to patrol the streets at night. I say again, would you ever have thought this would have been necessary in Britain, what, ten years ago? We have heard the Chief Constable of Surrey outline her views very clearly. She said that police officers on her patch and in our taxpaying county, may no longer bother with chasing car thieves or those driving away from petrol stations without paying. Devon and Cornwall police state that officers may no longer investigate anyone who "does a runner" from a restaurant without paying. So where is the incentive to stay on the right side of the law? It always costs more in the long run but as we know from years of cutbacks we are a country hell-bent on short-term thinking.

To cap it all, I read that Jeremy Corbyn's Shadow Chancellor, who nailed his true vivid red colours and views to the socialist mast many years ago, has stated that he would back demands to disarm anti-terror police and disband MI5. You do wonder just whose side he is on. Another appeaser, another misguided naive soul.

Before the light, there is the dark and not surprisingly, the dark comes in the form of Islam, IS, Muslim expansion. It is the single most worrying aspect of world peace and threat to western everyday life. I write the following under the thoughtful heading of "Who'd have thought it?" It is sub-headed, "A touch of Islam".

Not so long ago the Muslim Prisoners' Campaign Group organised a demonstration outside the Saudi Arabian Embassy that in a free democracy, they are entitled to do – although it still rankles! The pictures shewn in the newspapers at the time included that of young children waving Islamic flags and all of the protestors wearing full battle dress – well, certainly intimidating dress – completely covered in black with full face veils. Would anywhere else in the western world allow these people to demonstrate in a manner you find these people here. One can accept freedom of speech but the potential indoctrination of children does not bode well. Can you imagine the furore were there to be a BNP demonstration outside the Pakistan embassy, where the participants wore balaclavas and minors were similarly attired, screeching and waving Union Jacks. Christ Almighty, the Left go on about a Union Jack being hung from a town hall but then, what's good for the Islamic goose doesn't appear to be quite so good for the British pig.

We have witnessed Islamic fundamentalists creating mayhem on British streets – the London bus and tube bombings, the murder of a British soldier, literally in cold blood. A lesser-known case and only lesser known because it didn't result in murder, concerns a failed deportee, one Noureden Mailaky-Soodmand, an Iranian, double-barrelled. The authorities "lost track" of him after we failed to deport the cove as the Iranian Embassy was closed at the time and paperwork could not be completed. He had already been arrested for carrying knives in London. Earlier this year the 41-year-old Iranian ran amok with a curved knife in Stockton-on-Tees, one that is specifically designed for decapitating victims. I know the area isn't very nice but no-one deserves that on their streets. Unable to deport him, we release the bugger in the town of Stockton-on-Tees. Thankless bastard isn't he? Armed with a knife, he shouts out "I am ISIS and my people will cut off your balls, Christians." So, not an overly pleasant sort of chap, a view I suspect confirmed when you read that he approached a 22-year-old and shouted, (he does a lot of shouting) "I am Muslim". (Isn't half the population?) "And I'm going to chop your effing head off". I have to tell you now, that he actually said the complete "f" word! I know, no standards or class, is there. He admitted making threats to kill and two charges of possessing offensive weapons. He has subsequently been jailed for four years at our expense. Four years? The bastard should be given forty. That's assuming that we are still not in the position to deport the unwanted migrant.

Oh, and don't these coves know how to play the system. Back in October, a Syrian refugee – I use the term lightly – was jailed for 18 months for a sexual attack on a woman. This attack took place within two weeks of arriving in our country. Naturally he is now claiming asylum. When questioned, he apparently knew little about Syria and is thought to originate from Egypt. Quite what difference that makes is beyond me. It's all "over there" as far as I'm concerned. Just send the bugger back. He contributes nothing to the betterment of this country and during the two years that he has been in an immigration centre, the flotsam has cost the UK taxpayer £80,000, so he's not exactly good value for money. I really do hope these cases and thousands more like them are taken into account by those who vote in the EU referendum. Now, I know we've gone "off-piste", but Islam, the Middle East, immigration, crime and terrorism seem to play such a costly part in our everyday lives..

There is a horrendous case of a Muslim family living in Bradford who has converted to Christianity. Is that not their democratic right, in the same way that it would be the democratic right for someone to do the same thing, but arse about face. The family has been attacked by Muslim militants, furious with their decision to "leave the cause". The attacks have become physical and the husband is currently in hospital recovering from a broken kneecap, having been attacked outside his house by thugs wielding pick-axe handles. They have been forced from their home. So where is the democracy in all this and where are the police? Doubtless they won't want to upset the local "Muslim community", any more than they would, if it were a white under-age girl claiming grooming from Asians. Race always seems to be played down if it's black, or blackish, on white but not t'other way round. I use the word "t'other" because most of this grooming is done in the north and so anyone reading this in the northern territories is more likely to take comfort from the regional accent!

Of course, Muslim on what was Muslim opens up a whole new can of worms for the police but it still shows a level of intolerance for anyone not keeping to the pack rules.

Dr Andrew Parker, the Director General of MI5, states publicly his concern regarding "home grown" fanatics being "radicalised to the point of violence within weeks." I don't see our government appearing to pay much heed to these warnings. Of course, this is the MI5 that the Shadow Chancellor would seek to destroy, given half a chance. There are currently known to be 85 Islamic or Sharia courts in this country. If this is the figure accepted as "known", you can bet your bottom Middle Eastern currency that it is the tip of the minaret. There are stories of a senior cleric claiming it was wrong to prosecute men who raped their wives. A "court" official chuckled when a woman described being beaten and abused. How on earth and why on earth do we allow this alien and throw-back to the Middle Ages culture to co-exist with the laws of this country, laws that show a darn sight more equality for gender and race than ever these imported ones do. I suppose it's because the fear of racism should anyone be honest enough to speak out about it, might upset the newly arrived natives.

Ofsted are coming up against militant Islamic schools. A teacher at a school locked in the Trojan Horse enquiry led an assembly with the chant, "We don't believe in Christmas, do we?" Now, to be fair, many of us don't but this is indoctrination, not freedom of thought. Boys are segregated from girls during teaching and games such as tennis, so where are the feminists when you really need them. If they want a cause, pick one that matters, not appearing hell-bent on removing a statue of Cecil Rhodes. All mouth and no balls, some of these feminists!

As I write, a Muslim Academy Trust looks set to become one of the first in this country to take over three non-faith secondary schools. How can this be right? The Trust (and for me there is a distinct lack of it) has promised not to impose a religious agenda. So, would you trust them with this? No, neither would I. These people are dangerous. Anyone with an agenda is dangerous and this is an agenda fuelled and driven by a corporate desire to change and engulf western society in a manner we yet appear capable of comprehending. Sorry to go on, but it's not a palatable thought. What doesn't help is when that "all things to all people, but not the native inhabitants" or the BABC, refuse to refer to the IS killers as "terrorists". It's little irritants like this that make you wonder just whose side they are really on. So, to lighten the mood I will tell you about a little news story that's just come in regarding UK suicide bombers who are to go on strike.

Muslim suicide bombers in Britain are set to begin a 3-day strike on Monday in a dispute over the number of virgins they are entitled to in the after-life. Emergency talks between IS and Al Qaeda have so far failed to produce an agreement.

The unrest began last Tuesday when Al Qaeda announced the number of virgins a suicide bomber would receive after his death would be cut by 25% from 72 to 54. A spokesman said that increases in recent years in the number of suicide bombings had resulted in a shortage of virgins in the after-life.

The suicide bombers' union, the British Organisation of Occupational Martyrs (or BOOM) responded with a statement saying that the move was unacceptable to its members and called for a strike vote. General Secretary, Abdullah Amir, told the press, "Our members are literally working themselves to death in the cause of Jihad. We don't ask much in return but to be treated like this is a real kick in the teeth." Speaking from his gunpowder shed in Tipton in the West Midlands, Al Qaeda Chief Executive, Haisheet Mapants, explained, "I sympathise with our workers' concerns but Al Qaeda is simply not in a position to meet their demands. They are simply not accepting the realities of modern-day Jihadists in a competitive market place. Thanks to western depravity there is now a chronic shortage of virgins in the after-life so it's a straight choice between reducing expenditure or laying people off. I don't like cutting benefits but would hate to have to tell 3000 of my staff that they won't be able to blow themselves up." Spokespersons for BOOM in Aldershot, Portsmouth, Rochdale, Rotherham and the entire north-east of England stated that the change would not hurt their membership so much as there were very few virgins left in the area anyway. According to some industry sources, the recent drop in the number of suicide bombings had been attributed to the emergence of Scottish singing star, Susan Boyle. Many Muslim Jihadists now know what a virgin looks like and have now reconsidered their benefit packages.

Right, well we're almost there, the turn of the year, the end of the book. We must be, it's firework night all over again. They've been sporadic ever since Hallowe'en. They peaked on Guy Fawkes' remembrance day, came to the fore once more on Christmas Eve and are now beginning their annual performance on estates throughout the country.

You have probably noticed that once or twice I have mentioned migration and its effect on our once reasonably green and mildly pleasant land. Oh, you haven't, well, just to wrap things up on this front, an email came through within which there is a black and white photograph taken in the late 1800's of indigenous Americans, first nation Americans, Red Indians, Redskins ... which shows American braves on horseback traversing the plain. The photograph itself is a stirring sight, but a caption has been added to the two front braves. One says to the other, "I'm worried about all these strangers coming to our land. They have a strange religion and they refuse to speak our language." The other brave replies, "You're just being heartless and insensitive, let them in, I mean, what harm can they do ..." Mmmm.

A few things to do before I make us both a brew. Firstly, it's those hapless sods who are to be unceremoniously deposited in the "pit of pointlessness." In previous books we've had a list of those who would be put against the metaphorical wall and shot. The problem with that is that once shot, soon forgotten. This way, with the pit, you can make return trips year in and year out and hurl rotting fruit and veg at your favourite pointless person or persons. Naturally, there will be an unending supply and selection of your favourite fruit and vegetables, both organic and non-organic from participating stores. Now, who is the first for the pit? Yes, I really think it has to be Slob Geldorf, followed very swiftly by Jeremy Clarkson and Chris Evans. Yes, off you go. Mr. Geldorf is playing the part of the Pied Piper, leading his fellow arses on a one-way trip to the "POP". Ah, here he is, on time, Charlie Higson, followed by that nauseating duo, Ed Balls and Yvette Cooper (did they ever house Syrian refugees as they promised?) Behind them trudge Elton John and his ... well, you know who. Jonathan Davies is not happy about being included, but that shrill Welsh accent, it really is unacceptable to the ear. Davies is walking alongside that overly inflated Aussie, Aaron something, he appears on the BBC business section prior to the commencement of BBC Breakfast. I don't know his surname but he turned up as soon as a call for Aussie arses went out. Oh, they're now entering by the drove. The whole of the Royal Family has gathered, with the exception of Prince Charles and the Duchess of Cambridge, one of whom I feel sorry for and the other is cracking. I'll leave you to work out which is which. Behind them march the Royal corps of traffic wardens, humourless nonentities to a man and woman, smartly and closely followed by the bankers who let our country down so badly with their corporate greed and now we have some familiar faces of MPs. Yes, it looks like all of those who have publicly stated they will vote to remain. Who's that coming over the ridge? Ah, it's the brigade of lawyers who represent refugees, migrants, claimants, anyone who wishes to gain money for false claims of whiplash and mock car crashes, they're all there. In other words, the pointless working on behalf of the pointless – perfect pit fodder! Oh, they'd better move over as the LCA's are fast approaching. Yes, that mass of lycra-clad arseholes who are doing their damndest to remove all of those on foot who get in their way. They have scant regard for humanity, even pond life. Head down, unseeing, traffic light ignoring – what arses cyclists are and yet, what a service to humanity this pit performs. They really are arrogant sods. Now, I see before me prisoners. These are all prisoners serving sentences of over, well, just serving sentences will do. I mean, let's face it, you know that once they've completed their term in any prison they'll reoffend the second they are out. The pit puts a stop to all those shenanigans.

Oh, dear, even prisoners will feel clean alongside the next group. Yes, it's the Royal Corp of Land Developers, or soil rapists as I see them. "Yes, lads, that's it, the big hole over there with the rope ladder." One by one they enter, like lemmings to a cliff. Who can we now see approaching? Ah, it's the Corp of Camper Vans, Mobile Homes and Caravan Owners. At least they'll have somewhere to park, even if they're vehicle has landed on its side – 'tis a deep pit.

Excuse me a moment, I'll just have to go over and ask this sad looking bunch why they are lining up as I don't see anything obvious in their appearance. What's that? Ah, now I know. One of them has just spoken and they're forming the queue and it's now a long queue of those who drop their aitches and tee's. They were looking for the pit entrance. Sadly, none of them could pronounce pit or entrance, because both words have t's, so no hope there. I wonder if I'll spot Adele amongst their numbers? She could, of course, be singing her way up their rear.

I'll just take a break as this lot pass and frankly, with such deplorable diction meaningful conversation is impossible – ya' know wot I mean! A few minutes' relaxation with a good read. Firstly, I've got the "Commercial Motor Show Report" dated 26th September, 1956, to digest and after that, if time allows, there's a copy of "Titbits" from the 16th August, 1949. This edition includes

"The most complete pools guide and forecasts". Yes, I know it's all a bit dated but I hate throwing anything away and especially anything that harks back to a time when England was England. In similar fashion to the advert by Whiteleys Store in the Great Western Railway magazine, I am now savouring the review of the new models being offered by Austin, Morris, Wolseley, Riley, MG, Singer, Sunbeam, Humber, Hillman and not forgetting Jowett et al. Happy days, innocent days in many ways.

Right, time to prise myself from the Nostalgia Club. There are still thousands speaking badly and the hillside is expanding with bodies making their way to the pit. There's a group involved in health and safety that appear not to have been shot in 2010. They are naturally forming a very orderly queue, although I did hear someone asked if the pit had been properly inspected, registered as fit for purpose and had passed a business case study. No, it hasn't. It's a pit! Here's another section we haven't seen previously. This is a group involved in the food industry that was responsible for telling the public that they wanted fruit that ripens in the bowl. You purchase, you take home, you wait, you continue waiting, you check your fruit on an hourly basis, but no, still rock solid. Then, hey presto! You let the dog out of the back door for five minutes and it's already turned mushy.

There is a whole host of what look like non-offending cars heading towards the pit, so why are they … oh, I see, they've just started passing me and I can now see the rear windscreens. This is the "corps of arses" that insist that following drivers should be aware that they have a "Baby on Board", or a "Grandchild on Board", a "Little Princess on Board", a "Showdog", a "Pedigree Dog" … "Granny's Taxi Service" – bloody irritating! Do they honestly think that my driving manners should rise just because they are in the car in front? Ridiculous! To the pit with you and be damned!

Crikey, that's a large group assembling to my left. Now, that's the lot who believe that their beliefs override the beliefs – or otherwise – of others – bastards! Interestingly there is one individual trudging in the opposite direction who has seen a reprieve and that is David Walliams. Not one of my favourites by any stretch of the imagination but both Maureen and I very much enjoyed his acting skills in the light drama, "Tommy and Tuppence". So, hopefully, a second series will follow. If not, he can always be deposited in Part 2.

Now, we don't know the names of the following as sadly, their identities are kept very secret, within committees who do not make their findings public or have to justify their appointments. I want to wheedle out all those who give roles to under-qualified, over-paid chief executives, or CEO's, who head up banks, councils, care authorities, parole boards or one title I read, "Director of Regulatory and Democratic Services". I wonder what he or she does. The only certainty is that you know it won't be justified.

With specific regard to parole boards I would love to name and shame before depositing in the Pit of Pointlessness those who say "yay" to offenders who reoffend on licence, having been released early, presumably due to bad behaviour. So many re-offenders are reoffending, year in, year out. Who are these people, presumably of reasonable intelligence, who consider the inmate before the victim or the next victim-to-be?

The question I would like to ask is if judges are appointed on their ability to raise the nation's blood pressure when they preside over the fate of minorities and non-English miscreants. There are several lining up, nodding like donkeys at the side of the Pit. Clothed in all their regal finery. I am sure they will have either a field day down there or it will be the pits!

Ah, now there's a desperate group at the back. These are the ones who over- use words such as "pod", "hub" and describe shopping as an "experience."

Hang on a sec, won't be a mo'.... I'm just sending a text to Nigel Farage and David Cameron, as without the tireless work of the first and the brave yet suicidal decision of the second to hold a referendum we wouldn't be looking forward to 2016 in such positive mood. Whether we stay or whether we go, at least the public has had the right to voice their democratic choice at the ballot box.

And, don't forget – "election results" is an anagram of "lies let's recount".

A warning to all MPs, regarding the next pit that is being dug for Part 2 of this duo. Please do not use the phrase "hard working families". It will cost you dearly. There, they can't say they haven't been warned.

Talking of elections, if Mr. Trump succeeds there will be jobs aplenty for British brickies – that wall isn't going to build itself. Surely, justification for another series of "Auf Wiedersehen Pet – The Trump Months".

Well, as we wait for the transgressors to descend the rope ladders and spend the rest of their collective time wondering just where they went wrong, it is now New Year's Eve and as is our household tradition we will be in bed by ten to twelve with a Victor Meldrew DVD, playing as ever loud enough to drown out the sound of those bloody fireworks.

So, I'll leave you with a few thoughts. The first relates to Charlton Athletic. Our chances of survival in what I still refer to as the Second Division do not look good and you do not need a crystal ball to see where we're going.

I can't see me being given the opportunity to address any university group. Fancy having an opinion!

Good news ... no "Top Gear" with Jeremy Clarkson.

Bad news ... "Top Gear" with Chris Evans. He'll probably wheedle his way back out of the pit somehow. The man seems to thrive on career resurrections!

The New Year's Honours List has just been published with no mention of Carol Kirkwood. She should be given an honour – any honour, purely for making an old man happy! Dame Carol ... mmm....

Another thought – as time passes by, the authorities are still no further forward in finding Lord Lucan and the public are still undecided as to whether Jeremy Bamber is innocent or not.

Whilst I was thinking, I was washing my hair – don't want to start the New Year unable to face the world. I looked in the mirror and I'm sure there was more hair before I started washing. See, just where I'm pointing – yes, there – too much skin. As Harry Hill said, "I knew I was losing my hair when my face took longer to wash."

So, are you staying up for the festive irritation – Jules Holland – a lot of running about, music I've decided I really can't abide. Oh, you are? Fine. Remember to lock up, won't you.

As Bill Vaughn, an American industry writer, once said, "Youth is when you're allowed to stay up for New Year's Eve, middle age is when you're forced to." He's not wrong.

Happy New Year, I'll see you after the referendum for Part 2. Oh, by the way, I've just checked those nectarines, and they're still not ripe!

Nighty Night.